How Did Poetry Survive?

How Did
Poetry Survive?

The Making of
Modern American Verse

JOHN TIMBERMAN NEWCOMB

UNIVERSITY OF ILLINOIS PRESS

Urbana, Chicago, and Springfield

A companion anthology containing the full text of all the poems referred
to in this book is available through the University of Illinois Library's
scholarly digital repository, the Illinois Digital Environment for Access to
Learning and Scholarship (IDEALS), at http://hdl.handle.net/2142/26460.

Library of Congress Cataloging-in-Publication Data
Newcomb, John Timberman.
How did poetry survive? : the making of modern American verse /
John Timberman Newcomb.
p.   cm.
Includes bibliographical references and index.
ISBN 978-0-252-03679-8 (hardcover : alk. paper) —
ISBN 978-0-252-09390-6 (e-book)
1. American poetry—20th century—History and criticism.
2. Modernism (Literature)—United States.
3. Poetry—Authorship—Psychological aspects.
4. Poets, American—20th century—Psychology.
5. Social change in literature.
6. Social conflict in literature.
7. City and town life in literature.
8. Technology in literature.
I. Title. II. Title: Making of modern American verse.
PS310.M57N488   2011
811'.5209—dc23   2011027792

To the memory of my parents
Charles Elwyn Newcomb (1909–86)
Jane Ann Timberman Newcomb (1920–2005)

and always to Lori

Contents

Acknowledgments

When a project originally planned as one book becomes two, the acknowledgments multiply as well. All those I thanked in *Would Poetry Disappear?* are also part of this book, whether they like it or not. But I'm pleased to acknowledge these people who have had an especially important impact.

In their very different ways, my three intellectual mentors at Duke—Frank Lentricchia, Barbara Herrnstein Smith, and the late Bernard Duffey—instilled in me the belief that I had something to say in the world of American literature scholarship.

I am grateful to these colleagues at the University of Illinois for their support over a sometimes bumpy, but now happily smooth, road: Robert Dale Parker, Gordon Hutner, Bob Markley (fore!), Ramona Curry, Stephanie Foote, Martin Camargo, Sandy Camargo, Curtis Perry, Catherine Gray, Anustup Basu, J. B. Capino, Dianne Harris, Christine Catanzarite, Rick Powers, Carol Symes, Jim Hansen, Philip Graham—and most grateful thanks to two superlative colleagues, Bruce Michelson and Dale Bauer. Gardner Rogers, Ted Underwood, and Eleanor Courtemanche belong in that list, to be sure, but I trust they also know how much they mean to me personally. I haven't seen that quintessential academic jet-setter Cary Nelson very much since he ascended to the presidency of the AAUP, but he remains an abiding source of inspiration over on Lynn Street.

Researching this book was again a pleasure, thanks to the libraries and staffs of Duke University, the University of Delaware (especially Jesse Rossa), West Chester University, Indiana University, and most of all, the University of Illinois at Urbana-Champaign. Thanks also to the staffs of the Newberry Library, the Regenstein Library of the University of Chicago, the New York Public Library, the Museum of the City of New York, the New-York Historical Society, and the Chicago Postcard Museum. I'm grateful to the National

Endowment for the Humanities, West Chester University, and the University of Illinois at Urbana-Champaign for grants to travel to collections, for the duplication of materials, and for all-important release time.

I want also to extend my gratitude and continuing admiration to my former colleagues at West Chester, especially Michael W. Brooks, Carol Shloss, Christopher Buckley, Robert Fletcher, Cheryl Wanko, C. Ruth Sabol, John Thomas Kelly, and most of all Paul Maltby and Lynette McGrath.

Through their enthusiastic and sometimes skeptical responses to the many forgotten poems I've offered them over these many years, my undergraduate and graduate students at West Chester and Illinois have taught me more than I can say. I am especially grateful to Andy Thomas, Chris Corbo, Amy Murray, John Dixon, Juliet McCarter Latham, Tom McKibbin, David Amadio, John Kerrigan, Conley Wouters, George Conn, Ryan Cull, Matthias Somers, and Darren Penn. Bartholomew Brinkman has consistently inspired me with his intellect, decency, and pluck over these last five years. John Moore and Naida Garcia-Crespo, my research assistants for the past year, always made me feel that the tasks I gave them were pleasures rather than chores, which I greatly appreciate.

These far-flung friends from the Modernist Studies Association and elsewhere have given me lots of support and inspiration, even when they didn't always know it: David Chinitz, Celena Kusch, Miranda Hickman, Christopher Breu, David Earle, Pat Collier, Leif Sorensen, David Jarraway, Mark Morrisson, Andrew Goldstone, Benjamin Kahan, Robin Blyn, and especially Adam McKible, Suzanne Churchill, Leonard Diepeveen, and Edward Brunner.

Friends like Michael and Dianne Peich come along once in a lifetime—if one is very fortunate.

The enthusiastic support of the University of Illinois Press, personified by Bill "Goth" Regier, has meant a great deal to me in these uncertain times for academic publishing. I remember the first moment I imagined living the life of a scholar and professor: when as a teenager I idly picked up one of the Reader's Digest condensed volumes gathering dust on the shelves of our summer cottage in the North Carolina countryside and found a 1950s academic novel, *A Friend in Power* by Carlos Baker—now probably just about forgotten by everyone else—concerning a professor who discovers his closest friend has been angling behind the scenes for the college presidency, with ambiguous consequences. Bill will scoff at the idea that he is "in power," but I'm awfully glad to have him as a friend as well as a publisher.

Many thanks to Sarah Shreeves and the IDEALS program of the University of Illinois Library for making it possible to offer a companion anthology containing the full text of all the poems referred to in this book, which can be accessed at http://hdl.handle.net/2142/26460.

I continue to treasure my family: my brother, sister-in-law, nephews, nieces, cousins, in-laws, and the irreplaceable archivist of the Newcomb clan, my dear Auntie Eleanor Newcomb Rice. My relatives, past and present, have exhibited a remarkable affinity for things literary, photographic, and cinematic, with books, feature films, videos, radio and TV broadcasts, and bazillions of pictures, to their credit. Though I am probably more likely to see the movies and photos they shoot than they are to read my books, I am truly inspired by their example and their enthusiasms.

Last but certainly not least: after all these years, what new can I say to and about my dear spouse, Lori Humphrey Newcomb? She is my treasure and my guiding light, who makes everything fun.

A Modernism of the City

In 1850 poetry was the central genre of American literary culture. Fifty years later it was widely viewed as a mawkish refuge for dilettantes and sentimentalists. Its powers had been circumscribed by genteel custodians bent upon protecting it from the sullying forces of modern life: urbanization, organized labor, commodity culture. For several decades, cultural workers in other fields had been building the institutional and professional networks that still largely govern them today: prizes, fellowships, and commissions; academic units, disciplinary protocols, and credentialing bodies; wildly successful systems of mass marketing for popular genres including pulp fiction, song, and cinema. All the while, American poets were subjected to intense pressure to keep their work unspoiled by all that was mundane or sordid, especially the industrial city. After 1890, the standoff between poetry's immovable gatekeepers and modernity's irresistible force created a crisis of value that many commentators seriously believed would prove fatal. Some gloated, and others feared, that literary poetry in America seemed destined to end its days as the "rickety dream-child of neurotic aestheticism," a pathetic orphan in twentieth-century cultural marketplaces dominated by hypercommercialized ephemera such as mass-circulation newspapers, popular songs, and dime novels.[1]

As it turned out, however, American verse was on the verge of its greatest achievements. These conditions of crisis eventually eroded existing norms of poetic practice, and after 1912 the resulting vacuum of authority made possible bold new directions that were unimaginable a few years earlier. Unlike most previous scholarly accounts of the emergence of modern American poetry, my narrative locates this amazing reversal of fortune not in the individual accomplishments of a few titanic figures but in the collective efforts of hundreds of people involved in the New Verse movement between 1912 and 1925. These poets, editors, publishers, and readers renewed American verse by rejecting stifling prohibitions against topical entanglement and by delving into the technologies, spaces, social dynamics, and political problems of modern life. Taking over existing literary institutions and creating avant-garde alternatives, they found new ways to market and nourish poetry within twentieth-century cultural economies. Finding few useful predecessor poets aside from Walt Whitman, they drew instead from contemporary visual genres—painting, photography, cinema, and material culture—to elaborate a *poetics of metropolitan modernity* that embraced the very subjects that the genteel establishment had condemned as incorrigibly unpoetic. The importance of the visual arts in this process was evoked directly by a Chicago eveningscape of 1914:

> You are a painter—listen—
>   I'll paint you a picture too!
> Of the long white lights that glisten
>   Through Michigan Avenue;
> With the red lights down the middle
>   Where the street shines mirror-wet,
> […]
> And up in the air, high over
>   The rain-shot shimmer of light,
> The huge sky-scrapers hover
>   And shake out their stars at the night.
> […]
> Have I chalked out a sketch in my rhyme?[2]

Harriet Monroe's lines typify the thematic emphases and the tonal exuberance of the movement that changed the course of American poetry with remarkable speed and force beginning in 1912. Though this explosion of activity was given other names by later historians, participants called it the *New Poetry* or the *New Verse*.[3] In this study I employ these two terms interchangeably rather than *modernism,* seeking to avoid the proscriptive usage that limits the latter honorific to texts that use destabilizing stylistic innovations to express disdain for the benighted values of a mainstream readership—thus consigning all other verse of the period to some unnameable nonmodernist limbo. I use *high modernism* in a specific sense to designate the narrow canon of twentieth-century verse that dominated the American literary academy for a half century beginning in the 1940s. In contrast to modernism in this sense, the terms *New Poetry* and *New Verse* imply an inclusive field of many styles, political positions, and attitudes toward modernity that commingled in the American literary landscape between 1912 and 1925.

The first sentences of Amy Lowell's *Tendencies in Modern American Poetry* (1917) reveal the standard usage of the period ("When people speak of the 'New Poetry' . . .") and also the term's inclusive and eclectic connotations: "There is a 'New Poetry' today, and the new forms are part of its attire, but the body is more important than the clothing and existed before it."[4] Though Lowell's distinctions between the "New Poetry" and "new forms," and between content as "body" and style as "clothing," would have sounded deeply gauche during the high-modernist era of fetishized organic form, they remind us that the New Verse movement was catalyzed not only—or even primarily—by innovations of style but also by its polemical expansion of subject matter.

The belatedness of American poetry's turn toward the city intensified its force and diversified its forms. When poets began to explore urban subjects around 1910, they did so in every style available, from elaborately traditional forms and meters to big-boned *vers libre* to precise imagist miniaturism.[5] Their verse explored new forms, rhythms, and imagery, but it also used traditional forms against the grain as strategies of subversion and critique. For me, it's not a matter of deciding which of these approaches deserve the *modernist* honorific and which don't; I seek to show that by inventing new forms and by appropriating existing formal and thematic conventions to new uses, American poets of this decade participated in the socially responsive modernism described by Raymond Williams in his remarkable 1987 lecture "When Was Modernism?" Williams locates the origins of modernism much earlier than most, at the moment when the "great realists" of the 1840s (Dickens, Gogol, Flaubert) "devised and organized a whole vocabulary . . . with which to grasp the unprecedented social forms of the industrial city."[6] Williams meant this revisionist chronology to challenge the "late-born ideology" that has restricted *modernism* to twentieth-century movements predicated upon the "radical questioning of the processes of representation" and the "denaturalizing of language."[7] In his view, this modernism of stylistic innovation and deconstruction quickly "lost its anti-bourgeois stance" and became an elitist orthodoxy readily assimilated to the processes of twentieth-century capitalism, leading to a damaging segregation between modernist cultural production and modern social experience.[8]

Williams's revision of modernism around compelling *subject matter,* specifically the spaces, technologies, and social dynamics of the industrialized metropolis, carries momentous implications for the historiography of American poetry, in which style has nearly always been privileged over subject matter, the text as a self-contained verbal construct over its engagement with contextual forces.[9] By arguing that the astonishing revival of the 1910s was due primarily to American poets' newfound engagement with urban modernity, my account seeks to synthesize the rich interpretive tradition of New Criticism and its formalist successors with more recent historicist accounts of literary texts as inevitably and productively embedded within the sociopolitical horizons of their times. In this effort, I have been inspired by some fine scholarship (by Cary Nelson, Joseph Harrington, Mark Van Wienen, Cristanne Miller, Mark Morrisson, Jayne Marek, David Chinitz, Suzanne Churchill, Adam McKible, and Michael Thurston, among others) that reads twentieth-century verse in light of contemporary social and political concerns. But this study is the first to describe modern American poetry as a broad-based response, occurring across many styles and political positions, to the experience of living in the industrialized metropolis.

My effort to recover this American poetry of the city contains a polemical dimension, no less than the high-modernist histories that ruthlessly excoriated urban modernity as a horror show featuring "lethal and paralyzing traffic, physical decay and political corruption, racial and economic tension, crime, rioting, and police brutality. This is the lurid picture we are accustomed to, and even for those who have never heard of Dante or Baudelaire, it is the most natural of metaphors to speak of this scene of cruelty, ugliness, inhumanity, and despair as Hell."[10] Like Monroe Spears's *Dionysus and the City* (1970), too many accounts of twentieth-century verse have been narratives of repudiation—of the urban populace, of politics, of technology, of modernity itself. Such narratives reflect the postwar monumentalization of modernism as an exclusionary discourse tended by an academic clerisy dedicated to defending a residual form of elite culture. Dominant for half a century, this conceptual regime reduced the field of "modern American poetry," which had once consisted of dozens, even hundreds of writers intersecting in a rich multiplicity of ways, to a canon of barely half a dozen. This narrowing of the modern poetry canon was disastrous to the cultural standing of poetry in America. Sixty years ago, twentieth-century verse was central to the disciplinary discourses of American literature and modernism. Now, as Joseph Harrington has argued, American poetry barely even functions as "American literature" in the new-historicist academy.[11] Like the genteel gatekeepers of the previous century, custodians of the postwar high-modernist canon damaged American poetry by segregating it from modern social experience. This segregation means that—like the anxious commentators of 1900, measuring their pipsqueak contemporaries against the giants of previous generations—we cannot now imagine poets of our own day having the great cultural currency that such disparate figures as Carl Sandburg, Edna St. Vincent Millay, and T. S. Eliot enjoyed in theirs.

Every critical study creates its own canon, and readers will discover that mine has its clear favorites. But books that admit into their pages no more than three or four well-known writers, and books like this one that discuss texts by several dozen writers, make very different claims about the shape of their period and their discipline. One of my goals is to reveal any and all canonical configurations (including my own) as incomplete, and to suggest that around every neglected scholarly corner, in the pages of every forgotten magazine, we will find modern American poems worth reexamining. In other words, by describing the poetics of modernity developed in the New Verse of the 1910s, I am doing canonical recovery work, but in a fashion somewhat distinct from those scholars who have focused renewed attention upon poets suppressed to history by their race, ethnicity, class, or political affiliation. Though that kind of recovery is not absent from the pages that follow, I have more often found myself returning to a group of once-prominent writers whose standing was eroded by the post–World War II view of modern verse as necessarily experimental in form, hermetically intellectual in tone, contemptuous of any uninitiated audience, and opposed to the secular liberalism characteristic of urban-industrial modernity. These "popular modernists," a group headed by Masters, Lowell, Frost, Sandburg, Lindsay, and Millay, drew upon regional and urban vernaculars, colloquial diction and syntax, and realist modes of verbal representation to create a poetry of everyday experience that was widely accessible to nonspecialists, yet still sufficiently complex and nuanced to attract the admiration of literary professionals and connoisseurs. They will play significant roles in the narrative that follows—but so will a multitude of others never as famous.

As my argument developed, I found that prominent female poets—Millay, Lowell, Sara Teasdale, Harriet Monroe—needed particular recuperative attention after decades of belittlement.[12] If we survey the MLA Bibliographies of recent decades, we find that Hyatt Waggoner's complacent assumption in 1968—that "the three best-liked women poets of the 1920s," Millay, Teasdale, and Elinor Wylie, "are now nearly forgotten, except by a few . . . who were young when they were young"—has not exactly proved true.[13] But neither has it been challenged very forcefully outside the sphere of "women's poetry." Not much recent scholarship has refuted long-standing assumptions that verse by American women primarily explores emotive themes and interior states of consciousness, using symbolic natural, domestic, or mythic settings abstracted from entangling forms of historical and quotidian time. The reaffirmation of these once-devalued aspects of female poets' work, while entirely proper in itself, has not been accompanied by sufficient attention to their often powerful engagement with twentieth-century public life.[14]

I have no idea whether poetry's current disciplinary crisis in the American academy will lead to any further revival in the twenty-first century. But by recovering the surprising alliances, playful formal experiments, and insightful political commentaries that shaped the New Verse of the 1910s, I hope to demonstrate that the old, narrow high canon does not provide anything like an adequate picture of modern American poetry. The chapters that follow are designed to breach familiar authorial and canonical boundaries, mingling ultrafamiliar classics with ignored, even reviled, modes of verse. They represent my effort to "search out and counterpose an alternative tradition taken from the neglected works left in the wide margin of the century," in Raymond Williams's words.[15] Finally, I hope to make visible another possible past for modern American poetry—exuberant and combative, full of hope even while decrying things as they are—in which poets reached out toward a wide readership, nurtured visions of community rather than deriding them, and generated powerful social critique from their resilient vision of a humane modern future.

PART I

Inventing the New Verse

I had looked upon poetry as truly doomed, until the new poets
rose above the horizon. I was sick unto death of the endless
archaisms, the tedious harpings back, the spineless submission to
fetters. The new poets (yourself and the others) have cleared the
air. Thank God poetry is still possible.
—Edward Alden Jewell to Louis Untermeyer, November 30, 1915

One had to be a poet indeed a quarter of a century ago to
endure the attacking obloquy. One had to care. Nowadays it is
as natural and as reputable to write verse as to have one's shoes
polished.
—Witter Bynner to Eunice Tietjens, May 27, 1923

CHAPTER 1

American Poetry on the Brink, 1905–12

The status of poetry in the United States hit bottom between 1900 and 1905. Commentaries during these years routinely assumed that the art was in precipitous decline, and many questioned its very survival.[1] The genteel custodians of the nation's literary culture clung desperately to poetry as an anticommodity, something ostensibly above the frantic getting and spending of modern life. In this climate, any step toward organizing, professionalizing, or remunerating poets was likely to be disdained as degradation of a noble art. Thus in the early 1900s no one assumed sustained responsibility for the publicizing and reviewing of new books of verse, the identification of emerging poets and trends, or the preservation of periodical verses past their immediate moment of publication. No serial publications devoted themselves primarily to verse by living Americans. No ongoing national prizes remunerated poets. Following Edmund Clarence Stedman's monumental *American Anthology* of 1900, not a single anthology of serious literary verse by living Americans was published for twelve years.[2] The writing of poetry was not taught in institutional contexts, as architecture and painting and music now were, because nearly everyone assumed that poets were not made but born. Aspiring poets of these years, knowing they could hope to see a volume of their work only by paying for it themselves, felt isolated and useless, actively discouraged from writing for anyone except their own closeted muses.

The first attempts to challenge this dismal state of affairs can be detected beginning around 1905. The people behind these early initiatives, however tentative or traditional they might look to us now, were revolutionaries of a sort, the first to contest the obsolete ideal of amateur authorship used by the genteel literary establishment to barricade poetry away from commercializing and professionalizing forces of turn-of-the-century American life. While the immediate impact of these initial steps was mild at best, the forms they took and the fates they met reveal much about what American poetry had desperately lacked and what it would need in order to revive. All addressed crippling absences of access—to print, to time and money, to readers and other poets, to a vital national tradition. Disputing the widespread view of modern poets as preposterous dilettantes and seeking to reimagine them as productive artists, they proposed new methods of preserving published poems, networks of personal interaction, and incentives of money and publicity.

Outreaching into the Ether: 1905–12

The crisis in the years before 1912 was greatly exacerbated by a perceived vacuum of national tradition. For many Americans, the existing genteel canon, built around the six greatly revered "Fireside poets," had become an inhibiting, oppressive force.[3] The only viable alternative to this canon was Walt Whitman, who in the twenty years after his death in 1892 was transformed from a disreputable cult figure into an icon whose importance was acknowledged in nearly every arena of American literary culture. He dominated sizable chunks of scholarly and critical works of the 1900s, including Paul Elmer More's 1906 series of *Shelburne Essays,* Leon H. Vincent's *American Literary Masters* (1906), and John Macy's *The Spirit of American Literature* (1910). Among the many dozens of magazine pieces on the poet published between 1900 and 1912, several near-duplications of title and approach suggest that periodicals were actively competing for their share of the Whitman market.[4] Even the two bellwethers of the genteel "quality magazines," *The Atlantic* and *The Century,* were run by devotees of Whitman after 1900. *The Century,* whose longtime editor Richard Watson Gilder had befriended the Good Gray Poet during his later years, began around 1905 to give Whitman the same reverential treatment that the Fireside poets had enjoyed in its pages three decades earlier.[5] In November 1905 and again in September and October 1907, *The Century* offered extensive excerpts, more than forty closely printed pages in all, from Horace Traubel's hagiographic account of the poet's later years, "With Walt Whitman in Camden." This campaign survived Gilder's death in 1909, continuing with a portrait of the poet in March 1910 and then, in February 1911, "Some Portraits and Autographs of Walt Whitman," which, by emphasizing the "hitherto unpublished" nature of its images and manuscripts, portrayed Whitman's handwriting as treasured markings and his countenance as a source of nearly idolatrous power.[6] *The Atlantic* under Bliss Perry's editorship (1899–1909) was an equally strong supporter, averaging at least one piece a year on Whitman.

Perry would himself publish a monograph on the poet, *Whitman: His Life and Work*, in 1906.

Whitman meant multiple things to his growing ranks of admirers. Some, like the anthologist shaping an exclusive canon of nine dead eminences in *The Chief American Poets* (1905), sought to tame him within existing genteel paradigms of poetic value. But for many others, Whitman's work and persona represented a radical break with the late-genteel climate of inhibition and prohibition, pointing instead toward an American poetry open to the defining conditions of modern life. In 1907 in *Putnam's* (another quality magazine grown enthusiastic about Whitman), the critic Gerald Stanley Lee published "An Order for the Next Poet," a long two-part article setting out a "ground plan" for the twentieth-century poet that derived primarily from his admiration for Whitman.[7] This article, which could have been an outtake from the quirky volume Lee had published the year before, *The Voice of the Machines: An Introduction to the Twentieth Century,* argued that in "this modern world," old ideas of poetry were dying, and "the feat of being a Tennyson without looking ridiculous is getting more complicated every year," although Lee predicted eventual rapprochement between poetry and machines in a future in which "the distinction between the fine arts and the useful arts . . . should become extinct."[8] While most poets had "been content to regild the old gilding," Whitman had striven toward "[t]he only way a man can be a poet nowadays," which was "to do exactly what the machines are doing and do it better—to grip the hidden properties of matter."[9] Whitman epitomized the poet of modernity who "takes his cue from . . . silent machines" and hidden forces such as electricity, not to remove spirit and mystery from modern lives but to make them accessible to us once again: "The most modern poetry, like the most modern machinery, outreaches into the ether—into the symbolic, the invisible, the irresistible."[10]

Lee's argument that Whitman embodied an American poetry responsive to the motive forces of modern life was amplified by Horace Traubel, the most faithful and fervent of the poet's disciples. Publishing excerpts from his monumental day-by-day chronicle of Whitman's later life in *The Century, American Magazine, Appleton's, The Forum,* and elsewhere, Traubel sowed the poet's voice and influence throughout the nation's literary culture in the decade before 1912.[11] His 1911 essay "Sermon to Poets" in *The Writer* turned toward contemporary American verse, diagnosing its crisis as a failure to adapt to an unstable modern world. He indicted "books of idiotic rhymes and lying adjectives" produced by "verbal acrobats" from whom "the people have turned away"—but only because poets had "first turned away from the people."[12] Unlike many commentators of that moment, who assumed an unbridgeable opposition between poetry and modern life, Traubel saw the crisis as an opportunity to explore new forms and new subject matter. Instead of "all repeating each other" and "all repeating thousands who died before you lived," American poets needed to give voice to the conditions of modern life, to science, the machine, and "especially labor, the giant greatest force of all."[13] Though Traubel's sermon verged on hectoring, it did establish an important link between Whitman's experimental approach to form and an emerging poetics of modernity by arguing that "the message of the age can't be conveyed through alien forms" and "must create its own forms" integrally related to poetry's new social functions: "It will get its warp and woof from what it is intended to do."[14]

By the mid-1910s, Whitman's canonicity had become so thoroughly consensual that in the controversies between the genteel rear guard and avant-garde little magazines such as *Poetry: A Magazine of Verse,* both sides would claim his allegiance.[15] Participants across the entire spectrum of the New Poetry movement would find him an enormously generative model of formal innovation, social nonconformism, and openness to urban-industrial modernity. He did indeed provide, as Lee predicted in 1906, a "ground plan" for the poetry of the American machine age.

Before 1912, canonizing a single safely dead poet proved easier than devising new forms of support for living writers. Even so, faced with the rank futility of the rear guard's segregation of American poetry from modern life, some people did seek new modes of institutional organization for the art. The earliest attempt to take ongoing evaluative responsibility for contemporary verse was made by a young African American journalist, William Stanley Beaumont Braithwaite, who began in 1905 publishing in the *Boston Evening Transcript* annual summaries of verse that had appeared in the nation's magazines. He continued these summaries in the *Transcript* through 1912, and then from 1913 published a much-expanded version in book form as the *Anthology of Magazine Verse* (yearly through 1929, with occasional volumes thereafter). Braithwaite's tastes ran to fairly elevated tonalities and traditional forms, while his method of selecting and reproducing the magazine poems he judged "distinctive" was vulnerable to criticism as idiosyncratic and indiscriminate. Though he eventually accommodated himself to milder forms of innovation, including imagism, and maintained long-standing relationships with important figures such as Edwin Arlington Robinson and Amy Lowell, he would be eclipsed by Harriet Monroe and Louis Untermeyer as an arbiter of contemporary poetry well before the end of the 1910s.[16] And yet in his thankless effort to read and compile thousands of otherwise scattered texts, persevering despite continual financial struggles,

Braithwaite did more than anyone else before 1912 to assert contemporary poems as more than ephemeral page-fillers.

Others sought to build an ongoing institutional entity for poetry analogous to such recently founded disciplinary bodies as the American Institute of Architects (1857), the American Social Science Association (1865), the Society of American Artists (1877), the Modern Language Association (1883), the American Historical Association (1884), the National Arts Club (1898), the National Institute of Arts and Letters (1898), the American Philosophical Association (1900), the American Political Science Association (1903), and the American Academy of Religion (1909), among many others.[17] Harriet Monroe's founding of *Poetry* was the most momentous result, but this institutionalizing impulse emerged slightly earlier with the founding of the Poetry Society of America in New York in late 1909 and 1910. Among its leaders was Jessie B. Rittenhouse, who had published the only book-length critical study of contemporary American poetry since 1900 (*Younger American Poets*, 1904). Rittenhouse's account of the founding of the Poetry Society in her 1934 autobiography emphasized the need for (and the resistance to) new institutional structures for American verse. The effort began with an organizational meeting called by a wealthy Manhattan couple named Rice, who imagined a group "united largely through the hospitality of our hosts at whose apartments it was proposed we should continue to meet"—in other words, a private poetry salon.[18] Rittenhouse and Edward J. Wheeler, who became the mainstays of the Poetry Society, argued instead that the organization should be conceived "along national lines" and its events held "in a public rather than a private place"—whereupon the Rices promptly withdrew, affronted that their personal hospitality had been despoiled by modern bureaucracy and unseemly publicity.[19]

This contretemps etches a moment of transition between competing paradigms of poetry's social value. The Rices saw poetry as a pleasing accouterment of a genteel existence, enjoyed privately among one's social peers. Rittenhouse and Wheeler, who pushed the term "Poetry Society" over "Poets' Club," had begun to envision a role for poetry within a national public culture. Wheeler, the editor-in-chief of the digest periodical *Current Opinion,* used his association with the National Arts Club to obtain a meeting place, and in October 1910 the first gathering took place there, "the target of many gibes from facetious young reporters who were sent to write up 'The Poets' Union.'"[20] The idea of poetry as a private activity properly insulated from public intercourse was not confined to pert journalists. It was so thoroughly entrenched that, as Rittenhouse puts it, "Even the poets themselves were afraid of drawing attention to their art

by an organization in [poetry's] interest."[21] She remembers the young poet
Ridgely Torrence declaring "that he did not believe in organization for the
arts, but in solitary prosecution of them," and earnestly urging her not to
serve as the society's secretary, because an "alliance with a body sure to
be ridiculed" would "jeopardize [her] standing as a critic."[22] Torrence's
final appeal was that "'Will Moody would never have consented to join
such an organization.'"[23] Whether or not Moody would have joined the
Poetry Society, which was perhaps more likely than Torrence believed, the
anecdote suggests both parties' awareness that the cultural practices of
Moody's time were being superseded by new ones. After all, not only did
Rittenhouse become the society's secretary, but Torrence became a charter
member despite his objections. The Poetry Society of America would be
dominated by pedestrian East Coast versifiers, few of whom would play
even marginal roles in the New Verse except as foils against which avant-
gardists might define themselves.[24] But it did pioneer a model of institutional organization that, as Rittenhouse pointed out, was emulated over
the next twenty years by affiliated societies in nearly every state.[25]

In 1912 Braithwaite and Wheeler served as judges in another institutional
innovation: a contest and anthology called *The Lyric Year,* to be edited by
Ferdinand Earle, a wealthy dilettante and would-be patron of the arts, and
issued by Mitchell Kennerley, an erratic businessman who was the nation's
most adventurous publisher at the time. In its marketing, contents, and reception, *The Lyric Year* documents an embryonic moment of institutional
transition between genteel and modern paradigms in American poetry. Publishing one poem by each of a hundred poets, the anthology promised to be
"not just a book but 'an event'"—the first collection of serious contemporary verse in the United States since 1900, and the first significant contest
for American poets in decades, offering substantial sums (a total of one
thousand dollars) to three winners.[26] The volume, published in December
1912, featured a preface by Earle that asserted the need for new publishing formats for contemporary verse analogous to recent innovations in the
visual arts. *The Lyric Year* aspired to be "an *Annual Exhibition* or *Salon*"
of verse that would represent a fair cross-section of the nation's poetry at
a given moment, while also providing tangible incentives for poets.[27] Earle
also argued for greater contemporaneity of subject matter and diversity
of voices, noting that while the first series of Palgrave's *Golden Treasury,*
published a half century earlier in 1863, had contained only five poems
written by women out of 339, more than 40 percent of the poems in his
volume were by women. Unlike the many contemporaries anxious about
poetry's supposed feminization, he found this a happy development. He

further characterized the newest American verse as "democratic, scientific, humane," exhibiting "the liberating touch of Walt Whitman" and reflecting "the exhilarating trend that is sweeping over Continental music, painting and poetry."[28]

Despite these ambitions, the one hundred verses of *The Lyric Year* show relatively little spirit of stylistic experiment: only seven, for example, eschew rhyme.[29] But several took significant steps toward the expansion of subject matter that would soon energize the New Verse movement, including "From a City Street" (Armond Carroll), "New York: A Nocturne" (Florence Earle Coates), "Jetsam—In Memory of the Sinking of the 'Titanic'" (Herman Montagu Donner), "The Poet in the Market-place" (Margaret Belle Houston), "Pittsburgh" (James Oppenheim), "The Mob" (Edwin Davies Schoonmaker), "Caliban in the Coal Mines" (Louis Untermeyer), and "To a City Swallow" (Edith Wyatt). *The Lyric Year* also distinguished itself by its hospitality toward younger and less-established contributors. Thirty of the eighty-five contributors to whom C. Thomas Tanselle could assign birthdates were under thirty years old in 1912, and fifty-five of them were younger than forty. More than a third had published no books at the time.[30] Though, not surprisingly, most of its roster is now obscure, several participants would become important to the New Poetry, including Witter Bynner, Sara Teasdale, Arthur Davison Ficke, Vachel Lindsay, Louis Untermeyer, and the sensational twenty-year-old Edna St. Vincent Millay, whose "Renascence" narrowly missed winning a prize, creating the controversy that launched her meteoric career and gained her a private scholarship to Vassar College.

The traditional gatekeeping function of the anthology format was further challenged by the judges' decision to award the *Lyric Year* prizes "to three men whose names are absolutely unknown to the general reading public," as *The Dial* grumbled.[31] The anonymity of the prizewinners was mildly disputed by some other reviewers, who were aware of George Sterling and T. A. Daly, but all agreed on the obscurity of the first-prize winner. In keeping with Earle's aspirations to an American poetry engaged with modern life, the five-hundred-dollar award went to an ambitious if uneven poem of social critique, "Second Avenue" by Orrick Johns.[32] Like William Vaughn Moody's great poem of anti-imperialist protest "Ode in a Time of Hesitation" (1900), "Second Avenue" ironically contrasts the idealistic conviction of the Union dead in the Civil War to the empty capitalist greed dominating subsequent decades. Though it lacks a symbol as concentrated and resonant as the Saint-Gaudens statue of the Massachusetts Fifty-fourth regiment (used by Moody and by Robert Lowell in "For the Union Dead" in 1960), the poem does anticipate several key aspects of the New Verse in its emphasis on urban settings and imagery, its sensitivity to class stratification and conflict, and its juxtaposition of the mundane with the elevated. Johns portrays modern capitalism as a condition that impoverishes everyone, not only the immigrant underclass of subsistence laborers, who must "live from hour to hour" while "immured in living graves," but even its ostensible beneficiaries, who must endure a paradoxical condition of experience, both fragmented and routinized, in which "one year does not know the next, / And youthful still, the world grows old."[33] Although it deplores the exploitative structures of the capitalist metropolis, "Second Avenue" differs from the genteel anticapitalism that dominated American verse of the preceding decades by refusing to reject the city as the defining site of modern life, imagining the great twentieth-century poet as one who will discard obsolete accouterments ("cast his staff and horn away") and attend to "the clamoring will" of the "thousand thousand feet" who "[b]eat on through unreturning ways" of a world of "steel and steam and straining mass."[34]

Earle closed his preface to *The Lyric Year* by noting that he had personally examined "ten thousand poems by nearly two thousand poets"—an unexpectedly herculean travail that contributed to his departure for an extended stay in Europe in early 1913, scotching the plan to continue the project annually.[35] But the failure of his resolve did not make *The Lyric Year* a failed project. The enormous response to it confounded assumptions that poetry in America was withering away; as Harriet Monroe noted in her review in *Poetry,* the contest showed "how eager is the hitherto unfriended American muse to seize any helping hand."[36] Her hopes for *Poetry* must have been greatly buoyed by this evidence of widespread interest in contemporary verse, which she believed would emerge if only poets had a chance to be read and were not forced to starve in order to write.

Although the verses of *The Lyric Year* anticipate the New Poetry in their evident desire to reject the faded virtues of genteel verse, overall they lack the tonal strategies and formal tools of a more modern poetics. This same state of transition shaped the response to the anthology by a young poet excluded from it, William Carlos Williams, whose poem "On First Opening *The Lyric Year*" was published in the correspondence section of *Poetry* in June 1913. Williams mischievously compares encountering the anthology to the experience of overlooking a cemetery, the poems to "[a]ll the little two-yard-long mounds that vary / So negligibly after all"—a metaphor that affords him "a certain satisfaction."[37] The pedestrian sameness of the volume's contents leads him to reconsider his own desire to join a community, eventually a pantheon, of poets:

I remember once how I stood
Thinking, one summer's day, how good it must be to spend
Some thousand years there from beginning to end,
There on the cool hillside.[38]

But Williams's nonconformist imperative cannot be gainsaid, forcing him to recognize the too-high price of admission:

But with that feeling grew the dread
That I too would have to be like all the other dead.
That unpleasant sense which one has when one smothers,
Unhappy to leave so much behind merely to resemble others.
It's good no doubt to lie socially well ordered when one has
    so long to lie,
But for myself somehow this does not satisfy.

In these lines, Williams evokes the familiar topos of the modern artist as a rebel against complacent convention who embarks upon an intellectual journey that risks, even embraces, alienation rather than conforming to an oppressive "social order." But while the poem shows occasional evidence of the plainspoken diction and conversational cadences that would energize such later works as "Tract" (1916–17), its strained rhymes and indecisive rhythms suggest that Williams is still caught, like the anthology poets he scorns, between the desire to innovate and the lack of technical resources to do so. Furthermore, Williams's skepticism toward the whole idea of the anthology registers the continuing power of the late-genteel imperative to treat poetry as solitary rather than communal, dematerialized rather than worldly. For him in late 1912, as for Ridgely Torrence deploring the Poetry Society of America even while joining it in 1910, organization, community, and institution still signified intellectual drudgery, interpersonal strife, and artistic compromise—the very things one wrote poetry to escape. One of the crucial accomplishments of the New Verse movement of the ensuing years, in which Williams became a compulsive if often cantankerous participant, would be to establish such organizational innovations as benefits rather than contaminants to poetry.

Despite the efforts of Braithwaite, Rittenhouse, Wheeler, Earle, and others, no one in mid-1912 could have been confident of boom times just ahead for American verse. Kennerley and Earle had reason to feel aggrieved at the reception of *The Lyric Year*. Except for the qualified positive offered by Monroe in *Poetry* and the obligatory praise in Kennerley's own magazine *The Forum*, reviews of the anthology were remarkably negative. Reviewers complained about the method of choosing the contents, the anonymity of the prizewinners, and the overall mediocrity of the verse, while expressing almost no appreciation for the effort to publicize and remunerate American poets.[39] This sour response reveals the persistence of the evaluative climate that had inhibited American verse for the previous two decades, in which attempts at innovation were greeted with corrosive skepticism, the lack of institutional support for poets justified as a character-building virtue, and complaints countered by a rhetoric of overproduction holding that enough great poems had been written already, and contemporary poetry was just so much wastepaper. In December 1912, *The Dial*—not yet the champion of modernism it would become in the 1920s but still a vocal defender of the genteel tradition—attacked efforts to provide poets financial support such as *The Lyric Year* and *Poetry,* arguing that no "encouragement or incentive will be likely to increase [poetry's] amount and improve its quality."[40] Any increase in quantity was pointless, since already "hundreds of volumes of metrical exercises labelled poetry come under our observation every year," most of which were "the vapid outpourings" of unfortunates who combined "misguided taste with overweening conceit."[41] The hope of improving quality was equally futile, since no worldly incentive "has any potency to endow any singer with a higher rapture or a more authentically creative expression than would in any case be his."[42]

The situation of poetry in the book-publishing industry in the years before 1912 was no more hospitable. According to annual compilations by *Publishers Weekly,* the number of books classified as "Poetry and Drama" actually increased during the worst of the crisis between 1900 and 1910, reflecting a moment of great expansion in the nation's publishing industry. And yet in January 1911, as they surveyed a year in which the number of "Poetry and Drama" publications leaped to their highest levels yet, the editors of *Publishers Weekly* felt moved to complain that "[p]ure literature perhaps never made a poorer showing than this year, poetry of promise being especially lacking."[43] Such remarks suggest that the increase in volumes during these years was a sign not of renewed interest in poetry but of an improving economy that was enabling more middle-class Americans to subsidize their own publications with vanity and semi-vanity presses. Two conditions are clear: poets perceived the book-publishing market as anything but hospitable; and even high-toned firms routinely consented to publish contemporary verse only with subventions. In circulars aimed at potential guarantors of *Poetry* in early 1912, Harriet Monroe represented "[l]eading publishers of England and America" as saying that they "'almost never' publish a book of verse" unless the author paid the expenses; in 1913,

William Aspenwall Bradley likewise estimated that "[b]y far the greater part of the books of verse" were brought out in this fashion.[44] This entrenched subvention system allowed publishers to ensure a break-even result or even a small profit from the author's contribution, leaving little incentive to push their poetry list, especially if they genuinely believed there was no market out there to reach.

The prevalence of subventions can be charted by examining the early publication record of poets who became central to the New Poetry. Most had brought out books or pamphlets before 1912, but virtually all of these were noncommercially printed and subsidized by the authors or friends. Edgar Lee Masters's first volume, bearing the dreary title *A Book of Verses* (1898), was issued by a dubious Chicago firm, Way and Williams, which kept his manuscript for two years, agreed to publish only after he threatened to sue, and then went bankrupt on the very day his book came out—a nightmarish experience that soured him on poetry and publishers for the next decade.[45] Between 1900 and 1912, Masters issued several volumes of prose essays and plays under the imprint of Rooks Press, which he later described as "a little corporation of my own formation."[46] Carl Sandburg's professor and mentor at Lombard College in Galesburg, Philip Green Wright, issued four pamphlets of his verse between 1904 and 1910 under the Asgard Press imprint, future collector's items but hardly commercial propositions. Further south in Springfield, Vachel Lindsay had at least twelve pamphlets of his verse and artwork privately published between 1905 and 1913. Robert Frost's sole "book" before 1914 was an 1894 pamphlet called *Twilight*, of which only two copies were printed, for him and his wife-to-be Elinor.[47] Sara Teasdale's first book, *Sonnets to Duse*, was printed in 1907 by the Poet Lore Company, which charged her $290 for one thousand copies, while Elinor Wylie's first, *Incidental Numbers*, was printed anonymously at her expense in London in 1912.[48]

Even well into 1911, the American publishing establishment seemed perfectly certain that poetry had no market. In October of that year, only twelve months before the first issue of *Poetry*, Mitchell Kennerley, then virtually alone among American commercial publishers in his stated willingness to issue volumes of new poetry, rejected Harriet Monroe's manuscript using precisely the tone of complacent defeatism typical of the previous two decades: "*as we all know,* there is almost no sale for books of poems just at present" (italics added).[49] Kennerley also sent back the verses Monroe had offered to his magazine *The Forum*, regretting blandly that "at present we are hopelessly over-stocked."[50] His reply, dated only two days after Monroe's initial inquiry, suggests that he barely looked at them. Clearly, even the publishers most interested in contemporary poetry were routinely refusing the work of veteran poets without serious consideration.[51]

All Is Changed

In a remarkably short period after October 1912, the situation changed. By Christmas, *The Lyric Year* volume and the first three issues of *Poetry* had appeared. A poem in *Poetry*'s January issue, "General William Booth Enters into Heaven" by Vachel Lindsay, gained immediate attention, leading to reprintings and discussion in the March issues of *Current Opinion* and the *Literary Digest* and in *The Independent* for March 13. By July, the *Literary Digest* was already speaking of "a boom in poetry," citing "periodicals devoted exclusively to poetry, an increasing popular demand for volumes of verse, more and more space given up to poems in the popular magazines, and an improvement in the economic conditions of the poets themselves."[52] In that same article, the Poetry Society's president, Edward J. Wheeler, noted that some poets were beginning to find the idea of living on their verse imaginable, naming Arthur Guiterman, Berton Braley, and Lindsay, "whose stirring 'General Booth Enters Heaven' made him famous some months ago."[53] Clearly such claims sought not only to report a boom but to promote it. And yet the fact that they had become printable in reputable venues signaled a remarkable shift in the literary landscape; it's hard to imagine what evidence could have been summoned to support them in 1903 or 1908.

A month later in August, Arthur Ficke revealed the previous orthodoxy of subvention and the quickly changing conditions when he exulted at Kennerley's willingness to publish his latest volume without the author's help: "Good old Mitch Kennerley is going to stake his good coin on 'Mr. Faust.' Wouldn't it frost you—I don't put up a cent."[54] Before 1913 was over, Braithwaite had stepped into the void left by the disappearance of *The Lyric Year* and published the first of his annual anthologies of magazine verse, while Houghton Mifflin had issued a new anthology of work by living American poets, Rittenhouse's *Little Book of Modern Verse*. In a letter of November 25, Rittenhouse described the "remarkable response" to her volume: "[E]ven before the reviews have begun to come out it has sold its first edition. . . . People have sent back to Houghtons after ordering one copy, and taken half a dozen and in some cases ten."[55]

This exciting year in American verse was followed by an even greater one. In a *Literary Digest* piece for April 1914 entitled "Poets Again Best Sellers," the president of Macmillan, George P. Brett, described a "change in the public's attitude toward literature" that had come "with disconcerting suddenness" and produced such remarkable successes as Rabindrinath Tagore's 1913 volume of verse *The Gardener,* which had already sold more than a hundred thousand copies.[56] Even Harriet Monroe was now able to place her long-rejected manuscript (published as *You and I*) with a major firm—in fact, with Brett and Macmillan, who were now ready to proceed without any "commission" from the author. In May, the St. Louis magazine *Reedy's Mirror* began publishing *vers libre* epitaphs by "Webster Ford" about the lives and deaths of the residents of a small Illinois town. By the time they were collected into a Macmillan volume in April 1915, Edgar Lee Masters's *Spoon River Anthology* had become a genuine cultural phenomenon, "that rarest of publications, a poetry best-seller."[57] Nearly equalling it in notoriety was Lindsay's volume *The Congo and Other Poems* (1914), which he supported by indefatigable public performances—including a command reading for President Woodrow Wilson and his cabinet in 1915. Though she would not issue a volume until 1917, Edna St. Vincent Millay was already a national celebrity, an icon of the New Womanhood.

A new publishing economy for American verse was emerging that would have seemed an impossible dream a decade earlier. Over the next few years, volumes by American poets found sizable markets, among them Lowell's *Sword Blades and Poppy Seed* (1914), Frost's *North of Boston* (1915), Lindsay's *The Chinese Nightingale* (1917), and Millay's *Renascence and Other Poems* (1917). In April 1918, in the midst of a world war, the publisher B. W. Huebsch wrote to Louis Untermeyer about the first (and only) volume of verse by a twenty-two-year-old unknown, Alter Brody, which he would publish later that year as *Family Album and Other Poems.* Huebsch asked Untermeyer to relay to Brody his offer of a $1,500 advance on a proposed edition of 1,140 copies, which he called "the usual favorable terms for poetry"—terms that many poets would envy a century later.[58] The last years of the 1910s saw the publication of three highly successful anthologies of contemporary verse, all seeking to consolidate and cash in on the phenomenon of the New Verse: *The New Poetry* (ed. Harriet Monroe and Alice Corbin Henderson, 1917), *Modern American Poetry* (ed. Louis Untermeyer, 1919), and *New Voices: An Introduction to Contemporary Poetry* (ed. Marguerite Wilkinson, 1919). In 1917 alone the Monroe and Henderson volume went through four full printings, estimated by Craig Abbott as four thousand copies each, followed by at least one more printing every year through 1922.[59] In the fall of 1919 Wilkinson reported that her anthology was "selling with a surprising rapidity, even to my experienced publishers"—so well that she was planning a sabbatical year with its proceeds.[60] Over ten thousand copies of Monroe and Henderson's 1923 revised edition were printed in that year, followed by one or two further printings every year through 1928.[61] All three anthologies sold well enough to go into second editions by 1921 and would be updated and reissued into the 1930s.

Looking back in April 1916, Monroe meditated upon the astonishing change in poetry's fortunes in fewer than four years: "In January 1913, the art was still in the old era, and one saw few signs of a change of attitude among the constituted authorities. . . . Now all is changed."[62] She cited various specifics, the most impressive of which is an anecdote from a "well-known poet" who told of going into Brentano's bookstore "for the first time in years," heading for "the little table away back in a dark corner under the stair" where modern poetry had always been kept, and finding none there:

> "How is this?" I asked the clerk, "have you given up poetry altogether?" The man turned on me a withering glance—"Poetry," he said, pointing majestically, "is up in front."
>
> And up in front I found it, in high piles on the foremost table; and moreover crowds of people, three or four deep, were reaching over each other to buy it.[63]

The change of fortunes had been so sudden that Monroe worried about poetry "becoming the fashion—a real danger because the poets need an audience, not fitful and superficial, but loyal and sincere."[64] But the New Poetry was not a fad that would evaporate as soon as metropolitan elites were beguiled by some new trend. Along with the faddists had come deeply committed men and women who would establish stable institutional sites hosting a vigorous modern poetry—magazines, anthologies, prizes, organizations. Even by 1916 they had already done so much to rejuvenate the genre that, as Monroe claimed in another editorial later that year, "Never before was there so much talk about poetry in this western world, or so much precious print devoted to its schools and schisms."[65]

Little Magazines

This explosion of creative and institutional activity after 1912 took place in a wide variety of venues. The New Verse was published and publicized, argued over and defended, in periodical publications of many types, from the old "quality magazines" such as *The Century* to mass-marketed magazines such as *Munsey's*. Many publishers, including long-established firms such as Macmillan and Holt and innovative new ones such as B. W. Huebsch and Alfred A. Knopf, issued important volumes of contemporary verse between

1913 and 1920. But these creative energies were concentrated most power-fully in the "little magazine," which, despite a few abortive predecessors before 1900, was a distinctive twentieth-century format that reflected broad trends toward disciplinary specialization and niche marketing throughout the nation's print culture. Carl F. Kaestle and Janice A. Radway describe the period between 1880 and 1940 as one of simultaneous "consolidation and diversification" in which "technological innovations and changes in the distribution of literacy" combined with new "economies of scale and speed" developed by entrepreneurial producers to create a strongly standardized and consumerist print culture for a literate mass population, while also giving rise to myriad specialized print subcultures keyed to "professional and technical" disciplines, "emerging leisure-time pursuits," "specific hobbies and interests," and "the practice and publication of dissent."[66] The little literary magazine was one of the most important and characteristic manifestations of this specializing trend. After 1900 such publications could be produced with minimal capital outlay and distributed through easily identifiable venues such as the highbrow and bohemian bookstores springing up in major cities and through an increasingly cost-effective and quick national postal system. Small magazines often bought or swapped advertising space in the pages of their competitors, ensuring that readers of any one would quickly become aware of new entrants. Although many individual titles lasted only a few years or even months, after 1912 the little magazine as a field of literary production remained vigorous and stable.

Though long understood as playing a central role in twentieth-century American literature, little magazines have been misunderstood in two key respects: their sponsorship of later-canonical authors, and their supposed antipathy toward modern practices of professional writing and cultural entrepreneurship. The earliest scholarly interest in little magazines in the 1940s coincided with the campaign to create a lineage and canon for international high modernism, and their idiosyncratic and fugitive aspects were emphasized in narratives of modernism as rebellion against a benighted and commodified cultural mainstream. For nearly half a century after the landmark 1946 volume *The Little Magazine: A History and Bibliography,* the little magazine was treated merely as a "proving ground," as Frederick Hoffman put it in 1945, for a few titanic modernists who needed space and freedom to develop their unique experimental styles.[67] This era of critical "strip-mining, in which individual artists were extracted from the heterogeneous terrain in which they published, and singled out as the elite geniuses of modernism," obscured the complex roles played by groups and institutions and overlooked individuals in the emergence of modern American poetry.[68]

Few scholars supposed that attention to the activities of little magazines might reveal the evaluative machinery by which modernism was created, or how its canonical reputations were gained, challenged, maintained, and lost.

More recent scholars have begun to think of the little magazine quite differently. In 1989 Cary Nelson proposed that rather than merely extracting textual fragments from various magazines in order to complete authorial catalogs, scholars might read individual numbers or whole runs of magazines as themselves modernist texts offering us access to a moment when twentieth-century poetry was "undecided, unfixed, still exploring its potential and its possible alliances."[69] Jayne Marek's 1995 book *Women Editing Modernism* confronted long-standing disciplinary preconceptions by treating the female editors of little magazines such as *Poetry* and the *Little Review* as key modernist creators. Mark Morrisson's 2001 study *The Public Face of Modernism* challenged "the commonplace of modernism's inveterate antagonism to mass culture" by demonstrating the eagerness and skill with which such editors as Max Eastman and Margaret Anderson exploited the mechanisms of modern advertising to publicize their "little" magazines in mainstream spheres.[70] The ongoing Modernist Journals Project (www.modjourn.org), now based at Brown University and the University of Tulsa, has greatly aided scholars wishing to read little magazines in these new ways by digitizing and Web-publishing full runs (through 1922) of key titles, including *Poetry,* the *New Age,* and the *English Review,* as well as more specialized magazines not otherwise easy to access such as *Blast, Coterie,* the *Blue Review, The Owl,* and *The Tyro.*

Introducing their 2007 volume of essays *Little Magazines and Modernism,* Suzanne Churchill and Adam McKible emphasize the malleability and multiplicity of the climate that shaped and was shaped by these publications, arguing that "[l]ittle magazines provide a record of the large-scale conversation that became modernism, an odd and absorbing concourse that cannot be reduced to a single movement or coherent set of principles."[71] Their emphasis on the many faces and forms of "little magazines" (and, for that matter, of "modernism") is salutary. Like them, I am less interested in using such terms as gatekeeping generic boundaries than in describing a cultural field of continual and productive flux, in which a given publication might function as "little" or "avant-garde" in some contexts, and in others might resemble a specialized disciplinary journal or even a "quality magazine."

In that spirit, the remaining chapters of part 1 examine four publications that shaped the New Poetry movement of the 1910s, seeking to preserve their substantial differences and to highlight the powerful synergy among them. The first reevaluates the best-known yet often underestimated of American little magazines, *Poetry: A Magazine of Verse,* which combined into one stable and powerful entity the goals of the scattered initiatives of the previous decade: the preservative efforts of Braithwaite's annual reviews, the interpersonal networking structure of the Poetry Society of America, and the remunerative and publicizing functions of *The Lyric Year.* The following two chapters pair metropolitan New York magazines often viewed as opposites—*The Masses* and *Others*—to highlight overlooked commonalities of formal experimentalism and urban progressivism at the heart of the New Poetry. *The Masses* sponsored a poetics of social commitment in an eclectic mix of styles before transforming under duress into the more somber *Liberator* in 1918, while *Others* served as a lively laboratory of *vers libre* experiment from 1915 until fading into inactivity by decade's end. Both magazines sought verse that evoked the rhythms, voices, sensory stimuli, and spatial relationships that defined modern urban life. Both were socially engaged, and both were aesthetically experimental—just not exactly in the same way or proportion. The final chapter of part 1 examines the *Seven Arts,* a magazine straddling the avant-garde and the mainstream, which through its courageous campaign against the nation's war policy after April 1917 made modern verse into a powerful vehicle of sociopolitical dissent.[72] *Poetry* and *Others* took verse as their primary object of attention, belying the paralyzing assumption that publications founded on contemporary verse were economically unviable dreams. *The Masses* and the *Seven Arts,* placing verse alongside a variety of literary, political, and visual texts, integrated poetry into ambitious syntheses of modern culture and politics. Both approaches helped to rejuvenate American poetry by refuting the notion, endemic only a few years earlier, that contemporary verse was a pastime for an idle evening or a filler for a half-empty magazine page, practiced only by leisured idlers fastidiously detached from the lives of ordinary people.

By the end of the 1910s, despite the passing away of the faddists, the moderating popularity of some of the decade's poetic stars, and the repressive political climate, poetry in America had been thoroughly transformed. Poets were finding publishers willing, even eager, to issue their books. An ever-changing array of spirited little magazines printed verse in many different styles by writers both nationally famous and totally unknown. In the narrative that follows, I seek to show that the New Verse movement achieved this spectacular success by theorizing and demonstrating poetry's ability to speak not only to rarefied emotions and private fantasies, but to the public, the urban, the political—to every aspect of twentieth-century experience.

CHAPTER 2

Poetry's Opening Door

Harriet Monroe and American Modernism

Among the most familiar yet misunderstood moments of twentieth-century American literary history is the founding of *Poetry: A Magazine of Verse* in Chicago in 1912 by Harriet Monroe. *Poetry* has long been noted for its publication of nearly every key figure in Anglo-American verse of the period. But by focusing on the question of the magazine's openness or resistance to poets later viewed as important to high modernism, historians have misread its greatest importance, which was simply to create a space for contemporary American verse where none had been.

Poetry exemplifies the productive intersection between twentieth-century artistic avant-gardes and the forces of modern disciplinary specialization. The editorial discourse of its early years, mainly generated by Monroe, with notable contributions from Alice Corbin Henderson, Ezra Pound, Eunice Tietjens, Carl Sandburg, Edith Wyatt, and others, forcefully emphasized the living culture of the present over reverence for past canons and demonstrated a marked inclination for conflict with self-appointed gatekeepers of tradition. As they forged *Poetry*'s identity through antagonistic opposition to such "standpatters" as the "quality magazines," the American literary academy, the National Institute of Arts and Letters, and the Hall of Fame for Great Americans, Monroe and her colleagues made their magazine a crucial pioneer in the rhetorical self-fashioning of a twentieth-century American avant-garde. And yet despite abundant avant-garde energy, Monroe and her editorial colleagues did not see themselves as tyros disdaining worldly methods and goals. Instead they sought to create a publishing format for verse that combined the aesthetic refinement and emotional complexity of "high art," the modernized marketing practices of mass culture, and the targeted audience and professionalized demeanor of the disciplinary journal.

The announcement mailed to poets and interested parties in the summer of 1912 emphasized with great clarity the benefits of disciplinary specialization: "We offer [poets] . . . a chance to be heard in their own place, without the limitations imposed by the popular magazine. In other words, while the ordinary magazines must minister to a large public little interested in poetry, this magazine will appeal to, and it may be hoped, will develop, a public primarily interested in poetry as an art."[1] Monroe's understanding of the importance of niche marketing was an idea of its time; poetry was lagging well behind many professional disciplines and specialized pastimes that already supported one or more publications. But in a climate that kept poetry segregated from despoiling commercialism, her approach was revolutionary. Monroe was convinced that to immerse American poetry in the cultural economies of the modern metropolis would not ruin but energize it. This motivating premise was decisively vindicated by her magazine's immediate and lasting success. Barely a year after beginning the venture with no precedent or evidence that it could succeed, she had inaugurated what American poets and poetry lovers had long bemoaned as impossible: a stable and vigorous space that publicized virtually all the significant books of American and British verse, defended experiments in versification and subject matter, and insisted on paying poets for their work. Monroe personally maintained *Poetry* for twenty-four years until her death and left it so well-regarded that it continues to play a key role in the nation's literary culture a century after its founding.

Monroe's editorial career was an achievement of monumental proportions. Yet accounts of her role in the emergence of modern American verse have often been remarkably grudging. Perhaps inevitably the long-lived, steady figure who initiates a discipline or style will be taken for granted, becoming a foil for aspirants who need to differentiate themselves from encompassing elders. Monroe shares this role with distinguished figures in a variety of fields, among them William Dean Howells, Robert Henri, John Dewey, Franz Boas, Frederick Law Olmstead, Jane Addams, W. C. Handy, Duke Ellington, and Aaron Copland. But in her case something more, and darker, is involved in the question of reputation. The widespread unwillingness to credit Monroe personally as a modernist pioneer reveals long-standing gender biases that have tinged American literary history—particularly the notion that Ezra Pound was self-evidently "the most important figure in any venture with which he was associated," as Jayne Marek puts it.[2] *Poetry*'s complex, often fractious relations with Pound, and its sometimes reluctant (though by no means unimportant) support of certain poets within his orbit, have often been treated as prima facie evidence of the editors' insufficiently modern temperament, their desire to cling to the inhibitions of Victorian gentility.[3]

In the 1930 article "Small Magazines," Pound himself established this pattern for later historians by portraying Monroe as an unimaginative bluestocking who was merely in the right place at the right time. "Small Magazines" appeared in an unlikely but significant venue, the *English Journal*—which later became *College English*—where it would have reached a sizable audience of American college teachers over a period of years. Pound characterizes the true little magazine as above all a venue independent of "whether a given idea or given trend in art will 'git ads' from the leading corset companies" or "whether it happens to agree with what Aunt Hannah had heard from her uncle."[4] His argument simultaneously demonizes and feminizes genteel culture, situating the ideal little magazine into agonistic male opposition against forces of rank commercialism and closet conventionality supposedly embodied by women such as Monroe—his barely updated version of genteel Aunt Hannah, hankering after her uncle's Victorian bromides while also slavishly attending the accursed bottom line—who was only dragged toward modernism by Pound's stronger will and acuter taste. Pound uncharitably proposes that Monroe would be remembered only as a "meal ticket."[5]

Pound's metaphors suggest the strongly gendered subtext shaping literary-historical narratives that frame modernism as heroic rebellion against hidebound gentility. For decades, scholars of American poetry followed him in assuming unquestioningly that female movers and shakers of the period, the editors of *Poetry* above all, did little more than heed the advice and guidance of titanic males.[6] Valuable work by feminist scholars has begun, but only begun, to challenge what Marek has described as the "distorting lens" used by historians of the "Pound era," which obscured the central places of female editors in most of the important little magazines of the period.[7] Marek's book, along with fine essays by Ann Massa, Susan Albertine, and Robin Schulze, have now traced a distinctive and coherent intellectual genealogy for Harriet Monroe. Even so, the patronizing image of "Aunt" Harriet and other female editors following Pound's charismatic lead is foundational to the modernism we've known for a half century and is not easily dislodged. It lingers even in the volume commemorating sixty-five years of *Poetry,* where one of Monroe's successors as editor, Daryl Hine, describes her as "a strong-minded literary spinster" and "an anachronistic celebrant of the public virtues" of the nineteenth century whose lack of national prominence made the "inception of [*Poetry*'s] career" "not propitious."[8]

Such portrayals not only slight Monroe's initiative in founding and sustaining *Poetry* but also misrepresent her adventurous intellectual engagement with the conditions of early twentieth-century modernity. She was no "literary spinster," fluttery bluestocking, or reluctant modernist. Well before 1912, in both her experimental verse on modern themes and her resolute campaigns for the economic rights of authors, she was exploring new ways of understanding poetry's role in twentieth-century metropolitan culture and making herself the ideal person of her generation to found and edit a magazine committed to that revision. Monroe's modernism was obviously not the same as Pound's or Eliot's. A financially canny woman old enough to be their mother, she retained a genteel personal style while embracing modern industrial technologies and espousing the politics of midwestern progressivism. In short, she embodied a whole cluster of values antithetical to theirs. When the narrative of modernism as the era of Pound and Eliot was constituted in the Anglo-American academy after World War II, those such as Monroe who dissented from their pessimistic Olympian elitism were (and still are) often denied the honorific of *modernist* altogether. Challenging these long-standing preconceptions, as I aim to do here, does not mean converting Monroe into a traditional high modernist but reshaping our notions of modernism to account for her, and eventually a host of other important figures who can't be shoehorned into the Poundian model.

Monroe, *Poetry,* and the "Modern Subject"

Though many others contributed, *Poetry*'s distinctive character derived most directly from the tiny gray-haired figure who imagined it and ran it for a quarter century. Born in 1860 into a socially prominent but not wealthy Chicago family, Harriet Monroe was a woman of powerful and sometimes acerbic temperament, never to experience marriage or motherhood, who threw her prodigious energies into two interrelated activities: making a living in the arts, and contributing to the genre she loved best, poetry. Early writings, such as the 1889 verse "Cantata" and the 1893 essay "Chicago," articulate her fascination with boomtown Chicago and the forces of modern commerce that shaped it. Both pieces portray the city as a transformative environment offering access "[t]o realms that are rich for the souls that dare," combining unfettered ambition, democratic idealism, and dynamic gender relations: "[A]mong the women as well as the men, one finds the same love of conquest, the same desire to attain the impossible, for nothing is impossible."[9] Her lifelong identification with Chicago extended to an affinity for its business, cultural, and civic leaders such as her brother

William, an engineer whom she rhapsodized as a "builder of power-plants," and her brother-in-law, the eminent architect John Wellborn Root, whose biography she authored after his sudden death in 1891.[10]

Yet Monroe was no apologist for unbridled patriarchal capitalism. She inherited a fervent democratic idealism from her father, Henry Stanton Monroe, a man of deep principle who had turned down a lucrative partnership in a New York law firm to stay in Chicago "to act more for the needy and less for the affluent."[11] Her own politics drew from the more progressive leaders of civic modernism in Chicago, including Root, Louis Sullivan, and a group of female activists of whom Jane Addams is the best-known.[12] Yet her idealism was not the fantastical naiveté of a Vachel Lindsay but a pragmatic sense of "altruistic citizenship"—a commitment to improve society by using its own mechanisms of power.[13] Although Monroe seldom took overtly feminist positions, her actions throughout her life reveal a personality strongly committed to the emergence of American women into greater cultural and professional prominence. With its mostly female editorship, her magazine became one of American culture's most significant realizations of this principle. Indeed, one recent commentator, discussing *Poetry*'s significance to women's literary history, finds "a warm, rich, profound feminism" that derives from the editor's "immensely generous, incorruptible, democratic humanism."[14] Mary Biggs notes that during the years of Monroe's editorship (1912–36), 46 percent of the poets who appeared in *Poetry* were women, which she calls an "equality of literary opportunity that [women] had not had before and have probably not had since."[15]

The trajectory of Monroe's early career made her acutely sensitive to poetry's problematic status in modern cultural economies. She had begun the campaign that culminated in the founding of *Poetry* almost a quarter century earlier, with two early efforts to integrate poetry into the cultural life of Chicago: her 1889 verse "Cantata," commemorating the opening of an early landmark of modern civic architecture, Sullivan's Auditorium Theater; and her celebratory ode written for the World's Columbian Exposition, set to music by George W. Chadwick and performed with a large orchestra and chorus in October 1892. Though the Columbian Ode had but a brief public vogue, the experience gave Monroe a lifelong zeal for the rights of literary entrepreneurs, both authors and editors. Over the next several years, she sustained all the way to the Supreme Court a judgment against the *New York World* for an unauthorized and botched printing of the ode, a decision that helped to establish legal precedent for the rights of American authors to control their work.[16] After 1912, her commitment to authorial rights redounded in two central themes of *Poetry*'s editorial discourse and in its correspondence with poets and anthologists: a fervent conviction that authors should always be paid for their work, and an exacting insistence on *Poetry*'s own copyright claims against anthologies and other magazines. Both policies asserted poetry as a full-fledged participant rather than a charity case within twentieth-century cultural marketplaces.

In the inhospitable climate before 1912, Monroe struggled with only intermittent success to sustain a life connected to poetry. But it is crucial to understand that by the time she began her editorial career at the age of fifty-two, she was already familiar with the role of modern poet as provocateur who embraces unconventional styles and "unpoetic" subject matter. Quite early she had become convinced that American poetry needed to immerse itself in the conditions of urban-industrial modernity, and this view shaped her self-image as a poet, as for example when she pitched Mitchell Kennerley a volume in 1911 by remarking, "I will state certain facts. More than any other living American or British poet I have chosen modern subjects."[17] Indeed, around 1905, when almost no one in the United States was producing adventurous poetry, she had undertaken a self-consciously experimental series of verses portraying emblems of twentieth-century modernity, including "The Telephone," "The Hotel," "The Turbine," "A Power-plant," "The Ocean Liner," "Our Canal," "Night in State Street," and others.[18] Bliss Perry, the editor of the *Atlantic Monthly,* accepted "The Telephone" with enthusiasm in 1905 but conceded to Monroe later that year that the sonnet had "received sharp criticism in a good many quarters" for its marriage of traditional form with ultramodern content.[19] The most significant of her experiments was the unmetered poem "The Hotel," composed in 1907 and turned down by various periodicals before Perry accepted it in late 1908 "with particular pleasure" as one of Monroe's "very finest" works, while also predicting that "[t]here will be many doubters, of course, as to the propriety of your metrical scheme."[20] As Monroe noted in various contexts, "The Hotel" demonstrated her interest in verse without rhyme or regular meter several years before encountering the first such submissions to *Poetry,* and long before she met Ezra Pound.[21] When the controversies over *vers libre* erupted soon after *Poetry*'s founding, she was virtually the only American poet of the day who had been through a previous round.

Monroe's poems on "modern subjects" respond enthusiastically to accelerating technological advancements that she hoped were auguring an age of social progress. She shared with many Americans of her generation—though not most of its poets—a fascination with new modes of communication, transportation, and energy production, reading them as signs that humankind was overcoming fundamental limitations of time and space.

But she astutely perceived the modern condition to be fraught with new obstacles, not least for poets. Her 1911 essay "The Bigness of the World," also published in the *Atlantic,* addresses the quandary of the modern artist that *Poetry* would shortly attempt to ameliorate. She argued that while the arts had once resided in small spaces—city-states, courts, coteries—in which the issue of a national or global populace hardly arose, the advent of mass literacy and modern machine technology had rendered this model obsolete. The modern poet had to comprehend and address a much bigger world, an unprecedented task that was causing some once-promising artists to flounder. She was most perceptive, and most prescient of *Poetry*'s activist role, when she diagnosed modernity as a "vast immensity" of potentially "stultifying silence," in which "the poet's voice sounds hollow and impotent, for no one hears. Or if voices come back to him they are not stout cries from a hardy enemy, but vague, half-articulate whispers, unintelligent, irresolute, unauthoritative, coming from no-whither, mere intolerable confusion. He is . . . a creature silenced by silence, enfeebled by lack of response from friend or enemy, dispirited by the blasting loneliness of a wilderness without metes or bounds."[22] Monroe's modern poet is menaced less by enmity than by entropy, a systemic disintegration that creates "a corroding sense of inadequacy, a gradual loss of faith and power, ending in some kind of tragic impotence."[23] We can see the founding of *Poetry* as her attempt to combat this debilitating silence, to provide a site through which aspiring poets and poetry lovers could interact with kindred spirits and opponents across the far-flung world. Even if *Poetry*'s conversation would often be rancorous— which bothered Monroe not at all—it would challenge the greatest dangers of mass-literate modern culture: fragmentation and indifference.

In 1911, as Monroe and several friends pondered the idea of a magazine, her desire to get people talking about poetry led them to try an innovative method of funding in which one hundred guarantors would pledge fifty dollars per year for five years. This business model adapted the idea of high culture as a form of civic advertising that was then endowing the nation with many of its finest museums, orchestras, and theaters. While other editors of the 1910s attempted to find a single patron or small moneyed coterie to subsidize little magazines, Monroe proposed poetry as integral to twentieth-century civic culture and aspired to involve as many members of the Chicago community as possible. Her pitch to the city's business and cultural leaders combined high-toned idealism with hard-headed practicality, offering them an efficient way of advertising Chicago's (and their own) cultural capital. Having known these men and women all her life, she neither condescended nor kowtowed, and she understood which potential donors might respond to idealistic aesthetic appeals, which to ruthlessly pragmatic ones. She frankly analogized the magazine to other enterprises of civic culture, emphasizing the cost-effectiveness of a small magazine with nationwide distribution compared to a symphony orchestra or a world-class art museum: "We feel that the magazine is the most important aesthetic advertisement Chicago ever had. We are doing the same kind of work for the city which is done by the Art Institute, the Orchestral Association, the Chicago Grand Opera co., the two endowed theaters, etc. Indeed, our work is of more far-reaching influence, as poetry travels more easily than any other art."[24] Evidently such tight and worldly analogies appealed to her target audience, since in September 1912 she remarked with pleasure that the task of "securing . . . backers for our magazine" was "not such a hard one as I expected."[25]

This democratic and diffuse financial structure protected *Poetry* from the fate of little magazines dependent on single patrons, such as Alfred Kreymborg's *Others,* which went through one short-lived angel after another in its four years of hand-to-mouth existence.[26] To reassure guarantors that their faith in Monroe was not misplaced, the magazine was constituted with an advisory committee of three prominent figures of Chicago culture, H. C. Chatfield-Taylor, Edith Wyatt, and Henry Blake Fuller—all three loyal allies of Monroe, whose unintrusive behavior could not have disappointed one supportive guarantor, who hoped that the committee would be "quiet men [*sic*] who will keep their hands off the poetry."[27] Despite playing little active role in setting editorial policy, these three did lend their substantial personal authority to the magazine, insulating Monroe from potential meddling. All three served through the end of 1918, when Eunice Tietjens was added. The notion that Monroe's editorial decisions were inhibited by fear of her guarantors' disapproval became part of the myth of her timidity relative to Pound's genuine avant-gardism. From time to time various outraged individuals did noisily withdraw their support, but there is no significant evidence that grumbling guarantors ever exerted real influence on policy.

Monroe's funding method flew in the face of prevailing assumptions of poetry's necessary unworldliness and was ridiculed by contemporaries who objected to her willingness to mingle with the world of commerce. Though he disingenuously denied it, the young novelist Howard Vincent O'Brien lampooned her in *New Men for Old,* his facetious 1914 novel about a bohemian idler suddenly forced to make his way in Chicago's business world. One of O'Brien's subplots involves Muriel Bennett, "an acid person of many more years than she admits, who writes for newspapers or anyone who will employ her, on art and painting," who mounts an effort to "put a trellis on the failing vines of poesy in this degenerate day" by persuading "the men of commerce to subsidize the men of art."[28] She is nonplused to discover that half-literate philistines are eager "to be enrolled for public admiration" as supporters of "an ultra cultured movement," while more genuinely refined businessmen refuse her appeal with smug witticisms on the obsolescence of poetry ("'My dear Miss Bennett, we don't *write* poetry nowadays . . . we *build* it!'").[29] Here O'Brien is truly unjust to his real-life model, since Miss Bennett is thoroughly demoralized by having to acknowledge the truth of this judgment ("I've lost all my assurance for the purpose for which I'm working"), while the real Monroe had matter-of-factly engaged this problem a decade earlier in her verse play "The Thunderstorm" (1899–1900), whose main character, John Mather, sublimates his poetic genius into running a steel company with ambiguous results.[30]

In the autumn of 1912, as the moment of *Poetry*'s first issue neared, Monroe's acumen was tested by the announcement of a forthcoming Boston magazine also calling itself *Poetry*. To be published by Edward J. O'Brien and Edmund Brown of the Four Seas Company and edited by W. S. Braith-waite—then probably better known than Monroe due to his reviewing activities with the *Boston Evening Transcript*—this competitor posed a potentially serious threat, since nobody knew whether Americans would support one such venture, let alone two. Monroe responded by moving up the first issue a full month into early October, ensuring that her magazine, originally scheduled for November, would appear first. Another formidable Chicago woman of her generation, Harriet C. Moody, helped fill the pages of that premature issue by offering Monroe "I Am the Woman," a lengthy unpublished work by her late husband William, whose still-high reputa-tion bolstered *Poetry*'s initial impact, especially among Chicagoans.[31] On September 28, with the temporal priority of her *Poetry* assured, Monroe wrote to Edward O'Brien, urging him to "respect our priority of choice and publish yours under another name."[32] Clearly she understood that whoever controlled the preemptively simple name *Poetry* claimed the power to equate their particular publishing organ with the entire genre.[33]

Monroe wasted no time in advancing a strong position on the current status of poetry and its potential role in twentieth-century American life. The verse she chose to lead off the first issue, Arthur Davison Ficke's double sonnet entitled "Poetry," offered emblematic comment on the genre's chang-ing relevance. In the first fourteen lines, striking the fin-de-siècle attitude of George Santayana's 1890s sonnets, Ficke describes poetry as "a little isle amid bleak seas," a "refuge from the stormy days," and "an isolate realm of garden circled round / By importunity of stress and sound, / Devoid of empery to master these."[34] But the second sonnet counters that twilit reverie by portraying poetry as "a sea-gate" vibrating sympathetically with the motive forces of the world. In this guise, poetry "articulate[s] . . . the whole / Of ocean's heart, else voiceless" against the "blast of powers" that confront the "waiting soul." Ficke's two-part form foreshadowed the magazine's ecumenical character by portraying poetry not as one thing but as many. More importantly, the metaphoric trajectory from refuge to threshold encapsulated the decisive shift from the turn-of-the-century crisis to the post-1910 revival: from confining poetry as a vehicle of sentimental consolation or escapist fantasy to asserting it as a central expressive element of modern experience, a "herald" carrying idealistic "visions" and "incredible hopes" that would "shatter the bonds of sleep." In her editorials on literary value, traditions, and canons, Monroe would repeatedly draw upon the imagery of Ficke's second sonnet, emphasizing modern poetry as a locus of transformative possibility.

A few pages later, in the opening paragraphs of her first editorial, "The Motive of the Magazine," Monroe pursued these implications to position *Poetry* as a form of institutional opportunity for American poets corresponding to those in the visual arts, architecture, and music. She situated the twentieth-century poet in the same high-speed, complex modernity she had described in her 1911 essay "The Bigness of the World," whose every member, "through something he buys or knows or loves, [continually] reaches out to the ends of the earth."[35] Contrary to the notion that poetry needed protection from contaminating materiality, Monroe argued that the more heterogeneous and sprawling the modern world became, the more urgently poetry required "an entrenched place, a voice of power," else it become "lost in the criss-cross of modern currents, the confusion of modern immensities."[36] As she saw it, these challenging conditions were no excuse for resigning oneself to fin-de-siècle melancholy or cultish alienation. They required matter-of-fact acceptance and also implied a great opportunity. If poetry needed a worldly institutional niche to survive in modernity, the modern world in turn had an "immediate and desperate need" for a medium that could bring intellectual coherence and emotional resonance to "great deeds" and "triumphs over matter, over the wilderness, over racial enmities and distances" that would otherwise be left to instrumentalist forms of expression.[37] In other words, poetry was crucial precisely because the accelerated and chaotic character of modernity had left so little place for it.

But renewed relevance would come only if poets were intellectually and financially able to experiment with forms and subject matter expressive of those modern conditions. She did mean for her magazine to serve as a badly needed meal ticket, to insist upon the value of poetry by paying poets in an age when nearly everyone expected them to work for nothing. During her years in the wilderness after the Columbian Ode, Monroe had concluded that the self-righteous anticapitalism dominating genteel literary culture, particularly the idea that poetry should exist apart from "sordid" pecuniary considerations, brought poets no economic and only illusory aesthetic benefits. Instead it merely severed them from meaningful participation in the modern world. She also perceived that this position was itself deeply interested, benefitting entrenched institutional gatekeepers by allowing them to deny that worldly circumstances influenced the apportioning of cultural value. She was especially galled when traditionalists justified their complacent neglect of poetry as a moral virtue. By 1912, twenty years of fighting these battles had generated in her a deep antagonism toward established cultural institutions, which burst forth in the provocative positions that *Poetry* advanced from its first issue.

Avant-Gardism, Prairie Style

At the moment of *Poetry*'s founding, genteel venues of American literary culture were full of admonitions against the poet's need for money. In *The Nation* in August 1913, for example, an unnamed editorialist dismissed *The Lyric Year* and *Poetry*, arguing that "[t]he necessities of occupation in an unkind environment seldom rob us of anything of the highest value."[38] In fact, poverty and neglect are good for the poet, who will "find various sweet uses in his adversity—a close acquaintance with life, a call to perseverance, and the protection of his art from the soiling hand of money-grubbing."[39] The editorial concluded complacently that the poet's bread and butter is "the individual's problem, not the community's."[40]

The most searing of Monroe's avant-garde attacks on established cultural institutions targeted this attitude and its debilitating effects upon those who most needed encouragement: young, unorthodox, and socially marginal artists. In August 1914 she responded to *The Nation*'s complacency in an important editorial, also entitled "The Poet's Bread and Butter," by attacking the hypocrisy that purported to "protect" the poet like a feeble child from the "soiling hand" of the world of money but in actuality only "turn[ed] upon him the deaf ear and lift[ed] against him the stone wall."[41] In fact, she had been on this campaign since *Poetry*'s first issue, in which she had printed Pound's poem "To Whistler, American," as an homage to an American cultural pioneer ("our first great"), a self-portrait of the young artist expatriated for the cause of art, and, most sensationally, an opportunity to lambast the American bourgeoisie as a blinkered "mass of dolts."[42]

Monroe's decision to print such a poem in her inaugural number announced a marked inclination for conflict and a conspicuous unconcern for the feelings of her guarantors, whose names (including such pillars of the Chicago establishment as Palmer, McCormick, Freer, Pullman, and Insull) were listed near the end of the issue.[43] Most histories of modern poetry interpret the publication of "To Whistler, American" as a case of Pound appropriating *Poetry* as a proving ground for his developing avant-gardism, but I would reverse these evaluative valences and propose that Monroe found Pound's iconoclasm valuable in forging an avant-garde position for her magazine and for American poetry more generally. Not surprisingly, the poem's insult to the nation's readership drew flak from readers, but far from backpedaling, Monroe used the controversy to ramify further her avant-garde position, in the fifth issue tartly criticizing those who had attacked the poem for wanting to hear only "the sugar-and-water of compliment" rather than "the bitter medicine which possibly we need."[44] She continued by reaffirming Pound's characterization of the doltish American populace, especially in "our huge, stolid, fundamental indifference to our own art" that had "forced" young poets like him "into exile and rebellion."[45]

Two issues later, in April 1913, by publishing Pound's group in *vers libre*, "Contemporania," Monroe cemented *Poetry*'s avant-garde allegiances. "Contemporania" has been thoroughly discussed as a milestone in Pound's individual self-definition as a modernist, but its appearance in *Poetry* and the exceedingly strong responses it generated have not been fully appreciated as catalysts to the emerging field of the New Verse. Bruce Fogelman, for example, traces Pound's repeated reordering of the group as a formative moment for the "modern poetic sequence" but does not emphasize one notable consequence of the revised order.[46] Upon first submitting them, Pound had placed the two most stridently antagonistic pieces, "Tenzone" and "The Condolence," three-quarters of the way through, but his final reordering arranged them first and second, which meant that the sequence began with these lines:

> Will people accept them?
>   (i.e. these songs).
> As a timorous wench from a centaur
>   (or a centurian),
>
> Already they flee, howling in terror.
> Will they be touched with the truth?
>
>   Their virgin stupidity is untemptable.[47]

Poetry is cast here as a dangerous force, hypersexual and grotesque, whose effect on readers resembles an assault. Pound created the metaphor, but Monroe chose to print it. Even then, she could have chosen to bury "Contemporania" deep in the issue, but she placed it on the first page, ensuring that any unsuspecting reader who opened her magazine would be confronted by outrages not experienced in American poetry since the earliest verse of Whitman.

In the lines that followed, Pound affirms an iconoclastic solidarity with this great predecessor by unmistakably evoking his imagery and tone of voice:

> I mate with my kind upon the crags;
>   the hidden recesses
> Have heard the echo of my heels.

Later in the sequence, in "A Pact," he would pay open if ambivalent homage ("I make truce with you, Walt Whitman—/ I have detested you long enough. . . . / It was you that broke the new wood."[48] This kinship with Whitman has been generally overlooked, understandably in light of the ferocious elitism of Pound's later poetry and thought, but it pervaded the poems of "Contemporania," which persistently announce their sympathy with social underdogs. "The Garden" lampoons the emotional desiccation of the idle refined; "The Garret" concludes that "the rich have butlers and no friends, / And we have friends and no butlers"; "Salutation" contrasts the "generation of the thoroughly smug / and thoroughly uncomfortable" to jovial fisherman and their "untidy families" happily "picnicking in the sun."[49] "Commission" makes these allegiances explicit, beginning, "Go, my songs, to the lonely and the unsatisfied," and ending, "Speak for the free kinship of the mind and spirit. / Go, against all forms of oppression." Though even this early, Pound no doubt saw "forms of oppression" differently from Whitman and Monroe, the immediate effect was to assert poetry as a vehicle of avant-garde attack upon inhumane and absurd categories of social distinction. "Contemporania" thus powerfully supported *Poetry*'s developing avant-garde sensibility, in which antagonism toward established institutional structures intertwined with progressive social sympathies.

The reception of "Contemporania" and Pound's other early verses in *Poetry*, which created clear battle lines between traditional and radical factions of the nation's poetic culture, traces an American avant-garde sensibility at the exhilarating moment of its emergence. Monroe clearly anticipated the controversy that "Contemporania" would generate, remarking laconically just days before its appearance, "You will admit when you read EP, that it takes some courage to print him straight in his belligerent mood."[50] Some outraged members of the old guard responded by demonizing Pound as violently as Whitman had been a half century earlier. In November 1914, for example, the literary commentator of the Chicago publication *The Musical Leader* compared "the would-be poet to an orang-outang attempting to play the violin."[51] But Monroe's canny use of Pound's verse also galvanized rebellious generational feeling in the excited young writers who were following *Poetry*'s first issues, such as Witter Bynner, who exclaimed to Monroe on April 12, "Pound's 'Contemporania' immense! I devoured them, such edible soups."[52] And just a few days earlier, in an encomium in the *Chicago Evening Post Literary Review* for April 4, Floyd Dell had gushed to Pound that "Contemporania" ("Your poems in the April *Poetry*") had established him as "the most enchanting poet alive."[53] Two days later, writing to compliment Dell on this piece, Arthur Davison Ficke linked Pound's provocations in *Poetry* to the rebellious energy of a younger generation beginning to emerge from the genteel doldrums: "The praise or blame of the 'dolts' (see Ezra Pound) means nothing: but if a few of us find each other's work likeable, it's encouraging enough to make us intensify our purport to the point where even the dolts will get it."[54]

Though objections to *Poetry* sounded in many venues in 1913 and 1914, the most vocal adversary was *The Dial,* headquartered in the Loop a few blocks southeast of Monroe's offices at 543 Cass Street (now North Wabash Avenue). Monroe's long and not especially warm acquaintance with *The Dial*'s editorship, especially William Morton Payne, with whom she had participated in "Little Room" gatherings since the mid-1890s, may have exacerbated the antagonism between the two publications. Certainly *The Dial* treated the advent of *Poetry* as an affront to its status as an authoritative elder to which Monroe had once felt forced to defer.[55] *The Dial*'s initial remarks about *Poetry* in December 1912 pretended bland interest, but this was immediately undermined by skepticism toward the value of "doing something for poetry," as in this self-unraveling sentence: "We would not say a word in depreciation of any earnest effort to provoke the poetic spirit into activity, although the fruits of such an effort are likely to prove for the most part innutritive and insipid."[56]

Thereafter, animosity between the two magazines intensified as *Poetry* began enthusiastically violating the high-toned cultural standards that *The Dial* guarded. In mid-1913 the older magazine began direct attacks upon *Poetry*'s sponsorship of untraditional forms and iconoclastic content. Monroe quickly learned how to use these attacks as sources of valuable publicity and avant-garde energy. The first salvo in their feud was Wallace Rice's sweeping indictment "Mr. Ezra Pound and 'Poetry,'" in *The Dial* for May 1, which claimed that through its sponsorship of Pound, *Poetry* was "being turned into a thing for laughter."[57] Rice dismisses Pound as one "still occupied with youthful Bohemianism and impudence" who fails to understand that "formal rhythm is as essential to [poetry] as to its sisters by birth, Music and the Dance," and who consequently produces not poetry at all but prose.[58] Wasn't poetry, Rice demanded, first and foremost a recognizable "technic" of writing? If not, he argues, if "poetry have no technic and, left formless thereby, is at one with illiterary prose," then it is nothing at all, and a publication predicated upon it is a patent absurdity.[59] This line of attack on *vers libre* now seems quaintly absurd, but in 1913 such arguments were fundamental to how verse writing in America might—or might not—be reconfigured to the conditions of twentieth-century modernity. Would poetry be forever limited to the same forms and subject matter, guarded by those wishing to keep the "illiterary" modern world at bay? Or would the genre be opened to new forms and themes that might drastically alter prevailing notions of "the poetic"? *Poetry*'s pioneering effort to modernize and enlarge the horizons of possibility for the American poet, against opponents whose lack of intellectual dynamism was countered by their institutional entrenchment, was central to the success of the New Verse movement.[60]

If Monroe had positioned herself as an upstart by beginning her magazine in *The Dial*'s backyard without seeking its approval, her two replies to Rice's attacks printed in *The Dial* confirmed her as an active enemy of genteel Chicago and a champion of iconoclastic experiment. In the first she enacted the quintessential avant-garde embrace of the new, even the callow and inexperienced, over the established and overfamiliar, in the process ridiculing Rice's own editorial achievement: "'The editors who have never before edited' are less to be dreaded than those who have edited too much. Mr. Rice has edited so many anthologies—among them, 'The Little Book of Brides,' 'The Little Book of Kisses,' 'The Little Book of Sports'—that the keen edge of his judgment as an authority on poetry is somewhat worn."[61] In the second she rejected the implication that *Poetry* was failing "if it does not, in [Rice's] opinion, print a masterpiece or two each month," since poems "'of very great distinction' are not created often."[62] She understood this to mean the need of tolerating and encouraging "vital and provocative experiments," without which "the artist of any kind . . . can not go on."[63]

Continuing throughout 1913 into 1914, the feud between *Poetry* and *The Dial* marked a moment of epochal transition between two models of poetry's value in America. *The Dial* and its ilk still saw the genre as an instrument of moral uplift, now menaced by an ultramodern fringe that they called "Futurism," which in 1913 had become a catchall pejorative in American magazines, signifying everything that was threatening and incomprehensible about the modern arts. In April 1913, *The Nation* printed a letter by Raymond M. Alden (also a regular contributor to *The Dial*) that detected in Pound's "Contemporania" the "morbid banalities of Futurism," which he condemned as "products of distorted imaginations" and potentially' harmful to the impressionable young.[64] Alden read Pound's sequence through the embrace of modernity expressed in Monroe's editorial of the same issue, which had complained that most American poets seemed "as unaware of the twentieth century as if they had spent these recent years in an Elizabethan manor-house or a vine-clad Victorian cottage."[65] In October, *The Dial* again associated *Poetry* with "the bedlamite ravings of the futurists, and their nightmare creations of the pen and the brush," exemplified by Pound's verse and by F. T. Marinetti's notorious pronouncement, "We must spit upon the altar of art every day."[66] Speaking for those still invested in the notion that art should have an altar, *The Dial* interpreted *Poetry*'s editorial decisions—quite correctly—as irreverent expectorations toward long-standing artistic traditions and standards of value.

A few months later the feud reignited over another of *Poetry*'s most important early discoveries, Carl Sandburg, who first appeared in March 1914 with the group called "Chicago Poems."[67] As with "Contemporania" a year before, Monroe sought maximum avant-garde impact by leading off the issue with Sandburg's poems, and especially by placing his rough-edged portrait of the city, "Chicago," on the first page, where it became a self-defining editorial statement for this proudly Chicagoan magazine. From its first lines, characterizing the city as the "Hog Butcher for the World" and the "Stormy, husky, brawling, / City of the Big Shoulders," Sandburg's poem seemed to spit on the altar of art and provoked the most severe assaults yet on *Poetry*.[68] On March 16, *The Dial* condemned "Chicago" as an "impudent affront to the poetry-loving public," part of its dogmatic argument for keeping poetry sealed off from despoiling modernity. The unidentified editorialist insisted that "all definitions of art must say or imply that beauty is an essential aim of the worker, and there is no trace of beauty in the ragged lines" of "Chicago," which was therefore not poetry at all but another instance of the perversity of young pretenders to art for whom "the more freakish the form of expression, the more assured the triumph."[69] This specific attack on Sandburg formed the basis of a broader classist defense of genteel values against the barbarians at the gate: "We are told that the author 'left school at the age of thirteen, and worked in brickyards, railroads, Kansas wheat fields, etc.,' which we can well believe."[70] Having let this slip, *The Dial* nodded toward the egalitarian platitude that "[t]here are many ways of acquiring an education," but it still clung to rigid boundaries between the literary and the laboring classes, reiterating that "this author would be more at home in the brickyard than on the slopes of Parnassus."[71] For sponsoring such defilements of the "sacred precincts of the muse," *Poetry* was condemned as a "futile little periodical described as 'a magazine of verse.'"[72] The virulence of this and similar attacks suggests that in her use of Sandburg, Monroe had again succeeded in identifying her magazine with the most fiercely iconoclastic elements active in American verse.

The Dial's reckless attack on "Chicago" inspired the women of *Poetry* to further avant-garde polemic. The advisory-board member Edith Wyatt, needling *The Dial* for solemnly "'calling out the old guard' against new expression in poetry," questioned the old guard's reliability by citing an appreciative letter from Tennyson to Whitman.[73] In the more unbuttoned venue of *Poetry*'s editorial columns, Monroe mounted a devastating dismissal of *The Dial*'s Pecksniffian objections, in the process theorizing the little magazine as a dynamic vehicle of engagement with a modern world of constant, turbulent change:

> [W]hom and what has *The Dial* discovered? We have taken chances, made room for the young and the new, tried to break the chains which enslave Chicago to New York, America to Europe, and the present to the past—what chances has *The Dial* ever taken? What has it ever printed but echoes? For thirty years it has run placidly along in this turbulent city of Chicago, gently murmuring the accepted opinions of such leaders of thought as *The Ætheneum* and *The Spectator*. During all that third of a century it has borne about as much relation to the intellectual life of this vast, chaotically rich region as though it were printed in Glasgow or Caracas. Not only has it failed to grasp a great opportunity—it has been utterly blind and deaf to it, has never known the opportunity was there. Is its editor competent to define the word futile?[74]

In this fiercely avant-garde formulation, obeisance to "accepted opinions" led to irrelevance and futility. In contrast, *Poetry* sought canons of art vital to twentieth-century life, which meant sponsoring the sometimes jarring explorations of poets like Sandburg. Beyond merely endorsing Sandburg's right to be heard, Monroe's critique of *The Dial* drew rhetorical energy from his personification of "Chicago" as the turbulent, chaotic heart of modern experience ("under his wrist is the pulse, and under his ribs the heart of the people").[75] A few months later, *Poetry* reasserted its commitment to the radically modern values and styles Sandburg represented by giving "Chicago Poems" the first Levinson Prize, its biggest annual award.

In its vigorous defenses of Pound and Sandburg, *Poetry* staked out a radical position in the decisive culture war of early twentieth-century America, which Van Wyck Brooks would describe in 1918 as "a vendetta between . . . generations."[76] Despite the age of its editor, *Poetry* habitually took the side of youth, often employing a model of generational conflict to advance its avant-garde positions. Henderson's January 1915 commentary, "Contemporary Poetry and the Universities," decried the American academy's fetishization of the past and the repressive function of its poetry canons, to which most professors adhered so rigidly that they lacked any awareness of verse since 1890.[77] The academy's refusal of "direct contact with modern life," especially where poetry was concerned, meant that "[c]ollege students in literary courses remind one of rows of bleaching celery, banked and covered with earth; they are so carefully protected from any coloring contact with the ideas of the living present."[78] She concluded that "[a] scientific department conducted as a literary department is conducted, with no consideration of the achievements of the last thirty years, would be a disgrace to any college."[79] In this provocative analogy, the proper action of academic disciplines, literary no less than scientific, was not to closet themselves away with supposedly eternal verities but to keep up with the constantly changing climate of modern intellectual discovery.

If the literary academy inhibited new forms of artistic work, the National Institute of Arts and Letters and its inner sanctum, the American Academy of Arts and Letters, served as national canons having an even more exclusive function. These august bodies made for especially attractive targets in *Poetry*'s campaign of avant-garde self-definition. In January 1914, seizing upon an unfortunate description of the National Institute's purpose by one of its members as "the encouragement of sobriety and earnestness in all the arts," Monroe argued that such organizations would inevitably "be composed chiefly, not of exceptional high spirits in the arts, but of sober and earnest workers" who would "perpetuate their own kind" and reject "adventurous and original" work.[80] These conservatives, she noted sardonically, "are hardly to be blamed," since "they have no means of recognizing genius when it appears [and] honestly suspect original thought, original style. Thus with all possible good will toward genius in the abstract, and with much palaver of praise for entombed genius, they inevitably shut their door in the face of genius . . . embodied in an actual living young man or woman."[81] Hence the absurdity of an institute that promoted "sobriety and earnestness," which are "precisely the two attributes which need no institute to encourage them; without such aid they win most of the prizes and sit at most of the banquets."[82]

Monroe also hammered away at the racial and sexual exclusivity that accompanied such institutional self-importance. Thus far in their history, the

Institute and the Academy had belied even the lily-livered description that had provoked her response, since "their purpose is not even 'the encouragement of sobriety and earnestness in all the arts,' but only in those creations of art which proceed from sober and earnest males."[83] In contrast, she envisioned a desacralized national canon of greater diversity than was comfortable, no doubt, to much of the Institute's membership: "Either [such bodies] exist for the benefit and development of American arts and letters, or they do not. If they do, they are bound to admit to membership such American artists and men and women of letters as deserve the recognition, regardless of race, color, sex, or previous condition of servitude."[84] This formulation reveals the integral linkage Monroe saw between her specific avant-garde attacks on entrenched cultural institutions and a progressive social vision extending well beyond the narrow issue of economic opportunity for the American artist. Pound, in contrast, too often mistook his worthy immediate goals of helping artists he admired for a comprehensive social vision, with the result that his activism soured into bitterness against those who were not wealthy or enlightened enough to provide patronage to those favored few.[85] Rather than cursing the "mass of dolts" in their darkness, Monroe strove to promote their enlightenment.

Cultivating Genius

In its advocacy of institutional support for contemporary poets, *Poetry* reformulated central concepts of literary value—*genius, masterpiece, tradition, form, audience*—into a forceful poetics of avant-garde progressivism. Through her insistent references to the figure of the young poet ignored by the world, Monroe challenged the entrenched model of genius as a mysterious messianic force impervious to circumstance, arguing in her very first *Poetry* editorial that "[t]his art, like every other, is not a miracle of direct creation, but a reciprocal relation between the artist and his public. The people must do their part if the poet is to tell their story to the future; they must cultivate and irrigate the soil if the desert is to blossom."[86] In place of miracles, she offered a matter-of-fact analogy of culture as soil to be nourished, now perhaps consisting of underdeveloped grubs but with the potential to bloom into unexpected forms. This revisionist position was supported elsewhere in the opening number by Pound's portrayal of Whistler as the prototypical modern genius, inspiring not for the perfection of his work but for his commitment to experiment and willingness to fail ("You . . . / Tested and pried and worked in many fashions," "And stretched and tampered with the media").[87] The "searches" and "uncertainties" of Whistler's career reassured Pound of his own course of action and gave him continued "heart to play the game."

Poetry's revision of poetic genius, as it converged with the insistence upon exploiting the mechanisms of worldly power that were disdained by genteel models of value, precipitated terrific controversy. In August 1913, *The Nation* rejected the policy of prize giving, reasserting the desirable poverty of poets by opining that "the commanding figure, under modern conditions that make a Chatterton's fate almost impossible, will be discovered ere the shades of the counting-house close around him."[88] Because geniuses were not made but born, if none appeared this was not due to stunting cultural conditions but because the miracle wasn't meant to happen—a result virtually guaranteed by *The Nation*'s circular logic. Responding to this editorial in August 1914, Monroe polemically estimated that "alas, the modern Chatterton is not only possible but numerous."[89] In a particularly forceful passage, she anticipated Virginia Woolf's *A Room of One's Own* by subordinating genius to circumstance, arguing that Shakespeare born in an "unkind environment" would mean that "*Hamlet* is never written, and the *Nation* is not robbed of anything of the highest value, because even so divinatory an editor can not conceive of *Hamlet*'s being possible until *it has been written*. . . . How can the *Nation* and its kind hear in their hearts the unsung songs? How can they tell what the world has lost by silencing its poets and crucifying its prophets?"[90] In other words, the American literary establishment had failed not because geniuses had not appeared but because *all* young poets were inhibited from developing talents whose limits could not be known by anyone, least of all by *The Nation*.

But unlike the gloomy turn-of-the-century commentators who worried that poetry might really be disappearing, Monroe inverted the pessimistic logic of the Chatterton legend to support her activist argument. Redefining the "masterpiece of art" not as "a miracle of individual genius so much as the expression of a reciprocal relation between the artist and his public," she insisted that more genius would be generated by lifting the nation's overall level of education and artistic appreciation.[91] She concluded the editorial with one more salvo at the complacent institutions of American literary culture, arguing that self-professed lovers of poetry must do their part by offering poets tangible financial support: "Therefore let the *Nation* and its numerous rivals no longer be consoled by various flattering unctions as they 'watch the discomfort' of poets, but be up and doing to diminish that discomfort."[92]

This last point evoked *Poetry*'s insistence on the need to support poets financially, by paying for their work and awarding them monetary prizes whenever possible. Strange as it may sound now, this was one of the magazine's most controversial early positions. To many in the early 1910s, giving prizes to poets seemed perverse or dangerous because prevailing models of poetic value held that no benefits could accrue from remuneration. True genius could neither be deflected from nor helped toward its eventual destiny, yet ironically, lesser poets might be tempted into prostituting their gifts in pursuit of gain. In this climate, *Poetry*'s insistence on giving prizes was criticized not only by complacent editors but even by anxious poets who had internalized arguments for the necessary unworldliness of their art. Thus in "The Question of Prizes" (February 1916), Monroe wrote of a recent meeting of the Poetry Society of America at which her associate editor Alice Corbin Henderson "was almost the only speaker who advocated prize-giving for the encouragement of the art."[93] Monroe went on to note several recent objections to *Poetry*'s financial commitments, including those of Conrad Aiken, who had complained in the *Poetry Journal* "that there is a subtle corruption in a prize, the winner thereof becoming so consumed with self-satisfaction as to lose his artistic integrity."[94] To refute this position, she again employed her incisive analogical argument: "Why should a poet be 'utterly lacking in self-respect,'" as Aiken had grumbled, "if he accepts a fellowship, when so many painters and architects, scholars and scientists, have stood up nobly under the infliction?"[95]

Aiken's corollary complaint, that such awards were "creating not a poetry, but a *market* for poetry," reiterated the view that poetry's value depended absolutely on its freedom from soiling mercantile considerations.[96] In response, Monroe again took the most radical position possible for 1916: she flatly refused to accept any contradiction between the creation of poetry and the cultivation of markets for it. Addressing Aiken's pious disdain ("Miss Monroe led us to suppose she was building a cathedral—it now appears that it was a Woolworth Building"), she appropriated his architectural metaphors into an expression of avant-garde exuberance and regional affiliation: "A cathedral, did I? Modern cathedrals are second-rate—mere imitations. I would rather build a first-rate skyscraper! But not the Woolworth Building—the Monadnock, perhaps."[97] Rejecting the sacral and ancient connotations of the cathedral as a metaphor for poetic endeavor, Monroe cast her lot with the secular modernity of the (Chicago) skyscraper and the marketplace, believing that

> [g]reat art has usually been "popular" to this extent, that in the great periods of art the artists had their world behind them; . . . just as today we are in the midst of a great period of scientific discovery because every inventive mind

feels this push of his world. . . . It follows that if we want great poetry we must begin by preparing normal and natural conditions for the poet—by giving him, not the stone walls and stifling atmosphere of indifference, but light, air, freedom, neighbors who praise or curse—all things necessary for healthy growth and conflict.[98]

The tangible results of this position were *Poetry*'s prizes, among the earliest forms of the institutional support for American verse now taken for granted at all levels, from the National Book Awards to the ubiquitous undergraduate literary magazine. In *Poetry*'s first year, even before any permanent prize funds had been established, Monroe set aside $250 from her general fund for a Guarantors' Prize, which was given in late 1913 to W. B. Yeats at Pound's loud insistence.[99] Thereafter the magazine would administer and award various smaller and one-time prizes whenever money was available. The best-known of its ongoing awards was the two-hundred-dollar Levinson Prize (currently five hundred dollars), given annually since 1914 for the best poem published in the magazine by an American citizen during the previous year. Throughout his association with *Poetry,* Pound sought to control the disposition of award money for his favorites. At the other extreme, those such as Aiken condemned all monetary awards as appealing only to "second-raters."[100] As so often, Monroe's steady good sense prevailed in the long run: the first twenty Levinson Prize winners contain a remarkable proportion of important figures, including Carl Sandburg, Vachel Lindsay, Edgar Lee Masters, Wallace Stevens, Robert Frost, Edwin Arlington Robinson, Amy Lowell, Elinor Wylie, Edna St. Vincent Millay, Hart Crane, and Marianne Moore. The principle fought between Aiken and Monroe in 1916 was simple and crucial: did poets deserve, and would they benefit from, the same kinds of support enjoyed by the practitioners of other arts? By the early 1920s, with the establishment of such high-profile remunerations as the Poetry Society Award (which became the Pulitzer Prize) and the *Dial* award, as well as scores of smaller ones, Monroe's position on prize giving had won the day. Even Aiken deigned to accept his Pulitzer in 1930 for *Selected Poems.* The continuing wealth and variety of poetry produced by Americans vindicated her argument that in a condition of modernity, such financial rewards were not spiritual impoverishments but necessary resources.

If *Poetry*'s advocacy of prize giving was central to its ongoing critique of genteel models of literary value, so too was its forceful reorientation of the relationship between present verse and past canons. Monroe closed the magazine's second year by using her readership's allegiance to past masterpieces in support of *Poetry*'s economic agenda: "What do you owe, you who read this article, to Shelley? to Coleridge, Milton, Shakespeare? . . . to all the great poets whose immortal singing has incalculably enriched life, become an integral part of the mind of the race? . . . Is there any other way to pay your debt to the great dead poets than by supporting and encouraging the poets now alive?"[101] Americans who claimed to love poetry could best honor their canons "by staking something on their faith in those who practice it"—by subscribing to the magazine, or by endowing a prize for living poets.[102] This practical appeal had an important theoretical consequence: it recast canons and tradition as sources of energy enriching the dynamic present rather than the fixed and immutable standards that genteel culture had tried to barricade against that dynamism.

Monroe advanced this constructionist model of canonicity at many points, beginning with the key editorial of her second issue, "The Open Door" (November 1912), where she noted that present-day giants such as Keats and Whitman had been dismissed as minor by their contemporaries and resolved that "[t]he Open Door will be the policy of this magazine—may the great poet we are looking for never find it shut, or half-shut, against his ample genius!"[103] This metaphor of the open door clearly implies hospitality to works in modern forms, but it also implies a fundamentally unstable relation between contemporary work and past canons, recasting "the canon" from a jealously guarded sacred space into a temporal economy of constant flux. As she saw it, the proper role of a magazine of contemporary verse was to remain skeptical toward absolute judgments of brand-new works and continually to remind readers that posterity might see those same works in radically different ways.[104]

Poetry's advocacy of innovation extended to a potently avant-garde revision of the relationship between tradition and form. This effort began in the first issue with Edith Wyatt's essay "On the Reading of Poetry," which describes a rearguard reader who insists that "poetry may concern herself only with a limited number of subjects to be presented in a predetermined and conventional manner and form."[105] Such a position failed to grasp that "every 'form' was in its first and best use an originality, employed not for the purpose of following any rule, but because it said truly what the artist wished to express."[106] In "The New Beauty" in April 1913, Monroe returned to this theme by critiquing the traditionalist view of poetic form as "a matter of pleasing fancies and pretty patterns, which may be taken conveniently from the past."[107] In her view, adherence to old forms confined contemporary poets within a set of "ready-made conventions and prejudices" that had been created by their predecessors in response to specific and contingent circumstances, but were now treated as eternal

verities.[108] In contrast, her idea of a "New Beauty" emphasized originality of expression and modernity of attitude as the attributes necessary
for poetry to remain vital. Poets "should pay less attention to old forms
which have been worn thin by five centuries of English song" and "should
return rather to first principles, feel as if poetry were new, and they the
first to forge rhythmic chains for the English language."[109] Whether this
effort meant meter or *vers libre,* sonnet or collage, paled next to the poet's
willingness to "strain every sinew" to find forms adequate to the conditions of twentieth-century modernity.[110]

This position on form converged powerfully with *Poetry*'s avant-garde
appropriation of the canonical dead. Portraying those who initiated the
revered forms as rebels against the rules of their day, *Poetry* insisted that
modern poetic achievement would come not from reproducing the current
formal conventions of English-language poetry but from violating them.
Responding in 1913 to irate defenders of tradition, Monroe formulated an
avant-garde model of tradition as a reservoir of formal experiment. "We
confess little reverence," she asserted with typical bluntness, for pious adherence to canons based on "external form": "The men who made this grand
old English tradition little knew what they were doing. To them there was
nothing sacrosanct in their adventurous experiments; they never dreamed
of discouraging the adventurous experiments of others."[111] This argument
fixed *Poetry*'s critics in a double bind in which true reverence toward one's
canon entailed open-minded acceptance of change and innovation, since
one violated the spirits of the great writers by sacralizing and reifying their
exploratory and transgressive writing practices. Such formulations, portraying forms and traditions as culturally constructed rather than intrinsic,
anticipated and may have influenced Van Wyck Brooks's seminal modernist
argument of 1918 that the bankrupt academic-genteel American tradition
was not "the only possible past," and that it was feasible and necessary to
generate others: "If we need another past so badly, is it inconceivable that
we might discover one, that we might even invent one?"[112]

Poetry's avant-garde reorientation of genius, tradition, and form also implied a revision of the relationship between artist and audience, which was
emphasized on the back cover of every issue with a motto from Whitman:
"To be great poets there must be great audiences too." The adoption of this
phrase, buried deep in Whitman's notebooks, indicates Monroe's interest in
unmetered verse well before she was acquainted with Pound, since it comes
in a section headed "New Poetry" in which Whitman predicts the obsolescence of rhyme and traditional meters and imagines a future American
poetry emerging organically from the "more flexible" medium of prose.[113]

Poetry's motto became an object of derision, especially from Pound, who claimed that its primary message was one of capitulation to popular taste (audiences "great" in number) rather than, as Monroe conceived it, an admonition of poet's and reader's responsibilities to one another. By the beginning of the magazine's third year (October 1914), the fragile meeting of minds between Pound and Monroe was beginning to founder over this issue, and in their disagreement we can see the roots of his characterization of *Poetry* as pandering to popular tastes.[114] In a two-part editorial, "The Audience," they debated the meaning of the motto, elaborating their diverging models of modern poetic value. Pound read the motto as asserting that "[t]he artist is . . . dependent upon his audience," which he rejected on the grounds that popular writers ("my mutton-headed ninth cousin" or "any other American of his time who had the 'great audience'") were manifestly lesser artists than others who lacked "the popular voice," naming J. M. Synge, Whitman himself, and of course Dante.[115] Art only survived, Pound opined, because "in each generation" there are "a few intelligent spirits" who "ultimately manage the rest," who are mere "rabble," "aimless and drifting" without the artist.[116] Concluding that the great artist's only audiences are "the spirits of irony and of destiny and of humor, sitting within him," Pound evoked the literal sense of "genius" as a presiding spirit of place, but internalized this meaning completely, anticipating the high-modernist mantra that great writers are themselves their only audiences.[117]

Despite her castigation of popular versifiers such as Ella Wheeler Wilcox, Monroe did draw distinctions among various kinds of popularity and diverged from Pound's paranoid opposition between any poet reaching a substantial audience and the true artist. Her rebuttal to Pound describes a modernity defined by daunting physical immensity and by continual encounter with forces of heterogeneity, multiplicity, and otherness, a combination that paradoxically makes the world seem bigger and smaller at the same time: "Modern inventions, forcing international travel, inter-racial thought, upon the world, have done away with Dante's little audience."[118] In this condition of complex and sprawling interconnectedness, in which "nothing can stand alone, genius least of all," artistic flowering "is not an isolated phenomenon" but "the expression of a reciprocal relation between the artist and his public."[119]

A few months later she refined her portrayal of the American reading public by engaging an opponent on the other extreme of the issue: the "charmingly complacent" editor of a popular "uplift magazine" who had remarked in an editors' public forum that "these well-meaning neighbors of mine [*Poetry* and other nonmainstream magazines] don't give you [the public] what you want."[120] The first stage of Monroe's response was a "*Piers Ploughman* vision*,*" superficially Poundian, of "the huge easygoing American public following trampled roads, gulping down pre-digested foods, seeking comfortable goals, suspicious always of ideas, of torches, of climbing feet, of singing voices—a public which does not stone its prophets, finding it more effective to ignore them."[121] But rather than meeting the indifference of the American masses to the arts with contempt and antagonism, Monroe empathizes with them as "struggling, suffering, toilers who starve in body and mind, . . . who dream deep dreams which they dare not admit and cannot express, who grope for beauty and truth through tinsel trickeries and smug falsities."[122] Poets are not a breed apart from these crowds but "one with them," "plunging with such lights as they have into the darkness."[123] Monroe proposed that since "every man's heart, however perverse with ignorance, however cluttered with knowledge, makes a secret confession of the truth," then "[p]oets and prophets . . . appeal to him not quite in vain; and the appeal must go on so long as the race endures." She ended by envisioning a time in which popularity might be seen not as compromise and dilution of artistic integrity but as a matter-of-fact symptom of a healthy cultural life.[124]

For Monroe, that future artistic flowering was no pipe dream but a potentiality inherent in the emergence of global modernity. Her deep attachment to the American Southwest, well described by Robin Schulze, and her regional pride as a midwesterner led her to make *Poetry* a champion of what she called in 1922 "a strongly localized indigenous art."[125] Yet she also saw the insularity of national poetic cultures being inexorably dismantled by the impact of new technologies of communication and transport. The great poetry of the future could no longer be exclusively local or even national in its focus; its greatness would be measured by its ability to bring peoples of the world toward closer mutual understanding. Thus, for her the poet of 1913 who had "the keenest vision of the new beauty, and the richest modern message, not only for the millions who speak his mother-tongue but also for those far-scattered millions who carry Shakespeare's mother-tongue all over the world," was the Bengali Rabindrinath Tagore.[126] Monroe's use of Tagore to exemplify an emerging intercultural modernity was developed further in the following issue (alongside his own translations of his works), where she describes him as "the ideal poet . . ., the Ambassador Extraordinary from East to West, . . . speaking with supreme authority from race to race, writing a brave chapter in that epic of human brotherhood which must be sung around the world when locomotives and swift steamers . . . shall have opened wide the gates."[127] Within the year her enthusiasm for Tagore would be vindicated on a worldwide stage by the Nobel Academy.

Monroe's advocacy of Tagore was distinct not only from the Anglocentric provincialism of the genteel American literary establishment but from the nostalgic Eurocentrism of Eliot and Pound that became fundamental to New Critical high modernism. Although their poetic models included Italian and French, classical Greek and Roman, Chinese and Japanese, and even some South Asian elements, most of these came from the distant or orientalized past and had little to do with those cultures in the modern world. In contrast, the Americentrism of *Poetry* was tempered by humility and a commitment to cultural reciprocity. Thus for Monroe in 1913, Tagore's work "shows us how provincial we are; England and America are little recently annexed corners of the ancient earth, and their poets should peer out over sea-walls and race-walls and pride-walls, and learn their own littleness and the bigness of the world."[128] Scripting the poets of England and America as an audience benefitting from the manifold wisdom of cultural and ethnic difference that Tagore represented, this argument proposed poetry in the twentieth century as a sharing of self and other, familiar and new, native and foreign, across a world understood as irrevocably modern and inextricably interdependent. Such broad-minded formulations of poetry's potential for enriching twentieth-century life are strewn throughout the first ten years of *Poetry* and offer a bracing antidote to the ethnocentric, elitist, and often quite simply mean-spirited Poundian high modernism we have inherited.

Not all of *Poetry*'s myriad enthusiasms were equally successful or enduring, of course. Its belief in the importance of Vachel Lindsay and some other writers in the midwestern folk tradition proved a clear overestimation of their work. Its genuine interest in Native American chants as one of the nation's key indigenous poetic voices was compromised by the need to hear them translated by white writers such as Lew Sarett and Alice Corbin Henderson. But despite inevitable misses along the way, *Poetry* made a remarkable proportion of hits, and its eclectic interest in all aspects of contemporary verse constitutes an inspiring example of cultural leadership. Throughout Monroe's long tenure, *Poetry* maintained its support of experimental subject matter and styles and a broad-based commitment to progressive social positions. Despite the fine scholarly work already done, much remains unexplored about *Poetry*'s protean role in remaking the culture of American verse, particularly the magazine's complex and thoughtful response to the Great War, which involved poems, plays, and editorials by dozens of voices.[129]

When it began, *Poetry* was alone, but it did not remain so for long. Once it had demonstrated the appetite—the market—for new forms and subject matter in American verse, many other little magazines would follow, both emulating and resisting Monroe's and somewhat overshadowing its rebellious profile. But *Poetry* did a great deal more than provide a meal ticket. It generated a reservoir of energy that encouraged aspiring poets and editors in too many ways to count. It offered innovative expressive models in the work of Pound, Lowell, Sandburg, Eliot, Lindsay, Masters, Stevens, and a host of others. Quickly making itself notorious, it showed that avant-garde experiments might actually have a transformative impact upon American literary culture. Now more than ever, with its first ten years digitized and searchable through the Modernist Journals Project, this biggest of little magazines offers twenty-first-century scholars a rich archive for constructing alternative pasts for twentieth-century American verse.

CHAPTER 3

Young, Blithe, and Whimsical

The Avant-Gardism of The Masses

Between 1913 and 1917, several other little magazines enriched the New Verse movement by joining and competing with *Poetry* as vigorous venues of contemporary American poetry. The discussions of *The Masses* in this chapter and *Others* in the next aim to challenge the conceptual model dominating histories of modern American poetry from the 1940s, in which political and aesthetic radicalism are seen as mutually exclusive responses to twentieth-century modernity. In this binarized model, *The Masses,* putting ideology above artistry, placed itself beyond the pale of true modernism, while *Others,* sublimating its dissidence into formal experimentation, became important through its prescient sponsorship of a handful of later-canonical writers. The shaping force of this binary lingers even in scholarship that otherwise rejects the evaluative norms of high modernism, as in this 2006 description of American poetry of the 1910s as "ranging from the traditional verse of political journals such as *The Masses* to the free verse of avant-garde periodicals such as *Others.*"[1] Employing a familiar loaded opposition between *tradition* and *freedom,* in which ostensibly descriptive terms easily edge into proscriptive hierarchies, such formulations locate *The Masses* and *Others* not as multiply intersecting participants in a complex network of avant-garde culture but as mutually exclusive extremes.

My analysis of *The Masses* aims to revise the long-standing assumption that the verse published there was little but belated sentimentalizing or Marxist sermonizing with no significant role in the emergence of modern poetry.[2] The editors of the 1946 volume *The Little Magazine: A History and Bibliography,* for example, conclude airily that "we can scarcely say that [*The Masses*] offered a synthesis of the political and aesthetic points of view," diminishing it into a quaint episode of American bourgeois leftism instead of a serious and often successful attempt to create precisely that synthesis of radical politics and experimental aesthetics.[3] To identify *The Masses* wholly with radical politics and traditional forms misses its substantial institutional and aesthetic impact upon the New Poetry, just as limiting *Others* to a retrospectively constructed canon of experimental poetry overlooks the socially progressive force of its avant-gardism. Both magazines participated in the exhilarating climate of activism and innovation that emerged in the United States after 1910. Both sponsored verse that engaged urgent social themes, three in particular: the material textures and social dynamics of the industrial metropolis, the problems raised by machine-age labor, and the ideological forces behind the Great War. Resituating *The Masses* and *Others* as complementary rather than opposing helps us to see the New Verse as a dynamic discursive field committed to a synthesis of "political and aesthetic points of view."

Lunging at Specters

Although it published some verse from its outset in January 1911, *The Masses* became an important agent of the New Poetry with the arrival of Max Eastman as editor in December 1912, two months after the first issue of *Poetry*. By mid-1912 *The Masses* had gone through three editors in fifteen months and seemed destined to become one more short-lived radical initiative. But a group of artists and writers, including John Sloan, Art Young, Louis Untermeyer, and Mary Heaton Vorse, persuaded the charismatic young Eastman to assume the editorship, and after a three-month hiatus it resumed in December. Announcing "a radical change of policy," Eastman resolved "to make *The Masses* a *popular* Socialist magazine—a magazine of pictures and lively writing."[4] His organizing and fund-raising abilities, complemented by the acumen of the managing editor Floyd Dell, provided the stability to keep the magazine's disparate and mercurial personalities from whirling off into centrifugal incoherence. Through 1913 and 1914, its profile as a radical gadfly grew steadily, especially after withstanding threats of litigation from the Associated Press after it criticized the news agency's coverage of the bitter coal strike in West Virginia.[5]

Although cultural historians such as William L. O'Neill and Rebecca Zurier have noted that the sophistication, humor, and irony of *The Masses* departed from the pedestrian taste and earnest tone of the era's many other socialist publications, this important distinction has often been lost in American literary scholarship. Each month its masthead proclaimed *The Masses* "A revolutionary and not a reform magazine," and yet Eastman's first editorial in December 1912 had categorically renounced the sectarian squabbling and the "dogmatic spirit" hampering much American leftism, resolving instead to appeal to "both Socialist and non-Socialist, with entertainment, education, and the livelier kinds of propaganda."[6] Although commitments to the rights of the working class, women, and ethnic minorities informed the magazine's course at every important point, the editors refused to let entrenched injustice destroy their idealism. As O'Neill puts it, Eastman "and his friends had not become revolutionaries in order to usher in an age of cheerless conformity": "[T]he society they were building had to be fun as well as moral."[7]

Such cheerful self-contradiction was "a complete anomaly" within the American left and affronted such straitlaced members of the Socialist mainstream as future U.S. Senator Paul H. Douglas, who in November 1916 dismissed *The Masses* as mere "nastiness," "a horrible example of 'how not to do it.'"[8] *The Masses* encouraged this reaction by cultivating a provocative stance that we should recognize as avant-garde in the fullest sense of the term, leavening its serious critique of capitalism with irreverent satire of the foibles of conservatives, bohemians, and radicals alike.[9]

The magazine's mix of passion and playfulness is suggested by the statement that would appear in every issue from February 1913. Its first draft was composed by John Reed, who began, "We refuse to commit ourselves to any course of action except this: *to do with the Masses exactly as we please.*"[10] Despite coming from a *political* radical of legendary stature—the only American to be buried in the Kremlin—the statement contains virtually all the rhetorical touchstones of the *aesthetic* avant-garde: the whimsically impractical tone ("We intend to lunge at specters"); the declaration of independence from dogma and sectarianism ("We will be bound by no one creed or theory of social reform, but will express them all, provided they be radical"); the self-identification as a haven for work unprintable in more mainstream venues ("Poems, stories and drawings rejected by the capitalist press on account of their excellence will find a welcome in this magazine"); the utopian aspiration to realize an untapped audience by articulating new points of view ("We have perfect faith that there exists in America a wide public, alert, alive, bored with the smug procession of magazine platitudes, to whom What We Please will be as a fresh wind"); and an eager embrace of continual change and even self-contradiction ("Sensitive to all new winds that blow, never rigid in a single view of life, such is our ideal for *The Masses*. And if we want to change our minds about it—well, why shouldn't we?").[11] Eastman's final revision condensed these sentiments without weakening them, even reinforcing the tone of nose-thumbing avant-gardism with the parting shot that *The Masses* would "conciliate nobody, not even its readers."[12]

In cultivating this contradictory mix of attitudes, *The Masses* announced itself fully at home in a multifarious cultural marketplace in which politically radical artists like Art Young and John Sloan subsidized their activism by working for *Collier's, Cosmopolitan,* and the Hearst newspaper syndicate. Even in the earliest issues of 1911–12, with the founding editor Piet Vlag setting a more earnest tone than Eastman would, the influence of such commercial magazines as the *Ladies' Home Journal* was detectable in the layout and visual style.[13] In turn, the style of *The Masses* would influence a variety of later magazines, most prominently the *New Yorker,* as Eastman noted many years later.[14] Writers for *The Masses* were staff members of or regular contributors to such mainstream publications as the *American Magazine, Puck, Life, Harper's Bazaar,* and the *Woman's Home Companion.*[15] By emphasizing these links to both the aesthetic avant-garde and mass-commercial culture, I don't mean to condescend to its participants' radical commitments or denigrate its value to the American left. Just the opposite: I mean to challenge the distinctions often drawn between these realms of cultural endeavor and to enhance our sense of the dynamic openness of this moment of early twentieth-century literary history.

Understanding *The Masses'* dynamic relationship to mainstream culture and its willingness to harbor a wide range of relations to metropolitan modernity is crucial to reassessing its importance to the New Verse. However fervent its radical principles, *The Masses,* like *Poetry,* succeeded not because of its amateurism but because of its worldly effectiveness. Eastman found several private donors, but he also built a very healthy circulation for a little magazine.[16] As his December 1912 statement predicted, the magazine quickly attracted a wide range of readers, young and old, socialist and nonsocialist, metropolitan and provincial, middle-class suffragist and working-class immigrant, including literary celebrities such as George Bernard Shaw.[17] The reception of Louis Untermeyer's "God's Youth," one of the key poems of Eastman's first year, indicates that by mid-1913, only a few months after the magazine's makeover, its reach extended well beyond New York radical politics. On August 6, Edward J. Wheeler, the cofounder of the conservative Poetry Society of America and editor of the digest journal *Current Opinion,* wrote to the poet on his editorial letterhead that "'God's Youth' was delightful, as is everything I have seen of yours lately."[18] Four days later H. H. Peckham, a young academic from Indiana then employed at a small women's college in North Carolina, wrote Untermeyer that he enjoyed "both the form and the viewpoint. The idea of God as a creature with a sense of humor is fresh and delectable."[19] The following January 2, having just finished compiling his annual anthology of magazine verse,

W. S. Braithwaite wrote Untermeyer from the genteel literary backwater of Cambridge, Massachusetts, that the poem had "made a mighty and deep impression" upon him.[20]

Such cross-pollinations suggest that however revolutionary its mission, *The Masses* was understood at the time to be strongly integrated into a multifarious cultural climate that did not segregate political and aesthetic realms as later histories would do. Another measure of this integration, as Morrisson notes, is that magazine agents often packaged "combination subscriptions bringing together *The Masses* with mass market successes" such as *Cosmopolitan, Good Housekeeping,* and even *Business America.*[21] By March 1914 *The Masses* was advertising for subscribers in issues of *Poetry,* describing itself as

DESTRUCTIVE   ENTERTAINING
Impudent and Important
A Radical Monthly for Everybody. Written and Illustrated
by America's cleverest Writers and Artists[22]

Poetry reciprocated, advertising in *The Masses* in December 1916 using the context-appropriate (if perhaps gently tongue-in-cheek) pitch, "Are you a poet? / Everyone is these days, or would like to be."[23] In 1922, looking back at ten years of the New Verse, Harriet Monroe identified "*The Masses,* with its successor *The Liberator,*" as the monthly American magazines (apart from her own) that had been most "hospitable to modern poets, to 'the new movement.'"[24]

The hospitality to modern modes of verse that contemporaries saw in *The Masses* has been largely obscured to literary history, but it reemerges when one begins actually looking at its poems. *The Masses* was nominally run as a cooperative; anyone could attend the meetings at which submissions were discussed and sometimes voted upon, but Eastman and Dell, both skilled poets and critics, exercised the greatest influence over its contents, especially on literary questions. In their five years with the magazine, they published nearly four hundred verses in a wide variety of forms and styles, many of them exploring the material textures and social relationships of twentieth-century American life through a prism of radical social ideals. A host of *Masses* poems evoke the rhythms, voices, and spaces of the modern metropolis. They explore the dynamics of industrial capitalism, seeking to balance idealism and indignation. After August 1914 they contribute to the magazine's trenchant critique of the war in Europe. By ascribing to poetry such an important role in its radical project, while not insisting upon any single style or ideological function, *The Masses* significantly expanded the expressive range of the New Verse as a cultural movement.

This account of *The Masses* challenges the commonly held view that its attachment to traditional forms vitiates its impact on the history of modern poetry. The issue is important enough to require some specific attention. These assumptions are typically supported not by detailed examination of the magazine's pages but by reference to the narrower context of Max Eastman's literary-critical writings, such as the prose volume *Enjoyment of Poetry* (1913), which garnered substantial sales and positive reviews in genteel venues and briefly made Eastman into an icon of renascent romantic sensibility.[25] Later in the decade he continued to write against the excesses of *vers libre,* most prominently in "Lazy Verse" (*New Republic,* September 1916), which acknowledged the greatness of Whitman and a few others who eschewed meter but complained that the confusion of journalism and literature had fostered a "dilute variety of prosy poetry which is [currently] watering the country."[26] Though modern enough to argue that journalism was "the unique literary achievement of the age," Eastman still resisted the conclusion that a poetry unwilling to respond to journalism's achievement risked desuetude and irrelevance.[27] In 1920, contemplating Eastman's curiously retrograde position in the modern avant-garde, Alfred Kreymborg described him wryly as "preaching freedom wherever poetry *isn't* concerned," which "hurts Eastman so much more than anybody else" (italics added).[28]

But the relationship of *The Masses* to experimental verse is a good deal more complex. Floyd Dell, who as managing editor probably exercised the greatest influence over the magazine's literary contents, was much more sympathetic than Eastman to formal innovations such as *vers libre,* having been an early advocate of Vachel Lindsay and Ezra Pound in the Chicago *Friday Literary Review* between 1909 and 1913, before he came to New York. At times Dell played the role of half-unwilling defender of tradition against the more radical expressions of the New Poetry, but he resisted Eastman's a priori condemnation of the new forms themselves. His ambivalent but self-aware response to the prosy and sexually frank vignettes of Mary Aldis (discussed in the final chapter) indicates the effort he was making to keep an open mind. He began with the bemused observation, "I believe the *Masses* has the opinion of itself that it cannot be shocked: I know better. And you know that poor old Floyd, with his classical standards still fluttering in the cyclone of modernism, is very capable of it. Things like the pieces Mary Aldis sent in affect me with a vague uneasiness which I am candid enough to regard as shock."[29] Thus provoked, Dell fretted, "I do not understand the new ideas about form," and went on to judge that "[a]bout nine-tenths of the new art, in painting, in sculpture and poetry, seems to me to have no aesthetic values at all."[30]

Scholars have taken such moments of skepticism and incomprehension to exemplify the stance of *The Masses* toward new formal approaches. Even a sympathetic treatment of the magazine, O'Neill's anthology *Echoes of Revolt,* quotes Dell's comments and concludes disapprovingly, "One found neither Ezra Pound or James Joyce in *The Masses,*" as if such a thing were easily imaginable, an opportunity that the editors had inexplicably failed to act on.[31] Stranger still, O'Neill omits to note that later in the very same letter, Dell distances himself from the persona of Poor Old Classical Floyd and endorses innovation as a principle even, and perhaps especially, when he was not personally convinced of its value: "If the *Masses* were my own magazine I would print these things of Mary Aldis' on the simple theory that new things ought to be printed and some day we will have made up our minds whether we like them or not."[32]

In my reading of *The Masses,* this is the view that exemplifies its stance toward the New Poetry. Eastman published none of his attacks on *vers libre* there, probably because like Dell, he didn't see a "revolutionary magazine" as the proper venue for rejecting innovation and experiment. The verse in *The Masses* before they took it over was pedestrian in craft and didactic in tone, a left-wing counterpart to the genteel-homiletic verse that dominated American magazine poetry before 1912. After their arrival it immediately became more central to the magazine, growing in quality and quantity every year (from twenty-five poems in the 1913 issues to nearly one hundred in both 1916 and 1917). Imposing no simplistic litmus test of politics or style, Eastman and Dell published earnest radicals such as C. E. S. Wood, Arturo Giovannitti, Margaret Widdemer, and Sarah N. Cleghorn; adherents to fin-de-siècle traditions such as Joel E. Spingarn, George Sterling, and the latter-day "Vagabondian" Harry Kemp; and many poets associated with the New Poetry who typically worked in traditional forms such as William Rose Benét, Marguerite Wilkinson, Witter Bynner, Louis Untermeyer, and Jean Starr Untermeyer. But they also published a great deal of *vers libre,* including such standard-bearers as Carl Sandburg, Vachel Lindsay, Amy Lowell, and James Oppenheim. Many *vers libre* lyrics in *The Masses,* such as Helen Hoyt's "Menaia" (October 1915), Louise Bryant's "Lost Music" (January 1917), and Dell's "Summer" (February 1917), clearly exhibit imagism's influence, while Robert Carlton (Bob) Brown's playful *vers libre* sequence "Bubbles," appearing in *The Masses* for June 1915, could just as easily have seen the light of day in *Others,* which began the next month across the river in rural New Jersey. In June 1916, Dell and Eastman even published "The Conqueror," a cryptic love poem by the eccentric darling of the avant-garde, the Baroness Elsa von Freytag-Loringhoven. If not quite as eclectic as *Poetry*, *The Masses* featured a wider range of poetic styles than any other American magazine of the decade.

Old Bottles, New Wine

Many poems in *The Masses* bear out Cary Nelson's claim that some modern poems derive progressive or subversive force precisely through their use of traditional forms. Nelson's argument refers specifically to Claude McKay (who would publish several of his most powerful sonnets in *The Liberator*), but it has sweeping implications for contemporary scholars reconsidering the relations between the forms and the ideological meanings of modernist texts: "[McKay's poetry means] that we will never again be able to assume the sonnet form guarantees us the consolations of the dominant culture. It is sometimes precisely the unresolvable conflicts between the connotations of a received form and the new anger it contains that make his poetry interesting."[33] This position that a poet might use traditional forms for iconoclastic purposes, seeking to "destabilize those [old] forms from within," had no place in the high-modernist ideology of organic form, in which politically radical poems in traditional forms were doubly damned as benighted opposites to the only authentic modernism, which must be radical in form but free from the tentacles of ideology.[34]

The earliest *Masses* poem to suggest the value of traditional forms within a modern poetics of social engagement was Louis Untermeyer's insouciant satire of Christianity, "God's Youth" (August 1913), which begins: "I often wish that I had been alive / Ere God grew old,"

> . . . when He
> Was still delighted with each casual thing
> His mind could fashion, when His soul first thrilled
> With childlike pleasure at the blooming sun.[35]

Untermeyer had been an unofficial house poet to *The Masses* from its beginnings, but under Eastman and Dell he began to write more adventurously. "God's Youth" takes direct aim at a lingering *fin-de-siècle* mode of nostalgic melancholy that laments poetry's enfeebled position within a despiritualized condition of modernity, which was exemplified by the 1890s sonnets of George Santayana, one of which begins,

I would I had been born in nature's day,
When man was in the world a wide-eyed boy,
And clouds of sorrow crossed his sky of joy
To scatter dewdrops on the buds of May.
Then could he work and love and fight and pray.[36]

While imitating Santayana's tone, Untermeyer's poem moves in a very different direction, demonstrating American poetry's reviving savoir-faire by converting nostalgia into exuberant satire of an enfeebled theology. Once, God had made such "vast and droll experiments" as "the elk with such extravagant horns," "the animals like plants, the plants like beasts," and "the great impossible giraffe, whose silly head / Threatens the stars."[37] The poet elevates God's "vast mirth" at these "great jests," echoed by the heavens, into a principle of cosmic comedy that is "greater than His beauty or His wrath"—much as Wallace Stevens would propose a few years later in "A High-Toned Old Christian Woman" that the spheres' co(s)mic winking grows more intense as it affronts the delicate feelings of widows. But now, since God's back is "bent / With time and all the troubling universe," it is young radical poets instead who feel "young and blithe and whimsical." This displacement of enfeebled divinity by energetic human agency, a common trope in *Masses* poems, is realized in the conspicuously traditional form of blank verse, inevitably linked in English-language poetry to epic explorations of Christian or romantic cosmology such as *Paradise Lost* and *The Prelude.*[38] The animals of "God's Youth" embody a contradictory mix of the earthly and divine, majesty and absurdity: the giraffe whose feet "embrace earth" even as its head seeks the stars; "The paradox of the peacock," whose "bright form / Is like a brilliant trumpet" from the anthropomorphic heavens, while its actual sound is a bizarre inhuman screech, "a cackle and a joke."[39] We might fancy this satiric bestiary as a faint echo of Milton's motley cast of devils and angels, through which Untermeyer deanthropomorphizes the modern universe, seeking liberation from an inhibiting deity erroneously imagined in the image of humanity.

Untermeyer's use of blank verse to propose Christianity's modern irrelevance—a year before Stevens would do so in *Poetry* with "Sunday Morning"—is one of many *Masses* poems that adapt traditional formal strategies to provocative new uses. Later that year, in November 1913, *The Masses* published one of its most trenchant labor verses, "Paterson" by Rose Pastor Stokes, which refits Edwin Markham's famous poem of protest and warning, "The Man with the Hoe" (1899), for the world of the urban-industrial proletariat.[40] "Paterson" formed a bitter pendant to the extensive coverage *The Masses* had given to various labor actions of 1913, particularly the IWW-led strike of silk workers in New Jersey between February and July, which absorbed the attention of many New York artists and resulted in an avant-garde "strike pageant" at Madison Square Garden in early June, a triumph of bohemian-radical goodwill but a financial failure that didn't help the strike, which collapsed the following month.[41] Deflated hopes and barely contained rage fuel Stokes's poem. At the moment, the strike is over, the mostly female workers have returned in defeat to the looms, and the silencing of their aspirations is evoked through a striking oxymoron, "The air / Is ominous with peace."[42] Once again the equipment runs, and "[h]unger moves the Shuttle forth and back," but there is no reason to doubt that a much larger conflict lies ahead, since "[t]he product grows and grows." Those who oppose the strikers remain blind to these implications ("What we weave you see not through the gloom"), unable or unwilling to see that the true "product" of the looms is "a shroud of ghastly black." The strikers weave again because they must eat, but Stokes defiantly insists that they shall never weave "what you will." They weave not for their oppressors but for themselves, and their "bruised hearts" and "bitter hopes" drive the shuttle, whose action, "**sure** . . . **and fleet**," tropes the poet's conviction of an eventual proletarian uprising.

One might assume "Paterson" to be an artless cry from the heart, but in fact it is composed in an elaborate structure of four five-line stanzas, with a short added line ending the first and third. The poem's form is thus traditional in its use of rhyme and meter and innovative in its distinctive lineation and stanzaic structure. Its consistent iambics are rendered more tensile by the widely varying line lengths, which form a syllabic pattern of 10 / 2 / 6 / 10 / 6 / (2) in each stanza. Aurally and visually, this lineal arrangement evokes the weaving action of the yarn in the workers' looms. A speaking reader's voice will be heard in an oscillating rhythm of long, moderate, and short breaths, while a silent reader's eye will move first from far left to far right (l. 1), then back to the middle, where it is pulled rapidly downward by the short lines (ll. 2–3), then to another long horizontal pentameter line (l. 4), and finally back to shrinking verticals (ll. 5–6).

This structure of interlaced repetition and variation is reinforced by the rhyme scheme, ABCAAB / DBCDD / EBFEEB / GBFGG, which balances constancy (the B rhyme of each stanza's second line, the triple rhyme of lines 1-4-5) and continual change (the introduction of a new rhyme in each stanza, the anticipated but not supplied B rhyme of the "missing" sixth lines in stanzas two and four). These weaving effects are further enhanced by the oscillation between two contrasting registers of imagery: the elaborate allegorical conceit portraying the action of the shuttle as the historical progress of the proletariat; and the brutal simplicity of the B rhymes, set apart on their own lines—"The air" / "Beware!" / "Take care!" The symbiosis between the form of "Paterson" and its subject matter epitomizes the relationship between artistry and activism in *The Masses* more generally: often in tension, sometimes self-contradictory, but always striving for generative synthesis between the two.

This same nexus of themes that shape Stokes's poem—labor agitation, gender, and impending class war—drive a later *Masses* poem again adapting traditional formal strategies: "The Food Riots" (May 1917), by Marguerite Wilkinson, a lecturer on poetry to women's clubs who would publish *New Voices,* a successful introductory anthology of the New Poetry, in 1919. Wilkinson's poem refers to the riots that erupted in New York in February 1917, when hundreds of working-class women marched on city hall protesting exorbitant rises in the costs of staple foods sold by pushcart vendors.[43] Consisting of four stanzas of eight lines each, "The Food Riots" uses a meter that hovers between iambic and anapestic and a consistent but flexible rhyme scheme to advance the pointed political irony of people forgotten and starving in one of the world's richest nations. This irony is signaled in formal terms by the gap between the uniformity of stanza length and the striking contrast of line length from one stanza to the next. The first and third stanzas evoke the plentiful harvests and bursting stores of Keats's "To Autumn" in expansive tetrameter lines that seem to go on forever ("With wealth of the autumn the fruit trees were heavy—/ With burden of red and with burden of gold").[44] These leisurely lines contrast to the much shorter ones of the italicized second and fourth stanzas, as Mark Van Wienen notes.[45] Much as the American ideology of universal plenty is challenged by the presence of hungry rioters, the flowing tetrameter cadences of the longer lines are challenged by the staccato rhythms of the dimeter lines, in the same basic meter but cut short, running out of breath as they describe starving women, babies, and men who pant *"Give food or we die."*[46] Wilkinson's evocation of Keats, the greatest idol of the romantic-genteel poetic tradition, may be designed to implicate that tradition in the obfuscations of capitalism, but it also demonstrates the expressive potential of new uses of older forms in a decidedly untraditional venue such as *The Masses.*

In the long lines of the last verse, Wilkinson returns to that American ideology of plenitude ("Oh, fat is the land, East and West, far and wide, / And fair are the prairies and great is our pride / In the bounty that quickens, the beauty that thrills"), only to expose it as venal and false with the final refrain:

> But poor is the people
> Whose women must cry,
> "We work, but we starve,
> Give us food or we die!"

In *vers libre* the formal contrast between two alternating sections might register to some degree, but the more pointed clash between two similar yet strikingly distinct rhythmic structures—leisurely tetrameter versus breathless dimeter—would be lost. Juxtaposing themes of plenty and hunger within this traditional form helps Wilkinson get beyond liberal hand-wringing to articulate a forceful political point: that the fact of hungry people in a land of plenty renders all Americans poor. Such adaptations of old forms to new uses in *The Masses* and elsewhere should be reconsidered as significant modes of modernist innovation.

The War of Traders

Because the New York food riots were produced by wartime economic upheaval and opportunism, Wilkinson's text is a war poem, typical of the later verse of *The Masses* in exploring the wide-ranging consequences of this global catastrophe. Through 1916, the official U.S. policy of neutrality provided sufficient insulation for the magazine's sustained and passionate campaign against the conflict, which it treated as the horrifying yet logical result of two intersecting geopolitical formations: the modern capitalist economy, with its ceaseless need to expand markets beyond national boundaries; and the totalitarian nationalism that had become the primary ideological engine of a postdynastic Europe. This critique took many forms in the pages of *The Masses,* including traditional editorials, firsthand reportage from Europe, Marxist economic theory, fiction, and a wide range of artwork from gruesome battle scenes to sardonic lampoons of patriotic hypocrisies. The magazine's creation of a collage of genres built around a particular political position should be understood as a significant modernist innovation in itself, worthy of detailed study. But my primary concern here is with the substantial body of antiwar verse *The Masses* generated beginning in the fall of 1914. Over the next three years it published dozens of poems addressing the depersonalizing techniques, dehumanizing scale, and ideological mystifications of twentieth-century warfare. Arguably the strongest American antiwar verse of the period, this largely forgotten body of work by noncombatant radicals offers an intriguing contrast to the canonical version of elegiac "Great War poetry" produced by British combat soldiers. Certainly it belies the long-standing assumption that North American poetry about the First World War went no deeper than the stoical odes to duty that became most famous, particularly Alan Seeger's "I Have a Rendezvous with Death" and John McCrae's "In Flanders Fields."[47]

Above all, *The Masses* sought to challenge the legitimacy of the war by demonstrating how the conflict had been abstracted into a mode of capitalist trade, a fetishized national currency marketed to and consumed by European populations. And the magazine hoped to spearhead resistance to the selling of the war to the still-neutral United States. On both sides of the Atlantic, verse was playing a substantial role in the marketing of the war, most seductively in Rupert Brooke's enthusiastic romanticizing of the patriotic British soldier, and then by his convenient martyrdom to the cause. Brooke's sequence of six sonnets, "1914," completed in January 1915, celebrated the opportunity to escape from the putative drudgery and purposelessness of a peacetime world "grown old and cold and weary," populated by "half-men, and their dirty songs and dreary."[48] Like millions of young men of his generation, Brooke was so deeply invested in the high-toned rhetoric of abstractions such as "honor" and "valor" that he failed utterly to imagine the actualities of modern warfare. His portrayal of men about to go into hellish trench environments as "swimmers into cleanness leaping" is a travesty that Paul Fussell finds emblematic of the ironic and absurd character of the entire Great War.[49] Nevertheless, by early spring 1915, Brooke's sonnets had become a sensation in Britain, and after being evoked by the dean of St. Paul's Cathedral in an Easter sermon on April 27, they achieved the status of sanctified Englishness. Three weeks later the poet was dead in the Dardanelles—ironically, not in combat but from septicemia—providing the final ingredient for his "canonization and simplification . . . into a national symbol" in Britain and America.[50]

Brooke had made a dashing visit to New York and Chicago in the summer of 1914, and his glamorous persona had swept away many who met him, particularly Margaret Anderson, whose *Little Review* featured expressions of Brooke-worship in four of its first five issues, and several more thereafter.[51] After his death, the lore of his unfulfilled promise and noble sacrifice was accepted by most of American literary culture, even by many within the avant-garde. In May 1915, the *Little Review* mourned his "murder" as the worst yet of the war's "monster horrors" and in June published Arthur Davison Ficke's sonnet "Rupert Brooke: A Memory," while in the same month *Poetry* issued a different elegy by Ficke, "To Rupert Brooke," this one a sequence of six sonnets modeled on "1914."[52] In a commentary in the same issue, however, Harriet Monroe was more measured, noting with "regret" that Brooke's sonnets had "celebrated the old illusions," particularly "the romantic glamour which, as it has been made mostly by the arts, must be stripped off by the arts if war is to become as archaic and absurd as duelling is today."[53]

Floyd Dell of *The Masses* felt none of Anderson's hero-worship or Monroe's regret, finding Brooke's posturings revolting and his patriotic apotheosis dangerous grist for the propaganda mills. After seeing yet another elegiac celebration of Brooke's physical beauty, nobility of spirit, and sacrificial death (this one by Joyce Kilmer in the *New York Times Magazine* of September 12), Dell boiled over. In a letter to Ficke on September 16, he enclosed a furious sonnet, entitled "To Rupert Brooke," which asks,

> How does it feel, now your bright locks and curly,
> Are laid to rest under a tropic sky?
> Is this peace better than the life you tired of,
> Or thought you tired of, . . .
> This silence, than the "dreary songs and dirty"?[54]

Like his mocking misquotation of Brooke's line, Dell's choice of form exploits the disjunction between the elegant, familiar structure of Brooke's sonnets and his own scathingly iconoclastic content. Deriding Brooke as a "pretty little fool" and "Beauty Boy," the poet concludes that the proper "wages" for his warmongering "is the spittle / Of slobbering praise that drips into your grave."[55] His imagery condemns Brooke's delusional enthusiasm for the war as a form of nationalist currency, bought by those who were now busy fetishizing his death for their own purposes. For Dell, Brooke's life and death had become an appalling example of the conscription of literature into the patriotic and masculinist ideologies justifying the war.

Though Dell's poem was not published in *The Masses*, it accurately captures the magazine's critique of war propaganda of all genres, particularly how forms of propaganda affected societies structurally depersonalized by industrial capitalism's erosion of older communal bonds. Many of the strongest *Masses* poems explore the public relations of modern warfare through which governments induce their citizens to fight for patriotic abstractions.

These verses target politicized attempts to control war reportage, the rhetoric of masculine adventure that portrays combat as a harmless competitive sport, the ideological effects of martial toys given to American children, and above all the mass spectacle of the military parade. The military parade can be called many things—spectacle, diversion, advertisement—but it is perhaps best understood as the foremost *abstraction* of war that a nation can present to its populace, representing in stylized visual form the coordinated motion of soldiers advancing into battle and the distinctive objects they carry with them: clothing, regalia, equipment, weaponry.

But if the parade was a powerful form of propaganda, abstracting horrifying actualities into beguiling spectacle, in *The Masses* it became the subject of potent antinationalist critique. In November 1914, even before Brooke's bellicose sonnets had seen the light of day, the magazine printed a poem that anticipated his repudiation of the peacetime world but appropriated it to a radically different purpose. "A Breath of Life" by Clement Wood looks past incidental causes to the fundamental economic engine driving the war: pervasive class inequities that render the laboring man's life of "eleven servile hours a day, six days a week," so dreary and savorless that combat seems in comparison "a picnic, a vast game of chance," and "quick and bursting death" preferable to the "foul-aired routine" of a long life of drudgery.[56] With nothing in his life to "bind him to sanity and peace," Wood's working-class stiff needs little persuasion to join "the close-locked marching feet, / The music like great laughter, the rough comradeships" that enlistment promises. And yet by disconnecting the marching feet from their bodies, the poet emphasizes not the communal integration that parades are meant to foster but the callous impersonality of relations in the modern military that undermines the benefits of masculine comradeship. The lock-step marching of fragmented bodies thus becomes a trope of physical and psychic dismemberment, much as the spectatorial experience of a populace must be detached from their critical faculties to induce them to give over their lives to patriotic abstractions often utterly contrary to their actual interests. That fatal gap between marching feet and integrated citizenship was central to *The Masses*' synthesis of political activism and avant-garde aesthetics. If the ideological regimes of modern capital sought to make it easier to march than to resist, *The Masses* took as its mission to demonstrate that when people's lives could be made more rewarding, more whole, they would no longer throw them away in wars of traders.

Two issues later, Louis Untermeyer's "To a War Poet" (January 1915) again uses parades to explore the disjunction between actuality and ideology, addressing an unctuous noncombatant versifier whose "two-penny crav-

ing for gore" has inspired "hundreds . . . to their death"—anticipating the
critique of propaganda verse that Wilfred Owen would mount in "Dulce et
Decorum Est" a few years later.[57] Untermeyer's poem turns on the contrast
between two parades, first a splendid one in which young soldiers head off
to battle inspired by the words of the warmongering writer; and its ironic
obverse, a forlorn procession of "broken and spent" men, no longer young,
who drag past, their souls full of horror at the actualities he romanticizes.
Untermeyer urges the war poet—and, of course, the reader—to "learn from"
the parade of battered soldiers what war is really like, anticipating the
climactic rhetorical imperative of Owen's poem, which challenges noncom-
batants to understand war as a physical reality rather than an abstraction:
"If you too could see" what I have seen, then "you would not" promulgate
the "Old Lie" that dying for one's country is a sweet and fitting fate.[58]

Though emerging from a brave soldier's righteous fury and generating
enormous rhetorical power, Owen's syllogism is not in itself a sufficient
basis for an antiwar poetics. How short a step from his conviction that
if his readers could see the horrific sights he has seen, they could not support patriotic arguments for the war, to the absolute impossibility of seeing
truly—either by reader or poet—without actually being there. This barrier
between physical experience and intellectual understanding, which features
in so much twentieth-century war literature, threatens to inhibit a structural
critique of the less tangible forces behind the traumatic physicality of the
war. One of the foremost achievements of *The Masses* was precisely to create
a space where writers, artists, and readers might come to see the ideological truth of the war *without* being there. The final section of Untermeyer's
poem moves from the spectacle of the parades toward that more synthetic
critique, extrapolating from the physical experiences undergone by these
soldiers the eventual consequences of capitalist warfare upon all segments
of the populace:

> The dusk settling down like a blight,
> Screening unnamable hordes;
> Searchlights stabbing the night
> With blinding and bodiless swords;
> Of a sudden welter of cries
> And death dropping down from the skies.[59]

In careening martial anapests, these chaotic images emphasize what is unseen
and unseeable, evoking the chilling impersonality of twentieth-century war.
Unidentifiable hordes move about in the dusk, cries remain fragmented and
incomprehensible, and technologies of destruction become abstracted from

physical substance, no longer subject to barriers of matter and distance that limited the killing power of earlier weapons. Searchlights, like swords in their power to locate and penetrate secreted human bodies, are all the more sinister for being "bodiless." Indiscriminate air warfare on civilian populations, terrifying even in its infancy, promises to take the mechanization of killing and the dehumanization of the enemy to their ultimate levels, if not in this war, then in the next one. Faced with such long-distance technologies as these, *seeing* the war, in Owen's sense, seems almost beside the point. Reminding us that some things we can't see must be imagined nonetheless, seeking to move from physical results to ideological causes, Untermeyer envisions emerging military technologies and strategies eradicating all comforting distinctions between combatant and civilian, enemy and ally. Yet his frightening vision also carries an activist insight: to show that capitalist nation-states maintain their war powers through such disjunctions between concrete experience and ideological abstraction is to open that process up to critique.

Only a month later, in *The Masses* for February 1915, Carl Sandburg's "Buttons" pressed further the magazine's analysis of the depersonalization and abstraction that allow modern war bureaucracies to control their own populations. Here is the poem in full:

> I have been watching the war map slammed up for advertising
>   in front of the newspaper office.
> Buttons—red and yellow buttons—blue and black buttons—
>   are shoved back and forth across the map.
> A laughing young man, sunny with freckles,
> Climbs a ladder, yells a joke to somebody in the crowd,
> And then fixes a yellow button one inch west
> And follows the yellow button with a black button one inch west.
> (Ten thousand men and boys twist on their bodies in a red soak
>   along a river edge, Gasping of wounds, calling for water,
>   some rattling death in their throats.)
> Who by Christ would guess what it cost to move two buttons one
>   inch on the war map here in front of the newspaper office
>   where the freckle-faced young man is laughing to us?[60]

The opening phrase, "I have been watching," suggests that Sandburg's focus will be on the war as a spectacular form of modern mass culture and on the emerging science of selling it to a populace. It also signals that his representational strategy will be primarily cinematic, seeking to challenge obfuscating abstractions by turning words into pictures. The body of the poem consists of a simple but powerful juxtaposition of two cross-cut shots, depicting simultaneous events thousands of miles apart. The first is a jovially impersonal crowd scene in a bustling American metropolis in which a parade seems just around the corner and people follow the latest twists in the war's narrative precisely as spectators would gather at news offices to follow distant sporting events before radio and television. In a single striking line, the second shot concretizes the realities abstracted by buttons and maps. Sandburg then synthesizes the two images by asking, "Who by Christ would guess what it cost" to move these buttons an inch in one direction or another? The interrogative "who . . . would guess?"—the counterpart to the opening "I have been watching"—seeks to propel the reader away from passive spectatorship toward critical scrutiny of the ideological conditions that make the war narrative seem inevitable and necessary. Sandburg's method of juxtaposition and synthesis creates an effect very much like the "intellectual montage" Sergei Eisenstein would soon pioneer in *Battleship Potemkin,* which juxtaposes spatially and narratively discontinuous imagery in successive shots to reveal hidden structural relationships. Like Eisenstein's films (and indeed like the buttons on the map), the poem's political meaning inheres not in the individual shot or image but in the relationships among them, suggesting Sandburg's awareness of the necessity of understanding social realities not as atomized moments but as parts of larger relational systems.

The poem's concrete material imagery shows that Sandburg, like Wood and Untermeyer, had dug his way out from under the weightless abstractions of nineteenth-century poetic practice. But as I suggested of Owen's "Dulce et Decorum Est," such concreteness is the precondition for a structural critique of the war, not its fulfillment. Perhaps the most important political function of "Buttons" is to expose a paradoxical dynamic of modern mass society in which the more fully the individual consciousness is immersed in an ever-changing succession of quotidian moments, the more completely it cedes the power of abstraction to depersonalized entities—newspaper, government, military bureaucracy—whose ethical vacuity Sandburg highlights by noting the map's supplementary function as an advertisement. His poem targets a central problem of modern society, and arguably the primary ideological engine behind the Great War: the atomization of a populace who, like the laughing young man fixing the buttons, float through their lives doing their specialized jobs, minding their own small patches of business, no longer able to estimate the cost of being dominated by the depersonalizing institutions of capitalist nation-states.

The emphasis in these poems on the sinister pageantry of modern warfare is not surprising, given the profusion during 1915 and early 1916 of "preparedness" agitation in the New York streets traversed continually by those involved with *The Masses*.[61] President Wilson had initially opposed preparedness measures as contrary to the policy of neutrality, but after the torpedoing of the *Lusitania* in May 1915 he lost resolve, and by early 1916, as the nation gradually drifted from neutral toward combatant status, preparedness parades no longer seemed to protest national policy but to carry a quasi-official authority. *The Masses* had vigorously opposed the movement all along by arguing that such preparation would make American involvement more likely, even inevitable. As the atmosphere grew more oppressive, the magazine's dissident resolve increased, generating poems, cartoons, and essays in every issue of early 1916, including Martha Gruening's ferocious poem "Prepared" (March 1916), which melds the "patriotic" advocate of preparedness with the bloodthirsty lyncher of American blacks and Jews, and Pauline B. Barrington's verse "Toy Guns" (May 1916), which satirically castigates American bourgeois parents for cultivating "a new generation of militarists."[62] This campaign culminated in the July 1916 "Preparedness Issue," entirely devoted to a critique of the policy's logic and consequences.[63] The following month, the magazine offered perhaps its most insightful anti-preparedness critique in verse, "The Day of War: Madison Square, June 20th," by Arturo Giovannitti, which uses yet another military parade to demonstrate the links between the depersonalizing environment of urban modernity and mass acquiescence to the mystifications of capitalist propaganda.

Giovannitti's *vers libre* poem describes a "hawk-faced youth with rapacious eyes, standing on a shaky chair," who exhorts a ragtag crowd, "idle, yawning, many-hungered, beggarly," to embrace the cause of radical labor.[64] Giovannitti places him at the heart of the alienating skyscraper city, "in the roar of the crossways, under the tower that challenges the skies, terrible like a brandished sword." This bellicose young orator embodies the hard line of *The Masses*' revolutionary persona, as "his red tie flows tempestuously in the wind, the unfurled banner of his heart amidst the musketry of his young words." But he also possesses a human communicativeness otherwise lacking from the clamorous metropolitan environment, and he holds the crowd's attention through the intensity of his commitment. His humanity and vulnerability contrast to the other version of war that erupts upon the street, which is all the more intimidating for being fragmented and depersonalized:

> the blast of a trumpet, its notes ramming like bullets against the
>   white tower.
> The soldiers march up the Avenue. The crowd breaks, scatters,
>   and runs away, and only six listeners remain.

Though we get only this one fragmentary glimpse of the parade, its imposition of political authority disintegrates the "island of silence" the boy's voice had created amidst the "roar" of the city and sends listeners scurrying off to their various destinations, or wandering aimlessly toward some other temporary perch. As they drift away, Giovannitti acknowledges the difficulty of organized resistance to a capitalist modernity that enforces conformism by relentlessly isolating people from one another.[65]

Yet this story is not over: as Giovannitti repeats four times in the second half of the poem, "But he speaks on."[66] The boy's indomitability affirms the rightness of his cause, as does the one young woman who remains there transfixed, "her upturned face glowing before the brazier of his soul," showing that his words need not inevitably fall on deaf ears. At the end, the boy, the girl, and the white skyscraper "[a]re the only three things that stand straight and rigid and inexpugnable / Amidst the red omens of war." Though Giovannitti never names this building, he certainly has in mind the Metropolitan Life Tower (1909) on the southeast corner of Madison Square, at seven hundred feet the area's tallest by far and containing on its white walls the largest clock in the world. As I will detail in part 2, the Metropolitan Tower served as an extraordinarily powerful icon of urban modernity for American poets during the 1910s. We may initially assume that Giovannitti sees the skyscraper as just another daunting element of the alienating capitalist metropolis. Yet he associates it throughout with the radical orator who stands on a chair just beneath it, whose "shadow is heavy and hard upon their faces" while he exhorts the crowd, as the tower's must also be. At the poem's end, this affinity becomes explicit when the tower's great clock strikes twelve: "[O]ne by one drop at his feet the twelve tolls of the clock that marks time, the time that knows and flows on until his day comes." By associating the great timekeeping tower with the young radicals, Giovannitti implies a Marxist reading of industrial modernity as an era that has generated both greater exploitation and the class consciousness necessary for radical change, whose time is inexorably approaching. For him, as for many other leftist poets of the era, the skyscraper tower signifies not only the intimidating power of capital but the human race's ability to create things and ideas, eventually including a more just social order. The tower's size, strength, inexpugnability, and even its rebellious shape that "challenges the skies" make it an exemplary symbol, and "The Day of War" perhaps the exemplary verse text, of *The Masses'* revolutionary poetics of modernity.

The Postman Rings

Through 1916 and into the next year, the forces evoked in Giovannitti's poem intensified until American belligerency was inevitable. *The Masses* continued to challenge repressive patriotism with verse, editorials, artwork, and incisive articles such as Amos Pinchot's caustic "The Courage of the Cripple" (March 1917), which linked the interventionist Theodore Roosevelt to the bellicose German kaiser as figures driven equally by a transparent compulsion to compensate for their physical infirmities and emotional insecurities; and John Reed's essay "Whose War?" (April 1917), which analyzed the unholy alliance between belligerent American patriotism and organized religion. But after the declaration of war on April 6, *The Masses* was no longer protected by American neutrality and quickly came under government scrutiny. The Espionage Act of June 15 created the legal machinery for direct censorship against dissidence, and under its provisions the solicitor of the post-office department excluded the August issue of *The Masses* from the mails. *The Masses* obtained an injunction against the postmaster from the moderate District Judge Learned Hand in Manhattan, but before the issue could be mailed the post office took the extraordinary legal step of obtaining a stay against the injunction from a cooperative circuit judge in Vermont, effectively suppressing the August issue.[67]

Aware that without mailing privileges *The Masses* was done for, the editors elected, not without some contention, to go down fighting with more incendiary cartoons and articles such as Reed's "One Solid Month of Liberty" in the October issue, which chronicled the interlocking waves of governmental repression and "patriotic" mob violence that had swept the country in "the blackest month for free men our generation has known."[68] The final issue appeared (or mostly did not) in December 1917. By that time, the editorial staff, including Eastman, Dell, Reed, the business manager Merrill Rogers, the artists Robert Minor, Art Young, and Henry Glintenkamp—and even one unlucky young poet, Josephine Bell—had been indicted for sedition. The case would drag into the fall of 1918, but the *Masses* defendants, native-born, middle-class, personally charming, were more fortunate than many foreign-born radicals indicted under these shameful laws (including Rose Pastor Stokes, sentenced to ten years in May 1918 for making "unpatriotic" statements at a Woman's Club dinner).[69] Represented by excellent advocates, including Eastman himself in the second trial, they went free both times on hung juries. Except for Reed, who died a revolutionary martyr's death in the USSR in 1920, they would go on to lead long and varied careers in literature, art, and politics.

Their first significant act after the end of *The Masses,* even before the first trial convened, was to begin publication of *The Liberator* in March 1918. *The Liberator,* which ran until it merged with two other publications into the *Worker's Monthly* in late 1924, was a curious mixture of pragmatic capitulation and hard-line intransigence that echoed the contradictory character of *The Masses* but lacked the exuberance of the earlier magazine.[70] Seeking to circumvent the stranglehold the post office had achieved on *The Masses,* its first editorial pointedly acquiesced to the nation's participation in the war. Yet at the same time, *The Liberator* maintained an unquestioning allegiance to Soviet Bolshevism, endorsing Lenin's ruthless suppression of dissenting factions and civil liberties through 1920 and 1921.[71] The new venture was constituted entirely under the ownership of Eastman and his sister Crystal, and while Eastman's editorship never became a full-blown autocracy, the lively communal spirit of *The Masses* was largely missing. Though the mastheads of both magazines contain many names in common, the finest of the *Masses* artists, John Sloan, was gone from the scene due to a 1916 break with Eastman; John Reed resigned from *The Liberator* after a few months, unable to accept its capitulation on the war issue; and although Louis Untermeyer remained on the editorial board, he never played the leading role that he had in the verse of *The Masses.*

Despite outpacing *The Masses* in its circulation, which, according to Cary Nelson, peaked at sixty thousand, *The Liberator* never attained the eclectic readership or mainstream impact of its predecessor.[72] As associate editor, Floyd Dell was still in charge of the literary contributions, and poem for poem, the verse published there was stronger than that of *The Masses*: more varied in tone and technique, and more responsive to new formal developments. There were well-crafted poems of protest and commemoration, such as Michael Gold's "The Strange Funeral in Braddock" and rhapsodies to radical icons such as Eastman's sonnet "John Reed," Babette Deutsch's "Petrograd," and Witter Bynner's "Outlaws." *The Liberator* featured verse by such accomplished lyricists as Léonie Adams, Louise Bogan, and Elinor Wylie; experimental work by e. e. cummings and Jean Toomer; powerful sonnets by Claude McKay, including "The White City" and "America"; and poems in a variety of styles that dealt thoughtfully with twentieth-century urban life, such as Edna St. Vincent Millay's "To the Liberty Bell," Stirling Bowen's "Skyscraper," and James Rorty's "City Fear," among many others. All in all, *The Liberator* housed a rich, neglected vein of American leftist verse, which was anthologized along with poems from *The Masses* in a 1925 volume, *May Days,* edited by Genevieve Taggard.

And yet, despite the quality of its individual poems, as an agent of the New Poetry *The Liberator* was significantly less than the sum of its parts. In contrast to its predecessor, begun during a moment of unparalleled political idealism and cultural ferment, *The Liberator* was born from repression, paranoia, and bitterly compromised ideals and it operated in an era growing inimical to conjunctions of experimental aesthetics and radical politics. The American Socialist party underwent a devastating schism at its 1919 convention, and over the next two years this factionalism grew more debilitating as the nation's leftists scrambled to respond to a Soviet regime that was threatening to become almost as inhumane and brutal as the monarchy it had helped to overthrow—a scenario that appalled idealistic American radicals, sending some into doctrinaire denial and others into disgusted withdrawal from the entire political realm. O'Neill suggests that, by 1921, the American left as *The Masses* had understood it a few years earlier "was in ruins."[73] These accumulating burdens caused Eastman to hand management of the magazine over to others in early 1922 and drove Dell away a year later, in April 1923. But even well before those breaks, the synthesis of political activism and aesthetic adventurousness they had sought since 1912 was becoming less and less possible.

The Liberator offers its own sort of contradiction, this one less happy: though it frequently published good poems, poetry was not an important part of its program, as in activist magazines of the 1910s such as *The Masses* and the *Seven Arts*. In *The Liberator* we can see verse ironically drifting back toward the role of page-filler that it had played in the "quality magazines" before 1910. Much as the verse of those publications had reinforced their right-center ideological heritage, verse in *The Liberator* became an adjunct to its advocacy of revolutionary communism and Soviet Bolshevism. This is *not* to say (in either case) that the meaning of the individual verses appearing in these magazines can be reduced only to those respective ideologies. It is, however, to suggest that in some publishing venues, the function of such texts as purveyors of home truths to the converted can overshadow the wider range of meanings they might possess when encountered in other venues. This phenomenon produces, for me at least, a strange disparity between reading the poems in Taggard's anthology, where many of them glow with artistry and humanity, and reading them in issues of *The Liberator*, where they are like orphans lost on the page, sometimes difficult even to recognize as the same poems. There they seem ignored yet constrained by the material that surrounds them, which paradoxically makes their political sentiments sound more mechanical, less integrated into a larger social vision. I most emphatically do not mean by this that all such political contexts circumscribe the meanings of poetic texts in the same way or degree, or that poems can only realize their full potential if removed from the discursive networks where they first appeared. Far from it: the verse of *The Masses* generally speaks *more* vividly when read within its pages than when encountered elsewhere. Unlike its successor, *The Masses* managed to convey the sense that its poems, while seldom politically neutral (and better for not trying to be), were independent of any dogmatic control—and further, that both their passionate conviction and their independence helped to shape the magazine's spirited synthesis of politics and art.

   The Liberator's inability to make poetry integral to its radical project was not primarily a failure of individual artistic taste or radical will but a symptom of the encroachment of a binary model of literary value in which poets felt forced to choose between "art for art's sake" or "art for life's sake," between forfeiting social engagement to keep poetry safe from propaganda or compromising aesthetic nuance for accessibility and ideological purity.[74] Louis Untermeyer and Conrad Aiken staked out these polarities in the well-known "Ivory Tower" exchange in the *New Republic* in May 1919, a debate that sixty years later was still being cited as a formative moment in narratives of true "absolute" modernism rising up in rebellion against second-rate political versifying.[75]

   By 1925, only one year after *The Liberator* had been amalgamated with other publications into an all-purpose functionary organ of the American Communist party, this conceptual binary had taken firm hold, hampering Genevieve Taggard's attempt to commemorate the verse of *The Masses* and *The Liberator* in the anthology *May Days*. Her preface vividly registers this struggle, noting that in *The Masses*, "Social passion and creative beauty grew from the same tree branches. Now there has been pruning and grafting,—we have in consequence two trees—the air is sultry—there is no cross pollenizing. The artists who were attracted to the *Masses* for its art have gone one way; the revolutionists another. The two factions regard each other with hostility and suspicion. They consider themselves mutually exclusive and try their best to remain so."[76] As Taggard saw it, these polarities had created a "disheartening world" in which "the two trees wither for lack of each other."[77] The severance she describes would shape American poetry for decades to come. There were a few moments in which synthesis between the aesthetic and the political again seemed possible. In the mid-1930s, the American Popular Front sought to integrate high art and leftist politics, and while powerful verses by Muriel Rukeyser, Edwin Rolfe, Sol Funaroff, and others resulted, the effort was stifled by a series of horrific events after 1937, above all Stalin's show trials and the Nazi-Soviet Non-Aggression

Pact. Thereafter the ideal of integrating progressive politics and artistic ex-periment was virtually effaced by a polarized model of value that allowed New Criticism to control a "post-ideological" high ground of disinterested aesthetic judgment, in the process imposing its own potently ideological strictures and relegating *The Masses* and *The Liberator* beyond the pale of American literary history, an eclipse from which they are only now emerging back into view.

My analysis of verse in *The Masses* has sought to show that its eclectic and iconoclastic poetics of modernity was strongly aligned with the ex-perimental spirit later valorized by historians as *modernist*. In the next chapter, I approach the same issue from the other side and argue that the verse of *Others*, the quintessential aestheticist-modernist little magazine of American poetry, emerges from and responds to the same climate of progressive social engagement. One can find instances of tone-deaf piety in *The Masses* and narcissistic frivolity in *Others*—and vice versa. But to frame modern American poetry as an incommensurable dualism between social commitment and aesthetic integrity drastically underestimates the complexity of the New Verse. The sizable common ground between these two magazines, and among other publications of the 1910s, suggests the inadequacy of binaries of life versus art and helps us to see the New Verse as a movement defined by unlikely alliances and overlaps, in which wildly different figures rubbed shoulders in the same magazines and poets could be accepted by their contemporaries as fully modern while still reaching substantial nonspecialist audiences.

CHAPTER 4

There Is Always *Others*

Experimental Verse and "Ulterior Social Result"

If *The Masses* was written out of the history of twentieth-century American poetry, *Others,* published in New Jersey, New York, and Chicago between July 1915 and July 1919 by Alfred Kreymborg and various friends, was written into it in a peculiarly narrow way that underestimates the magazine's range and misrepresents its goals. The circulation of *Others* never much exceeded five hundred, yet its roster of contributors features a remarkable proportion of poets who later became canonical, including Pound, Eliot, Stevens, Williams, and Moore in its first six issues.[1] A single issue—the "Competitive Number," edited by Williams in July 1916—contained work by Pound, Williams, Stevens, and Moore, as well as Conrad Aiken, John Gould Fletcher, Amy Lowell, Mina Loy, and Carl Sandburg. With such a record, *Others* has been particularly subject to the "critical strip-mining" by which the "elite geniuses of modernism" were extracted from the multifarious landscape of the New Verse.[2] Until recently, historians have equated the magazine's historical importance entirely with the involvement of these later-canonical figures rather than understanding it as a dynamic avant-garde intervention involving a wide range of people and views, intensely committed to challenging the literary and social conventions of 1910s America.

The standard portrayal of *Others* in postwar scholarship was established by the 1946 volume *The Little Magazine,* which asserted that "the significance of . . . *Others* is *no greater or less* than the estimate that one places upon the desirability of securing the reputations of such poets as Williams, Moore, and Stevens" (italics added).[3] Nearly everyone else involved, including its founding editor Kreymborg, has been lumped into a category of self-indulgent bohemians, the perpetrators and victims of antibourgeois frivolities and outright hoaxes, their real accomplishments reduced to flukes. *The Little Magazine* again established this pattern by condescending to

Others as "a place for those whose poetry has not appeared, or has appeared only infrequently, in *Poetry*. Because of this almost accidental 'policy,' it publishes verse which is more boldly experimental [than that of other magazines]."[4] This notion of the "accidental" experimentalist, no less than the reduction of *The Masses* to a merely political organ, served the high-modernist project by attributing all artistic and historical agency to the few writers who later became canonical, denying credit to other individuals of importance, and stunting understanding of the editorial practices, material contexts, reciprocal influences, and ideological affinities that link *Others* to other magazines of the American New Verse. Jacqueline Vaught Brogan's 1991 lively anthology of "American Cubist Poetry" and fine recent work by Suzanne W. Churchill and Cristanne Miller have begun to correct this narrow view by examining a wider range of the magazine's participants and contexts. Churchill's book in particular establishes that *Others'* commitment to stylistic experimentation possessed a strong social dimension, but while she focuses on issues of gender and sexuality, my account emphasizes the magazine's distinctive response to the climate of metropolitan activism that links it to *The Masses*.

The reduction of *Others* to the aestheticist avant-garde was made easier by the magazine's refusal to supply any substantial editorial commentary, an extraordinary policy at a moment in which grandiose manifestoes and internecine battles of little magazines often overwhelmed their literary contributions. *Others* offered no earnest statement of purpose, no attacks on other magazines, no outraged letters from readers, no snippets of literary news, almost no reviews or critical essays, and no polemical surveys of the contemporary poetry scene until its final issue. Most of its twenty-six issues contained no prose at all except for an occasional brief announcement and a laconic motto of avant-garde allegiance, "The old expressions are with us always, and there are always others."[5] If every little magazine of the 1910s had been as unwilling to articulate a program, American poetry could not have emerged from its crisis with such vigor. Yet *Others'* single-minded pursuit of the new and "other" through verse itself, refusing the consensus view of poetry's subservience to prose, was also its greatest contribution to the New Verse.[6] Kreymborg's refusal of prose polemic and explanation should be considered a significant modernist choice, consciously made, expressing his distinctive personality and carrying specific aesthetic and ideological consequences: no more an accident than Harriet Monroe's decision to start her magazine in Chicago rather than New York, or T. S. Eliot's decision to name his quarterly *The Criterion*.

In August 1915, a month after the first issue of *Others,* Kreymborg pub-lished an article in the *New York Morning Herald,* "Vers Libre and Vers Librists," which sought to build on some bemused interest in the magazine among the New York newspaper press. This essay devotes paragraphs to sev-eral of the now-obscure poets prominent in his magazine's first phase, such as Hester Sainsbury, Horace Holley, Skipwith Cannell, and John Rodker, but finally it reads more as enthusiastic publicity for the whole Anglo-American *vers libre* movement—including well-informed accounts of imagism, the Chicago school, and vorticism—rather than as a manifesto for *Others,* which is described modestly as "the latest venture in the field" without further elaboration.[7] Kreymborg never printed this piece, or anything like it, in the magazine itself. In *Others,* verse would do the talking.

Over the years, various prose pieces have been pressed into service as explanatory manifestoes for *Others,* but none of these correspond well with what the magazine actually did. After the magazine underwent a series of improbable revivals in late 1918 and early 1919, William Carlos Williams was put in charge of a July 1919 issue, despite being fed up with the whole project. He produced two prose commentaries that he hoped would make another resuscitation impossible. Probably nothing in a final issue should be taken as representative of a whole magazine, but certainly Williams's vitriolic valedictions "Gloria!" and "Belly Music," ranting about *Others* as a nest of "vermine" [*sic*] soon to be "blasted out of existence" and indicting American poetry criticism as "sophomoric, puling, nonsensical," say much more about his own preoccupations of that moment than about the maga-zine's overall editorial posture.[8] In fact, the scatological ferocity of these pieces could hardly be further in tone from the genial, ironic understatement, exemplified by the motto, that Kreymborg had cultivated for *Others* over the previous four years.

The prose statement most congruent with the role *Others* came to oc-cupy in American literary history is Baker Brownell's "Irrational Verse," in the December 1918 issue. In this sophisticated but rather narrow essay, Brownell defended *Others* from populist-minded detractors such as Louis Untermeyer by connecting it to contemporaneous experiments in literature and the visual arts that sought to detach language from the ostensible op-pressions of referentiality for the "freedom" of pure sound: "'[O]thers' are etudes in cadence and word tone, experiments in the sound values of words intentionally segregated from the logical sequences of grammar."[9] Brownell's argument anticipated two key rhetorical strategies of later high-modern formalism: He sealed off stylistic and social realms from one another, positioning *Others* as an apolitical aestheticist faction interested only in "limited and intimate matters of workmanship" without reference to "ulterior social result."[10] And he used the imagery of social conflict to describe a struggle of the imagination in which the fetishized power of words as sounds became the crucial weapon in a revolution of technique: "The 'others' are struggling for the liberty of words against the tyranny of word definition."[11]

Like Churchill, I am suspicious of taking Brownell's essay as representative of *Others*' poetics or politics, though perhaps for reasons different from hers.[12] Its appearance at the tail-end of a very late issue militates against taking it as a comprehensive policy statement, as do the many rhetorical markers of distance between the authorially and temporally specific utterance entitled "Irrational Verse" and the much larger, temporally diffuse, collaborative body of discourse we call *Others*. Brownell himself insists repeatedly that he is "not an 'other,'" and indeed, he never published anything else there.[13] Repeatedly using such qualifiers as "I should guess that," he concedes that he has "read none of their prefaces or apologia nor even their latest book"—presumably the 1917 version of *Others: An Anthology of the New Verse*.[14] The only poet Brownell names as exemplifying these "others" is Walter Arensberg, who had not appeared in the magazine since its third issue more than three years earlier (September 1915). His assumption that Arensberg's Steinian verses were typical of *Others* may derive from their positioning at the head of the first two *Others* anthologies—but in those alphabetically arranged volumes, such prominence doesn't mean much. Even if his argument accurately represented Arensberg's work, it did not for the verse of *Others* as a whole. By December 1918 the magazine had published over a hundred poets, most of them not personally acquainted, writing in many *vers libre* styles, very few of them engaging in any radical linguistic deconstruction. Nor did much in the anthologies besides Arensberg's verses fit Brownell's model of poetry as pure sound "segregated from the logical sequences of grammar."

Brownell's argument for the asocial aestheticism of *Others* verse was also undermined by Kreymborg's typically minimal editorial statement at the head of the same December 1918 issue, which begins: "The newest issue of *Others* brings a recrudescence of the magazine as a monthly publication. The present policy will merely carry on the old, under the initial motto, 'The old expressions are always with us, and there are always others.'"[15] Kreymborg continues by reiterating his habitual refusal to exclude or factionalize, emphasizing individuality of expression but saying nothing to discourage socially engaged work: "It has been said in many places that the contributors to *Others* . . . are members of a group, a school. This is not true. Collectively or separately, they eschew everything which approximates ismism. . . . The curriculum is taboo; the only question asked is: 'Does a man express himself, and if so, how well?'"[16] This statement flatly contradicts Brownell's implication of a unified collective of poets called "Others" and reestablishes the inclusive stance against doctrine and dogma that *was* representative of the magazine's entire lifespan. By throwing all his editorial weight behind the values of skill and individuality regardless of theme or politics, Kreymborg implicitly affirms the feasibility of using verse as social commentary, even and especially in the newest styles.

My claim that *Others'* commitment to stylistic experimentalism possessed a strong social dimension would mean little if its pages were not peppered with verses addressing the conditions of urban-industrial modernity. But there they are, page after page, issue after issue. Just as American literary history has underestimated the importance of *The Masses* to avant-garde modernism, so has it overlooked or excluded the social engagement of the verse of *Others*. The rest of this chapter, juxtaposing familiar and forgotten verses from the magazine's pages, will describe its poetics of modernity as it extends across three interdependent registers: *formal, thematic,* and *metapoetic. Others* contributed to the expansion of modern poetic form by cultivating a distinctive innovation, the *vers libre* variation sequence, which was premised upon an understanding of twentieth-century experience as perceptually disjunct and socially heterogeneous. Like *Poetry* and *The Masses, Others* sponsored a great deal of verse exploring the defining themes of American life in the 1910s: the daunting cityscapes of the industrial metropolis, the explosive dynamics of Machine Age labor, the catastrophe of global warfare. Finally, in lieu of prose manifestoes, *Others* cultivated metapoetic verses that theorize poetry's changing functions and expanding reach in the sociomaterial landscape of twentieth-century America.

Sequences

The meanings of *Others*—its poetics and its politics—are best read through its verse rather than through the idiosyncratic and belated prose characterizations of Brownell, Williams, or Kreymborg himself, whose 1925 autobiography, *Troubador,* generated various myths for *Others'* high-modernist legacy, as Churchill notes.[17] I will begin by going back to the magazine's initial utterances—where a manifesto would conventionally appear—treating the verse of the first issue (July 1915) as an implicit statement of purpose. Like most that followed, this first number contains no editorials, no mission statement, and no reviews. Yet the selection and juxtaposition of its verse expresses a distinctive editorial vision committed to searching for forms and themes capable of speaking to twentieth-century life. To call Kreymborg's vision "distinctive" is not to call it self-consistent: indeed, much of *Others'* distinctiveness comes in the editor's tendency to yoke together discordant or incongruous elements. Kreymborg's whimsical personal style and his proclivity for faux-childlike verse became deeply unfashionable during the New Critical orthodoxy, which demanded emotional austerity and textual complexity, resulting in widespread dismissal of him as a mildly ridiculous figure. But the modernist editorial sensibility that inaugurated a new magazine with Mary Carolyn Davies's "Songs of a Girl" followed by Mina Loy's "Love Songs" deserves serious reconsideration. Each of these initiating texts expresses central elements of *Others,* and so too does their jarring juxtaposition.

"Songs of a Girl" is a sequence of eight *vers libre* lyrics of two to fourteen lines, featuring commonplace diction and a naive tone. The persona created by Davies is childlike, wide-eyed, earnest even when attempting to be flippant, and absorbed by her own emotions. She communicates with intangible entities and abstract concepts that possess shape, form, volition, consciousness, and voice (the sequence begins, "There is a morning standing at my window, looking into my room, and saying: / 'What will you do with me?'"[18] Following hard upon these rather cloying gestures were the original four of Loy's "Love Songs," which begin:

> Spawn of fantasies
> Sitting the appraisable
> Pig Cupid his rosy snout
> Rooting erotic garbage
> "Once upon a time"
> Pulls a weed white star-topped
> Among wild oats sown in a mucous membrane
> I would an eye in a Bengal light
> Eternity in a sky-rocket
> Constellations in an ocean
> Whose rivers run no fresher
> Than a trickle of saliva[19]

From Davies's use of poetry to articulate naively explicit emotion, we are thrust into a verse of hallucinatory eroticism, wrenching juxtapositions, bizarre metaphoric leaps, and unconventional punctuation and spacing. Seen through the narrowing prism of a century of modernist history, "Songs of a Girl" and "Love Songs" seem to have little in common, and I suspect that they were arranged to produce maximum cognitive dissonance in their original readers. But examining them together against the poetic conventions of 1915 reveals commonalities that illuminate *Others'* contribution to the remaking of American poetry in that decade.

In their drastically different ways, both poems assert a central premise of the New Poetry: modern verse must express the full range and intensity of female consciousness. Despite its chaste romanticism, Davies's work is modern in challenging reductive or essentialized conventions of female identity, instead framing "partial views of the self" that confound our ability "to decipher a coherent representation of the speaker's identity," as Churchill puts it.[20] Loy's work explores female consciousness in just about the most aggressive way imaginable for 1915. By announcing her sequence as "Love Songs," Loy evokes conventional assumptions of "female poetry" only to explode them, making no bones about the pleasure that the female takes in fantasizing and performing her sexuality, even its "wanton," "profane," and "promiscuous" aspects.[21] The unforgettable opening image of male and female sexual organs—the snout of "Pig Cupid" rooting in "erotic garbage"—rejects once and for all the Victorian denial of female sexuality. The second of Loy's "love songs" violates these taboos even more outrageously by evoking the deflating discordance between the conventional orgasmic pace of male and female, as the male sexual organ ("skin-sack") is redefined into "a clock-work mechanism / Running down against time / To which I am not paced." Obviously Loy's work represents a much more dramatic reconception of poetry by and about female experience than does Davies's. But both assume that articulating the intimacies of female consciousness, independent of any controlling male principle, is a central function of poetry in the twentieth century.[22]

Beyond their self-identification as songs, the Davies and Loy works exhibit important formal similarities, particularly the *vers libre* that in the summer of 1915 was still an object of controversy carrying strongly gendered elements. The powerful synergy in that decade between changing gender norms and the emergence of *vers libre* was largely lost later on, as such high-modernist polemics as John Crowe Ransom's "The Woman as Poet" (1937) feminized traditional forms as "meretricious decoration" while canonizing the unmetered verse of Pound and others as the "free" expression of the virile masculine imagination.[23] But in the 1910s, the situation looked quite different. As Churchill points out, for women in the early years of the New Verse, "writing was both a means and sign of emancipation, and poetry—especially free verse—was a favored form of expression."[24] Together, the Davies and Loy works thus established a foundational link for *Others* between changing gender attitudes and emerging experimental forms, demonstrating that the range of tone and voice available through *vers libre* is at least as great as through more traditional styles.

Perhaps even more significant than their prosody is the two poems' common structural arrangement: multiple sections headed by Roman numerals, combining natural and emotive imagery around a central theme or frame. Eschewing linear narrative for the juxtaposition of obliquely related elements, this form demands the reader's active participation in linking them. Such nonlinear sequences of juxtaposed elements became the signature form of *Others* and represent its most significant formal contribution to the New Poetry. This sequence form is distinct from conventionally numbered stanzas of equal length—as in, say, Stevens's "Sunday Morning," in which the sections advance an argument or narrative possessing some degree of linear progression. Clearly the variation-sequence poems in *Others* owe something to Whitman, who used versions of it in *Song of Myself* and elsewhere, but the form was otherwise quite uncommon in American verse before 1915. *Others'* cultivation of this form contrasts to the faux-sequences published in *Poetry,* many of whose prominent early poems were opportunistically grouped under catchall titles such as "Contemporania" (Pound), "Chicago Poems" (Sandburg), or "Pecksniffiana" (Stevens). In most of these groupings in *Poetry,* each section had been composed individually and would be published separately in later volumes of the authors' work. But in the Davies and Loy sequences, the individual elements are not designed to stand by themselves and cannot do so without significant loss: both register as organically conceived works comprised of distinct yet nonlinear components.[25]

Except for three poems by Horace Holley, every work in the first issue of *Others* employs some version of this structural principle, quickly establishing it as the magazine's signature mode. The Davies and Loy works were followed by "Olives," a sequence of fourteen miniatures of four to nine lines by Orrick Johns. Rather than using Roman numerals, Johns gives each Olive its own title, a single word or brief phrase, arranged graphically to the left of the verse's body. This structure lends a graphic and conceptual complexity to what might otherwise seem scattered or frivolous observations. Unlikely as it sounds, "Olives" combines the breathless naiveté of Davies and the hypersexualized worldliness of Loy, suggesting the importance of both expressive modes to the developing poetics of *Others*. Here are the final two units:

SOME	Now I know
WHERE	I have been eating apple-pie for breakfast
	In the New England of your sexuality.
A	It lasted a month,
MOON	We had one moon . . .
	You took it for a baby
	And when it cried
	For a bib and a bottle,
	All was over.[26]

Churchill links "Olives" to Gertrude Stein's work, noting that its structure splinters into a depiction of "discontinuous, cubist space characterized by shifting planes and perspectives."[27] I would propose further that the phrases in capitals can be seen as a whimsical alternative text, no less coherent or more self-parodic than many experimental *vers libre* sequences soon to appear in the pages of *Others* and elsewhere:

FIN-
GERS

SHOE-
STRING

BEAU-
TIFUL
MIND

MIG-
GLES

A
ROOM

BLUE
UNDER-
SHIRTS

IN
BED

IN THE
SQUARE

AT THE
DOOR

ON THE
TABLE

IN THE
STREET

IN THE
ORCHARD

SOME
WHERE

A
MOON[28]

In becoming a fanciful acrostic in two columns that invites the reader to proceed horizontally, vertically, or in both directions at once, "Olives" uses the sequence principle to challenge basic assumptions of what poems are and how we read them.

After the three Holley poems, the juxtapositional structure of the first three *Others* sequences was picked up again by Kreymborg's "Variations." As its formalist title suggests, "Variations" is an exercise in nonlinear structure: eight *vers libre* pieces between two and five lines long, each with its own brief title, offering a single haiku-like image or impression concerning a love relationship. The first consists of five lines entitled "Wizardry":

Your hands,
so strong,
so cool,
wizards
improvising sleep. . . .[29]

The paradox of hands that "improvise" most magically while the conscious mind sleeps tropes the decentered conceptual structure of the whole sequence: variations and only variations, with no unifying theme in sight. Kreymborg reinforces this sense of pregnant absence by feinting at a theme in the two-line second unit, "Till you came—/ I was I." And yet this apparent stripping down to the relationship's most basic meaning is belied by the section's aggressively formalist title, "Variation," which insists that what follows has no special priority but is simply one more variation among many. Such a structure of variations refusing a theme (as opposed to a hidden or secret theme, like Edward Elgar's *Enigma Variations*) responds to the disjunctive textures of modernity by shedding nostalgic yearnings for origin and coherence in favor of a productive deconstruction of center and margin, figure and ground, beginning and end.

"Olives" and "Variations" are experiments in form without strong reference to the modern social world, but often in *Others* the variation-sequence principle would serve as a vehicle for social comment. Certainly this is true of the final work in the first issue, Kreymborg's "Overheard in an Asylum," which has no Roman numerals or offset titles but nonetheless employs a variation structure. The poem is framed by an official voice, a doctor or superintendent, addressing visitors:

> And here we have another case,
> quite different from the last,
> another case quite different—
> Listen.[30]

We then hear four italicized quatrains of a confined woman's wistful song to a lost or imaginary infant, urging him to "drink," "rest," "sleep," and "dream" in turn. Each verse juxtaposes these maternal murmurings with references to war and soldiering, creating a sequence of variations on the loss of husband, baby, and sanity to the war. The official voice then offers a final fragmentary gloss on her state of mind—"We gave her the doll"—before going on to announce briskly "another case, / quite different from—."

This framing structure exemplifies and theorizes the *vers-libre* variation sequence as a form expressive of the fragmented nature of modern experience. The tour of the asylum implies a procession of "cases," all "quite different" from one another yet linked through the common theme of lives and minds destroyed by the war. To the professionally detached guide, the woman's song is merely one of these many cases, and it is exactly because the woman's lament is treated so indifferently by authority that poetry must imbue it with the power to move the overhearing reader. Each of the woman's verses hopefully proposes that "the war is over" but also contains discordant notes signifying her awareness of her plight and the impossibility of this hope, such as the comparison of the baby's feeding to that of pigs ("*Baby, rest, / the war is over. / Only pigs / Slop over so*") and the arrival of "Daddy" with "a German coin" that tropes the metal object that we must assume has killed him. In the final verse, the tension between maternal and martial elements turns openly menacing:

Baby, dream.
The war is over.
You'll be a soldier
too.

The war will appear to end, and the baby will survive, at least in the woman's delusional imaginings; yet no other outcome for his existence is imaginable except to become a soldier in another war, where others will be forced to replicate the agonizing loss she feels.

In these lines, Kreymborg is in no sense seeking to liberate the sounds of his words from the "tyranny" of referential meaning. He is advancing a frankly dissident position toward the war and its presumptive successors as products of the callous and impersonal forms of modern life, exemplified by the asylum and its keepers. His use of *vers-libre* sequence form gives this critique a horizontal and vertical dimension. The horizontal-synchronic trajectory implies room after room of melancholy cases in the present-day asylum, the present war; the vertical-diachronic trajectory imagines generation after generation of future lives ruined by wars of other days. By combining the emotional immediacy of the former with the reflective capacity of the latter, Kreymborg seeks to build from the vivid but scattered figurations of modern social experience a ground for more systematic understanding.

In its first year alone, *Others* published more than a dozen *vers libre* sequences of juxtaposed miniatures, including John Rodker's "Dutch Dolls," Ferdinand Reyher's "Kaleidoscopics," Edward O'Brien's "Hellenica," Skipwith Cannell's "Ikons," Adelaide Crapsey's "Cinquains," Wallace Stevens's "Six Significant Landscapes," Carl Sandburg's "Louis Mayer's Ice Pictures," Davies's "Later Songs," Bodenheim's "Images of Emotions," Muna Lee's untitled sequence, Adolf Wolff's "Fireflies," and Horace Holley's "Divinations." Collectively they made an important contribution to the New Poetry's ability to address the experiential textures of twentieth-century modernity. They reveal American poets learning to balance the stripping away of decoration wrought by imagism against the continued desire to create larger structures. Sequence poems negotiate this challenge by being nonlinear yet integrated, every individual element discrete yet contributing to a whole greater than the sum of the parts. They acknowledge the fragmentary and disjunctive conditions of twentieth-century experience while still inviting active readers to discover unexpected affinities and relationships. Akin to cinematic montage and cubist collage in that their meaning inheres less in any one component than in the juxtapositions among the various components, these sequence poems can be seen as among the earliest steps toward the verbal collage forms from which many of the monumental works of later twentieth-century American verse were constructed.

The magazine's cultivation of this form culminated with the publication of a twentieth-century masterpiece by Wallace Stevens that first saw daylight alongside sequence poems by Baxter Alden, Mary Carolyn Davies, and David Rosenthal in the December 1917 issue. "Thirteen Ways of Looking at a Blackbird" is a magnificently Stevensian original, one of his most distinctive works. But it is also exemplary of the many *vers libre* variation sequences that *Others* published throughout its four years. The structural basis for "Thirteen Ways" came not only from Stevens's knowledge of the Armory show and Japanese printmaking, as is often asserted, but also from the mostly forgotten variation sequences of *Others,* of which he was a faithful reader and frequent contributor. Probably its most immediate poetic model is Kreymborg's "Variations" of July 1915, which uses titles rather than numerals but features similar imagery and almost the same distinctive voice, at once laconic and intense and whimsical:

> "Willows"
> The air is drenched with the sound of wind.
> I with the noise of you.[31]
>
> II
> I was of three minds,
> Like a tree
> In which there are three blackbirds.[32]

In demonstrating how much technical mastery and conceptual ambition could be contained within a rigorously miniaturist juxtapositional structure, "Thirteen Ways" provides a critical link between the embryonic experiments with poetic sequence found in *Others'* early issues and the great collage works of modern American poetry: *The Waste Land, The Cantos, Paterson, A, The Maximus Poems.* But—equally important—its strong resemblance to an earlier poem by a nearly forgotten figure reminds us that even the most individual and titanic creators did not carve their formal innovations out of nowhere. They drew inspiration and example from the richly experimental climate that surrounded them in *Others* and other venues of the New Poetry.

Otherness

The exhilarating climate of social engagement that shaped *The Masses* was hardly absent from *Others*—it simply took different forms and tonalities.

Cristanne Miller argues that, in stark contrast to the Eurocentric elitism and frequent anti-Semitism of the *Little Review*—often treated as the essence or totality of modernism—*Others* nurtured a climate of progressive cultural "pluralism" in which "the hybrid position of the immigrant and Jew [is] vitally associated with that of the new poet."[33] This sensitivity to social otherness is clearly evident from the first issue of July 1915, where the Davies and Loy sequences flouted patriarchal stereotypes and explored the independent female consciousness as poetic subject, while Kreymborg's "Overheard in an Asylum" critiqued the war's incomprehensible cruelty by linking it to the social construction of mental illness.

Over the next year, *Others* would explore the potential of the little-magazine format for expanding the range of modern poetic identities, publishing special issues around verse by outsider groups: the "Spanish-American Number" of August 1916 and the "Woman's Number" of September 1916. A "Negro Number" was advertised in the December 1917 issue but never materialized, probably because the magazine's funding collapsed again shortly thereafter, making possible only two issues during all of 1918. Churchill notes the lack of formally experimental verse by African Americans before 1920 as another reason for the failure of this initiative, although late in its life (between January and May 1919) *Others* did publish eight poems by the Chicagoan Fenton Johnson who, although only thirty, was in the last phase of his career as a publishing poet.[34] In his three previous volumes, published between 1913 and 1916, Johnson had worked in conventional lyric and dialect forms, but *Others* drew from him a new and experimental spirit. Perhaps the most powerful of all his poems is "Tired" (*Others,* January 1919), a bitter satire of "civilization" as defined by whites that confronts the reader with this Swiftian sentiment:

> Throw the children into the river. Civilization has given us too
>   many. It is better to die than it is to grow up and find out
>   that you are colored.[35]

Most of Johnson's *Others* poems, including "Aunt Jane Allen," "The Barber," "The Gambler," "The Drunkard," and "Aunt Hannah Jackson," depart from his previous practice by exploring modern urban scenes in long *vers libre* lines:

> Despite her sixty years Aunt Hannah Jackson rubs on other
>   people's clothes.
> Time has played havoc with her eyes and turned to gray her
>   parched hair.
> But her tongue is nimble as she talks to herself.

All day she talks to herself about her neighbors and her friends
    and the man she loved.
Yes, Aunt Hannah Jackson loved even as you and I and Wun
    Hop Sing.[36]

Though it portrays a life marked by racial oppression, "Aunt Hannah Jack-son" does not register as a poem of misery or self-pity, especially in the context of *Others*, whose affirmation of what Miller terms "linguistic and cultural mixing" is reflected in Johnson's open-hearted reference to a second denigrated racial other, a move that asserts the essential equality of all races and peoples.[37] His urban verses, which Lisa Woolley describes as combin-ing "near-despair with realism, humor, and a celebration of survival," owe something to the gritty social realism of Sandburg, while also anticipating in their tonal complexity the empathetic vernacular vignettes of African American city life that Langston Hughes would begin to publish in the 1920s.[38] Johnson receded from the scene of the New Poetry shortly after publishing these verses, but he would be evoked as a pioneer of socially engaged African American urban verse by Kreymborg in his 1929 survey of American poetry *Our Singing Strength* and by J. Saunders Redding in *To Make a Poet Black* (1939) as "the earliest recorder of the Negro in the city."[39]

Apart from the two special numbers of 1916, general issues of *Others* would feature a great many poems engaging with the material and social landscapes of the twentieth-century metropolis, most of them taking point-edly nonconformist positions. The magazine's temperamental iconoclasm toward orthodoxies meant that some of its verses—Johnson's "Tired," Jean Davis's "Our Camilla," Mary Aldis's "Beans," Arthur Davison Ficke's "The Dancer"—could just as easily have found a home in *The Masses*. Even the most canonical issue from a high-modernist perspective—the "Competi-tive Number" of July 1916, containing all those titanic figures mentioned above—exhibits a rich and varied engagement with urban modernity, featur-ing poems about a city pet shop (by Padraic Colum), industrial workhorses on their way to be destroyed (John Gould Fletcher), two urban laborers bent over needle and thread (Adolf Wolff), the ruminations of a "penniless rumsoak" roaming the skyscraper streets (William Carlos Williams), and the auctioning-off of Walt Whitman's Long Island homestead (Witter Bynner).

As *Others'* climate of experiment would inspire Fenton Johnson to his strongest moments as a poet of the twentieth-century city, so it invited some bourgeois white Americans, such as the Iowa-raised Harvard graduate and practicing attorney Arthur Ficke, to explore social otherness more vigor-ously than they were able to do in other contexts. Churchill and Miller have provided excellent accounts of the Spectra hoax perpetrated by Ficke, Witter

Bynner, and Marjorie Allen Seiffert between 1916 and 1918, in which the hospitality of *Others* to unknown writers and offbeat styles played a central role (Kreymborg, not in on the joke, gave over the entire January 1917 issue to "the Spectric school"). Both scholars find that although the Spectrist trio initially intended to satirize the poetic avant-garde, they discovered that "the taking on of fluid and foreign identities [freed] them to write a kind of poetry they would otherwise not have attempted."[40] Miller notes in particular that Ficke's Spectrist persona Anne Knish, obviously female, "explicitly cosmopolitan and implicitly Jewish," embodies a modern verse "born out of generative contact with difference": a premise I see as central to *Others* as a whole.[41]

Even before Spectra, however, Ficke in his own person had used the iconoclastic venue of *Others* to look critically at social distinctions and to identify himself with otherness. His poem "The Dancer" (March 1916), a portrait of a "little half-clothed painted cabaret performer," targets his own class, the "godly people" of the American haute bourgeoisie, "Substantial citizens / With their virtuous wives" who goad the speaker to dance with the cabaret artist after he expresses unguarded admiration of her performance.[42] When the speaker responds to their spite by remarking that "for a nickel I would" dance with her, one of the "respectable" women maliciously produces a coin, inspiring him to identify himself with the dancer's precarious social and economic circumstances. The poem thus approaches the potent insight that prostitution in all forms speaks not to personal immorality so much as to economic inequities and the callous distinctions of class. One wonders how this portrayal went over in the country clubs of Davenport, Iowa, but it corresponds precisely to typical treatments of prostitution in *The Masses* (by Max Eastman, John Reed, Emma Goldman, and others), which were undoubtedly romanticized yet still constituted one of the period's most significant critiques of the links between gender inequality and economic exploitation.[43] Ficke's insight is reinforced by the ambiguity of the dancer's situation: she is not literally a prostitute but is demonized into that role by the bourgeoisie who seek to demonstrate their own ostensible freedom from the economic forces that shape her life. The experience of dancing with this untouchable, "Before the gaping herd of my respectable fellow-townsmen," reveals to the speaker the inhibitions and hypocrisies of his own class, and as he escorts her back to her table, he flouts respectability yet again by turning and kissing her.[44] The woman in the poem remains a symbol of the male persona's release from stultifying social restriction and never gains a voice of her own. But even with this notable blind spot, such attempts to reimagine traditional relationships of gender and class contributed to the climate of change and possibility that rejuvenated American gender-reform movements after 1910.

As Ficke's experiments with alternative poetic personae suggest, the openness to heterogeneity that poets discovered in *Others* didn't result only in formal and prosodic experiments; they also generated bold ways of imagining the poet's role in the modern social world. In "Prison Weeds" (November 1915), the anarchist writer and sculptor Adolf Wolff pressed this expansion by positioning the modern poet as politically incarcerated subject.[45] Wolff's poem, a record of his thirty-day confinement in the Blackwell's Island workhouse in September 1914 for IWW associations and parole violations, vividly demonstrates the potential of the *vers libre* sequence form for advancing dissident social critique.[46] Written in twelve juxtaposed sections, the poem has a discernible beginning—an establishing image of a "chain" of "isles of evil odors" on the river—and a sense of an ending, as the speaker contemplates his impending release.[47] But the ten sections in between do not form a linear narrative and could be arranged in almost any order—an appropriate structure for an experience defined by repetitive and largely meaningless actions, from which only the beginning and end stand out as discrete events. The second section explores this theme by using the simplest verbal materials, two phrases repeated and extended through most of a page, representing in spatial terms the seemingly infinite repetition of numbing tasks that produce no alteration in the speaker's world:

> I break stones
> in the stone shed
> big ones
> into little ones
> big ones
> into little ones
> big ones
> into little ones
> big ones
> into little ones
> I break stones
> in the stone shed

This Sisyphean sense of purposeless repetition returns in other sections, sometimes describing monotonous physical actions ("they carry the buckets to the river / with heads bowed / with trembling hands / they carry the buckets to the river"), at other times functioning phatically to express the speaker's bewilderment at the world he finds himself in:

He never speaks
he never reads
he never laughs
always silent
always brooding
always sad
deep sunken eyes
black beard
noble brow
he resembles a German Christ
no one knows why "he's up"
no one knows when he came
no one knows when he'll go
they say
"nobody home"

This withdrawn figure, half-Christ, half-Bartleby, haunts the poem; the intractable mystery surrounding him emblematizes for Wolff the power of the capitalist legal system to erase people's social existence without meaning or memorial.

The early sections of "Prison Weeds" maintain a close focus on bodily experience. One of them ponders the irony of convicts "weeping" as they eat onions, their emotive response to their imprisonment simultaneously released and masked by the chemical effects of the onions. Another describes the indignity of having one's body stripped, scrutinized, and rendered criminally legible:

a row of naked men
standing against a wall
waiting
a desk
a scribe
a centurion,
they are recording
marks of identification.

In the section that follows, the pathos of the men's naked bodies is forcefully juxtaposed to the broken body parts of beasts—"Bones / a barrel of bones," discards from "last week's stew"—through which, the speaker realizes in horror, some creature is rooting ("No—/ it's not a dog / it's not a cat / it's a man / a man / made in the image of God").

The poem's second half shifts from immediate bodily experiences toward personal reflection and social critique. Representatives of officialdom, priest and warden, are portrayed not as evil so much as professionally callous, with a strong sense of their own performative function: "*investigators* / go away / with nothing / but the best / to say / they're satisfied / beyond expression / *the warden* / made such good impression." When a prisoner calls out to the unheeding priest, "Father! / the Christ is in the cooler," the specific reference is to the silent bearded "German Christ" of the earlier section, but the line also positions all the imprisoned as martyrs to an unjust social order, worthy of empathy and even capable of visionary spirituality through their suffering. In the poem's final unit, Wolff synthesizes these bodily and meditative dimensions, anticipating with "strange unease" the imminent "separation / from my cell" as resembling the separation of soul from body at the moment of achieving "eternal life." Understandably, the prospect of being released feels a lot like going to heaven, and yet Wolff may also suggest that the experience of being imprisoned—the loss of control over one's body and movements, the uncanny solidarity with others so situated—has revealed an intensely integrated level of experience not otherwise easily accessible in a social order that depends on segregating self from other, intellect from emotion, body from soul.

Poems about asylums, prostitutes, and prisoners are not linguistically nonreferential or politically inert. They remind us that perhaps the best way to understand the politics of *Others* is through its title and motto, which have usually been read in an aesthetic register but carry strong sociopolitical resonances if we listen for them. Kreymborg, the child of working-class Catholic immigrants, grew up on Manhattan's Lower East Side with minimal formal schooling. In the literary world he was very much a social other and acutely aware of the fact.[48] His poem "New York" (*Others*, December 1916), an ambiguous exploration of social difference, exemplifies his distinctively understated style of articulating this defining sense of otherness. The first of its three sections reads:

> There is a difference
> wider than a city block
> between the House of Moses
> on Second Avenue
> and the Chapel of the Immaculate Virgin
> on Third.[49]

After this initial assertion of difference, the second section appears to make the familiar universalizing turn of much lyric poetry:

They wait under the same sky,
on the same level,
through the same rain—
honest humans crawl to both—
but

The final word "but" hangs there unmoored and unpunctuated at the end of the paragraph, signaling a further turn to come. The last verse paragraph does indeed turn, but backward into a verbatim repetition of the first, as if to deny that the universalizing platitudes of the second have produced even the least effacement of difference. The poem's understated political complexity is enhanced by the pairing of two religious minorities, each possessing its own historical trajectory in the United States but both signifying social otherness, suspended between segregation and assimilation. Nowhere in the poem is there any hint of a normative social stratum of native-born WASP "Americanism"—all is difference and otherness. "New York" may lack the exuberant directness of the typical *Masses* verse about class, but it says no less about the complexity of social difference in the United States as a disorienting oscillation between seemingly intractable distinctions of ethnicity or religion and pressure toward an "American" sameness that is both ideological and attractive, illusory and inexorable.

This laconic ode to a hometown and an immigrant heritage tells us much about the socially engaged modernism advanced in *Others* by Kreymborg and his various associate editors William Carlos Williams, Lola Ridge, William Saphier, and Maxwell Bodenheim—all of them first- or second-generation immigrants, as Cristanne Miller notes.[50] In contrast to the persona of the proletarian modern artist as brawling roughneck (personified by Arturo Giovannitti, Michael Gold, and Bertolt Brecht, among others), Kreymborg, small of stature and at times delicate in health, had to find a different path to an artistic and social identity. His strategy from an early age was to associate himself with signifiers and practitioners of avant-garde high culture: opera, experimental poetry, esoteric small magazines, abstract painting, modern-primitive sculpture. But his affinity for the hypermasculinized intellectuality of competitive chess suggests steel underneath his mild-mannered appearance, since the meek and weak do not supplement their income in New York's chess clubs and parks, as he did for years.[51] All things considered, we can no longer take for granted that Kreymborg's unassuming but resolute commitment to avant-garde otherness could not generate a viable progressive modernism, nor should we underestimate that commitment as a shaping force upon *Others*. Loy's sexual outlaw, Ficke's dancer, Wolff's prisoners, the woman confined in the asylum, the chronically alienated cast of characters haunting Bodenheim's urban verses, Williams and his restive demand for a "tincture of disestablishment," Ridge and her fervent Christian Marxism: all these disparate figures and more, clustered around Kreymborg, othered by choice or circumstance, suggest that we've unduly dismissed a potent social dimension of his magazine.[52]

The verse in *Others* returns insistently to iconoclastic treatments of three socially resonant themes that were also central to *The Masses*: the material textures and social dynamics of the metropolitan cityscape; the character and meanings of machine-age labor; and the catastrophic fact of the Great War. The first of these categories includes, among others, Robert Swasey's "The City in Summer," Bodenheim's "East Side Children Playing," Douglas Goldring's "Maisonnettes," and William Carlos Williams's "The Young Housewife," all of which strive for imagist clarity of line and a photographic authenticity that carries an implicit social critique. Swasey's poem (January 1916) may initially seem one of atmosphere rather than social comment. But as it accumulates a series of closely observed details—a skulking cat, a "withered vine," a "newspaper / Shambling in the gutter," and finally a "ragged child" and "hungry dog" standing side by side, "[l]ooking in a dust can"—it comes to resemble strongly the contemporaneous urban photography of Lewis Hine, which, as Alan Trachtenberg and Miles Orvell have argued, generates powerful social commentary by eschewing the typological manipulation of Jacob Riis in favor of a modernist authenticity of unique moments that see and reproduce actual conditions so powerfully that they cannot be gainsaid.[53] Appearing in December 1917, Bodenheim's poem about East Side children is extraordinarily reminiscent in tone and imagery of Dorothy Day's "Mulberry Street," which had appeared in *The Masses* five months earlier. Bodenheim evokes social-realist photography by focusing on silent, ambiguous gestures of face and body: a "lame boy" who "stares at an orange on a push-cart," a shabby girl who "swings her candy stick," two boys who "calmly slap each other's cheeks," and a "twisted" old man who "[d]rags himself past" as the "children smile at him."[54] The meanings of these gestures, the children's smiles in particular, are as radically open, as unsusceptible to being circumscribed in words, as those in such Hine photos as "Newsboys: Midnight at the Brooklyn Bridge" (1912), which depicts a group of six youths composed from waist-length, capturing both their distinctive body language and the strikingly ambiguous expressions on their faces.

Examined alongside these poems in the context of *Others*, "The Young Housewife" (December 1916), Williams's well-known portrait of the yearn-

Lewis W. Hine, "Group of Newsboys on Frankfort Street near World Building" (ca. 1908). Courtesy of the Library of Congress.

ings of an emotionally inhibited middle class, also takes on a strongly photographic character from a series of silent, ambiguous bodily gestures, seen or imagined by a motorist-observer-poet who passes by repeatedly: a young woman "tucking in / stray ends of hair" as she speaks to delivery men or wandering about "in negligé behind / the wooden walls of her husband's house."[55] These gestures create a social subtext that speaks to repressed desires and repressive gender norms. The foregrounding of the housewife's poignant lack of emotional ownership of her own domicile and her attenuated role in the world, which seems to preclude crossing the boundary of the curb into public space, reveal an empathetic if conflicted identification across gender that Williams explored in several poems of this period, notably "To Elsie," "Portrait of a Woman in Bed," and "K. McB."[56] This empathy is complicated but ultimately affirmed by a final silent gesture, this one the speaker's, who bows and smiles as he passes once again. His courtliness maintains patriarchy's benevolent facade, as does his self-consciously poetic comparison of the wispy young woman to "a fallen leaf." But the final sentence combines these seemingly innocuous elements into a moment of self-examination that contains a potent critique of patriarchy:

The noiseless wheels of my car
rush with a crackling sound over
dried leaves as I bow and pass smiling.

These last lines mark the speaker as a figure of no special insight or empathy, merely one more in a series of departing men who strand the young
housewife behind barriers of curb or walls, heedlessly assuming her content-
ment (her husband) or maintaining a decorous distance (the delivery men).
Through the persona of the speaker-motorist-doctor, Williams also turns his
critique toward poetry as a cultural discourse. The metaphor of the fallen
leaf, which becomes the symbolic means of crushing her, reminds us that the
speaker's gentility is complicit with his ability to leave her there while he
moves freely about the city—as is the poet's nearly surgical ability to probe
and excise moments from her life, actions undertaken more for his benefit
than for hers.

Another group of city poems in *Others,* influenced less by social-realist
photography than by the extreme rhetorical strategies of futurism, portrays
the capitalist metropolis as a landscape of hallucinatory violence. Max
Endicoff's sequence "New York Etchings" (January 1916) juxtaposes four
disparate metropolitan environments: subway tunnel, harbor, public library,
and railway terminal. Futurist violence prevails throughout, as "[y]ellow-
blotched things of steel" dart through the dark tube "[w]ith a crunching,
grinding cry," a "leviathan" ocean liner "spits from a thousand mouths"
its contempt for the toiling tugboats that surround it, and "ghouls" prowl
furtively about in the library, "Peering into the barren homes of the dead."[57]
Endicoff's imagery of expulsion and putrefaction (the ship's bilge as sputum,
the library as "mausoleum," books as "coffins") culminates in the outra-
geous metaphors of "The Terminal," portrayed as a "[r]avenous stomach
of stone and steel / Gulping in / Sizzling, steaming morsels." These morsels
may have begun as discrete organic beings and mechanical objects, but in
railway modernity, where an arriving train becomes "a string of wooden
sausages / Hurl[ing] itself / Into the deep, cavernous maw," everything
terminates as undifferentiated muck to be consumed and expelled: "And
a moment later / A hissing, stenchful mass / Is vomited forth." Comparing
dispersing passengers to particles of projectile vomit is so far over the top
that we may well wonder whether to take the poem straight or as self-
parody. Either way, the verse of *Others* can hardly be portrayed as ignoring
the material—social and bodily—realities of modern life for some realm of
decathected nonreferential soundplay.[58]

Though labor verse is associated more closely with the noncanonical ghetto of "political magazines" like *The Masses,* the poets publishing in *Others* also lived through the exhilarating, often heartrending activism of the early 1910s, observing and often participating. A substantial number of the magazine's poems deal with environments of modern machinery and with the bodily experience of industrial labor, again suggesting that Kreymborg never sought to repudiate "ulterior" social engagement in verse but to nurture new modes for writing it. Two of these poems, Lelia Miller Pearce's "Machine Made" (March 1916) and Adolf Wolff's "Mending" (July 1916), portraying women at toil over loom and needle, respond intensely to the issues raised by perhaps the seminal radical labor verse of the decade, Rose Pastor Stokes's "Paterson," published in *The Masses* in 1913. Wolff's "Mending" is a well-mounted imagist vignette of two women doing nocturnal needlework:

Night
a shop window
two women
mending
doing invisible mending
the light
close to their eyes
their eyes
close to their work
wearing out their eyes
mending
wearing out their life
mending
doing invisible mending[9]

Where Stokes had used an intricate oscillating pattern of lineation and rhyme to evoke work at an industrial loom, Wolff threads repeated words and phrases—"mending," "close to," "their eyes," "wearing out"—into lines of varying lengths and rhythms that evoke the repetitive but always slightly varying movements involved in hand stitching. The tension in these lines between continual reconfiguration and endless repetition intensifies the political irony of the scenario, in which the women's own bodies and lives are worn out through the ceaseless work of restoring damaged objects—but always objects belonging to others. This irony is further enhanced by the repetition of the poem's lone characterizing adjective, "invisible," which carries three interlocking meanings: the mending will become increasingly invisible to them as their eyes wear out; it will remain invisible in the sense of never having any transformative impact upon their lives; and most broadly, their labor will remain anonymous and unremembered by the vast enterprise of capitalist industry that relegates their bodies to invisibility in out-of-the-way storefronts and sweatshops. Meanwhile, the way the women are framed and lit positions the observer (speaker, poet, reader) as a passerby glimpsing the scene from outside, someone far enough removed spatially and socially that the women's work is not fully visible—yet not so distant as to preclude an empathetic response.

Pearce's five-stanza poem in *vers libre,* "Machine Made," takes a different approach to the iconic figure of the sewing woman, beginning with an unpromising oracular gesture ("I am the woman at the loom—") but soon becoming more immediate by emphasizing the bodily consequences of repetitive labor.[60] The immersion of the laboring body within industrialized space is so complete that the woman who makes things with machines feels herself "Machine Made," "fathered" and "moulded" by the huge mechanisms, her body rendered "[g]aunt and unwomanly," her future seeming "a vista with no end, / Grey and unlovely," sloping forever downward. The final stanza, set at dusk, "frees the woman from the loom," stilling the machines and allowing her a taste of a different, "[w]heel-weaned" life. But even this interval of release cruelly contributes to her life's unending drudgery, as she spends her nights "dread[ing] the Dawn's / Call." The poem's most intriguing structural element is its shifting narrative perspective: the first two stanzas speak in first-person singular as one woman, "I," caught in the midst of the "great wheels." The next two shift to first-person plural as the speaker gives voice to "we," a class of "dull, wan humanity, / Soul-starved." The final stanza shifts yet again, now to an indirect third-person narrator who describes "the woman" as a "loom-daughter." This narrational instability suffuses a poem deeply grounded in social-realist premises with the juxtaposed but disjunct multiple perspectives exhibited in so many *Others* sequence poems, suggesting how modernist forms such as "cubist" polyphony contributed to the magazine's poetics of socially engaged experimentalism.

In "Machine Shop Notes" (June 1917), William Saphier places the magazine's signature sequence form in a setting of industrial labor, creating a gallery of modern craftsmen that complicates conventional assumptions of the deadening monotony of machine-age work, not unlike William Carlos Williams's much later poem "Fine Work with Pitch and Copper" (1936).[61] Saphier emphasizes machine-shop work as a struggle between men and machines, but it seems a mostly fair fight in which individuals retain substantial agency, signified by active verbs and powerful, iconic bodily gestures. In "At the Anvil," Dan, a silent man with eyes like "blooming, black roses" and arms "like oak trees in winter,"

> shapes a woman's dream
> with a sledge
> out of a bar of red-hot steel
> on his anvil.[62]

Likewise, in "A Dream," a man at a tempering furnace has the power of God over life and death as he precisely manipulates chunks of cyanide. In "At the Lathe," this motif of individual agency in the industrial environment culminates in a lathe operator, "boulder-shouldered," who "twirls a steel shaft / that will roll out gold," "shoves the tiny hard tool deeper / into the heart of the steel / and smiles at the moaning shaft." The sexualized imagery of his worklife reflects this man's pride in his familial potency as he thinks of the "new baby in his home." Only in the final section, "At the Vice," does a note of more grinding servitude creep in, as the operator "is swayed" and "held tight" by the vice, "his days" cut by a sawtoothed "bastard file." Unlike the others, this man has "long ago passed the scratch / that means stop / and he moves on as if blind," no longer in control of his body's action on the machines or their action on it.

Despite the dark turn at the end of "Machine Shop Notes," Saphier's individuation of the men's faces, gestures, and skills remains at heart a celebration of creative labor, foreshadowing the series of iconic photographs of master machinists and other industrial workers done by Lewis Hine beginning in the early 1920s.[63] Saphier's idealization of hypermasculine machine-age labor obviously has its naive aspects, but we would be mistaken to assume that his poem constitutes an apology for hierarchical capitalism rather than exemplifying a key visual topos of the period that signified across the ideological spectrum. The dominant futurist-industrial aesthetic of the Soviet avant-garde through the 1920s, for example, reveals that such iconography often functioned to support radical collectivist positions, as this comment from Hine's preface to *Men at Work* also suggests: "Cities do not build themselves, machines cannot make themselves, unless back of them all are the brains and toil of men."[64] Juxtaposing Saphier's poem and Hine's photos with *Others* verses portraying women working with textiles reminds us, however, of the unevenly gendered standards of much machine-age labor. These male workers, skilled craftsmen whose precision and attention to detail means the difference between a project's success and failure, enjoy much greater imaginative scope and freedom of movement than the female loom operators and piecework menders of Pearce and Wolff's poems—which makes the gynocentric emphasis of the latter two all the more valuable.

Perhaps the most ambitious of all the labor verse in *Others* is Daphne Carr's "Steel Town" (April/May 1919), which steps back from the close focus used by Saphier, Wolff, and Pearce to portray an industrial environment on a larger canvas reminiscent of an Ashcan cityscape. The poem is divided into two alternating styles of *vers libre* that convey the tension between life and work in an industrial town. The first of these styles creates a strongly vertical texture with short indented lines occupying the middle of the page:

> Gray
> as with time
> and austere
> as the colonnades of a ruined temple
> stand the steel-mill chimneys
> at sundown.
> Curved
> knotted
> stems of fleur de lys
> rise the gray smoke columns
> to blossom in blackening mist.[65]

The second structuring element counters this verticality with unindented longer lines of more uniform length:

> While the trams course along the dull streets
> Flashing at intervals with bill-boards,
> While sooty Jews sell second-hand furniture
> And ladies go on buying laces,
> Till the little shop-girls flitter home
> Shivering under their cat-furs.

The contrast between these two graphic structures on the page corresponds to other differences. The vertical sections focus on the steel mill and its furnaces but also evoke a consciously poetic realm of metaphor and mythic allusion—the chimneys seen as a "ruined temple," the rising columns of smoke as decorative arabesques on some classical artifact. The horizontal sections eschew metaphor for sheer description as they portray the life of the townspeople away from the mill, particularly the cheerfully scruffy material culture that occupies their leisure hours—billboards, five-and-dimes, dance halls, "cinema screens," newsies and milkmen doing their early morning work. The stylistic contrasts between the alternating sections imply a radical disjuncture between work and life, despite the spatial proximity of mill and town. These people, unlike the "woman of the loom" in Pearce's poem, are at least somewhat able to detach themselves from work while not working, and they seem not wholly dominated by dread of the morning. Even so, the two horizontal "town" sections are structurally enclosed by the three vertical "mill" sections, and the last of these is an almost verbatim repetition of the first section, which begins, "Gray / as with time," suggesting the deeply redundant character of industrial workdays.

The most challenging element of "Steel Town" is the association of metaphor and myth with the poisonous effluvium of the mill, which is the source not only of omnipresent soot and "unchanging" labor but also of poetry. If nothing in the work directly indicts poetry as complicit in the exploitative environment of capitalism, nothing links it to any enriching element of the town's life either. Poetry, at least in its traditional guise, remains entirely disconnected from the daily life of ordinary people, as austere and uninviting as the stark beauty of the chimneyscape whose "blossoms" generate nothing but clouds of besmirching soot. Much as *The Masses* was enlivened by its cultivation of self-contradiction in defiance of dogmatism, *Others* poems such as "Steel Town," like Williams's "The Young Housewife" and Kreymborg's "New York," become more compelling as they scrutinize the generic ground of their own existence—without ceding their claims to iconoclastic social engagement.

Along with these potent responses to the urban landscape and the dynamics of machine-age labor, *Others* built its poetics of social engagement by responding to the Great War, beginning in the first issue with Kreymborg's "Overheard in an Asylum." Five months later, the first of Marianne Moore's eight poems in *Others*, "To Statecraft Embalmed" (December 1915), critiqued what Sandra Gilbert calls the "masculinist swagger" behind the war by combining the ibis, representative in Egyptian mythography of Thoth the scribe, with the imagery of heraldry, a potent symbolic expression of patriarchally structured societies, as Bonnie Costello notes.[66] Moore's analysis of the disastrous recent failure of European statecraft, in which kindred nations suddenly turned on one another as mortal enemies, culminates in the devastating closing images of the enfeebled ibis-scribe

> Staggering toward itself and with its bill,
>   Attack[ing] its own identity, until
>   Foe seems friend and friend seems
>   Foe.

As its bill metamorphoses from inscribing pen into penetrating weapon, its visionary wisdom curdles into "the wrenched distortion of suicidal dreams."[67]

If in late 1915 Moore is still grappling with the outbreak of war and the incomprehensible self-immolating conduct of all the nations involved, by late 1917 we find Maxwell Bodenheim addressing the menacing domestic implications of American belligerency in "Parade of Conscripted Soldiers." The theme and imagery of this poem link it closely to several antiwar poems in *The Masses*—Louis Untermeyer's "To a War Poet," Clement Wood's "A Breath of Life," Arturo Giovannitti's "The Day of War"—all of which use military parades to trope the war's danger not only to individuals but to the whole fabric of American democracy. Like Bodenheim's "East Side Children Playing," with which it is paired on the page, "Parade of Conscripted Soldiers" is highly photographic, glimpsing a series of individual faces as a mass of men march by:

> One soldier's face is flat stone
> With bitter hieroglyphics of silence
> Cut deeply into it.
> Another soldier's face is a twitching white bird
> Suddenly clawed by a long-taloned question.[68]

Scarcely resembling the stalwart recruits featured in propaganda materials, these conscripted men yearn to lash out at those who have commandeered their lives for this dubious nationalist imperative, but personal decorum and military discipline prevent this, instead driving their anguish inward to play poignantly upon their faces and bodies. No less than in the *Masses* poems, the parade is here exposed as a spectacle of imperial capitalism with one purpose: to sell the war. Such spectacles require buyers, to whom the poet turns in the final lines:

> O silent stiff-fingered people on the curbstone,
> You do not see this, but you feel
> Unspoken words from the marching conscripts
> Striking your faces like weakened fists.

The elusive sensation of being beaten by feeble fists offers a final trope for the "unspoken" protest signified by the soldiers' facial gestures, which silently indict a misguided national policy and an acquiescent populace.

Carl Sandburg, who had produced a compelling series of poems analyzing the war's ideological conduct in *The Masses* during 1915, found *Others* an equally congenial venue for his antiwar verse. In "Statistics" (March 1916), Sandburg returned to the themes of "Buttons" (*The Masses*, February 1915) by confronting the ghost of Napoleon, the greatest warmonger of an earlier era, with a modern war of

> "Twenty-one million men,
> Soldiers, armies, guns,
> Twenty-one million
> Afoot, horseback,
> In the air,
> Under the sea."[69]

Numbed by this recital of enormous yet abstract statistics, the emperor fails to see any connection between modern war and "'[t]he world I marched in'" and returns to his silent sleep "[i]n the old sarcophagus," while

> The aeroplanes
> droned their motors
> Between Napoleon's mausoleum
> And the cool night stars.

Napoleon may let himself off too easily by denying his role in the European territorial history that produced the Great War, but Sandburg's more urgent goal is to emphasize not its continuity with earlier wars so much as its apocalyptic break from them. However brutal previous conflicts may have been, they remained within certain limitations of space and scope. Such limits mean nothing in the domain of modern warfare in which men, machines, and noise threaten to fill every available physical and psychic space, from beneath the earth's surface right up to the night stars.

Though Sandburg reluctantly supported American entry into the war after April 1917, he continued to write against its premises and effects. In the brilliantly ominous "Long Guns" (April/May 1919), he further pursued this bitter insight that modern technologies have overcome previous barriers of space and time only to generate wars of unlimited reach. Like Untermeyer's frightening vision of searchlights and aerial bombardment in "To a War Poet" in *The Masses,* "Long Guns" portrays advancing technology as the symptom and the engine of modern catastrophe. Sandburg's focus is on the making of "twenty-mile guns, sixty-mile guns":

> Then came, Oscar, the time of the guns.
> And there was no land for a man, no land for a country,
>> Unless guns sprang up
>>> And spoke their language.
> The how of running the world was all in guns.[70]

These lines evoke the concept of *lebensraum* (living space), coined by the German geographer Friedrich Ratzel in 1901 and popularized by the military theorist Friedrich von Bernhardi in the 1912 book *Germany and the Next War,* which would provide a key ideological rationalization for German policy throughout the Great War and its successor. But the poet doesn't limit the mania for gun-based nationalist expansionism to Germany, proposing it as the grim governing principle of twentieth-century geopolitics. In such a world, all previous terrestrial, human, and cosmic laws ("The law of a God keeping sea and land apart, / The law of a child sucking milk, / The law of stars held together") are vacated by the imperatives of the long guns, which take on a self-perpetuating force beyond any instrumental or local goal.[71]

The poem's final section turns toward the effect of a world of guns on future generations, imagining the rise of a vengeful boy with a Hitlerlike hunger for destruction:

> There was a child wanted the moon shot off the sky,
>> asking a long gun to get the moon,
>> to conquer the insults of the moon,
>> to conquer something, anything,
>> to put it over and run up the flag,
> To show them the running of the world was all in guns.[72]

Curiously, through all these unnerving turns, the poem's narrative structure remains one of reminiscence, in which the speaker addresses "Oscar," presumably a young boy being told about past events. Yet Sandburg offers no way out of the "time of guns," and the poem ends with the chilling implication that even human interiority, the space of dreams, has been colonized by machines of destruction: "They dreamed . . . in the time of the guns . . . of guns." Though "Long Guns" obviously condemns the vast waste of the Great War, its publication in *Others* in the violent postwar moment of early 1919 also makes it into a prescient comment on the grim progress of twentieth-century geopolitics.

Sifting

In lieu of prose manifestoes, the many verses in *Others* about the modern city, machine-age labor, and the war comprised its poetics of social engagement. This poetics was theorized most explicitly by a group of metapoetic verses that assert the obsolescence of the genre's traditional function as a source of uplift or consolation and propose the modern poem instead as a useful object, speaking sometimes uncomfortable but necessary truths and bringing illumination from unlikely places. Perhaps the most trenchant attempt in *Others* to reconceptualize the elemental matter of poetry is William Carlos Williams's "Epigramme" (February 1916), which begins by asking its implied reader, "Hast ever seen man / Dig gold in a manure heap?"[73] This provocative image is an early instance of Williams's fascination with othered spaces—the backwaters and dumping grounds of the industrialized American landscape—as sources of poetic material, which he would pursue over decades in key poems including "Between Walls," "[by the Road to the Contagious Hospital]," "To Elsie," and of course *Paterson*.[74] The first line announces that the activity of "seeing" is the point of his urging to the reader: if one is willing to "open two eyes," as the poet has tried to do, one may "turn up this nugget" from the most marginal and unexpected sources.

Along similar lines, "The Microscope" by Jeanne D'Orge (May/June 1916) figures the elemental matter of modern poetry as a collection of microscopic "slides," visual fragments arranged in no preordained order, a metaphor that tropes the juxtapositional sequence form employed by so many *Others* poems:

> Only to look—
> To take at random slide after slide of life,
> Put it under the lens,
> Observe the blood of nation's heart [*sic*].[75]

The modern artist must be like the scientist in his or her dispassionate willingness to observe everything without flinching, from "[t]he bloom on the wings of emotion" to "[t]he clear still wriggling of obscenity." Only from such incisive, inclusive, unprejudiced attention to the external world will come self-knowledge, which D'Orge conceives in the most materialist sense as the Whitmanesque ability to perceive "section by section, the changing cells / Of one's own soul."

Other metapoetic verses in the pages of *Others* seek to reconceive poetry for the twentieth century by revisiting the anxieties that grip American poems written between 1890 and 1910, but they depart from those incurably self-alienated utterances by ebulliently embracing modernity, alienation and all. "Nostalgia" (January 1916) by Joseph Warren Beach enacts this process with particular intensity, beginning in anxious reverie over the loss of past verities and ending in meditative equanimity with a modern condition of irreversible change. In the first part, the speaker describes a dream in which "my father sent me into his garden / To gather an armful of flowers."[76] But this child of modernity finds "no flowers at all / nor any garden" and returns in infantile supplication "with empty hands outspread." The father then takes him in hand through a threatening landscape populated by creatures who jostle and scurry "[l]ike maggots deep in the cracks of a mouldy cheese." In the father's benevolent presence, however, each one "raise[s] an eager and lustrous face," and he gathers them all into his arms, speaking "the name of each with lingering relish—/ The names were courage, love, endurance, faith—." This perfect Victorian patriarch, radiating absolute conviction in his values, assuages the "struggle and pain" of all he meets, including his son, and the dream ends in almost narcotic tranquillity, the father smiling exactly "as mother used in her summer garden / To speak of jonquils or of marigolds."

To this point, one might call the poem a *Snow-Bound* for the Freudian era, wistfully remembering a lost patriarchal order of coherence and homogeneity. But ultimately the contrasts outweigh the resemblances. For Whittier in *Snow-Bound*, the bittersweet nostalgia of childhood memories is an unambiguously real and beneficial element of his emotional life, which he invites his adult readers to embrace as their own. Although Beach experiences the attractions of nostalgia intensely, he distrusts them even more fiercely. He contains nostalgia's siren song by specifying these memories as dreams signifying the infantile urge to return to the protection of all-powerful parents, while his use of "Nostalgia" as the title adds an analytical dimension to the dream experience, as if diagnosing some clinical condition.

The poem's second part, only six lines, elaborates this skepticism toward nostalgia in vividly imagistic fashion:

> II.
>
> A thousand fountains in a thousand valleys
> Bubble and leap and run from the fountain-head,
> And never a one turns back to its cradled spring.
>
> The shining and circling planets
> Never unravel the magical web they have woven,
> Fixed to the irreversible shuttles of fate.

Beach has moved far from the jagged emotions and surreal transformations of dream psychology to two elegantly composed images of a cosmic coherence that paradoxically comes only through acceptance of limitation and dispersion. The first image proposes that while we may imagine a single source of all life—father, God, fountainhead, cradle—all that finally matters is the inexorability of the dispersive flow away from origins toward myriad possible destinations. Likewise, the planets move in fixed patterns of interdependence, achieving a magical equilibrium that is as reliable, as absolute, as anything we can hope to experience and upon which our existences depend. Yet the only principle that fixes them is fate, irreversible but not preordained, no less real for being random. Through these images Beach finds a liberating equanimity toward cosmic indifference, the same serene agnosticism that Stevens's "Sunday Morning" had articulated on a grand scale in *Poetry* in 1914 and that Williams would call "a strange courage" in *Others* for December 1916:

> It's a strange courage
> you give me, ancient star—
> shining alone in the sunrise
> toward which you lend
> no part.[77]

Beach's poem asserts a metapoetic premise that motivates several key *Others* verses: the fact of modern dispossession from all sources of permanence, which requires and enables new functions for poetry. "The Peddler" (June 1917) by Marjorie Allen Seiffert elaborates this premise by exploring the artist's alienated place in a commercialized culture of modernity. Seiffert figures the modern poet as an itinerant vendor of goods, a "curious young magician-peddler" who "wanders through the city" swapping

> useful tin-ware
> For all the ancient metal
> You have left to rust
> In the dim, dusty attic
> Or mouldy cellar
> Of your soul.[78]

This metal detritus evokes symbols of genteel cultural value that were once crucial but are now obsolete: "Rusty nails, / Which may have played their part / In a crucifixion" and "andirons / Once guarding hearth-fires of content, / Now dusty and forgotten." In facilitating the exchange of these grand but superannuated symbols for commonplace objects of use—spoons and teakettles—Seiffert's peddler anticipates Williams's red wheelbarrow as an emblem for a functionalist aesthetics of twentieth-century poetry.

Still, when offered an "antique bowl / Fashioned to hold / Wine or roses," the peddler-poet's eyes glisten with hope and excitement. Like Pound exploring obscure corners of literary history, or Van Wyck Brooks aspiring to reconstruct a usable American past, he does not blindly repudiate tradition but searches through its detritus for something still valuable. Seiffert proposes wittily that to uncover such treasures requires the use of "acid" to "reveal" what lies hidden beneath deceptive or decorative surfaces—the same analytical imperative evoked by D'Orge's microscope. For such a "golden bowl," the modern poet will gladly "give" away all the instruments of his creative being: hands, eyes, soul, even "[h]is young, white body." If, more likely, he doesn't find it, then he will offer something more whimsical that the reader of *Others* should recognize:

> A mocking laugh
> And a bright tin sieve
> To hold your wine
> And roses.

The sieve is a comical but serious emblem of the avant-garde poem, genially inviting the readers of *Others* to join the poet's quest to sift and reclaim unfamiliar materials that might speak to the distinctive needs of modernity. *Others* thus offers its readers poems as useful objects but does not pretend to promise that they will function exactly as expected or hoped (the sieve may hold the roses but never the wine).

Seiffert's use of ordinary material objects to reorient poetry from decoration toward function may remind us of a key theoretical statement of American modernism, William Carlos Williams's assertion in *The Wedge* (1944) that "a poem is a small (or large) machine made of words."[79] In this formulation, as in much of his mature work, Williams suggests how the modernist revision of words as objects meaningful in their own materiality might lead not to Brownell's aestheticist poetics of nonreferential verbal play segregated from "ulterior social result" but toward a productive synthesis of formal experiment and social engagement. For Williams, the poem is not *like* a machine, in the sense that the verbal constructions of Apollinaire or the Dadaist structures of Picabia might approximate the appearance or motion of a machine. Instead the poem *is* a machine, what Cecilia Tichi calls a "system of component parts" that is constructed to address some purpose in the world.[80]

Williams's "To a Solitary Disciple" (February 1916) theorizes that account of the modern poem with elegant reference to the visual arts. Constructed from short lines that create a forcefully vertical shape on the page—appropriate for the soaring steeple that will be its main visual image—"To a Solitary Disciple," like "Epigramme" and "The Microscope," emphasizes differing ways of observing the material environment (its verbs, in order, are "notice," "observe," "grasp," "perceive," "see" twice, and "observe" three more times). The first half reorients the observing imagination toward an aesthetic of modernity by rejecting such ornamental strategies as alluring colors and gratuitously beautiful similes. The speaker urges the disciple to apprehend abstract visual relationships much as a modern painter might—

> Rather notice, mon cher,
> that the moon is
> tilted above
> the point of the steeple,
> than that its color
> is shell-pink

—and to note simple facts without adornment ("Rather observe / that it is early morning").[81]

Once this elemental level of perception is established, the observer's images become more architectonic and dynamic:

> Rather grasp
> how the dark
> converging lines
> of the steeple
> meet at the pinnacle

Exploiting the running pun on "lines" as the common medium of painter and poet, Williams offers a soaring modernist design of form, line, and movement in place of an obsolete aesthetics of ornament, playfully evoked by his reference to a "little ornament" on the steeple that "tries to stop" the lines from meeting but fails:

> See how it fails!
> See how the converging lines
> of the hexagonal spire
> escape upward
> receding, dividing!

So far, Williams has theorized modern poetry as a medium that, like painting, can reveal the governing structural principles underlying the densely sensory textures of perception. But at this moment of greatest abstraction, the act of metaphor reemerges in startling fashion as he describes the converging, ascending lines of the steeple as "sepals / that guard and contain / the flower!" The metaphor is risky in readmitting the self-consciously beautiful flower into his crisp architectonic arrangement. But Williams is unwilling to give up metaphor altogether, as few poets are. His goal now is to reorient the metaphoric imagination, as the first part of the poem had reoriented the observing eye. If the steeple's lines are like sepals (a sepal is a steeple without the †), the flower they contain becomes "the eaten moon" framed "motionless" "in the protecting lines." Despite the flower, the metaphor is still primarily structural rather than decorative in emphasizing the visual relationship between moon and lines, an emphasis reinforced by the notably unbeautiful figure of the "eaten moon." The sepal's biological function is to shield the flower from being eaten, but the "protecting lines" have "failed" at this. Thus the decorative and sentimental associations of the metaphor of sepal-line and flower-moon dissolve, leaving the architectonic correspondence of a central mass partially enclosed by ascending, converging verticals.

If this stage of the poem recuperates metaphor for use in a modernist aesthetics of underlying structure, the final lines do the same for the coloristic aesthetic that had been rejected earlier:

> It is true:
> in the light colors
> of the morning
> brown-stone and slate
> shine orange and dark blue
> but observe
> the oppressive weight
> of the squat edifice!
> observe
> the jasmine lightness
> of the moon!

The poet concedes that colors are legitimate elements of observation if they emerge from the full environmental context of light and shadow, rather than seeming painted on, as the "shell-pink" moon had. Even so, following the early cubist preference for muted palettes that would not distract the eye from structural relationships, he turns away from color yet again toward contrasting forms, masses, and shapes: the "squat edifice" of the church and the jasmine-light moon. Yet as he ends by again reinvoking the metaphor of moon and flower that he has just problematized, Williams cheerfully affirms that giving up ornament does not mean that poems must lack metaphors or even flowers. Nor does becoming aware of the powerful materiality of words and verbal forms mean that the words no longer carry equally powerful referential meanings. What these changes do mean for Williams is a poetics of modernity enduring in its materiality, beautiful in its lack of redundancy, capable of comparing a poem to both flower and machine—a poetics that generated the greatest individual verse *oeuvre* of the American machine age.

By tracing overlapping affinities and goals between *The Masses* and *Others,* I have not meant to imply that their poetics or politics were identical: their differences are as important to the New Poetry of the 1910s as their similarities. But neither are the links between them arbitrary or casual. Both publications featured a poetry responding to the twentieth-century cityscape, to machine-age labor, to the physical and psychological brutality of global warfare. Both nurtured a climate balancing social engagement and formal experiment. Among poets, they shared at least twenty contributors, including William Carlos Williams, Amy Lowell, Mary Carolyn Davies, Helen Hoyt, Marjorie Allen Seiffert, Arthur Davison Ficke, Max Endicoff, Joseph Warren Beach, Laura Benét, Witter Bynner, Florence Kiper Frank, Haniel Long, Horace Holley, Mary Aldis, Eunice Tietjens, Robert Carlton Brown, Marguerite Wilkinson, and perhaps most importantly, Carl Sandburg.

The simultaneous importance of Sandburg to *The Masses* and *Others* demonstrates that a poet could be political enough for the first and avant-garde enough for the second, without compromising his distinctive style. More broadly, I find it nearly impossible to overstate, and perhaps equally impossible to convince people today, how deeply Sandburg's poetry was respected as artistry by almost everyone involved with the New Poetry during the 1910s.[82] By the end of the 1910s he had gathered a remarkably diverse readership, ranging from fellow avant-garde poets to key impresarios of the New Poetry such as Monroe, Untermeyer, and Lowell, to pioneering academic scholars of American literature such as Duke's Jay B. Hubbell, to American Federation of Labor organizers who read his works at their meetings.[83] He had also begun to garner laurels from institutions of established culture, sharing the first and third Poetry Society of America Prizes (the forerunner of the Pulitzer) in 1919 and 1921.[84]

Sandburg's reputation suffered perhaps more than any other American poet's during the Eliot-Pound era, whose historians wrote him out of the main line of modern poetry. Still treated as a key figure through Horace Gregory and Marya Zaturenska's 1946 *History of American Poetry,* he barely appears in most academic discussions of modern poetry after that date, and is seldom taken seriously when he does.[85] The campaign to reduce Sandburg to an avuncular purveyor of folk songs and populist platitudes was so successful that, although most literate Americans will still recognize his name in 2012, to many literary academics one must insist quite vigorously upon his claim to be a serious artist at all, let alone one of the most important poets of his era.[86] Sandburg's decanonization deprived modern American verse of one of its most socially responsive figures, but this loss may not be irreversible. I will return to individual Sandburg poems often in part 2, but I will close the discussion here by proposing that in the American New Poetry of the 1910s, Sandburg, not Pound, is the central figure: most threatening to the genteel establishment, broadest in his appeal to various popular and avant-garde constituencies, and most representative of the fears and hopes that defined those times. His simultaneous importance in so many disparate avant-garde venues and his great popularity among nonspecialist readers evoke an exhilarating moment of American avant-garde culture before high modernism's aesthetic and ideological pigeonholes, when any alliance still seemed viable, any goal possible.

CHAPTER 5

Volunteers of America, 1917

The Seven Arts *and the Great War*

In contrast to *Poetry,* celebrating its centennial in 2012, the *Seven Arts* lasted only twelve tumultuous issues between November 1916 and October 1917. Yet perhaps even more than *Poetry* and *The Masses,* the *Seven Arts* challenges conventional views of the modernist little magazine as a fugitive publication whose amateur status redeems it from the capitalist marketplace, making it a haven for formally experimental work. Based in Manhattan, the *Seven Arts* enjoyed substantial financial backing, found a broad audience, proposed an ambitious synthesis of genres into an integrated national culture, and sought to impact American politics at the highest level. Yet these "mainstream" attributes did not keep it from exploring avant-garde, even radical positions. Like the three magazines discussed in previous chapters, the *Seven Arts* was inspired by an idealistic conviction in the promise of twentieth-century modernity, but even more than the others, its existence was deeply shadowed by the Great War, and its end resulted directly from its principled stand against governmental policy after the declaration of war in April 1917. The magazine's life divides rather neatly into two halves, an initial phase of utopian cultural nationalism between November 1916 and March 1917, followed by a steadily intensifying oppositional phase between April and October. Its demise provides disturbing evidence of the limits and weaknesses of American free-speech traditions and marks the end of the utopian moment of early American modernism. But its odyssey from cheerleading nationalism to radical dissent also demonstrates the possibility of a modernism passionately engaged with a politicized public sphere. The central role played in this project by verse texts and by "poetry" as a metaphor for national identity reveals the cultural impact of the New Verse movement in a particularly striking way.

In its initial phase, the *Seven Arts* combined the Progressive-era cultural nationalism catalyzed by Herbert Croly's 1911 book *The Promise of American Life* with the emerging generational consciousness articulated in such works of "Young America" as Randolph Bourne's *Youth and Life* (1913) and Van Wyck Brooks's *America's Coming-of-Age* (1915). Croly and several colleagues had established the *New Republic* as an organ of political commentary along progressive-nationalist principles in 1914, and in some ways the *Seven Arts* sought to become a *New Republic* for the arts, covering newer modes of expression for a self-consciously modern readership. But even from the beginning there was a substantial divergence: those in charge of the *New Republic* were middle-aged technocrats who had little to do with the artistic avant-garde or with radical politics, while the editors of the *Seven Arts,* all well under forty, responded strongly to innovations in artistic and political spheres alike. Van Wyck Brooks joined the advisory board of the *Seven Arts* and eventually became an associate editor, as did Waldo Frank, whose *Our America* would make a notable if slightly belated contribution to the discourse of cultural nationalism in 1919. Also on the advisory board were prominent younger figures from a range of artistic fields: the dramatist Edna Kenton of the Provincetown Players; the violinist and music educator David Mannes; the modernist theatrical designer Robert Edmond Jones; and three poets, Robert Frost, Kahlil Gibran, and Louis Untermeyer. True to its name, the *Seven Arts* would feature an eclectic mix of fiction, drama, reviews, and prose commentaries on everything from reminiscences of the Victorian novelist Samuel Butler to contemporary Italian religious cinema to "Two Views of Ragtime." Still, the editor-in-chief, James Oppenheim, and half the advisory board were primarily poets, suggesting the central role poetry would play among the seven.

Cristanne Miller notes that the *Seven Arts,* with Oppenheim, Frank, Untermeyer, and the journalist and music critic Paul Rosenfeld within its inner circle, was essentially run by progressive Jews.[1] The magazine's strong affiliation with a cultural pluralism sympathetic to Jews and immigrants and its connection to the geographic locale of lower Manhattan give it a lot more in common with *The Masses* (in which Untermeyer was also a central figure) and with *Others* than most historians have realized. Ironically, the forgotten figure on the magazine's roster is its editor-in-chief, Oppenheim, a prolific writer of *vers libre* and enthusiastic advocate of the New Poetry movement, whose later career was shorter and less noteworthy than those of the magazine's other key participants. Despite his virtual disappearance from literary history, it would be a serious error to consider Oppenheim peripheral to the *Seven Arts*. Almost all material on the magazine's editorial pages is either signed or initialed by him, or else bears no signature and must be assigned to him in lieu of evidence to the contrary. Oppenheim's progressive idealism and rhapsodic voice shaped the magazine's course at every important point, especially its momentous decision to oppose American belligerency after April 1917.

The twelve issues of the *Seven Arts* offered an impressive cross-section of the American New Verse, including work by Robert Frost, Vachel Lindsay, Carl Sandburg, Amy Lowell, Alfred Kreymborg, James Oppenheim, Arthur Ficke, Maxwell Bodenheim, Witter Bynner, Sherwood Anderson, Stephen Vincent Benét, Wallace Gould, Alice Corbin (Henderson), Babette Deutsch, Helen Hoyt, Eunice Tietjens, Louis Untermeyer, Jean Starr Untermeyer, and Claude McKay (writing as Eli Edwards). But the magazine's importance to American poetry has ultimately less to do with its individual verse offerings than with its use of "poetry" as a locus of symbolic and historical meaning in its account of modern national culture. Unlike *Poetry* and *Others,* built entirely around verse, the *Seven Arts* was conceived, as its title suggests, as a general magazine exploring the relationship between various artistic forms and twentieth-century modernity. In the United States between 1890 and 1910, such a project would likely have sought to involve poetry as little as possible, or not at all. But by late 1916, the genre had already been so thoroughly rejuvenated that in the *Seven Arts* the term "poetry" no longer signified a quaint form of emotional pablum but became the central metaphor for a "body of social theory," an "American vision" defining the nation's identity and potential.[2]

Idealism: A Poetry of Nations

The initial premises of the *Seven Arts* emphasized the reciprocal interaction of artist and audience through a self-defining slogan reminiscent of *Poetry*'s: "The *Seven Arts* is not a magazine for artists, but an expression of artists for the community."[3] The announcement sent to prospective contributors and subscribers in the summer of 1916 and reprinted in the opening number offered this ringing affirmation of America's potential: "It is our faith and the faith of many, that we are living in the first days of a renascent period, a time which means for America the coming of that national self-consciousness which is the beginning of greatness. In all such epochs the arts cease to be private matters; they become not only the expression of the national life but a means to its enhancement."[4] For the next five issues, the *Seven Arts* continued to pursue a utopian vision of modernity understood in powerfully national terms. In January, for example, Oppenheim's editorial portrayed America as "the land of large-scale life—of the vastest crops, the tallest skyscrapers, the largest railroad trackage, the heaviest tonnage, the most complete personal comfort. It is the land of Bigness. It is the land of Kindness. It is the nation wrought out of all nations."[5] He acknowledged that such celebrations of sheer magnitude betrayed a lingering state of cultural "adolescence" but still saw the nation's vast scale as evidence that "everything is possible" in these "days of high ambition, of unresting activity."[6]

Oppenheim wasted no time in integrating the New Verse movement into his magazine's cultural agenda. In the first issue, November 1916, responding to Max Eastman's polemic against *vers libre* in the September *New Republic,* he argued that far from being an aberration from unalterable poetic tradition, *vers libre* was a defining innovation of art in the twentieth century, analogizing it to crucial developments in modern music: "[I]f [Whitman's] symphonic use of rhythms is formless, then in music, Wagner and Debussy and Stravinsky are formless."[7] This analogy posited an intergeneric and international account of modern artistic form that refused to rely on "neat little molds, ready-made," in favor of forms that grew organically out of particular verbal or musical ideas.[8] In the effort to devise forms adequate to the conditions of twentieth-century life, Oppenheim saw the New Poetry as America's main contribution so far. In an editorial statement a month later, Oppenheim returned to this theme, finding in the formally adventurous and iconoclastic temper of contemporary American verse precious hints of a nascent national culture that would be idealistic, secular, and egalitarian. He argued that the "'new poetry'" was "[e]xtremely significant for our future" in "spring[ing] directly from many levels of experience" that represented the diversity of the American populace, rather than being imposed from a single elite class or foreign culture.[9] The other arts in the United States were showing some signs of vernacular renewal, but only in poetry was there anything like "a large tendency, an integrated movement" making a concerted attempt "to break through the class-crusts, to be assimilated back into the universal experience of life." Thus in its poetry resided America's "great hope for a national art."[10]

Though all twentieth-century expressions of nationalist feeling may warrant scrutiny, it is also important to distinguish among their various implications. Even at its most callow, the progressive nationalism advocated by Oppenheim and his colleagues differs greatly from the ugly patriotic fervor that swept through combatant nations of the Great War. The nationalism of the *Seven Arts* owed much to the progressive political movements of early nineteenth-century Europe, adapted to an American modernity understood as secular, democratic, and cosmopolitan, shaped by continual interchange with many other cultures: a "nation wrought out of all nations."[11] A crucial source of inspiration for this view was Randolph Bourne's essay "Trans-National America," published in *The Atlantic* in July 1916, just as the *Seven Arts* was being organized, which rejected "melting-pot" models of assimilation and argued instead for a pluralism that cultivated and celebrated cultural diversity as the basis of the nation's utopian potential.[12] This pluralist understanding of nationalism led the *Seven Arts* to pay persistent attention to cultures well outside the Anglo-American world, such as the self-translated verse of the Lebanese-born mystic Kahlil Gibran, which appeared in each of the first four issues. The issue of April 1917, as the United States was about to declare war on Germany, featured the poems of a Jewish-born antinationalist German expatriate, Heinrich Heine, as translated by a leftist American Jew, Louis Untermeyer. In this context, Heine's poems implied a simultaneous protest against German militarism, anti-German hysteria in America, and anti-Semitism in both cultures. The *Seven Arts* also explored how the modern generational consciousness shaping "Young America" was enriching other cultures, commissioning and publishing essays on "Young Japan" (Seichi Naruse, April), "Young Spain" (John Dos Passos, August), "Youngest Ireland" (Padraic Colum, September), and "Young India" (Lajpat Rai, October).

In its delineation of a vigorous cultural pluralism, the *Seven Arts* framed American modernity as a struggle not between natives and foreigners, bourgeoisie and proletariat, or Christians and heathens but as a conflict between generations in which idealistic youth collectively rejects the poisonously narrow materialism that its elders had foisted upon it. This model of cultural change—each generation defining and energizing itself by repudiating its predecessors—was emerging as a crucial catalyst for twentieth-century artistic avant-gardes. *Poetry*'s editorials on behalf of the New Verse had employed it prominently since 1912, and Brooks's 1915 book *America's Coming-of-Age* had brought it to national attention. Brooks imported his generational argument into the *Seven Arts* in the second issue (December 1916) with the essay "Young America," which traced a genealogy back to the European liberation movements of the early nineteenth century. For Brooks, a strong generational consciousness in the young was a defining characteristic of modernity and represented "a warm, humane, concerted and more or less revolutionary protest against whatever incubus of crabbed age, paralysis, tyranny, stupidity, sloth, commercialism, lay most heavily upon the people's life, checking the free development of personality, retarding the circulation of generous ideas."[13] "Young America" of the nineteenth century, faced with establishing basic material comforts and economic prosperity, had channeled its energies into commerce rather than culture. But Brooks now saw this rudimentary acquisitive phase passing away as people "discovered the inadequacy of business to fulfill their spiritual needs."[14] The concept of Young America had thus once again become meaningful for expressing "some prodigious organism that lies undelivered in the midst of our society, an immense brotherhood of talents and capacities coming to a single birth."[15]

Despite or perhaps partially because of its exuberant naiveté, this generational rhetoric became a source of tremendous iconoclastic energy that greatly aided American poetry's rejuvenation after 1912. In the *Seven Arts* it generated a potent critique of the canons of nineteenth-century American poetry and an alternative canonical narrative with Whitman at its center. In *America's Coming-of-Age*, Brooks devoted an entire chapter to the stunting influence of "'Our Poets,'" "commonly six in number, kindly, gray-bearded, or otherwise grizzled old men" who had erected "an immense, vague cloud-canopy of idealism" that obfuscated the emptiness of existence in a culture of unbridled capitalism.[16] The "essence" of their poetics was its escapist disengagement from modern experience, its insistence that poetry "had and could have no connection with the practical conduct of life."[17] In the April issue of the *Seven Arts*, Brooks continued this attack in "The Culture of Industrialism," arguing that Longfellow, Holmes, and their peers had taken in hand "all the difficult elements of human nature and [put] them under chloroform," thereby providing a "free channel" for the voracious pioneers who built America into an industrial power.[18] But in doing so they had "shelved our spiritual life, conventionalizing it in a sphere above the sphere of action," stunting the nation's growth in every other area.[19] Brooks drew a sharp evaluative distinction between these inhibiting figureheads of established culture and a few outsiders, Whitman above all, whose work had responded vigorously to urban-industrial modernity. Other challenges to the Fireside poets would emerge during the mid-1910s, but Brooks's critique of the "genteel tradition" catalyzed an influential canonical narrative that would be adopted by many American literary historians over the next three decades and consolidated in 1941 by F. O. Matthiessen's magisterial study *American Renaissance*.

Brooks's canonical revisionism underpinned the magazine's alternative history of the nation's poetry with Whitman as the central figure and *vers libre* as the formal breakthrough. In Oppenheim's advocacy of the New Poetry in the first issue, he had demonstrated the rhythmic richness and affective subtlety of unmetered verse by discussing lines from "When Lilacs Last in the Dooryard Bloom'd"; over the ensuing months this poem became a particular source of inspiration for the *Seven Arts*.[20] Elsewhere in the first number, Whitman's importance to twentieth-century life was evoked in a statement of support from another of the editors' intellectual heroes, the French pacifist novelist Romain Rolland, who saw the poet as originator of a great national culture: "Behind you, alone, the elemental Voice of a great pioneer, in whose message you may well find an almost legendary omen of your task to come,—your Homer: Walt Whitman."[21] In issue after issue, Whitman would function as crucial precursor, spiritual parent, native genius, and secular deity. In Paul Rosenfeld's November article on American composers, Whitman was the artist who best incarnates the "spirit of a community, of a nation"; Waldo Frank's December article, "Concerning a Little Theater," began by evoking "Whitman's man of the 'divine average'"; in January, Brooks's commentary, "The Splinter of Ice," echoed Rolland in referring to "our Homer (Walt Whitman)."[22] Oppenheim, who repeatedly evoked Whitman's work as a kind of sacred text, began his May editorial: "[T]he other night, after a hard day, full of confusion, I opened my Walt Whitman," as a clergyman might refer to opening a Bible or Talmud.[23] The May issue of the monthly cultural supplement "The Seven Arts Chronicle" was headlined "The Fifth-Month Poet," following Whitman's frequent method of designating months, and the unsigned text beneath the headline, beginning "May is Walt Whitman month," celebrated his synthesis of the moral authority of the prophet with the empirical integrity of the scientist.[24] A July commentary praised Thoreau by rating him with Whitman as fellow iconoclasts challenging the conventions of their times.[25] Finally, the September issue offered the great man's voice itself, courtesy of extensive excerpts from the fourth volume of Horace Traubel's long-running chronicle "With Walt Whitman in Camden." Clearly, in the *Seven Arts* every month was Walt Whitman month.

Whitman's persona and his reservoir of imagery were also central to the *Seven Arts'* utopian vision for the modern secular nation. An unsigned but very Oppenheimian statement entitled "The American," published in April, just prior to the nation's entry into the war, posited that "at the moment when we might despair of nationality, we discover that there is something great in our life: that there is a spirit permeating our land. It is unlike the spirit of any other land, for by the miracle of our destiny it is not a god and it is not a divine king, nor is it any ghostly visitant. It was thumped together and thumbed painfully into shape out of the common clay of middle America."[26] This American "hero of the folk" was a mythic amalgam of Whitman and Lincoln for a secular egalitarian society, "born humbly, in a manger, a hut, a cabin": "Once the marvellous thing was that this hero was a man of magic, a god, and was worshipped. With us, the marvellous thing is that he really lived this life, that he was one of us, that he remains one of us, and that his is a greatness not aloof, not of heaven, not something we must gain by mystic devotion and a separation from life, but a greatness possible to men here on earth, in this life."[27]

In the following issue, Oppenheim sought to mold this position into verse. His poem "Memories of Whitman and Lincoln" proposes an intimate connection between these two figures by evoking Whitman's elegy to the president yet again. As the nation entered another spring fraught by war and self-doubt, Americans might be comforted by these symbolic national parents, "two great shadows in the spacious night, / Shadows folding America close between them, / Close to the heart," for whom "[l]ilacs shall bloom" as long as "yet America lives."[28]

Another editorial comment in the April issue, again unsigned but clearly by Oppenheim, revealed the role that the term "poetry" played in the *Seven Arts* by applying it to this canon of originary American creative spirits. On this occasion, the editor evoked Thomas Jefferson as "[u]ndoubtedly . . . our first national poet," whose words in the Declaration of Independence—"our first national poem"—generated an American spirit that Lincoln and Whitman had each developed further.[29] A page later, Oppenheim returned to the metaphor, calling these three figures "our national poets of the first order."[30] Just as Whitman had generated an utterly distinctive verse style out of disparate nontraditional sources, Lincoln and Jefferson had invented new political forms from raw materials largely without precedent. Now in 1917, with the nation's policy of constructive neutrality collapsing, "the old America" of these figures "exists no longer."[31] But this devastating turn meant no retreat to aristocracy, church, or royalty; instead it required re-doubled commitment to the ideals embodied by these three. The editorial concluded by calling for a "poet and prophet" who might "project a vision" of a twentieth-century future: "[T]he time has come. A new poet must appear among us."[32] Such formulations reveal the remarkable accomplishment of the New Verse movement in only five years. "Poetry," until recently a term signifying unworldliness and ineffectuality, could now be used without apology as a metaphor for the ideas upon which the nation's—and the world's—future depended.

Contradiction: Dark Converging Paths

In its initial utopian phase, the *Seven Arts* relied implicitly on America's neutrality in the war. To celebrate nationalism while opposing an unprecedented war driven by nationalist rhetoric required all available evidence of America's freedom from atavistic European traditions. This premise was supported by Rolland's benediction in the first issue, which portrayed the war as proof of the bankruptcy of European cultures and America as the best hope for rebuilding the world in a progressive direction.[33] Through the first five issues, these premises encouraged an exceptionalism that, although often critical of arrested American development, envisioned a great future in strongly national terms. Oppenheim's editorial of March, for example, embedded a rationale for neutrality within Young America's critique of the nation's culture under unbridled capitalism: "Nothing has given us a clearer picture of ourselves than the glare of the Great War, whose fierce fires burning round the world show us to be thin silhouettes moving about without real purposes and meanings. This is the disillusionment of Midas, whose touch turned everything to gold. Our younger generation is sick of it: it turns with disgust against the soft ideal of universal comfort and the ennui of a colorless social life, a purposeless round of petty sensations."[34] In this formulation, Oppenheim sought to separate progressive national feeling from jingoistic patriotism by revising conventional youthful rejections of the stale peacetime world (such as Rupert Brooke's sonnet sequence "1914"). Repudiating the empty acquisitiveness and absurd social rituals of the prewar world led his idealistic young American not to Brooke's belligerent patriotism but to a "willingness to serve" by means other than fighting, such as working for the "league for peace" President Wilson had proposed.[35]

Still, no rhetorical acrobatics could change the fact that the nationalist program of the *Seven Arts* rested upon a potentially crippling contradiction. Before April, the magazine was largely unable to speak this contradiction, and its prose and editorial commentaries repressed the unnerving awareness that nationalism and isolationism were not viable responses to the global condition. But in the less earnest and guarded venue of verse, this repressed material returned in discordant or self-confuting moments that darkened but also enriched the magazine's response to the catastrophe. The sense of inhabiting a realm of intractable contradiction emerged with particular force in poems by two key figures of the New Verse whose work is often not thought to engage sociopolitical questions, Robert Frost and Amy Lowell.

In the magazine's first issue (November 1916), which is otherwise full of ringing idealist proclamations, Frost's poem "The Bonfire" dramatized the impossibility of keeping the war from affecting even those not directly involved. In its imagery, tone of voice, and blank-verse cadences, this poem strikingly resembles, but also revises, Frost's earlier allegory of territorial conflict, "Mending Wall." Though "Mending Wall" was published in *North of Boston* in May 1914, before the outbreak of hostilities in Europe, it

presciently imagines an irrational animosity between neighbors, emerging
from no issue of compelling importance, focused on the spatial borders
separating and conjoining them, and finally driving its speaker into fantasies
of demonization and violence that transform rocks into projectiles, human
arms into weapons, and a longtime neighbor into an "old-stone savage."[36]
Similarly, "The Bonfire" is built around a ritual of rural life that carries
communal and antagonistic meanings, through which Frost explores the
perverse human desire to commit meaningless acts of destruction, even as
every rational impulse demands staying away, keeping out. But "The Bonfire," written under the pressure of an actual war, carries Frost beyond the
comfortable limits of allegory into one of his most genuine and thoughtful
responses to the twentieth-century world.

The poem's speaker and the children in his charge ponder a "'reckless'"
assault on the brush they have collected by lighting a giant dry bonfire
without waiting for rain "'to make it safe.'"[37] The adult speaker leads the
way in this discussion, while the children merely react with a few brief questions, making it clear that Frost sees the pyromaniac impulse not as some
quirk of heedless youth but as integral to mature manhood. The speaker's
motivations are as murky as they are frightening. One part of him desires
to antagonize his neighbors, exulting as he imagines alarmed and furious
figures standing helpless at their windows, "'saying what they'd like to do
to us'" for endangering their lives and property. Another part of him wants
to "'scare ourselves'"—to be put in a position where he cannot control the
results of his actions, to make sure that

> " . . . nothing but
> The fire itself can put it out, and that
> By burning out, and before it burns out
> It will have roared first and mixed sparks with stars
> And sweeping round it with a flaming sword,
> Made the dim trees stand back in wider circle—."

The bonfire the speaker contemplates will become his own private war, a
"flaming sword" he can brandish against his neighbors, the surrounding
forests, and the earth itself. He knows that if a wind chances to come up
at the wrong time, he risks causing great destruction, yet he still desires a
draft that will "'bring on / A wind to blow in earnest'"—in other words,
to make the fire a blindly self-perpetuating force with no motivation or
meaning beyond its own continuation. By November 1916, the notion of
unstoppable, unending destruction detached from the desires or intentions
of its participants could hardly fail to evoke the Great War, just as Frost's

imagery of a firestorm that incinerates everything in its path, gouging out bare spaces from forested areas, inevitably tropes the blasted landscapes of western Europe.[38]

With this narrative frame in place, the outcome in suspense, Frost shifts to a long middle section in which the speaker recounts memories of another fire he had started one April long before, for no discernible reason beyond the desire to "'walk . . . once round it in possession.'"[39] This phrase recalls the powerful thrall of ownership (of rocks, apples, cows, space, and ideas) that drives the animus between neighbors in "Mending Wall." The speaker treasures the earlier fire as something fully and exclusively his own, and this same possessive imperative drives his opening proposition to the children—"'The pile is ours: we dragged it bough on bough / Down dark converging paths'"—words implying that their proprietary claim justifies doing exactly as they wish with brush and fire, regardless of the possible detriment to the community.

The speaker tells us that he stopped his earlier fire in the nick of time. But the experience has left him unrepentant, even exultant in having gotten away with it:

> "They looked about for someone to have done it.
> But there was no one. I was somewhere wondering
> Where all my weariness had gone and why
> I walked so light on air in heavy shoes
> In spite of a scorched Fourth of July feeling."

These extraordinary lines imply that setting and barely extinguishing this fire made the speaker feel not only happier and more powerful but more American. The poet thus proposes that the links between organized aggression and national identity, so often clothed in the weightless abstractions of personal honor and patriotic pride, are instead ignited by a dark convergence of irrational desires. This account of humanity's visceral compulsion toward violence might have given pause to both smug "pragmatic" rationalists who were advocating American intervention so that they could control the war for human good and the naive isolationists hoping that Americans were somehow excepted from such a will to destruction.

The last section of "The Bonfire" contains a surprise: Frost registers the pressure of the Great War by departing from his lifelong mode of analogical-allegorical nature verse and adopts a mode of more direct statement. Unlike "Mending Wall," "The Bonfire" cannot be fully decontextualized from its geopolitical register because of the moving final lines, which reveal a Frost much less emotionally guarded—and perhaps more appealing—than his usual persona of canny, detached New England yeoman. To the children's question about the oversized bonfire they contemplate, "'If it scares you, what will it do to us?'" the speaker responds:

> "Scare you. But if you should shrink from being scared,
> What would you say to war if it should come?
> That's what for reasons I should like to know—
> If you can comfort me by any answer."

> "Oh, but war's not for children—it's for men."

> "Now we are digging almost down to China.
> My dears, my dears, you thought that—we all thought it.
> So your mistake was ours. Haven't you heard, though,
> About the ships where war has found them out
> At sea, about the towns where war has come
> Through opening clouds at night with droning speed
> Further o'erhead than all but stars and angels.—
> And children in the ships and in the towns?
> Haven't you heard what we lived to learn?
> Nothing so new—something we had forgotten:
> *War is for everyone, for children too.*
> I wasn't going to tell you, and I mustn't.
> The best way is to come up hill with me
> And have our fire and laugh and be afraid."

The children's belief that war is "not for" them echoes the exceptionalist neutrality upon which the cultural agenda of the *Seven Arts* had been premised. The speaker's final response is powerfully conflicted, simultaneously hiding and confessing the bitter truth learned since 1914: that in the condition of modern global warfare, civilians, neutrals, and innocents no longer exist. As the bonfire suddenly diminishes to a harmless antic compared to the much scarier events beyond sheltered New England forests, the poem ends by questioning whether the analogical-allegorical methods Frost had adopted were adequate to the enormity of twentieth-century history.

Along with Frost's dark fantasy, the inaugural issue of the *Seven Arts* contained the first of two poems by Amy Lowell readable as thoughtful meditations on the nation's precarious neutrality. In public life, Lowell made no secret of her advocacy of the Allied cause.[40] Yet "Flotsam" (November 1916) and "Orange of Midsummer" (April 1917) follow several of her wartime works published elsewhere, notably "Patterns" and "September 1918," in employing ambiguous imagery of prone, broken, or constricted bodies that evoke the devastation of the war with great force. Both *Seven Arts* poems feature scenarios of seduction and incipient annihilation in which bodies and objects undergo surreal transformations that trope the nation's impending involvement in the war as a perverse will to self-destruction.

In "Flotsam," the transformed body is that of a young man sitting mesmerized at the feet of a beguiling female figure who toys with his heart in a startlingly literal way, making it her plaything for the afternoon:

> She tapped it gently,
> Held it up to the sun and looked through it,
> . . .
> Tossed it into the air and caught it,
> Deftly, as though it were a ball.[41]

Finally tiring of these trivialities, she tosses it back to him, but his infatuation has dismembered him irrevocably, and he "only laid it on the ground beside him / And went on gazing." As she often does, Lowell draws here upon the surreal textures of the fairy tale, but she also evokes the immediate prewar moment with the languorous garden-party posture of the young couple on the lawn. The final lines shift toward a sardonic joke that suggests the delusiveness of their idyll, as a maidservant cleaning up after her social betters finds the discarded heart and, thinking it a "pretty thing,"

> . . . ran a ribbon through it
> And hung it on the looking-glass in her bedroom.
> There it hung for many days,
> Banging back and forth as the wind blew it.

Here Lowell's fascination with the transformation and deconstruction of bodies tropes battlefield triage, as the ribbon is run through the vital organ not to mend it but to display it as decathected aesthetic object. The heart, given for an overwhelming and (at least to the giver) noble cause, has been reduced from essence to gift to trophy to toy to "pretty thing" severed from all connection to its human source. As even its trinket appeal wanes, it becomes an overlooked piece of brute matter, lifted and strewn meaninglessly by passing breezes. In this context, the title, otherwise difficult to link to the scene or imagery of this landlocked poem, begins to make sense. The currents of air moving the heart at the end evoke the currents of water tossing flotsam, the residue of shipwrecks seen floating and broken throughout the seas, existential reminders of human mortality and folly. The title thus becomes a strategy for evoking contemporary world events and gives the poem an intractably contextual register of meaning. Many believed, at the time and later, that America was driven toward belligerency against Germany most powerfully by the trauma of seeing thousands of its neutral citizens lost at sea in 1915 and 1916, on the *Lusitania* above all. By incarnating all the lost bodies and broken lives of those maritime disasters into this single heart, sacrificed and then itself forgotten as flotsam, Lowell allegorizes the emotional logic for America's seduction into the conflict and hints at its fatal flaws and bitter outcome.

In the April issue, as the United States was about to declare war, the *Seven Arts* published another of Lowell's enigmatic responses to the war, "Orange of Midsummer." This poem's scenario resembles that of "Flotsam" but is narrated in first person, from the perspective of the naive figure beguiled by an incipiently sinister object of desire. Lowell's habitual use of elaborate color schemes here generates powerful allegorical resonance. Various hues— saffron, pearl, rose—are splashed across the first section as the speaker is beckoned through the iridescent world of early spring. Yet all are finally reduced to monotone by the single-mindedness of the speaker's attachment to the beloved, which is figured as a blurring of vision: "[T]o me it was all one / Because of the blue mist that held my eyes."[42] In the longer second section, except for a field of "yellow wheat," midsummer is tinted almost exclusively red. The color of "red-hearted summer" comes from a "field of poppies," and the desired one sits under a tree, "plaiting poppies for a girdle." Finally the lover offers the speaker a libation colored "scarlet and crimson," again the color of poppies. The speaker exclaims in distress and yearning, "'It looks like blood,'" whereupon the desired one replies with seductive menace:

> "Like blood, . . . Does it?
> But drink it, my Beloved."

Here Lowell draws upon the powerful homology between the bodies of dead soldiers and the wild red poppies thriving in the embattled landscapes of the western front, an equation made everywhere during the Great War, most famously in John McCrae's poem "In Flanders Fields" (first published in *Punch* on December 8, 1915), which begins: "In Flanders fields the poppies blow / Between the crosses, row on row, / That mark our place."[43] Because seeds of the wild poppy can remain long dormant but then sprout vigorously when neighboring plants are killed or uprooted, they bloomed in profusion on the churned-up earth of battlefields, creating the fanciful impression that they were somehow generated by the bodies of those who had shed blood there. This association became so strong that Great Britain and Canada would adopt the poppy as their official symbol of war remembrance after the Armistice (Canada currently prints portions of Mc-Crae's poem on its ten-dollar bill). By 1917 this symbolism was already so widespread that any English-language verse of that year featuring poppies became an allegory of the war. The final offering of "drink" the color of poppies evokes the stupefying narcotic effects of the opium-producing species. Coupled with the "girdle" of poppy blooms, which recalls the oppressive function of girdling garments in Lowell's "Patterns," this imagery makes the beloved's hold over the speaker's body and spirit, like Frost's bonfire, into a sinister trope for the war's magnetism upon those who might have remained apart from it.[44]

Lowell's color palette contains an allegorical twist that foregrounds the curious relation of the poem's title to its contents. Although summer is colored red and yellow, no orange is found inside the poem, an aporia that suggests a significance beyond visual decoration to "Orange," that curious word that refuses to rhyme with any other. Unlike the red battlefield poppy, a symbol generated out of the physical spaces of the war itself, "Orange," both word and color, is a historical symbol that evokes nearly a thousand years of territorial conflict among the elaborately interwoven ruling houses of Europe, including those of France, Germany, England, and the Low Countries.[45] These associations make "Orange" a fitting allegorical signifier for a poem written during and about the last and most horrific of these dynastic wars, set in motion during the heady midsummer days of July 1914. If the ubiquitous phrase "in Flanders fields" invoked the patriotic resistance of Belgium and the Allies to German aggression and supposed atrocity, the phrase "Orange of Midsummer" in Lowell's composition tropes the whole proud tower of European dynastic society, whose intermingled lineage and seductive pageantry generated complex and powerful national identities before destroying itself with the "war to end all wars." The speaker invited to drink this intoxicating mix of blood and symbolism occupies a position not unlike that of the neutral United States, linked by its syncretic origins and variegated population to every side of the conflict, induced in a thousand different ways to quell its misgivings and join the parade.

Opposition: Volunteers of America

The *Seven Arts* was not to realize its modern American utopia. Its most profound achievements were more bitter, but no less meaningful: dissent from U.S. war policy and critique of the national exceptionalism that had underlain its own founding. The wishful belief in America's superiority to Europe, always fraught with contradiction, began to crumble as the Wilson administration began to shift from neutrality to belligerency in early 1917. This change of national policy brought forth from the *Seven Arts* an unexpected capacity for self-critique and a dissident resolve. Only hinted at before April, this critical position intensified in every issue thereafter, catalyzed by the fiercely moral and intellectual figure of Randolph Bourne, who had previously been associated with the *New Republic,* where he had published at least seventy items since November 1914. That magazine's enthusiastic advocacy of intervention alienated him from the editor Herbert Croly and eventually from his intellectual mentor John Dewey. Reduced to doing book reviews in the *New Republic*'s back pages by the fall of 1916, Bourne turned to the *Seven Arts* as the main outlet for his antiwar convictions.[46] Beginning with "The War and the Intellectuals" in June 1917, he advanced a passionate balance of dissidence and idealism that dominated the magazine's final five issues. Meanwhile, Oppenheim contributed copious editorial commentary and, in one of the most fascinating experiments of the New Poetry movement, produced antiwar editorials in verse that exemplify a poetics of engagement very different from the refusal of political entanglements later canonized as the only valid form of modernism.

The emergence of this oppositional stance was unexpected because of how much the *Seven Arts* owed to the progressive intellectuals who had embraced with alarming enthusiasm the Wilsonian line of "making the world safe for democracy"—many even before Wilson himself. The *New Republic* in particular showed that shifting away from isolationism could redound into a messianic narrative in which the exceptional American nation must intervene to save the world from its own irrationality.[47] The *Seven Arts* could easily have followed its immediate intellectual ancestors Croly and Dewey in advocating this national destiny. Sheltered in this way, given its financial support and strong base of circulation, it might well have become as central to the nation's cultural life as *The Dial* was during the 1920s, conceivably as long-lasting an institution of American intellectual culture as the *New Republic* itself.[48]

Instead, James Oppenheim followed his conscience and led the *Seven Arts* away from naive nationalism toward dissident internationalism. This dissenting role began tentatively enough, in uncertainty and contradiction. As late as March, Oppenheim was still clinging to the notion that "[i]t is in nationality today that the race finds that larger self to which the individual may give all and so become human," a sentiment that he wishfully linked to President Wilson's stated resolve to remain a constructive mediator by supporting a league of nations.[49] But he also included in this March issue a note of powerful antinationalist critique in Carl Sandburg's poem "Grass," which bluntly negates the seductive consolation of so much war propaganda: that the patriotic dead will live eternally in the national memory. In 1917, bodies are being piled high at Ypres and Verdun just as in earlier wars at Austerlitz and Waterloo and Gettysburg. Yet no matter the place or time, Sandburg's grass gets on with its sardonic business:

> Shovel them under and let me work.
> Two years, ten years, and people on passenger trains ask
>   the conductor:
>   What place is this?
>   Where are we now?
>   I am the grass. Let me work.[50]

Like many of Sandburg's poems of the war years, such as "Buttons" in *The Masses* and "Long Guns" in *Others,* "Grass" challenges the ideologies of national identity, patriotic duty, and *lebensraum* that drove the conflict. Spreading indiscriminately, the grass generates a denationalized landscape that will render today's geopolitical borders and fatal disputes irrelevant tomorrow. Sandburg's imagery also evokes the ubiquitous wartime bromide that ground spilled with patriotic blood becomes nationally sanctified, as in Rupert Brooke's "The Soldier," which begins, "If I should die, think only this of me: / That there's some corner of a foreign field / That is forever England," and ends by anticipating "an English heaven."[51] Whether or not Brooke is Sandburg's explicit point of reference, the stark indifference of the shoveling and the inexorable action of the grass signify a devastating reality: nobody will really remember the wrenching sacrifices of today, and before long all signs of them will vanish from the earth. It is hard to imagine a more forceful challenge to the patriotic rhetoric of the moment, or a clearer rationale for not entangling oneself in a nationalist war of obscure motivation.

A month later, with America's belligerency imminent, the odyssey of the *Seven Arts* away from complacent nationalism toward principled opposition began in earnest. In the April issue, Oppenheim portrayed Wilson as "the last of the Jeffersonians," who had begun "bravely enough with the old reiterations" but had been forced "to abandon one position after the other" and was now being challenged as severely as the great prophets of America's past had been.[52] This too-hopeful portrayal of Wilson was more accurately a description of the magazine's own journey toward internationalism, in which "we realize that America is becoming not so unlike every other nation and also we are no longer isolated, but merely a fragment of a world, a state in a greater federation."[53] As he announced flatly that "the role of Messiah-nation is ours no longer," Oppenheim distinguished himself from most American intellectuals of the day, including the president, in responding to the failure of isolationism not by taking refuge in national exceptionalism but by rejecting it.[54]

Thenceforward until its end in October, the *Seven Arts* sustained a lonely challenge to American war policy and the repressive climate it engendered. Oppenheim's May editorial, the first written after the American declaration of war on April 6, echoed with agonized confusion at the overthrow of the magazine's utopian premises. He began by describing "successive waves" of contradictory thoughts: sadness at the loss of the peacemaker role; skepticism of the technocrats scheming to convert the conflagration into a "social workers' affair"; the chastened realization that the war's challenge to naive American optimism might somehow be an "experience we need"; and worry that America was an "amateur nation" being manipulated by "keen transatlantic statesmen."[55] In response to this clash of impressions, Oppenheim turned again to Whitman. Although Whitman functions as a role model as usual, Oppenheim uses him here to highlight divergences between the situation Americans faced in 1917 and the analogous moment in 1861. As he traces the phases Whitman underwent as the nation spiraled into civil war, Oppenheim marvels at the poet's "intense conviction" in the Union cause but also notes that even in the bellicose early *Drum-Taps* verses, Whitman exhibits a moral seriousness that contrasts to the venal congressmen who had just declared war, who according to newspaper reports had "lounged in their seats, even 'joshed' some of the speakers, and had to be admonished that they were not 'at a vaudeville performance.'"[56]

Reading further into *Drum-Taps,* Oppenheim encounters "Long, Too Long America," a poem hoping that Americans might "learn from cries of anguish" how to "show to the world what your children en-masse really are."[57] But the idea of war as a crucible of character that "brings national greatness" was one that Oppenheim could not finally accept, since it did not "explain the barren epoch . . . since the Civil War," in which the nation languished, "spiritually burnt-out"—except, of course, for "our Industrial Captains" who were hard at work for themselves even "while the nation fought and bled."[58] Pursuing this critique of expedient justifications of the current war, Oppenheim turns finally to Whitman's "Reconciliation," a poem from the last somber phase of *Drum-Taps* which posits that all the war's great deeds "must in time be utterly lost" and imagines a kiss between the speaker and the enemy he has killed. Oppenheim again uses Whitman to draw a contrast between the wars: because of their own failures, Americans of May 1917 have no healing reconciliation to look forward to, only "bitter experience and great sorrow" as they "go into the great fires, learning what was learned before."[59]

Oppenheim's refusal of reconciliation even as a future possibility adumbrates the resolutely dissident position that the *Seven Arts* was moving toward. By June he was more confidently measuring his distance from Wilsonian liberalism, describing the war as "a throwback of fifty thousand years" that no amount of earnest American intentions could ameliorate.[60] The spiritual primitivism it revealed was all the worse for using "the best products" of human intellect to create "machines of destruction whose horror is beyond our imagination."[61] Clearly American isolationism had been "a failure," not really peace but "a mere absence of war," the consequence "of a century of shallow living."[62] Supporters of American involvement were now busily manufacturing logical continuity between the nation's previous self-positioning as enlightened neutral and its current one as the savior of democratic civilization. But Oppenheim and the *Seven Arts* refused to pretend that one policy followed logically or ethically from the other. Like all the other nations, America's going to war revealed its disastrous failure at maintaining peace: "We too must know war because we could not volunteer and meet together as human beings to create great peace and great persons."[63]

Through the summer of 1917, the editorial pages of the *Seven Arts* registered with growing alarm the ascendancy of what Randolph Bourne called "the war-mind": a totalitarian paradigm of conformity, paranoia, and rationalization in which anything can be justified by official proclamations of state emergency.[64] Bourne's crucial essay of June, "The War and the Intellectuals," announces in its first paragraph his severance from his former allies and indicts American intellectuals as having colluded in the failure of neutrality: "To those of us who still retain an irreconcilable animus against war, it has been a bitter experience to see the unanimity with which the American intellectuals have thrown their support to the use of war-technique in the crisis in which America found herself. Socialists, college professors, publicists, new-republicans, practitioners of literature, have vied with each other in confirming with their intellectual faith the collapse of neutrality and the riveting of the war-mind on a hundred million more of the world's people."[65] The self-delusion of "new-republicans" like Croly, Dewey, Walter Lippmann, and Woodrow Wilson himself, who argued that intervention would allow America to control the war to rational and humane ends, demonstrated to Bourne the bankruptcy of traditional liberalism and demanded a disruptive intellectual persona who would work to puncture the words of "leaders who tell us that we go to war in moral spotlessness, or who make 'democracy' synonymous with a republican form of government."[66] This dissident personage, finding in war propaganda "no consolation whatever," would "sneer at those who buy the cheap emotion of sacrifice."[67] However disillusioned, this figure refuses his enemies the power to destroy his utopian hopes for the future and makes his dissent constructive through "heightened energy and enthusiasm for the education, the art, the interpretation that make for life in the midst of the world of death."[68] Bourne ends by urging whoever "retains his animus against war" to work to "divide, confuse, disturb, keep the intellectual waters constantly in motion," and never to accede to the militarization of American life.[69]

Thenceforth Bourne ramified and concretized this activist position month by month. In July's "Below the Battle," he describes a young American, neither coward nor pacifist, who feels only "smouldering resentment at the men who have clamped down the war-pattern upon him."[70] Yet while rejecting the rhetorical "shafts of panic, patriotism, and national honor" aimed at him, he maintains a "personal and social idealism" that "cannot be hurt by the taunts of cowardice and slacking."[71] Of course, this formulation describes the position that Bourne and Oppenheim were seeking to maintain: firmly in opposition to the compromised official ideals of the nation, yet adamant in preserving an idealist perspective of their own. In August, Bourne's "Conspirators" described the trials of three students from Columbia and Barnard who had been arrested and indicted for planning to issue a manifesto urging young men not to register for the draft.[72] This issue also featured an unsigned editorial defense of *The Masses,* recently denied the use of the mails under the newly passed Espionage Act. The worst part of this oppressive policy was its deliberate cultivation of paranoia and self-entrapment: the post office refused to pass advance judgment on a particular issue even when asked to do so, but it then had the power not only to deny any periodical the use of the mails but to indict their editors for sedition after the issue was printed.[73] To Bourne and the *Seven Arts,* the three students and *The Masses* editors were martyrs to the war-mind threatening the democratic principles that the nation had reputedly joined the war to defend.

As Bourne was elaborating his activist stance, Oppenheim's sense of poetry's role in modern life was also evolving, and in August he inaugurated the most innovative function of verse in the *Seven Arts.* For nine months after the magazine's founding, he had observed the conventional distinction between his verse and his prose editorial work. But this boundary collapsed under the pressure of America's entry into the war, and in the final three issues Oppenheim composed verse editorials that employ the rhapsodic and metaphorical capabilities of poetry to develop a symbolic vocabulary for Bourne's position of negative activism. The formatting and layout of these verse editorials show that Oppenheim sought to present them not merely as poems of political commentary or prophecy but simply as the voice of the *Seven Arts*. Without changing a word, he could have given these pieces different titles, signed rather than merely initialing them, and placed them elsewhere in the issue, where they would have readily supplemented the antiwar prose of Bourne, John Reed, and others surrounding them. Instead, they sit underneath the magazine's name, logo, and masthead, where official editorial comments had always been placed. On subsequent pages they are headed not with the title on the verso and the author's name on the recto, as other pieces typically were, but simply with "*The Seven Arts*" on both sides. The use of verse for such a purpose may seem puzzling or absurd, given our critical tradition distrustful of political statement in poetry. But it followed logically from Oppenheim's contention that not only Whitman but also Lincoln and Jefferson were America's greatest poets, their foundational civic utterances its "national poems."[74] To take this metaphor seriously meant imagining the obverse: poems seeking to articulate political ideas crucial to the nation's present and formative of its future.

The first verse editorial appeared in August alongside a double-barreled blast of antiwar prose: Bourne's "The Collapse of American Strategy," anatomizing the intellectual and ethical failures that had eroded Wilson's resolve to maintain neutrality, and John Reed's ferocious piece "This Unpopular War," indicting the imperialist motives beneath the nation's altruistic claims. In his editorial, bitterly disappointed by the lack of dissent in the United States yet still seeking a locus for his idealism, Oppenheim found possibility in the throwing-off of Czarist oppression by the Russian people, an act that he celebrated as a "glimpse of the splendid sun in the black battle-smoke, / Thou shining health, thou virtue in the insane death-shambles."[75] Oppenheim's nationalism had been crumbling for some time, and here he breaks through into utopian internationalism, proclaiming that to Russia

> the leadership has passed.
> From America to thee has been handed the torch of freedom;
> Thou art the hope of the world, the asylum of the oppressed,
> The manger of the Future

that would "[c]all us to the Day of Man, to the Planet of Humanity."[76]

In the magazine's final two issues, September and October, prose and verse commentaries worked interdependently to demonstrate how far the

Seven Arts had traveled from exceptionalist nationalism toward radical internationalism. In September's "A War Diary," Bourne sought to imagine a future beyond the war but foresaw that the loss of America's political equilibrium was likely to generate a powerful drive back toward isolationism.[77] If America was to "retain its spiritual integrity," he insisted, it could not allow itself "any smug retreat from the world, with the belief that the truth is in us and can only be contaminated by contact."[78] The only withdrawal should be from America's messianic self-positioning, since "it is absurd to try to contribute to the world's store of great moving ideas until we have a culture to give."[79] In October, Bourne contributed "Twilight of Idols," demonstrating how the ethical weakness of John Dewey's pragmatism had led Dewey to rationalize American belligerency, while Bertrand Russell's "Is Nationalism Moribund?" advanced the magazine's ongoing critique of its own intellectual heritage by portraying fervent national feeling as a historically specific symptom of the dislocating effects of modernity that would soon obsolesce in a world moving inexorably toward internationalism.[80]

Meanwhile, Oppenheim composed verse editorials for both issues. September's adopted Bourne's notion of negative activism as a response to the coercive pressures of the moment:

> Our task today is to hold against panic and loneliness,
> To put from us the temptation of the drums and the bayonets,
> To shut the gates of the heart against the seducing myth
>   of Slaughter,
> To be, each one of us, a rallying-point, a call and a summons
>   to the War beyond War,
> To the fighting civilization we shall create.[81]

Oppenheim's fiery *vers libre* cadences and martial imagery acknowledge the power of the war-mind, manifested in parades and propaganda, strengthened by paranoia and isolation, which had seduced potential dissenters into a sheltering national mythos that authorized slaughter as a moral good. But he is careful never to frame the struggle as hopeless or oppositional ideals as futile. One way he maintains this precious sense of possibility is to appropriate patriotic rhetorical conventions into expressions of counterpropaganda that seek to discredit "[t]he foul lie of the glory of war, / The lie that dying in a war of traders is worthy of a man."[82] This September editorial ended with a powerful instance of such counter-rhetoric, commandeering the elegiac "forever England" imagery of Brooke and others to repudiate nationalism and messianism in favor of secular internationalism:

If we must have a sacred land to die for,
It shall be no acre in France or in Indiana,
But the Earth—only the Earth itself is sacred to us.
If we must have a religion,
Our God shall not be a Chosen People in the shape
    of a Thunderer,
Our God shall be a man, in every land, of every people.[83]

In October, Oppenheim's final verse editorial, "After a Stormy Twilight," further advanced Bourne's dissident ethics by offering a speaker who repudiates his former urge for the "approbation of the herd, / Crowd-comfort for my loneliness" that had tempted him "to say 'Yea, yea' to the public that I might go safe," and who resolves instead to

turn from will-to-power
And seek will-to-inner-power,
Deal with my own body and my desires until I walk freely.[84]

As for Bourne's negative activist, for Oppenheim the self-understanding necessary to renounce dominion over others will bring not withdrawal into narcissistic isolation but a redoubled commitment to work in the world. In the last and finest moments of his editorial career, Oppenheim broadened this personal goal into a utopian prophecy in which all people might "cease being tyrant over another, / And in freedom cease being slave of another." The result of such a turn would be "[a] race of volunteers seeking each to present the gift of a great Self unto the world."[85] This metaphor of dissident volunteerism would resonate in American progressive circles for decades, through the Abraham Lincoln Brigades of the Spanish Civil War, the Peace Corps and other global initiatives, to the antiwar counterculture of the 1960s, where it would be celebrated explicitly in Jefferson Airplane's revolutionary antiwar anthem "Volunteers" (1969). Here in the *Seven Arts* it functioned as a humane counterdiscourse to the coercive climate of wartime America, in which individual lives and freedoms were being sacrificed to the state, political opinions measured along a repressive axis of patriotism, and all forms of information mined for their propaganda value. In such a climate, to dissent from authority while also volunteering the best elements of oneself was to insist that the individual still possessed an ethical force not circumscribed by the carceral structures of nationalist modernity.

How do we place Oppenheim's verse editorials—so distant in intention and effect from classic autotelic modernism—within the New Poetry movement? The literary-historical norms of subsequent decades would have dismissed them as aesthetically inferior to the "purer" poetry found in the *Seven Arts* and other magazines, and certainly Oppenheim was never considered as fine a poetic artist as other Whitmanesque writers such as Sandburg or even Lindsay. But it is important to understand that people living through the period would have seen strong continuity between his roles as editor of an oppositional political magazine and as writer of rhapsodic *vers libre*. The declamatory tendency of nearly all his verse, now difficult to appreciate in the pages of his volumes, is better suited to the highly rhetorical format of the editorial. And his conviction that poetry was the best vehicle for his political critique indicates how thoroughly the genre had been rejuvenated in a decade. Less than twenty years earlier, it was widely declared that poetry no longer had any social function in a accelerated modern world of efficient prose. If poetry was to survive at all, it would be merely to provide beguiling "bagatelles of fancy" that we could use "now and then to forget the awful burden of our responsibility for the world's welfare," as one commentator had declared in an 1898 piece entitled "Have We Still Need of Poetry?"[86] Now in 1917, the editor of a publication predicated upon the need for Americans to shoulder those burdens had embraced poetry not only as his secret love or avocation but as a primary vehicle for articulating public positions on issues central to the world's welfare.

Bourne's centrality to the wartime poetics of the *Seven Arts* was reinforced by the memorial verse "Randolph Bourne," published by Oppenheim in *The Liberator* in February 1919. The occasion of the poem was one of the bitterest ironies of a bitter time. After the demise of the *Seven Arts* in late 1917, Bourne had spent 1918 writing prolifically for *The Dial* and other magazines, horrified at the oppressive national climate and fearful of being prosecuted for sedition but still attempting to sustain the role of public "irreconcilable." The Armistice provided him a last moment of hope, and his temperamental optimism sprang up again in a letter to his mother on November 21: "Now that the war is over people can speak freely again and we can dare to think. It's like coming out of a nightmare."[87] He was engaged to be married and had prospects for a position of real importance, since Scofield Thayer had asked him to head a political division of a reconstituted *Dial*.[88] But a month after Bourne wrote those hopeful words, he was dead from influenza at the age of thirty-two—small consolation that he was spared seeing the repression and social chaos of 1919. His untimely death may have had a profound effect on the modernism of the 1920s by depriving the decade's most important little magazine of its political catalyst. By the time Thayer took charge of *The Dial,* he and his editors had decided to forego politics and limit themselves to "literary, artistic, and philosophical matter."[89] Edward

Abrahams insightfully describes this episode as evidence of a fundamental "rupture that took place in American life in 1919," in which the integration of artistic experiment and social engagement that had energized the *Seven Arts* and its contemporaries was suddenly no longer viable.[90]

In Oppenheim's poetic elegy (and also in Floyd Dell's prose obituary in the *New Republic* for January 4, 1919), the legend of Bourne's martyrdom to noble ideals in an evil time had already begun to take shape. Oppenheim describes him as having "a passion for humanity / Almost terrible," a soul "that writhed over injustice and sham and the masquerades of virtue," and a mind capable of "vivid play over the world, a realism penetrating a keen blade."[91] In his opposition to the war, Bourne became increasingly isolated and friendless, "unswerving, dreading and fearing prison and persecution, / Yet continuing in [his] own truth" until despair overmastered hope, and "[w]hat was there left to do, but die?" The poem's inexorable momentum toward this conclusion verges on fatalism, but Oppenheim maintains oppositional energy by drawing upon the tradition of political jeremiad, traceable back through Moody's "On a Soldier Fallen in the Philippines" (1900) to Whittier's antebellum abolitionist verse, to assert that Bourne had became a symbol of the ideals worth remembering and rebuilding after the "whole rotten structure" of imperial America "shall crash to ruins." In other words, by speaking with unmatched honesty the horrifying failures of modern American democracy, yet also insisting on the continuing possibility of utopian alternatives, Bourne had made himself into a national poet to join Jefferson, Lincoln, and Whitman.

As for the *Seven Arts* itself, the hysterical wartime climate spelled its demise in the most mundane of ways: its chief sponsor, Mrs. A. N. Rankine, became exasperated with its antigovernment stance and withdrew the needed financial support, whereupon the magazine quickly ceased after October 1917. Compared to the high-profile indictments of the editors of *The Masses* under the Espionage Act, the end of the *Seven Arts* was quiet, an instance of modern capitalism's tendency to suppress by economic rather than legal means.

But the significance of the magazine's demise is more complex and poignant than the simple loss of a financial angel. It is complex because of the conflict among the various editors, which will probably never be fully understood. In 1937 Waldo Frank suggested that the *Seven Arts* could have continued on after the departure of Rankine's money by adopting some sort of joint editorship. He identified the removal of Oppenheim as sole editor as a precondition for the continued support proffered by "[m]any wealthy men and women," including Scofield Thayer.[92] By the time Frank wrote, Oppenheim was no longer around to offer his version of these events—nor was Thayer, whose mental problems drove him from the literary scene before 1930. But if Thayer admired Bourne strongly enough to offer him *The Dial*'s political division, would he have been intent upon dismissing Oppenheim, whose views were so strongly aligned with Bourne's through the summer and fall of 1917? Those attacking Oppenheim's continued control were likely prepared to capitulate to the fact of American belligerency to ensure the continuation of the magazine, as the editors of *The Liberator* would soon do. If so, Oppenheim's refusal to allow this compromise becomes not, as Frank insinuated, mere stubbornness and ego but an act of principled dissent with devastating personal consequences, since he never again held a position of editorial importance and faded into obscurity even before his early death in 1932. The demise of the *Seven Arts* is poignant because it had made an impressive start at envisioning and promoting American culture not as a bunch of atomized artists and genres but as an integrated whole with a distinct character—in which poetry would play a central role. From complacent cultural-nationalist beginnings, it redefined itself in internationalist terms while mostly avoiding the common American pitfall of messianism. For six months it had withstood enormous ideological pressure to conform to an oppressive war mentality and had striven with notable success to articulate modernity's tragedy and promise.

The heady atmosphere of the early 1910s—radical labor agitation, woman's-suffrage and birth-control movements, the exhilarating effrontery of avant-garde art—germinated potent subject matter and techniques for a socially engaged American poetry. If this utopian-activist moment of the New Verse was epitomized by *Poetry*'s redefinition of the literary canon as an unstable motley of rebels violating the conventions of their day, and by *The Masses*' exuberant use of verse to advance radical perspectives on contemporary issues, the odyssey of the *Seven Arts* from cheerleading nationalist to trenchant dissenter signals a shift in the primary social role of modern poetry. In an era of conscriptive world war, officially sanctioned repression of freedoms of speech and movement, and widespread demonization of social otherness, a viable poetics of modernity would require some element of dissent to maintain credibility. But opposition does not have to mean withdrawal into "apolitical" high-modernist disillusionment. The *Seven Arts* discovered a form of dissidence that came from redoubled commitment to the struggle needed to realize its utopian ideals.

In other words, the oppositional poetics I am describing here does not mean monotonous ranting about the evils of modernity, industrialism, or capitalism. The four little magazines discussed in these chapters maintained a self-questioning mode that allowed them to accommodate many positions and expressive forms and to demonstrate that twentieth-century verse could address the urgent questions of the modern world as powerfully and thoughtfully as any literary genre. Writing in June 1917, Randolph Bourne had diagnosed the intellectuals who had capitulated to prowar pressure as being unable to cope with the "dread of intellectual suspense."[93] Bourne felt that this suspense, inherent in the national policy of neutrality, had eventually become an "object of loathing to frayed nerves" craving "certitude" above all else, leading to the collapse of American poise.[94] Such a condition of intellectual suspense seems to me integral to the experience of modernity itself. If so, then Bourne's insistence on the need to keep the intellect "supple" is perhaps the most fully realized modernist response of all.[95] For Bourne, as for Whitman and Baudelaire in 1860, for Stephen Crane and William James in 1895, and for Harriet Monroe and Floyd Dell and Alfred Kreymborg and James Oppenheim and many others at their best moments during the 1910s, the challenges of modernity required no return to bankrupt certitudes but *more modernity*—fuller acceptance of uncertainty, continual readjustment to constant change, and a skeptical, sustained belief in the possibilities of life in a modernized world.

PART II

Keys to the City

The poetic spirit has usually had a quarrel with modernity, and has turned for solace to nature or a romantic past.
—Anonymous editorial comment accompanying Chester Firkins's poem "A Cry in the Market Place" in *Current Literature* (1907)

Iron structure of the time,
Rich, in showing no pretense,
Fair, in frugalness sublime,
Emblem staunch of common sense,
Well may you smile over Gotham's vast domain,
As dawn greets your pillars with roseate flame
For future ages will proclaim
Your beauty, boldly,
Without shame.
—Sadakichi Hartmann, "To the 'Flat Iron'" (1904)

CHAPTER 6

Gutter and Skyline

The New Verse and the Metropolitan Cityscape

So far, my narrative of the New Verse movement has focused on the little magazine as the discursive innovation that catalyzed the dramatic change in American poetry's fortunes after 1912. The three remaining chapters complement this institutional history with an interpretive history, focusing on the struggle of American writers between 1910 and 1925 to fulfill the little magazines' call for a poetry of modern life by casting off long-standing generic strictures of style and subject matter and immersing their work in the industrialized metropolis. Soon after 1910, an astonishing range of poets—William Carlos Williams, T. S. Eliot, Joyce Kilmer, Amy Lowell, John Reed, Sara Teasdale, Claude McKay, to name only a few—suddenly began to produce verses about life in the modern city. Over the next fifteen years, dozens and even hundreds of individuals produced a huge archive of verse intensely engaged with the defining social forms of twentieth-century metropolitan experience.

This turn toward urban subject matter marked a decisive shift in American poetry's relationship to modernity and an epochal departure from national traditions. With the signal exception of Whitman, most literary verse in the United States throughout the nineteenth century, and most commentary upon it, had expressed powerful antipathy toward the modernization transforming the nation and the leading signifier of that process, the industrialized city. Urban and modern subjects were tolerated to some degree in departments of self-designated light verse featured in various magazines such as *Munsey's* and *The Century,* but any serious poet taking up an urban subject or setting felt great pressure to reassert a hierarchized opposition between urban and pastoral realms.[1] Sadakichi Hartmann's celebration of the brand-new Flatiron Building, appearing in an obscure self-published volume in 1904, anticipated the poems resisting knee-jerk condemnation of the city that began appearing in certain American magazines around 1905.[2] By the summer of 1912, this city poetry had become a trend sufficient to provoke the indignation of traditionalists such as René Laidlaw, who wrote to *The Century* condemning partisans of "gutter verse" for taking meretricious delight in "anything in poetry, or painting, that drags in Brooklyn Bridge, the Third Avenue Elevated, or a boxing exhibition under the Frawley Act. . . . 'How clever he is!' we say of the young poet, 'to have heard iambic pentameters in the racket of Times Square, or to have vibrated with a rhythmic beauty in the McAdoo Tube.'"[3] For Laidlaw, the outrage of "gutter verse" was exemplified by a sonnet published in *The Independent* in September 1910 that would also exercise other commentators: "The Subway (96th Street to 137th Street)" by, of all people, Joyce Kilmer.[4]

The integral connection between these new developments in verse and the visual arts is revealed in the terms of Laidlaw's objections, such as the parallel construction "anything in poetry, or painting," and the derisive epithet "gutter verse," recalling the sobriquet applied to a group of American painters working with modern urban subject matter whose February 1908 show had divided the New York art world into modern and antimodern camps as never before: the "Ashcan Artists."[5] The imputation of radical modernity to Kilmer—later singled out by the New Critics as the period's quintessential purveyor of meretriciously accessible doggerel, the antithesis of the great modern poet—reminds us that the impact of the New Verse came from its aggressive embrace of new subject matter as much as from its new styles.[6] In poetry no less than painting, realist and even sentimental approaches to urban subjects were perceived as avant-garde provocations and should be seen now not merely as resisting the transformational energies of modernism but as helping to initiate those energies.

The urgency and the difficulty of learning to represent urban modernity in verse became the theme of many American poems between 1910 and 1925. Such poems seek meaning from the city's welter of discordant material, but not by effacing anxieties over emotional dispossession and social heterogeneity. Instead they posit ironic forms of coherence built from the jagged contradictions of experience in the twentieth-century metropolis. "The City" by William Rose Benét, first published in *Munsey's* in February 1920, exemplifies this thematics of urban representation in two key emphases: on the city as the inescapable site of modern experience; and on socially charged acts of seeing as responses to this modern condition. Benét begins by announcing the twentieth-century poet's aspiration to portray the urban scene:

I went forth to sing the city, today's city—
The blank stone sphinx, the monster search-light-eyed,
The roaring mill where gods grind without pity,
The falling torrent, the many-colored tide.[7]

These goals—to capture the city's intimidating physical textures, the growing heterogeneity of its population, the moral challenges of industrial capitalism—imply a poetry that asks searching questions about class, ethnicity, gender, economics, and all the forces that form and deform modern lives. But the speaker's initial unreadiness for this task is signaled by the conventional genteel metaphor of poetry as "singing." Hampered by old expressive conventions that are now inaudible in the vast "roar" of today's city, the poet is assailed by the fragmented textures of modern experience—"tiny toils both frail and idle" and "itching needs and each small thirst and lust"—that soon have "fogged every wonder" about him. Losing the ability to wonder and decry, to hold the city's contradictions and possibilities in view, he verges upon the same blindness to modernity that had afflicted nineteenth-century American poets.

But even as they frame the speaker's poetic crisis as a failure of vision, these lines enact a crucial metaphoric shift from singing to seeing. Acknowledging that in the modern city "all misprision / Flourished and fattened," and "fear-struck" crowds move fitfully about "lashed as by a scourge," Benét's speaker is saved from total blindness by epiphanic "moments of bewildering light" that erupt unpredictably even in the midst of his distress. He envisions an ideal alternative city—no fantasy metropolis far above the street but a "strange vision" that exists incipiently within this world,

As on the instant ready to emerge,
But ever foiled—and still forever trembling
Just past the reach of mind, the urge of will.

Recasting the relation between the present flawed city and the unbuilt ideal city from opposition to immanence, these lines propose the urban scene as a locus of transformed vision. In the ensuing lines, "once again, almost against desire, / The appalling city unsealed the eyes she sealed," the speaker perceives that the very complexity and incoherence of modernity, the overwhelming "[s]um of all jaded aims and drab dissembling," make it possible to imagine an ideal city one day emerging into the actual world. In the final stanza, the poet is no longer a singer but a seer, his eyes remaining "unsealed" to the city. The importance of the shift to visuality is clinched by the last thing he sees: the eyes of its crowds, looking back, "fixed on mine forever, /

Eyes of dark pain and unfathomable will"—continual reminders of the need, and the hope, of creating that better world "unbuilded, to be builded still!" This unbroken reciprocal gaze between poetic observer and urban other challenges the scopic imperiality of so many modern acts of looking. As it portrays the modern metropolis as source of both crushing disappointment and continuing utopian possibility, Benét's poem exemplifies the struggle of many American poets during these years neither to reiterate the obsolete romanticized past nor to flee the relentless capitalist present but to seek, as Raymond Williams puts it, "a modern *future* in which community may be imagined again."[8]

Benét's poem does not fit familiar prototypes of the "modernist poem," which is one of my main points. Learning to represent the machine-age metropolis after 1910 did make American poets modern—but not all in the same way. Some adapted traditional prosodic modes to new uses, others experimented with new forms; most tried both approaches at some point in their career. Whatever avenues of stylistic experiment they take, whichever material spaces and social dynamics they portray, the city poets of the 1910s seek greater precision and particularity in their representational strategies. Their search for new modes of poetic vision suited to the metropolitan environment carries them away from the weightless abstractions and consoling platitudes of their romantic-genteel inheritance and toward questioning the aesthetic and ideological verities of class, ethnicity, and gender underlying that heritage. Collectively, these city verses build a poetics in which prohibition gives way to provocation, in which the very instability of the material environment enables new forms of individual and communal experience.

Painting the Town in Verse

As they investigated the city as a subject, poets of the 1910s found few usable resources from predecessors. Instead, as Benét's revision of his work from singing to seeing suggests, they found inspiration in the visual arts. Their poems engage the same concerns addressed by contemporaneous paintings, photographs, films, and postcards: the spatial and symbolic relationships created by urban structures, the counterpoint between the verticality of buildings and horizontality of streets, the chiaroscuro of light and shadow playing across socially charged spaces, the complex visual and social patterns created by moving masses of people and vehicles. Twentieth-century American poetry and the visual arts have been linked by some fine scholarship, but most has focused upon the influence of European cubist and abstract traditions in painting upon the work of individual canonical authors, particularly Pound,

Williams, Stevens, and Moore.[9] Instead of this approach, I emphasize poets' adaptations of the many styles for portraying modern urban space that enriched the nation's visual arts after 1890, many of them representational and broadly realist, which included the impressionism of Childe Hassam, William Merritt Chase, and many others; the socially insightful photography of Alfred Stieglitz and Lewis Hine; the Ashcan-school urbanism of John Sloan and George Bellows; the exuberant American futurism of John Marin and Joseph Stella; the machine-inspired precisionism of Georgia O'Keeffe, Charles Sheeler, and Elsie Driggs; and the expressionist-tinged social realism of Edward Hopper, Reginald Marsh, and Ben Shahn.

My emphasis on stylistic eclecticism in poetry and painting is meant to carry a good deal of polemical weight. Just as an influential strain of American-poetry scholarship equates modernism with extreme segregations of technique from subject matter and social context, a familiar hegemonic narrative of art history identifies modernism with the fracturing of realist surfaces beginning in the late nineteenth century, privileging cubism and abstraction as teleological destinations while dismissing twentieth-century representational styles as aesthetically and ideologically retrograde. The similarities between these two disciplinary formations are not coincidental: their common framing of the modernist work as radically autotelic object reflected a mid-twentieth-century desperation to fend off totalitarian attempts to reduce the arts entirely to their propaganda value. The long-term danger of this retreat from representation has been to render modernism—so it often seems—entirely irrelevant to the social and political lives of most people. In "When Was Modernism?" Raymond Williams seeks to redress this loss of social purchase by positing an alternative version of modernism initiated by social-realist fiction before 1850 and defined by its intense pursuit of new ways of "seeing"—particularly new ways of *seeing the city*.[10] Analogously, though from very different theoretical premises, Jonathan Crary argues that modern conditions of visual representation, which traditional art history has typically located in the temporal nexus between impressionism and abstraction (roughly 1870 to 1910), should actually be traced much farther back into the nineteenth century to a series of optical techniques and devices—the photograph, to be sure, but also less-remembered inventions of the 1820s such as the stereoscope and the phenakistoscope. Achieving their effects by exploiting various quirks in the human visual apparatus, these devices signaled the displacement of an Enlightenment model of vision as stable and objective, which had been exemplified mechanically by the camera obscura, by a paradigm of "subjective vision."[11] Crary calls this shift a "transformation in the nature of visuality probably more profound than the break that separates medieval imagery from Renaissance perspective."[12] No longer could reality be assumed as ever-present and stable; it now had to be sought through conscious acts of vision or constructed through the effects of style in paint or words.[13] This rupture underlay a host of disparate developments in visual art, mass culture, and optics through the later nineteenth century, including the proliferation of new artistic techniques and the search for radically individual styles—although the work of J. M. W. Turner suggests that the paradigm of subjective vision had begun to take hold well before 1850.

Perhaps Crary's boldest insight is to reject the widespread view that the drive toward modernism in the traditionally elite genre of painting represented a reaction against the emergence of photography and other optical technologies of positivist mass culture. He proposes instead that all forms of modern visual experience, artistic and technological alike, were participants in a "single social surface on which the modernization of vision had begun."[14] This argument challenges "great divide" binaries that pit avant-garde art against mass culture and allows us to recast modernism in terms of multiple intersecting spheres of cultural production, all of them inextricably and productively engaged with their times.

The ascendancy of the paradigm of subjective vision also led to one consequence not directly addressed by Crary: it intensified the drive to name and render visible the fundamental constituents of matter. To his list of transformative nineteenth-century optical instruments I would add the microscope, invented centuries earlier but attaining a new level of importance with the rise of cellular and atomic theory, modern anatomy, and sanitary engineering. Faced with a new age of nonomniscient vision, both scientists and artists went microscopic, seeking explanatory clarity at cellular, molecular, atomic, and eventually subatomic levels. This modern understanding of matter as comprised of innumerable particles, individually insignificant or imperceptible yet collectively adhering to describable structural principles, informs a host of new artistic and scientific practices throughout the nineteenth century: the conspicuous brushstrokes of Edouard Manet and the dots of Georges Seurat, the copper plates of Louis Daguerre and the hand-cranked filmstrips of the Lumières, the atomic theory of John Dalton and the quantum theory of Max Planck. This fundamental change in the understanding of human vision, and the particulate model of reality it helped to engender, also strongly inflected the material from which modern poetry was created.

The transformative technologies and styles of visual experience in the nineteenth century—the improved microscope, the camera and stereoscope, impressionist and postimpressionist painting, the cinematic apparatus—all seek to enhance human vision by revealing underlying structural components or patterns beneath fragmented or chaotic surfaces. Yet ironically, they do so only by establishing reality as something *unseeable,* demonstrating the subjectivity and incompleteness of vision by revealing objects too small, fast, or elusive to perceive with the naked eye. In the first decades of the nineteenth century, atomic theory posited invisible particles as the basis of all matter, and better microscopes confirmed that there were further levels of visual experience to explore. In the 1820s the phenakistoscope exploited the anatomical quirk of optical persistence to create the illusion of moving objects, while a decade later the stereoscope used the troubling phenomenon of binocular disparity, in which "each eye sees a slightly different image," neither of them equal to what is seen through both eyes at once.[15] Beginning in the 1850s, impressionism and subsequent styles of painting rendered objects and light in nonliteral ways that sought to capture underlying structures of material reality. In the 1870s, the sequential photography of Eadweard Muybridge revealed information about the locomotion of people and animals that cannot be seen by the eye alone. In the 1890s, the cinema, also exploiting optical persistence, captured and projected particles of light that depicted moving objects, not least the observing eye in motion, with unprecedented verisimilitude. Collectively, these vision-enhancing techniques promised, and to a great extent delivered, the elemental components of material reality and organic life to our perception. Yet as they spoke to fundamental questions of matter and energy, they reminded us that we cannot rely upon our own senses and instantiated a central paradox of modernity formulated by Georg Simmel: "[C]oming closer to things often only shows us how far away they still are from us."[16]

Something of this overarching paradox of modern visuality is evoked in the experience of the poet-figure of Benét's "The City," who can only perceive the better world he yearns for as a peripheral phantasm that vanishes when looked at directly ("ever foiled—and still forever trembling / Just past the reach of mind, the urge of will").[17] Such images address a conundrum of modern artistic creation as well: how to reduce the vast modern world to a manageable scale of individual experience. As Harriet Monroe argued in 1911, the twentieth-century artist can no longer ignore the vast world that lies outside small circuits of patronage, court, or coterie.[18] Yet at the same time, modern mass society can never be portrayed completely, not even with thousands of artists working through thousands of lifetimes. This problem is utterly unresolvable, but the unresolvability itself becomes a valuable subject for the modern artwork, especially for a genre such as poetry, in which meaning emerges through emblems and evocations rather than through logic or proof.

Many early twentieth-century cityscape verses negotiate these paradoxical grounds of their existence by focusing not only upon what is actually visible but upon things not seen yet still apprehended as present, and upon the conditions by which anything can be seen in the first place. In both cases, the position, experience, and function of the observer becomes an integral part of the visual transaction, but for the most part, the disembodied, godlike omniscience of the eighteenth-century observer gives way to acts of observation that are more local, fugitive, and contingent, in which the imperfect nature of vision is a necessary and productive element of the experience.

Acts of observation in American cityscape verse operate at both microscopic and panoramic levels. One group of poems seeks the fundamental constituents of matter and meaning on the pavement and in the gutters, focusing on things lost, overlooked, thrown away, or too minute to be seen with the naked eye. Another group examines the conditions of modern vision through sweeping views and collocations of disparate objects that evoke the city in its totality—panoramic perspectives epitomized by the metropolitan skyline. I will discuss each of these apparent extremes of visual scale in further detail, but I want to establish at the outset that poems of gutter and skyline are not mutually exclusive or even functionally opposed but complementary within an emerging poetics of urban materiality. Many poems posit some synthesis between microscopic and panoramic imagery, some discovery of each in the other. Poems of pavement and gutter, asserting that reality consists of microscopic particles and rejected objects that carry hieratic or emblematic meaning, propose that apprehending the formative particles of all matter will provide the means to see comprehensively. Such poems pursue the same imperative to the modern poet articulated in Jeanne D'Orge's "The Microscope," described in chapter 4 ("Only to look—/ To take at random slide after slide of life, / Put it under the lens"), which seeks to "observe" the external world intensely enough to reveal "section by section, the changing cells / Of one's own soul."[19] Conversely, the panoramic skyline, whether seen as painting, photograph, or actual prospect, takes form only through the collection of innumerable visual fragments: buildings, signs, street pavements, paint strokes, photographically captured patterns of light and shadow. Building their panoramic wholes from such fragments, skyline poems seldom portray individual objects in their entirety, yet they still propose to represent integrated compositional wholes.

Much as Crary argues that painting, photography, and other nineteenth-century forms of visual experience were part of a "single social surface" that transformed the conditions of seeing, both gutter and skyline poems work with dialectics of particularity and wholeness, dialectics that register the changes urban-industrial modernity had wrought upon key sociospatial relationships: between part and whole, individual person and social mass, motion and stasis, mimetic surface and underlying functional structure. Both the microscopic and panoramic perspectives in these poems foreground enhancements to human vision offered by machines such as the microscope and camera, and by new adaptations of artistic media—paint, words, film. They seek to envision the city from its most minute particulars by using several interrelated types of imagery: uncountable fragments of matter, organic and mechanical, that suggest atomic or molecular units; gaps or negative spaces charged with meaning; and visual events broken into elemental components, such as light seen in particulate form.

Crary's study stresses the oldest etymological sense of the verb *observe*, "as in observing rules, codes, regulations, and practices."[20] His observer is one who sees but "more importantly" is a Foucauldian subject who "sees within a prescribed set of possibilities, one who is embedded in a system of conventions and limitations."[21] But to account for any sociohistorical change, must we not allow observers, including artists of all sorts, some degree of nonconformist agency? Though clearly the majority observes most of the conventions and norms of any given moment, there must also be individual or group deviations, some of which may lead to sweeping alterations of prevailing disciplinary conditions. Indeed, Michael Leja has recently characterized urban experience at the turn of the twentieth century as "looking askance"—that is, learning to "process visual experiences with some measure of suspicion, caution, and guile," a process in which both "the fine arts and the larger visual culture of commercial amusements, photographic illustrations, and pictorial advertising" played an important role.[22] The earliest cityscape poems, castigated as "gutter verse" by readers who perceived their aggressive refusal to observe prevailing norms of poetic subject matter, participated in this process of skeptical looking. While I would not argue that every individual city poem between 1910 and 1925 carried progressive ideological implications, I do propose that collectively cityscape verse had transgressive and progressive effects in helping to transform American poetry's relationship to the conditions of modern experience. These verses challenged their early readers to consider whether the act of observing, at its root an act of obedience and conformity, might instead catalyze productive deviation and discontinuity—or put more affirmatively, might generate skepticism toward prevailing conditions, leading to unexpected insights and new avenues for change.

Poems of the Pavement

Orrick Johns's 1917 volume of verse, *Asphalt and Other Poems,* employs a familiar titling convention, but the reader will look in vain for a poem called "Asphalt." Johns's playful aporia defines all the poems in his volume as bits of asphalt and the asphalt of the city street as a poem. It creates a productive slippage between the textual object and the objects portrayed therein and implies the modern poet's embrace of the material world of urban modernity. Johns didn't write an asphalt poem, but several others did. Their "gutter verses"—which I mean quite differently from the disdainful detractors of the early 1910s—express the defining incoherence of modern urban life by means of a microscopic focus upon the disintegrated objects, negative spaces, and cryptic markings of the street, down to and including its particulate surfaces such as stone and asphalt. Thus in Carl Sandburg's "Broadway" (1916), the lost dreams of passersby are preserved in "the dust of . . . harsh and trampled stones," while in Maxwell Bodenheim's "Advice to a Street-Pavement" (1919), the patterns of "[l]acerated gray" and "heavy stains" on the pavement become "hieroglyphics" of the "[l]ittle episodes of roving" that comprise human existence.[23] The best-known of these early gutter verses is perhaps "Preludes" (1917, though written several years earlier), in which T. S. Eliot describes fragmented objects, surfaces, and verbal signifiers—broken chimney pots, "sawdust-trampled streets," the "grimy scraps / Of withered leaves . . . / And newspapers from vacant lots"—as the base materials, "the thousand sordid images" from which the modern "soul was constituted."[24]

For these poets writing a century ago, when the materials used to create photographic images were much more varied and tangible than they are today, the links between covering surfaces such as asphalt and the process of recording information were not wholly metaphorical. Throughout the nineteenth century, particulate materials, especially such invented composites as macadam and paving asphalt, had functioned as powerful signifiers of modernization, new forms of matter that promised access to new spaces, experiences, and forms of information. Asphalt had even figured in some of the earliest successful efforts to capture images photographically in the 1820s by Joseph Nicéphore Niepce.[25] Verses using these and other microscopic materials of the gutter define modern experience as heterogeneous and fluid. For some poets, notably Eliot in his preconversion youth, this condition of material instability means the disappearance of divine presence ("some infinitely gentle / Infinitely suffering thing") and a devastating apprehension of cosmic blankness in which "the worlds revolve like ancient women / Gathering fuel in vacant lots."[26] For others, this condition of relent-less flux implies not only fragmentation and indifference but transformation, growth, and liberation as well.

The struggle to gain understanding of the city through the fragments and negative spaces of the gutter is exemplified by a poem in *Some Imagist Poets* for 1916, John Gould Fletcher's "The Unquiet Street." Fletcher's title frames the street scene in terms of what it isn't, and his opening lines cluster together a series of negative constructions: "By day and night this street is not still"; the rumble of buses and taxicabs at all hours negates distinctions between day and night, and leaves those who live there "no time for sleep."[27] Initially such images seem to evoke the specter of modernity as Eliot's soul-nullifying rat race, a sinister inversion of the analogical-pastoral mode of genteel verse, now seen as an ominous mirage: "On rainy nights / it dully gleams / Like the cold tarnished scales of a snake: / And over it hang arc-lamps, / Blue-white death-lilies on black stems." And yet in this alienating environment, the imperfect material surface of the pavement, defined by gaps, gouges, and missing pieces ("corrugated with wheel-ruts," "dented and pockmarked"), becomes modernity's authentic emblem through its very lack of wholeness. This ironic illumination brings the poet no easy consolation or escape, but it does generate a productive dialectic between the city's material surfaces and the observing subject, as the street

> heaves its old scarred countenance
> Skyward between the buildings
> And never says a word.

The scars are not only the street's but the observer's of the street. They signify a deeper level of vision that transcends genteel hand-wringing over the city's incoherence and disintegration. Read in this microscopic sense, Fletcher's metaphors of flora and fauna become not merely symbols of a poisonous and obsolete pastoral but signifiers of modern visuality. The street-pavement, which within the old analogical mode seems a snake sym-bolizing the city's satanic power over its inhabitants, now becomes a visual trope of the snake's scales, the fantastically intricate, perhaps even beautiful, elements of a complex functional system. Likewise, the blue-white gas-lamps are no longer primarily the ghastly flora of some symbolic underworld but material sources of particulate light that defamiliarize and refresh the street scene. The materiality of the city, disorienting and even menacing, remains the only viable environment for the observing poet, who affirms his engage-ment by continuing to inhabit and observe, open-eyed and uncomplaining like the street itself.

"The Unquiet Street" tropes the street-pavement as both the object of observation and the observing "countenance." In several gutter verses of the 1910s, the street surface likewise functions in this double sense, as observing subject and documenting text, at once visual and lexical, dispassionately recording the entirety of modern experience. Typically the textuality that results from this process is silent, hidden, cryptic, or otherwise unreadable, yet it becomes meaningful through this very incomprehensibility, its hidden and missing pieces integral to its design and function. In Ridgely Torrence's "Three O'Clock" (1925), for example, the material surface of the street contains a silent but ineradicable record of the life lived in that space:

> The stones keep all their daily speech
> Buried, but can no more forget
> Than would a water-vacant beach
> The hour when it was wet.[28]

Here human experience is imagined as matter imbuing each stone of the street with some residue of every person who touched it. These stones, which function as both individual and collective objects not unlike Whitman's "grass," observe and record the life of the street much as a poetic consciousness would do. Yet they also become the textual record itself, never fully legible but still meaningful to our imperfect observational powers. Torrence's final metaphor redoubles this emphasis, comparing the speech-laden stones to bits of sand once infused with water molecules, still possessing a perceptible residue of wetness even after the water has evaporated. The constituents of both dispassionate matter and human experience are thus posited as microscopic monads that observe physical laws yet also retain some unfathomable residue, some level of meaning that is not fully encompassed or explained by those laws.

Though many poets of the period spent time poking around in gutters, the American New Verse movement featured one character positively obsessed with the ignored and discarded matter of city streets: Maxwell Bodenheim. His poems, strewn with fragmentary objects, garbage, mottled surfaces, checked patterns, and jumbled words, portray reality as fragments continually coalescing into unpredictable new shapes. These particles and fragments, laden with "hieroglyphic" meaning, become Bodenheim's governing metaphors for all human experience, which often amounts to little more than the production and inexorable dispersal of debris. Not surprisingly, at times this metaphoric framework leads him, like Eliot in *The Waste Land* a few years later, into despairing repudiation of modernity. The sonnet "City Streets" (1922), for example, bleakly updates "Ozymandias" for a modern urban environment populated by anonymous masses, seeing the "pavement and the sordid boast of stone / And brick" that lines the street as "martyred symbols" of a futile "dream of permanence for flesh and bone."[29] But since life consists of nothing but "jumbled, furtive anecdotes of lips / And limbs" that must inevitably "subside to fragments of defeat," the poet concludes that city streets are nothing but mementoes or even agents of human mortality, "waiting to disperse / With ruins the fight and plight of earthly pains."

At other times, however, Bodenheim's objects carry a hieratic significance capable of resisting the forces of class distinction and commodity fetishism that inhibit modern lives. In "Garbage Heap" (1920), new forms of matter arise from the chaotic mingling of natural and constructed objects, often within single lines ("Green weeds and tin cans").[30] These things never quite become personified in the usual literary sense, and yet they seem to pose in cryptic, evocative gestures: "brilliant labels" that "peeped from the weeds," a "bone reclined against a fence-post," a "woman's garter" that "wasted its faded frills / Upon a newspaper argument," "[t]he shipwrecked rancor of bottles and boxes." As these "disfigured complexities" of matter register in gnomic silence the indignity of their treatment in the human world, they bring the observer no self-evident or all-encompassing insight but remain intransigently *there,* uncanny and self-composed, hinting at meanings that remain always just out of reach. The uncanny vitality Bodenheim finds in fragmented objects, enigmatic in "Garbage Heap," becomes explicitly affirmative in "Street" (1928), where they offer release from sealed material surfaces that represent stifling bourgeois conformity, such as houses seen as "[r]ows of exact, streaked faces, / Each afraid to be unlike the other," and "[g]lass globes on signs and in shops" that encompass "the small souls" who own them.[31] Willing even to damage his own body in the effort ("Let me batter different shapes into you / With cracked knuckles!"), the poet relishes the idea of dashing this speciously integrated world back into its elemental constituents, a deconstruction that will generate scintillating new forms possessing authenticity and even beauty, as he imagines the glass globes shattering into "showers of falling splinters and sparks!"

Bodenheim's celebration of disintegrated materials in "Street" implicitly affirms social difference, a theme foregrounded in his most ambitious poem of the pavement, "South State Street: Chicago," from *Advice* (1920). This poem invites the reader to "[w]ander with me" through a motley panoply of "pawn-shops and burlesque theatres" that is strongly evocative of contemporaneous Ashcan school cityscapes such as John Sloan's "Election Night" (1907) or William Glackens's "Christmas Shoppers, Madison Square" (1912).[32] Bodenheim builds this sprawling social canvas out of disintegrated fragments, a "livid confetti" of discarded, variegated, or patterned objects: "violins, / Cut-glass bowls and satchels," mingled together in pawn-shop windows; a tough guy "[w]hose fingers waltz upon his checkered suit"; a woman "nibbling bits of sugar"; the "tangled dresses" of other women; pin-pointed "[t]iny lights" arrayed above a cabaret entrance; the black stubble on a vagrant's face. He animates these innumerable material fragments with phrasings evoking repeated or arpeggiated motions, tintinnabulating noises, quivering bodily sensations, and coruscating effects of light and shadow: the brawny man's waltzing fingers, the crowd's "clattering," laughs clank-ing like "softly brazen cow-bells," "[m]omentary sounds" that "crash into night" and then dissipate. This "mottled nakedness" of Bodenheim's objects and surfaces tropes the city's social motley, which is portrayed neither as appealing nor repulsive but as microcosmically containing every element of human experience—and therefore as the primary object of the modern poet's attention. The variegated scene of State Street culminates in an instant

Chicago's State Street at night, ca. 1915. Author's Collection.

of random violence—a drunken man leaping from a blazing doorway and "[s]mashing into the drab sidewalk"—but this startling appearance and immediate disappearance merely provide momentary punctuation in a spectacle that continues without finality or denouement.

If the city street is an exemplary signifier of modernization, then asphalt and other paving surfaces are exemplary modern substances. In Bodenheim's epic of State Street, the pavement tropes the poet's page and the photographer's plate, intrinsically blank material surfaces that accumulate indentations and stains, lexical pen strokes and indexical traces of objects. These traces, which Bodenheim calls "lacerated" and Fletcher "scarred," are likely far from beautiful and may even be lacerating to the observing eye—but those very qualities make them forcefully authentic signifiers of twentieth-century experience. Like Jeanne D'Orge's trope of the poet as observer of microscopic slides, William Carlos Williams's search for poetic "gold in a manure heap," and Whitman's positing of a transcendent commonality of human experience through the common atomic structure of all matter, these poems of the pavement seek to exclude nothing, to observe everything, to build a panoramic understanding of the modern world from its tiniest material fragments.[33] Exploring visual nulls and negations, imagining the stains on the pavement as hieroglyphic clues to understanding, "gutter verses" propose modern poetry as an expressive form striving to grasp the fundamental constituents of physical matter and human meaning.

City Lights and Lines

In contrast to verses of the gutter and street pavement, skyline poems seek to represent the metropolitan environment in panoramic form. Like so many photographs and paintings produced by Americans during these years, such poems are artifacts of widespread fascination with the rising skylines that had since 1890 altered the visual scale of urban experience and created dramatic new spatial arrangements, visual perspectives, and temporal measures for architects, engineers, city planners, and artists.[34] Thomas A. P. Van Leeuwen notes the widespread use during these years of a precise phrase, "the ever-changing skyline," which became a "standard code" signifying "the accumulation of the city's collective wealth" and, more broadly, a progressive narrative of modernity itself.[35] In such epochal visual works as Alfred Stieglitz's photograph "The City of Ambition" (1910) and George Bellows's painting "New York" (1911), and equally in innumerable images of material culture such as postcards and advertisements, the Manhattan skyline became a paradigmatic visual trope, a "mirror" of modern American life, as in this remark of 1914: "The skyline is confused—like America's destiny. The style is mixed—like the people on the sidewalk."[36] After 1910 these unprecedented metropolitan geometries began to shape American poetry as well. Skyline poems of that decade chart the modern city's transformation of the relationships between individual and mass, self and other, the human observer and surrounding objects. Often they work by exploring two forms of visual contrast: between the vertical thrust of individual elements and the horizontal sweep of the whole; and between images of light and shadow, especially in nighttime panoramas of lights that rendered the city's underlying structure strikingly visible.

We should not underestimate the initial difficulty writers faced in trying to alter American poetry's long-standing antipathy to the modern city. They had to teach themselves how to see the skyline, whatever other meanings they might attach to it, as primarily a *material space*. The romantic-genteel poetic tradition they had inherited not only carried a powerfully anti-urban force but imposed an observational discipline that inhibited their ability to see the city in material terms. The key literary trope in this accommodation was *analogy*, through which Bryant, Emerson, and their contemporaries detected the controlling hand of a benevolent deity in the workings of nature. This analogical poetics, which dominated American poetry from 1840 into the first decade of the new century, determined the conditions of seeing for nearly a century of American poets and poetry readers.[37] Those under its sway were unable to see objects as material facts in themselves; such objects only took on meaning and value when they could be situated into a reassuring framework of analogical meaning.

In the American poetic culture of the late nineteenth century, this poetics of dematerialized analogy functioned as an enforcer of genteel categories of social distinction.[38] The poetic cityscape would eventually become a site of resistance to this analogical mode of seeing, but overcoming its disciplining force would not happen easily or seamlessly. If soon after 1900 the Manhattan skyline was being perceived by visual artists as "among the most breathtaking of man-made wonders," in literary spheres it was still readily situated within an anti-urban analogical framework as a self-evident emblem of modernity's despoiling force.[39] Perhaps the best-known of these disciplining uses of the skyline came in 1907, just as city verses were beginning to appear in American magazines. A titanic American-born novelist, visiting his hometown after many years abroad, had looked at New York across the bay and seen an uncontrollably growing "monster" flinging its great "web" "under the sky and over the sea," becoming a "colossal set of clock-works, some steel-souled machine-room of brandished arms and hammering fists and opening and closing jaws."[40] To Henry James, fascinated and horrified, skyscrapers were "[c]rowned not only with no history, but with no credible possibility of time for history, and consecrated by no uses save the commercial at any cost."[41] The jagged line they traced across the sky was the most powerful signifier of modernity, yet this signifying power negated all it touched. My point is not simply that James's antipathy toward the skyline in *The American Scene* exemplifies the conventional anti-urbanism of turn-of-the-century elite culture, though it certainly does. Even more important are the potently regressive assumptions about social class contained within these anti-urban conditions of observation. James's conflation of body parts and mechanical parts ("brandished arms and hammering fists"), signifying the replacement of God's guiding hand by the baleful machines of Mammon, equates modernity's dehumanizing forces with the spaces occupied and the actions performed by othered working-class bodies, an equation clinched by his brilliant but chilling adjective "steel-souled."

In this context, the panoramic perspectives of skyline poems, developed gradually over a decade by a variety of American poets, represented an important modern negotiation of changing conditions of seeing. These poems resist, more or less successfully, the disciplining force of analogical poetics by asserting the act of observing not as Christian spiritual vision or romantic "spot of time" but simply as the investigation of material facts. Many find meaning in acts of imperfect or even failed seeing by rejecting analogy for metonymy, the distinctive detail or partial view that in its intensity and specificity evokes the entire integrated design of the city that can never be represented in its totality.

Not surprisingly, some poems that aspire to see the modern city anew are eventually disfigured or paralyzed by the pressure of residual anti-urban tradition. For example, in "Sunrise from the Jersey Shore" (1918) by Walter Prichard Eaton, the bifurcated form of the sonnet dramatizes the poet's ambivalence between seeing the modern city as an exciting material object of desire and as a shaming analogical sign of human hubris. Eaton's octave rhapsodizes the city's architectonic beauty in apparently wholehearted fashion:

> Across the salt-cool, restless river way,
> Manhattan stands up ragged on the sky,
> Each crag-like tower lined majestically
> Against the kindling east, each building gray
> A ruddy herald of the new-born day;
> The cañoned cross streets where the night lamps die,
> Are sun-pierced gorges to eternity;
> And high above the cloudy smoke plumes play.[42]

The array of buildings in the skyline creates a "ragged" pattern that is incipiently textual, inviting the observer to discover a hidden significance, much as Bodenheim's hieroglyphics of the pavement encode a cryptic but meaningful language. The poet's sensitivity to individual elements is suggested by the repeated use of "each," yet the scene as a whole possesses notable structural integrity. The skyline here, offering images of "eternity" while also illuminating the restless "play" of passing ephemeral moments, becomes a "herald" not only of a single sunrise but of a "new-born day," a transformed and appealing world of individual parts integrated with collective wholes.

But in the sestet, the repressive analogical tradition returns upon the observer-poet, whose enthusiasm for the metropolitan skyline is arrested by spasmodic guilt at being seduced by the city's powers. In these six lines, Eaton follows James by reducing the skyline to the signifier that negates all meanings, retreating into a conventional contrast between human constructions and those of "mightier Nature," against which the skyline seems no more than "small mounds to mimic mountain heights," mementoes of the "stubborn will" of "fretful man." Still compelled to seek an absolute form of visual understanding not subject to the disintegrated textures of the modern city—yet able to muster only the monolithic abstraction of capital-N "Nature"—the poet winds up nullifying all of the octave's relish of complexity and contradiction.

"Sunrise" is an especially revealing failure because Eaton left a prose record of the same observational experience. In a striking passage in *New York,* his illustrated celebration of metropolitan modernity published by the Grolier Club in 1915, Eaton observes the city from the New Jersey side of the Hudson, admiring the infinite variety of form and color in the skyscraper landscape:

> When the sun rises behind lower Manhattan the spectator on the River or the Jersey shore sees the cross streets as deep gulfs of molten gold, and each building, sharply outlined in the new-washed air, bears its steam plumes like salmon streamers high aloft, while every divergence of building material tells as an individual note of color. The New York atmosphere, indeed, is sharp and unpolluted . . . much of the time, and from the gray street haze and the parti-coloured pedestrians, street cars, and shop windows, up along towering walls of red and white and brown and yellow to the gay flags and the slit of blue sky, the entire panorama of the Lower Town is spread in a thousand tints, with another thousand yet of transforming shadows.[43]

The visual perspective and the observed objects here are virtually identical to those of the sonnet. But this observer, operating in a prose discursive formation no longer dominated by the disciplining function of analogical tradition, feels none of the compunction that paralyzes Eaton's poet-persona. These sentences contain within them an expansive observational paradigm for the modern urban subject: limited and incomplete in their perceptions, yet still capable of evoking a composition of structural integrity in which a sweeping panorama of water, buildings, and sky is built from microscopic fragments of matter, "parti-coloured" and thousand-tinted, infinitely divergent yet still "unpolluted," a collection of sharply outlined "individual notes" that nonetheless comprise a satisfying whole, an "entire panorama." In contrast to the horrifying social difference that James had found in the city's unending differentiation of forms and materials, this appreciation of visual difference implies an openness to the social heterogeneity of the "parti-coloured pedestrians" populating the twentieth-century metropolis. Eaton's inability to sustain in verse what he so ebulliently achieved in prose allows us to measure the residual force of inhospitable genteel conventions upon the poets of the era and to appreciate the achievement of those verses that remained open to metropolitan modernity.

One such poem comes from a writer ten years older than Harriet Monroe, Florence Earle Coates, who in "New York: A Nocturne" (published in *The Lyric Year* in 1912) compares Manhattan favorably to fabled cities of the past, seeing "[m]iraculous by night, / A city all of gold. / Here, there, and everywhere, / In myriad fashion fair, / A mystery untold / Of Light!"[44] To describe how metropolitan modernity has altered fundamental relationships of light to darkness, order to entropy, and mystery to understanding, Coates turns to particulate imagery: "Night, birth-fellow to Chaos, never wore / A robe so gemmed before." These gems are the innumerable lights that stud the nighttime skyline, a metaphor likely drawn from contemporary skyline paintings and photographs that feature what Merrill Schleier calls "the jewel-like effects of electric lighting."[45] This perception of light as a tangible material substance leads the poet to conclude that the modern skyline rivals the celestial sky in its architectonic elaboration of constellated patterns:

> The splendor streams
> In lines and jets and scintillating gleams
> From tower and spire and campanile bright.[46]

The city's jumbled and innumerable materials are at night clarified into an elegant grid of light. Yet even as the modern skyline evokes celestial spectacle, Coates contrasts it to the stately and cyclic temporality of the sky, instead portraying the modern experience of time as streaming, a condition of flux so relentless that the objects around us are constant only in changing every time we look at them. Unlike William Chapman Sharpe, who sees the poet's

The luminary geometry of New York City from the Woolworth Building. From *Above the Clouds and Old New York,* Woolworth Building Visitors' Brochure, 1913. Author's Collection.

perspective as "Olympian," "literally superior, in a god's position" to the skyline vision she describes, I take the poem to be gripped by a dynamic of revelation and mystery that acknowledges that the city's spaces can never be fully visible or utterable.[47] And yet in this atmosphere of gemlike splendor, the lack of full comprehensibility reinforces the sense that all previous limits to human progress are suspended in a world of modern artificial light.

"New York: A Nocturne" acknowledges an ongoing tension between the skyline's aesthetic and social meanings, conceding that the apprehension of the modern city's "splendor" requires that its "squalor" be "hid from sight."[48] By opposing the transfiguring splendor of the city lights not only to squalor but also to "opulence," however, the poem does reject the conventional genteel binary of modern ugliness affronting timeless beauty and seeks instead a new form of splendor based not on decorative appeal but on a bracing vision of the city as a site of transience, change, and challenge. Such strategies signal the emergence of what Harriet Monroe in an early *Poetry* editorial termed the "New Beauty": an aesthetic of modernity rejecting the Victorian values of comfort, decoration, luxuriance, and familiarity, and embracing instead qualities that the night skyline offered in abundance: precision, complexity, integration of form and function, continual change, and infinite particularity.[49]

Giving up the ungrounded omniscience of the romantic poetic consciousness meant redefining vision as relative and unstable, foregrounding the observer's relation to observed objects. When those objects were other people, particularly those marked by class or ethnic difference, the central question posed by skyline poems—how fragmented constituents form integrated wholes—took on greater social urgency. With the exception of Whitman, most American poets from Bryant onward had participated in a form of observational discipline in which the poetic consciousness, seeking God's perfect ability to be everywhere and see everything at once, judges other people, particularly those marked by social otherness, as they imagine God might do. The result was a poetics of distinction and exclusion that enforced the social prejudices and presumptions of the Anglo-American bourgeois male as those of God Himself. By adopting panoramic yet non-omniscient perspectives, skyline poems of the 1910s refuse those corrosive distinctions and reopen American verse to the exploration of social difference. Laura Benét's "Gardens of Babylon" (*The Masses,* March 1914), refreshing the hackneyed antimodern metaphor of the city as wicked Babylon, illustrates poetry's renewing power to explore class relationships through objects charged with social meaning. In the first two stanzas Benét occupies a distant observational perspective from which a jumble of differently angled chimneys and roofs comprise a miniaturized skyline metonymically representing the whole city:

> Huddled chimneys grey, forlorn,
> In the deadened light of a city morn,
> Roof tops ranging, red and high,
> Tenement windows glaring, dry.[50]

In these lines the observer is everywhere and nowhere, not quite omniscient but not clearly grounded in the scene, a perspective perhaps approximating that of the well-meaning middle-class social worker—which the poet was during the 1910s.

But as she describes the "[g]aily caparisoned flower pots" arrayed on tenement fire escapes as a modern "hanging gardens" "[n]odding against the sky," Benét aligns her observer with the perspectives of those who actually live in the scene:

> Vines spring up in a single night,
> Old faces soften, children stare
> At the slender gardens in the air.

The multiplicity and heterogeneity of these flower pots become affirmative signifiers of social difference, like the "thousand-tinted" skyline of Eaton's *New York.* Benét takes the further step of imagining multiple individual acts of observation, each with its own validity, which create the meaning of this communal event. To share, even tentatively and momentarily, the perspectives of the old people and children who live in the tenement district, to see the "gardens" as they see them, represents something of a breakthrough for skyline poetry, demonstrating that the poetic observer need not be the Olympian judge scrutinizing all others as God might do while remaining inaccessible him- or herself.

The modest but real achievement of such a poem can be measured by examining others that try but fail to achieve similar goals. In "Lunchtime along Broadway" (1920), Laura's brother Stephen Vincent Benét, the youngest of the three sibling poets, uses panoramic skyline imagery to represent the urban phenomenon of masses in urgent motion but cannot finally shed a corrosive judgmental gaze upon the objects of his observation. He begins promisingly with geometrical imagery of objects arrayed in series multiplied almost to infinity:

> Twelve-thirty bells from a thousand clocks, the typewriter tacks
>   and stops,
> Gorged elevators slam and fall through the floors like water-
>   drops
> From offices hung like sea-gulls' nests on a cliff the whirlwinds
>   beat.[51]

The falling elevators imagined as water-drops, the thousand bells chiming simultaneously, the microscopic particularity of thousands of typewriter strokes in offices arrayed all across the city skyline—this powerfully visual imagery prefigures the unforgettable descent from elevated office to terrestrial streets with which Hart Crane would begin *The Bridge* a decade later. Benét then accelerates into a vivid montage of various lunchgoing venues ("white-tiled caves," "subterranean holes," "restaurants where lily-voiced women feast") that draws from the cinema's metonymic ability to portray events in many characteristic spaces simultaneously. But at the moment when human bodies are first seen in the poem, he loses this intensely visual focus and lapses into an incongruous, obsolete image system, allegorizing the roiling mass of hungry office workers to an "octopus-crowd" whose greedy "tentacles crawl for meat." His development of this unprepossessing analogy is cold and scattershot, comparing those under his gaze to various beasts of land, sea, and air: octopus, wasps, bees, cats, and a prehuman "feeding brute as he pads by the cooking-fires." Despite the poem's innovative experiments in perspective, its observational consciousness remains firmly rooted in the speaker's own revulsion, and consequently it fails to say much about the scene of urban modernity except that masses of rushing, ravenous people are pretty unattractive.

Though it cannot finally save Benét's poem, the movie camera, with its capacity to portray simultaneous multiple perspectives, provides other poets of the 1910s a powerful observational model for exploring the structural relationships undergirding the vast space of the metropolis. In Edith Wyatt's "To a City Swallow" (1912), a constantly moving bird's-eye perspective represents the multifarious life of the modern city, "the myriad souls' abode and the roads of my trading town." Once an emblem of timeless and placeless natural beauty (evoking "the ways of the jasmine far"), the swallow has now adapted to urban life, making it a fitting symbol of time-bound urban realism ("the hours that are") and a symbol of the poet's own emerging commitment to "the housetop sea" of the metropolis.[52] Tracing the bird's swooping and soaring movements, the poem traverses the city in dynamic dactyls, balancing panoramic and microscopic imagery, outlining the abstract geometry of the skyline, but also dipping low enough to mark particular human interactions:

> Up from the South, swallow, fly to the North, over the roof-top
>   miles,
> The pillaring stacks and the steam-cloud racks and the telegraph's
>   argent files,
> Rich man's and poor man's and beggar man's town, odors of pine
>   and pitch,
> Marbles and chalk on the hop-scotch walk, and racketing rail
>   and switch,
> Over a thousand close-housed streets with a million steps arow,
> Where the nurses walk and the children talk and the light-
>   gowned women go.

Wyatt ends by imagining the swallow flying "afar, afar" over the "roof-top sea" of a distant city, reaching another woman who will look out and say, as she herself had done, "A swallow flies in my city skies and cries of the city May!" As her swallow evokes Whitman's emphasis on the shared physical experiences of urban life, Wyatt adapts nineteenth-century transcendentalism to a utopian modernity in which new technologies of communication and transportation, and new strategies for representing social intercourse and physical motion, might bridge the social and spatial boundaries dividing individuals and groups from one another.

Wyatt's balancing of the cityscape's abstract visual patterns with the material traces of urban lives implies an openness to social heterogeneity, but still her poem represents only a few relatively classless individuals rather than considering class as a defining social category. Other verses of the period explicitly map observer and cityscape onto class space, demonstrating American poetry's renewed ability to explore problematic social dynamics, even if the process is seldom easy or the results cheering. In "Morning at the Window" (1916), T. S. Eliot experiments with visual perspective to evoke a hypostatization of social class entering a chronic stage. Although Eliot hardly epitomizes cross-class empathy among twentieth-century poets, "Morning at the Window," like much of his early verse, exhibits a productive tension between disdain and yearning for class otherness. His speaker, gazing from an upstairs window, hears the distant rattling of breakfast plates in basement kitchens and senses "the damp souls of housemaids / Sprouting despondently" at the gates below.[53] Despite this patronizing description, Eliot's observer is notably sensitive to these nearly stifled sounds and invisible movements, perhaps because he himself is equally confined, the lonely figure at an upstairs window made emblematic of modern city life by "Prufrock" and later by Edward Hopper's tableaux of metropolitan isolation. He seems to yearn for release from this frozen posture, for contact with the "twisted faces from the bottom of the street," but remains immobilized in his tower, unwilling to relinquish his bourgeois redoubt. "[B]rown waves of fog" convey light and images up to him, but only in distorted and disintegrated forms, notably an "aimless smile" torn from a female passerby whose freedom of movement he seems to envy. From her perspective on the street, the speaker would appear a statuesque shape framed and monumentalized into an element of the skyline—the Olympian omniscient observer reduced to madman in the attic. Thus her smile, which "hovers in the air / And vanishes along the level of the roofs," wafts through Eliot's city detached from human agency and meaning, a wistful sign of undesirable but insurmountable class disconnection. Appropriately, the poem ends without resolution. The speaker in his vertical tower will continue to gaze upon the morning street; the smiling woman will continue to pass horizontally; they'll never intersect.

Shadow Skylines

Wyatt's soaring swallow and Eliot's immobilized speaker represent limit cases of cityscape verse. The former expands the mobility and agency of the observer by linking her to the free-flying bird, and implicitly to the cinematic camera-eye, in order to envision a transcendent modernity without boundaries. The latter doubts that any such transcendence is possible, but in its compositional precision and its critique of the Olympian observer, it reveals a complex engagement with its dystopian urban environment. Both these portrayals, utopian and dystopian, are valid, even necessary responses to metropolitan modernity, but neither tells the full story of the New Poetry and the cityscape. The most characteristic poems fall between them on the tonal spectrum, shadowed by incoherence and antagonism, highlighting contradictions and disruptions of closure, enacting contingent or incomplete acts of observation that nonetheless vividly express the character of modern experience.

One of the best-known treatments of urban modernity's shadowy revelations of social difference is Claude McKay's sonnet "The White City," from *Harlem Shadows* (1922). William J. Maxwell notes that McKay echoes Wordsworth's "Composed upon Westminster Bridge" (1802), which for a century had served as a nostalgic parable of the preindustrial city ruined by modernity.[54] But McKay's title and imagery evoke another frame of reference as well: the utopian strain of American urbanism that inspired Whitman's celebrations of the city such as "Crossing Brooklyn Ferry" and the architectural fantasia of the Columbian Exposition in Chicago in 1893–94. The official Exposition, of course, was popularly called the "White City" due to its uniformly gleaming white surfaces and neoclassical detailing. McKay's usage forcefully reminds us of another significance of "White City," phrase and symbol: a homogenized conception of national cultural value defined by its denial of color.

As for Whitman's vision of "the mighty city," McKay admits that

> [t]he strident trains that speed the goaded mass,
> The poles and spires and towers vapor-kissed,
> The fortressed port through which the great ships pass,

are "sweet like wanton loves" to him.[55] But for the racial other, acts of observing the city become expressions not only of love but of disobedience, refusing to observe the disciplining convention that prohibits blacks from looking into the eyes of whites. Such an observer sees the city "through a mist" that shadows the phenomena that majorities perceive as normal and transparent. And yet such a veil of otherness can illuminate as well as obscure, and this outsider sees "the white city" as no insider ever could, defined not by commonalities of experience or sympathy but by the enmity of "the white world's hell," which becomes the "muse" that feeds him "vital blood." The bond between this man of color and the white city is thus one of inversion, the defiant negative to Whitman's hopeful picture of urban modernity. Yet the speaker's triumph is to keep the searing knowledge of that structural inversion from destroying his sense of self-worth. Maxwell and

Cary Nelson have noted the powerful political charge carried by McKay's traditional forms, particularly the sonnet.[56] Here, as the poet speaks his mind in the language of a culture that would silence him, his use of the sonnet—symmetrical, rigidly formalized, reaching back through four centuries—gives tangible form to his refusal to "bend an inch," his resolution to look the white city and its literary tradition straight in the eye.

The trope of inversion that structures "The White City" also shapes another group of cityscape verses that address the depersonalizing scale of modern mass society by observing not the skyline directly but its shadowy inverse: the shifting patterns of light and shade that the overbuilt metropolis traces on the ground. One might imagine light and shadow as artistic rather than social issues, but as early as 1900 the shadows cast by tall buildings were perceived as a serious socioeconomic problem in New York and other large cities.[57] The campaign for height restrictions and setback requirements, which in New York produced the landmark zoning restrictions of 1916, were driven primarily by economic concerns over the potentially catastrophic effects of new buildings upon nearby properties deprived of direct sunlight and fresh air, which could become virtually unrentable overnight, as Keith Revell notes.[58] Almost two decades of debate over this issue culminated in the furor over the infamous Equitable Building on lower Broadway, which was originally planned to occupy virtually its entire lot and rise 909 feet straight up, while still complying with existing building codes.[59] The final design by Ernest R. Graham reduced the Equitable to 542 feet, but when completed in 1915 it still occupied virtually its entire one-acre lot all the way to the top. A monolith "casting a noonday shadow four blocks long and six times its own size," the Equitable inflicted what Rem Koolhaas calls "grim deterioration—both financial and environmental" on adjoining spaces.[60] Koolhaas describes the result in terms of a radical bifurcation between the good life lived inside and the hyperalienating environment just outside: "Its lobby is a sybaritic arcade lined with social facilities such as shops, bars, etc. The surrounding streets are deserted."[61] It is striking to hear this description, depressingly familiar from the post-1945 discourse on urban decline, suburbanization, and gentrification, applied to the very moment of the vertical city's greatest cultural prestige and economic dynamism.

Often the economic issues raised by the skyline were transposed into aesthetic, medical, and ethical registers, as the looming shadows of tall buildings signified not only an absence of sunlight and air but the presence of toxic matter. As early as the 1890s, critics of the skyward trend had argued that concentrations of tall buildings prevented "the dissipation of noxious effluvia," which, if trapped in inhabited space, would produce "endemic disease

The Equitable Building, lower Broadway, 1910s. Author's collection.

and a high death rate."[62] In 1913, during the Manhattan zoning debates, a Harvard professor of sanitary engineering, George Whipple, measured dust at various levels of New York skyscrapers, finding that air near the ground contained eight to ten times more particles than the air at the top.[63] The following year, in a piece entitled "Restraining the Overambitious Skyscraper," C. P. Cushing drew a sharp distinction between the visual "poetry" of the skyline seen from a distance and the actual life lived in its shadows.[64] Cushing baldly entitled one section of his essay "The Skyscraper as a Menace," arguing that unregulated construction had made city streets into "cheerless cañonlike" spaces in which the tall building, like some voracious capitalist buccaneer, "rob[bed] its neighbors of light and air."[65]

Filtering through into poetry, the well-intentioned critiques of public-health officials might seem to reinforce the problematic homology of spaces and classes made by Henry James, in which those forced to live in the dark spaces and bad air created by the skyline are portrayed as invisible or inhuman. But some poems of the 1910s work hard to challenge that equation, scrutinizing the spatial politics of the metropolis by portraying patterns of light and shade as seen by those living amongst densely juxtaposed structures. Maxwell Bodenheim's "The Rear Porches of an Apartment Building" (*Others,* September 1915) explores abject spaces that have "never known sun, moon, or stars."[66] But unlike, say, the awesome depopulated blankness of Paul Strand's 1924 photograph "The Court, New York," Bodenheim's poem emphasizes human activity and incipient solidarity. His observer contemplates people on the porches of different floors of the same building caught in vivid yet stubbornly ambiguous gestures. The "lavender-white eyes" of a servant girl are no longer alive, yet she still wistfully sings "of pear-trees in the sun"; two old women "[w]hose faces have the color of brown earth that has never felt rain" knit patriotic decorations and "nibble cakes"; children play a curious game of "gravely kissing each other's foreheads." From across the way, the observer sees them all at once, but they can't see those above or below. This distinctive spatial arrangement of observer and objects tropes the fear that as the city's buildings grow higher, its tenements denser, its green spaces fewer and farther between, people's ability to connect with others, even those living right next to them, may diminish to nothing.

Bodenheim's composition may owe something to George Bellows's classic Ashcan canvas "The Cliff Dwellers" (1913), which likewise depicts people on different floors of crowded multistory tenements. But Bellows's sprawling cityscape offers an integrated plenitude of experience, as many of his figures lean out of their windows, palpably engaged with the heterogeneous life of the street below. If not altogether effacing distinctions of class, the painting renders them relatively innocent. In tone, Bodenheim's cityscape falls somewhere between the darkness of Strand's and the vivacity of Bellows's, but it certainly denies readers the comfort of imagining that people living in the rear porches are unaffected by arrangements of urban space. Although Bodenheim's human figures are by no means the robotic masses flowing over London Bridge in *The Waste Land,* the prognosis for their emotional lives can't be too hopeful in the perpetual gloom of rear porches where

> [t]he death of the afternoon to them
> Is but the lengthening of blue-black shadows on brick walls.

Like Eliot's confined speaker in "Morning at the Window," they have been deprived of the ability to observe those near to them, and more broadly to gather the city's fragments into integrated understanding. That synthesizing effort, the ability to inhabit multiple perspectives and imagine alternative subject positions, falls to the observing poet, a responsibility that Bodenheim carries out with unsentimental empathy.

A few years later, Louis Untermeyer's "Playground" (1923) again uses constantly shifting patterns of light and shade to portray the lives of city children as paradigmatic of modern experience. In this poem, a snake-like "length of sunlight" uncoils through a particular patch of the skyscraper city until a certain "corner boils with brilliance," and

> [s]hop-windows and a crowd of children raise
> Their loud hosannahs like a victory
> Of blazing banners.[67]

Every element of this environment—chimneys, sparrows, an "old, moth-eaten tree," the "tall / forbidding spires" of the parish church, even the "stone clouds" themselves—is transformed by this sudden illumination into something fully alive. But the spatial configuration that permits the sun to burst through the concrete canyons will cause it to disappear just as suddenly, and as light reaches the playground where a group of "parish girls" has just arrived, its "dancing benison" is halted by "hard, unyielding black," personified by two impossibly grave nuns who twirl a jump rope "with lifeless eyes / And frigid regularity." The girls jumping rope, denied the sun by the alienating urban environment and importuned by the "deepening rhythm" of parochial submission, are incipient observers but also the objects of a potent disciplinary regime. They are being taught to observe merely in the sense of obeying imposed precepts rather than learning to see skeptically, to ask why they must live in spaces where the sun only shines for a few moments a day.

Bodenheim and Untermeyer both use the shadow skyline to suggest that life in the modern city is an ongoing process of emotional desiccation promoted by the harsh physical environment and by the exploitative social dynamics that define it. In "Pastoral" (*Others*, December 1916), William Carlos Williams composes observer and skyline into an ingenious examination of the fraught relation between these class dynamics and the social function of the twentieth-century artist. This poem's observer strolls

> back streets
> admiring the houses
> of the very poor:
> roof out of line with sides,
> the yards cluttered
> with old chicken wire, ashes,
> furniture gone wrong.[68]

The jagged horizontal arrays of backyard debris and jerry-built structures evoke the visual drama of the city skyline in miniature. This miniaturizing conceit intertwines two modes of inversion, of visual scale and social status: the most monumental constructions of the capitalist metropolis are represented by its tiniest fragments, its pinnacles of worldly achievement by the shreds and patches of an imaginatively deprived populace. Despite the strongly composed quality of its imagery, however, the poem is no mere experiment in abstraction but an intense exploration of observer-object relations in an environment defined by vast class inequity. Williams's observer takes an aggressively active role, identifying himself with the abject traces of this populace. No longer afflicted by the youthful urge to "make something" of himself in the city of ambition, he now feels free to admire these scenes for their striking juxtaposition of shapes, forms, and hues, especially a weathered bluish-green that "pleases" him "best of all colors." Despite this aestheticizing impulse, Williams invests powerful meaning into the detritus of disoriented and even desperate lives whose improvised recycling of old junk into new structures ("fences and outhouses / built of barrel-staves / and parts of boxes") expresses the obdurate desire to "make something" *for* themselves. At the poem's end, he predicts grimly that "[n]o one / will believe this / of vast import to the nation." But he has discovered a powerful new function for the modern poet: to see past the disciplining ideological frame that equates the ostensibly deficient taste of the poor with their lack of character or worth to reveal a complex ingenuity and significance beneath the seemingly chaotic surfaces of their creations.

A final variant on the observer-object dynamic operative in nearly all skyline verses takes us back toward the poems of the pavement with which I began this chapter, but with a key difference. If the skyline is the jagged horizontal pattern formed by densely spaced tall buildings as seen from a panoramic perspective, then we can use the term *groundline* to refer to the patterns of lines, buildings, figures, lights, and shadows on the street as seen from an elevated prospect. The observers in groundline poems look down at the streets much as one looks into a microscope, probing beneath concealing surfaces to discern individual elements and the whole they comprise. This attempt to balance extremes of visual scale proved a particular challenge for poets, especially when coupled with the godlike implications of an elevated panoptical perspective in which observed individuals are reduced to tiny insectlike figures. One of the earliest twentieth-century attempts at a groundline poem, James Oppenheim's "New York, from a Skyscraper" (*American Magazine*, January 1909), begins promisingly by attending to the city's material structures, describing a "[p]lateau of roofs by canyons crossed: windows by thousands fire-unfurled."[69] But when the observer begins to enumerate "each strange type" who is "[w]alking your Night's many-nationed byways," the poet's focus blurs from sharply etched materiality into pedestrian social typology, and he retreats toward the seductive stance of godlike omniscience, seeing everything and nothing, radiating impersonal sympathy toward everyone in the abstract and no one in particular. More effective is Armond Carroll's "From a City Street" (*The Lyric Year*, 1912), which foregrounds the uncanny aspects of the groundline perspective by describing gargoyle-observers that perch on the "crags which high uplift / Their steel-knit skeletons" above "the surfs that surge and shift."[70] These "harpies of our modern time" are observers who both "mock the futile restless waves / That surge in great affair below" and "hail to wide oblivious graves / The victims of the undertow." Through their simultaneous mocking and hailing, Carroll implies that a society gets the imaginative icons it deserves. These harpies, grotesque and derisive, are faithful emblems of the depredatory culture that has constructed the crags they inhabit, and thus their mocking is appropriate commemoration for its victims.

The poet for whom the groundline perspective proved most productive was Carl Sandburg, who in two poems from *Smoke and Steel* (1920), "Hats" and "People Who Must," uses it to articulate a poetics for mass urban society, problematizing and affirming the observer-artist's role. If McKay's primary frame of reference in "The White City" is the nation's racial divide, Sandburg's is an inhospitable urban condition defined by sociomaterial categories, class in particular, so vast and diffuse that they daunt comprehension. Yet he resists the troubling idea that modernity accommodates only the disciplined observer who watches passively within accepted ideological frameworks. The observers in both these works survey the city from rooftop perches, but rather than just gazing upon the visual drama of the skyline, they focus on the groundline, pondering what relationship they might have with the microscopic creatures below. In "Hats," the speaker perched "[o]n the rim of a skyscraper's forehead" can see nothing but an abstract pattern of "fifty thousand hats."[71] At such a distance, this perception of humans as indistinguishable particles of matter carries an alienating force, and the poem ends abruptly with another unanswered plea, this one resonating with bleak irony: "Hats: tell me your high hopes." These hats do speak, but only to remind the speaker of his distance from the anonymous bodies underneath. As mass-produced objects effacing individuality past a certain distance, they both hide and hint at a bitter truth of the American social ethos. Still, Sandburg has reason to hope that the poem might yield the reader something more productive than the hats yield the observer: heightened awareness of national ideologies of individual success which flatten out Americans' multifarious experiences and aspirations into a single mass-produced model, the derby-clad man of business.

In "People Who Must," Sandburg's focus upon the groundline produces a particularly thoughtful meditation on the difficulty of observing and representing class dynamics in the skyscraper city. Here is the poem in full:

> I painted on the roof of a skyscraper.
> I painted a long while and called it a day's work.
> The people on a corner swarmed and the traffic cop's whistle
>   never let up all afternoon.
> They were the same as bugs, many bugs on their way—
> Those people on the go or at a standstill;
> And the traffic cop a spot of blue, a splinter of brass,
> Where the black tides ran around him
> And he kept the street. I painted a long while
> And called it a day's work.[72]

Sandburg foregrounds the question of this observer's class status yet leaves it intractably ambiguous: is he a workman painting part of the building, or an artist painting a canvas? This central indeterminacy undergirds the poem's meditation on the role of the arts in atomized mass society. The painter-as-artist observes swarming masses in ant-black, counterpointed by a single traffic cop, "a spot of blue, a splinter of brass, / Where the black tides ran around him." Abstracting a complex cityscape into a simple, striking pattern of color, form, and motion, Sandburg acknowledges the influence of modern painting and photography upon poets seeking to represent the city. Yet as in visual texts, abstraction can become merely a means of disconnection, and Sandburg evokes that anxiety by using, as in "Hats," verbatim repetition to end the poem.

The uncertain achievement of the painter-as-artist flatters the honest day's labor done by the painter-as-workman, and indeed this blurring of class distinctions between worker and artist was one of Sandburg's foremost goals as a writer. But it doesn't ease the poet's anxiety over a modern city that places artists at this unfathomable remove from audiences. Nor is this anxiety relieved by the unstable connotations of the title, which may sound initially as a cheerleading slogan for modern achievers "on the go" but soon takes on darker notes of economic determinism: the people swarm through the city because they must, the cop directs traffic because he must, the painter-as-workman must do a day's work to get by. All are products of the swarm, the forces of modernity that move them in ways that they can't control or understand. The observing painter-as-artist also *must* create, in the hoariest cliché of the psychology of creativity. But this imperative remains disconnected from the artist's actual insight into his materials, and Sandburg fears that he's just putting in time and "call[ing] it a day's work"—another phrase that turns worryingly ambiguous when pressed.

The only figure resisting this swarming motion is the traffic cop, no more than a microscopic "spot" of color, a "splinter" of light nearly overwhelmed by the panoramic tides of black surrounding him. And yet the cop "keeps the street," conducting the traffic and giving visual integrity to the artist's composition. Sandburg thus proposes that his four intermingled observing personae—cop, building painter, artist, and speaker—inhabit the street not only because they must, but because they can. Persevering against the pressures of capitalist modernity, balancing individual with collective, will with obligation, these fellow workers in the city suggest that the struggle to represent the ambivalent life of the skyline city has proved productive for Sandburg despite its dark revelations. If the roofbound speaker remains worried over the artist's place in twentieth-century mass society, the groundline poet achieves a measure of control over these anxieties without dishonestly shrugging them away. As Bodenheim in "The Rear Porches," Wyatt in "To a City Swallow," and McKay in "The White City" all resolve to do in different ways—and as Eliot perhaps despairs of doing—Sandburg remains a modern worker in the city, striving to observe in an active sense, recording and commemorating everything, his eyes wide open to his twentieth-century world.

CHAPTER 7

Footprints of the Twentieth Century

American Skyscrapers, Modern Poems

The most potent icons of modernity in the early twentieth-century city were great buildings, structures of unprecedented scale and grandeur that punctuated the skyline and symbolized the metropolitan ethos. Unlike the grandest structures of the Gilded Age, which were mainly private houses for the super-rich, the iconic buildings after 1900 were venues for business, transport, or amusement—public not necessarily in ownership but in function and spatial accessibility, designed to accommodate a large number and variety of occupants, both permanent and transient. Twentieth-century analogues to the small-town churches and schoolhouses around which the lives of most Americans had once revolved, these great structures served citydwellers as clocks and compass-needles, as gathering places and repositories of civic pride.[1] Housing every sort of interaction from the ruthlessly commercial to the frivolously recreational, carrying a vast range of symbolic meanings, skyscrapers and other great buildings laid forceful claim on anyone seeking to represent urban modernity: painters, photographers, sculptors, commercial artists; manufacturers of postcards, souvenirs, toys, every imaginable genre of material culture—and the many Americans who began writing city poems in the early 1910s.[2]

Challenging the Skies

No less than visual artists, American poets of the 1910s were fascinated with several types of modern great building—railroad station, department store, hotel, theater, sports arena—but most of all with the skyscraper office tower, which for more than a century has been the most spectacular visual symbol of urban modernity. Between 1885 and 1910, during the childhood, adolescence, and young adulthood of the Americans who created the New

Verse, a breathtaking acceleration in building height transformed the visual scale of metropolitan life from street level to hundreds of feet in the air. The tallest structure in Manhattan for many decades was the 284-foot spire of Trinity Church (built 1846) on lower Broadway, whose primacy had once asserted "the material claim of the church on the territory between Earth and Heaven," as Thomas van Leeuwen puts it.[3] But by 1890, Trinity had begun to function as a "mere yardstick for any new skyscraper that was thought fit to carry the name."[4] The economic imperative that one commentator in 1902 called "the capitalization of the air" had come to dominate the most desirable commercial areas, such as lower Manhattan and the Chicago Loop, in which rents were "prohibitive" and the purchase of land "impossible."[5] The combination of two breakthrough technologies—steel-frame construction made practical by the falling cost and rising quality control of steel, and the high-speed electric elevator—brought the era of the all-masonry skyscraper to an end in 1893 with the completion of the massive Monadnock Building in Chicago, which rose only 197 feet. Successful early experiments such as the nine-story Home Life Insurance Company Building in Chicago (William LeBaron Jenney, 1884) and the ten-story Wainwright Building in St. Louis (Louis Sullivan, 1890–91) had shown that the steel-frame tower could look good, inspire public wonderment, and make its owners money.[6]

After 1890, the residents of larger American cities observed with wonder as voracious buildings colonized their airspace. The world's tallest inhabited structure in 1900, the Park Row Building in lower Manhattan (R. H. Robertson, 1899), rose 383 feet (thirty stories), while the most distinctive building in the artistic landscape of New York City before 1905, the Fuller Building, better known as the Flatiron (D. H. Burnham Co.), was completed in 1902 at twenty-one stories, just under three hundred feet high.[7] The dimensions of these pre-1905 skyscrapers sound paltry by later standards, but the drive to the skies was irrevocably under way. This first major phase of skyscraper construction culminated with three lower-Manhattan behemoths, each in succession the tallest building in the world, which became magnetic icons of the city for writers, painters, and photographers: the Singer Tower (612 feet, Ernest Flagg; completed 1908, demolished 1967), the Metropolitan Life Tower (700 feet, Napoleon LeBrun and Sons; 1909), and the Woolworth Building (792 feet, Cass Gilbert; 1913). In this decade before 1914, as new buildings were shooting up hundreds of feet higher than existing ones, commentators foresaw cities densely packed with towers a thousand, or even two thousand, feet high.[8] As it turned out, these heaven-storming years marked the zenith of people's belief in modernity as boundless progress and growth. Because of the more height-restrictive zoning laws of the mid-1910s and the economic constrictions brought about by the war, the Singer, Metropolitan, and Woolworth towers would remain the three tallest inhabited buildings in the world until after 1920, and the seven-hundred-foot mark would not be eclipsed again until 1930.[9]

Virtually everyone who approached Manhattan from the south or west during the later twentieth century remembers, now painfully, seeing the bland but unmistakable twin towers of the World Trade Center as the first visible signs of the city. A century ago, the very tallest buildings were even more prominent signifiers of the metropolis, visible from nearly every prospect. Until 1930, the Singer, Metropolitan, and Woolworth towers dwarfed surrounding buildings by several hundred feet and thus "command[ed] an uninterrupted view of New York, with no other skyscraper obstructing the vision in any direction," as was said of the Metropolitan in 1909.[10]

The Woolworth's publicists claimed that a clear view from the top extended for twenty-five miles in every direction and noted (like their colleagues down Broadway at the Singer) that their tower when illuminated could be seen from forty miles out in the open sea.[11] An early booklet for the observation deck on the fiftieth floor of the Metropolitan Tower claimed plausibly that from there one could see "the homes of over one-sixteenth of the entire population of the United States."[12] The reverse must also have been true: millions of people would have seen the Metropolitan, Singer, and Woolworth nearly every day of their lives.

Commanding this degree of visual prominence, the early twentieth-century skyscraper carried tremendous, if profoundly paradoxical, signifying power. Soaring into the heavens, taking up whole city blocks, housing many thousands of people, it was understood as an exhilarating emblem of modernity, "the footprint of the twentieth century," as *Munsey's* remarked in 1899.[13] Its herculean scale was matched by its complexity as a technological, social, and economic system, which required precise mastery of "thousands of intricate details" by planners and engineers.[14] The fascination of machine-age Americans with the qualities of visual intricacy and structural accessibility, described by Cecilia Tichi in *Shifting Gears,* was gratified by the cunning stylings of such creations as Cass Gilbert's Woolworth Building, admired by the architectural critic Montgomery Schuyler for allowing people hundreds of feet below satisfying visual access to the detailing of the uppermost floors in all its "distinctness and sharpness."[15] In 1911, Edgar Forbes estimated this combination of enormity and intricacy to be "the most marvelous thing about a tall building"—"that it has been made in millions of pieces in different parts of the world and yet, when the pieces are brought together, they all fit!"[16]

The skyline of lower Manhattan, ca. 1914. Woolworth Building, left foreground; Park Row Building, left center; Hudson Terminal Building, right center; Singer Tower, far right. Author's collection.

But even as the skyscraper's synthesis of enormity, intricacy, accessibility, and coherence was read as a triumph of modern system building, its rampant verticality challenged Enlightenment models of rationally planned cities built in low-rise radial shapes, dominated by single-use properties, providing healthful but convenient boundaries between work and home environments. The powerful if nostalgic appeal of these horizontal models of urban space was signaled by the popularity during those years of the Garden City and the City Beautiful movements, but in economic terms neither of these could compete against the vertical-skyscraper model, in which the clamor of the streets was kept at bay by technologically advanced towers of modular design and theoretically unlimited size, so fully meeting their inhabitants' needs that leaving them might prove altogether unnecessary.[17] What future was augured by the fact that "a man might live in a modern skyscraper year in and year out, luxuriously, too, with every want richly supplied, and never pass beyond the revolving storm doors at the street entrance," as Ray Stannard Baker wondered in 1899?[18] One ominous response came from the guidebook and travel publisher Moses King, whose postcard "Future New York: The City of Skyscrapers" (1910s) offered a futurist-primitive cityscape—later a staple of dystopian science-fiction films from *Metropolis* to *The Fifth Element*—consisting of buildings so tall and densely grouped that they appear to give no access to the ground at all.

The unprecedented scale and complexity of these constructions also reminded observers that rationalist and individualist models of cultural value were being transformed by the imperatives of consolidating industrial capitalism. It was well known that most skyscrapers were built as "cold, hard, business propositions," "advertising buildings" for enormous corporations.[19] Walter Prichard Eaton was one of many commentators to frame a tight parallel between the growing enormity of buildings and the magnitude and impersonality of the firms behind them: "The phrase 'Big Business' has leapt into the language, because the thing itself has shot up into the economic structure, even as our skyscrapers have shot up on every street."[20] For every oversized personality like F. W. Woolworth, driven to construct, in the words of *Citizen Kane*'s sardonic newsreel, "the costliest monument a man

"Future New York: The City of Skyscrapers," 1910s. Postcard produced by Moses King. Author's Collection.

has built to himself," there was at least one Metropolitan Life or Equitable Insurance Corporation, using sober actuarial paradigms to calculate the value of its skyscraper in rentable office space and public-relations impact. And even Woolworth's vast fortune was built from hundreds of millions of cheap tiny things, sold to millions of people five and ten cents at a time.[21]

In other words, skyscrapers foretold a new phase of capitalist modernity on a vast scale in which the individual, even the exceptional one, mattered less than the forces of the corporate, the aggregate, the mass. Eaton's response upon first seeing the skyscraper city, for example, was to apprehend the microscopic insignificance of the individual consciousness: "The very mass of it bore down upon me like a weight. Who was I amid these millions?"[22] This perceived loss of individual agency was articulated by many commentators, including Arthur Goodrich, who in 1902 called the drive to the skies an "inexorable force over which its makers have no control," and Eaton, who saw the skyscraper city's inhabitants as "midgets who have moulded mountains and who have then been moulded by them, played upon by the environment they have created."[23] The wonder and anxiety provoked by skyscrapers was often articulated through ritualized litanies of numbers that listed their staggering number of component parts, or recombined these parts into new forms: thirty-five million bricks in the Metropolitan Life Tower and 2,462 miles of telegraph and telephone wire, enough to stretch from New York to Denver; 541,000 terra-cotta floor blocks in the Singer Tower, enough to cover the ninety-seven miles from New York to Philadelphia if placed end to end; enough glass in the Woolworth Building's exterior windows to create a giant awning extending over all of Madison Square; enough horsepower in the Woolworth's giant boilers to lift a hundred Statues of Liberty at one time.[24] These transformations of one type of mass into another, however incongruous, evoked the insignificance of any individual element—even the owner—compared to the daunting scale of corporate modernity.

These tensions between individual and mass also indicate that as the early skyscraper spoke to its observers of global communication, efficient management of resources, and a rational future without boundaries, it also carried a powerful charge of irrationality and mystery, becoming what Rem Koolhaas calls "the great metropolitan destabilizer" and "the instrument of a new form of *unknowable* urbanism" in a modern condition of "perpetual programmatic instability."[25] Even the skyscraper's overwhelming materiality contributed to an otherworldly or miraculous quality in which a structure such as the Woolworth Building could be seen both as "a larger *mass* than ever constructed before" and "as disembodied [or] antigravitational."[26] Taking shape from "an enormous puzzle of interwoven lines and numerals and hieroglyphics worked out on many broad drawing-boards," the skyscraper evoked a realm of hermetic codes and uncanny signs, put new mysteries into play, and confounded full comprehension of its functions and meanings.[27]

These contradictions were exemplified by the opening ceremonies for the Woolworth Building in 1913. On the evening of April 24, hundreds of feet off the ground, a group of eight hundred guests gathered, including not only the expected industrialists and bankers but members of the Wilson cabinet, various foreign diplomats, and nearly 20 percent of the U.S. Congress from twenty-eight states. When everyone was seated, all the building's exterior and interior lights were extinguished, and precisely at 7:30 P.M., President Wilson at the White House pressed a single button, igniting all eighty thousand lights at once, "enough to illuminate the entire 40-mile waterfront of Manhattan"—an effect no doubt as stunning to the crowds watching for miles around as to the dignitaries inside.[28] This dramatic event conjoined a variety of political, commercial, technological, and aesthetic meanings into a thoroughly ambiguous spectacle. On the one hand, it demonstrated that a single skyscraper's reach extended not only throughout the metropolitan area but to the seat of national government. The fact that the building so confidently, competently *worked* promised a progressive epoch driven by the unending advance of industrial technologies and organizational skills. On the other hand, mystifying an enormous labor of design and construction into a magical instant of illumination, the event demanded that observers accommodate a modernity so massive and abstruse that only a tiny class of experts would ever understand how it could function.

Even before 1900, the contradictions surrounding skyscrapers had given rise to a mythic-anthropological rhetoric that associated them with exotic premodern environments of hermetic insularity. Often their inhabitants were imagined as "modern Cliff Dwellers," a metaphor that drew upon the turn-of-the-century fascination with the Anasazi peoples who had built aerie-like dwellings high on the mesas of New Mexico, Colorado, Arizona, and Utah at some distant time (later determined to be between the eleventh and fourteenth centuries).[29] In the late 1880s, anthropologists and mountaineers were beginning to explore, photograph, and write about these spaces, emphasizing the architectural acumen, tactical ingenuity, and sheer nerve of those who built and lived in them.[30] Commentators were fascinated by the Anasazi Cliff Dwellers' unknown anthropological origins and by their seemingly unmotivated disappearance from places that seemed nearly impregnable even by much later standards. Adding further to their uncanny appeal was the belief that their remains showed a puzzling mixture of physiognomies and their artifacts a marked eclecticism of style and sophistication, which implied a greater degree of intercourse with the outside world than their hermetic living spaces seemed to admit.[31]

In 1893, the Anasazi were brought to the consciousness of millions of machine-age Americans through an exhibit at the Columbian Exposition in Chicago featuring a massive composite simulation of a cliff, along with relics and "portions of the real houses" taken from a dig in Colorado.[32] Outside the Exposition's boundaries as well, the idea of using the Cliff Dwellers to describe the new spaces of the skyscraper metropolis was in the Chicago air. Later that same summer, the well-known Chicago novelist Henry Blake Fuller published *The Cliff Dwellers,* among the earliest integrations of the skyscraper setting into the tradition of social-realist fiction. Fuller's most original stroke was an introduction in mock-ethnographic language that describes a fascinating and exotic space that had produced a new people to be named, a new culture to be studied:

> Between the former site of old Fort Dearborn and the present site of our newest Board of Trade there lies a restricted yet tumultuous territory through which, during the course of the last fifty years, the rushing streams of commerce have

Composite simulation of the homes of Anasazi Cliff Dwellers, World's Columbian Exposition, Chicago, 1893. Author's collection.

worn many a deep and rugged chasm. . . . Each of these cañons is closed in by a long frontage of towering cliffs, and these soaring walls of brick and lime-stone and granite rise higher and higher with each succeeding year, according as the work of erosion at their bases goes onward—the work of that seething flood of carts, carriages, omnibuses, cabs, cars, messengers, shoppers, clerks, and capitalists, which surges with increasing violence for every passing day.[33]

Fuller's facetious archaeology of the Loop centers on the Clifton Building, a fictional eighteen-story skyscraper housing "four thousand souls" and fea-turing wonderful elevating devices that "ameliorate the daily cliff-climbing for the frail of physique and the pressed for time."[34] His portrayal precisely captures the skyscraper's distinctive combination of variety and monumen-tality, spatial openness and hermetic inaccessibility. The Clifton's "tribe" is remarkably fluid and "heterogeneous," containing all walks of life from bankers to janitors, all of whom seem to be recent arrivals from elsewhere.[35] As a matter of course, the building enables state-of-the-art communication so that "the warriors" of commerce may transmit "their messages, hostile or friendly, to chiefs more or less remote."[36] Yet in gathering a vast variety of functions and resources into a single space, the Clifton aims above all "to be complete in itself," to make it "unnecessary" for its inhabitants, their archaeologist, or his readers to "go afield either far or frequently."[37]

Much journalistic writing on skyscrapers over the next thirty years echoed Fuller's ambiguous synthesis of hypertechnologized urban space with the unknowable, uncanny, and hermetic landscape of the western desert. In 1898, a writer in *Munsey's* noted that many streets "are already darkened by the huge cliffs of masonry that rise above them"; in *Collier's*, C. P. Cushing deplored the "cheerless cañonlike streets" created by the skyscrapers; in the *Technical World*, a venue we might expect to embrace the skyscraper, C. F. Carter remarked on the menace to health and life from "the crowded war-rens of the cliff dwellers towering . . . three hundred feet into the air on either side of the narrow slits called streets."[38] In 1911, Mildred Stapley detailed the economic imperatives inducing builders to maximize rentable space right up to the property line by building "sheer vertical wall[s] deviating neither outward nor inward," which created the sunless and cheerless "cañon streets" of lower Manhattan.[39] There are dozens of similar references to cliff and canyon (usually spelled *cañon*), which became consensual metaphors for the urban spaces being remade by skyscrapers. In 1911 Forbes synthesized these images and anxieties into a vision of the future skyscraper city as "a collection of towns and villages under separate roofs," each "complete unto itself," its streets "canyons of a depth varying from 200 to 400 feet, through which the wind will sweep like gales"; "the sky will be practically blotted out" from this "city of electric lights" inhabited by businessmen who will seldom glimpse any element of the natural world.[40] Four years later, Walter Prichard Eaton summarized the effects of these new skyscraper spaces in terms of irony and contradiction: "Through the cañons he has made, Man hustles and bustles, creating more perplexities than he can solve."[41]

Yet as skyscrapers darkened the canyon streets of lower Manhattan, they also begat new aesthetic styles and accounts of beauty. Eaton's 1915 description of his evolving attachment to the skyscraper city reveals an important link between its sheer lines, massive forms, and constantly changing conditions, and an emerging mode of aesthetic perception we can identify instantly as modernist. Upon first arriving in the city, Eaton had seen "miles and miles of ugly dwellings, cave dwellings where people lived in layers."[42] But he soon came to love the "mortared Himalayas" of Manhattan's streets, and he credits skyscrapers and the spaces their presence created—"great crags in the walls of a man-made cañon"—for providing him with an aesthetic

"Canyon" streets of lower Manhattan, ca. 1910. Author's collection.

appropriate to the twentieth century, which repudiates "symmetry" and "conformity" and instead embraces ceaseless variety, "stirring challenge," "endless surprises," "sudden revelation . . . amid apparent ugliness," and anything that "rouses the eye to keener attention."[43] These are, of course, the very qualities that drew the eyes, brushes, and cameras of so many visual artists to skyscrapers and cityscapes. The painter Robert MacCameron made this affinity explicit in 1912 by noting that the lines and forms of the skyscraper city were creating a twentieth-century aesthetic, a "freshening of the vision" that was sure to catalyze "fresh problems and solutions in other forms of art."[44]

Like their contemporaries in the visual arts, American poets of the 1910s and early 1920s would perceive the allure of the great building and explore those new notions of beauty. Skyscrapers and other great buildings carry a wide range of emotional and ideological meanings in their work, from capitalist intimidation to revolutionary praxis. Some poems read the skyscraper city as an image of bleakly depersonalized modernity, others as a locus of utopian possibility. Most bear the traces of both these responses, portraying skyscraper space as a symbol of contradiction, instability, and challenge. As they perceive the metropolitan grid as an arresting abstract pattern of lights and lines rivaling the creations of nature, poets ponder how to balance this detached aesthetic perspective with empathy for other people. As they feel the skyscraper city hurtling them into a future of unimaginable marvels, they question whether the constantly mutating metropolis would allow any meaningful connection with the past. As great buildings provide them with new metaphors for portraying mass society, they worry that a society defined by masses—people and buildings—might prove inaccessible to the powers of poetry. As they sense its transporting power, they wonder whether the skyscraper would carry us anywhere we wanted to go.

Abyss, Eternity, Threshold

One group of poetic responses represented skyscrapers looming ominously over more humanly scaled structures, symbols of modern capital at its most unaccountable and self-congratulatory. In the 1920s, as an architectural critic for the *New York Times,* Orrick Johns, would write admiringly of skyscrapers, but in 1912 in "Second Avenue," he deplores their ever-expanding array as a "jagged line of mist-enshrouded masonry" that "you, my people, reared and built / To be a temple and a shrine / For gods of iron and gilt."[45] Likewise, in "Lines to the Woolworth Building" (1913), the anarchist poet and sculptor Adolf Wolff admits that the just-completed skyscraper "awes my soul" but quickly goes on to term it a "[m]onstrous sacrilege" because never "[h]as thing so big been made for end so small."[46] Wolff plays here with the incongruity of a five-and-ten-cent store housing itself in the world's tallest building, but his more serious goal is to proclaim the venality of the Woolworth's commemoration of nothing but "the priests of lucre."[47] Appropriately, the building's "pallor" is "like in color to the tint of bones," its "slender, upright lines" "[s]o much like children's bones."[48] Wolff ends with a passionate but banal condemnation of the building to the dust of history: like the pyramids, "tyrants' tombs, built by a million slaves," before long "[t]hou'lt be the relic of an age gone by." Drawing upon late genteel poetry's hoary reservoir of antiquarian imagery, such castigations of the idolatrous skyscraper rehearsed the conventional antimodern sentiments that American poets had long been expected to produce. But they were not typical of verse of the 1910s, which more often acknowledged the intimidating potential of these great buildings and also their allure as creations strikingly expressive of modernity.

For obvious reasons, the skyscraper often signified massive size and strength, but it proved a remarkably tensile symbol, even serving as a harbinger of Marxist revolution. Like Arturo Giovannitti in "The Day of War" (discussed in chapter 3), radical poets in the orbit of *The Masses* tended to see the skyscraper as a symbol of the limitless possibilities of collective human effort. John Reed's sonnet "Foundations of a Skyscraper" (*American Magazine,* 1911) portrays its construction as a "ghastly" inferno of exploitative labor ("Thunder of drills, stiff spurting plumes of steam,—/ Shouts and the dip of cranes, the stench of earth").[49] And yet he finds the completed skyscraper a site and emblem of utopian possibility in which "men give a vision birth, / Crawling and dim, men build a dreamer's dream." Effectively balancing the utopian vision of "[a] phantom of fairtowers in the sky" with the grittier assertion that the "foundation" of the skyscraper is human labor, Reed turns in the sestet to a striking image of the building in the strenuous posture of one of the workmen who builds it—"Naked, a giant's back, tight-muscled, stark, / Glimpse of mighty shoulder, etched in steel." In contrast to James in *The American Scene,* who diminishes the bodies of workers to mechanical instruments and their souls to steel, Reed uses the shapes of buildings and the motion of machines to elevate the figure of the worker into iconic status, much as Lewis Hine would do a few years later in his photographs of the workers constructing the Empire State Building.

Worker constructing the Empire State Building. Photograph by Lewis W. Hine, 1931. Reprinted by permission of the New York Public Library. Photography Collection, Miriam and Ira D. Wallach Division of Arts, Prints, and Photographs, New York Public Library, Astor, Lenox, and Tilden Foundations.

Reed's reference to "the clamor of unknown tongues" in the skyscraper's construction site evokes the heterogeneous ethnic makeup of its workforce and the class-consciousness that such an enterprise might promote, no doubt in spite of its developer's desires. Two poems published in *The Liberator*, Raymond Corder's "The Skyscraper" (1921) and Stirling Bowen's "Skyscraper" (1924), pursue this line of thought by celebrating the modern capitalist tower as an empowering icon of collectivist labor and incipient radical consciousness. Corder's poem begins, "All that steel frame-work bristling in the sun / Is something we have done."[50] The physical labor of construction ("We sweated, we plugged, and built it, span by span") has enabled workers to think of themselves as the building's "creators" and therefore, its rightful owners: "And every rusty beam that skyward towers / Is ours—we built it—It is ours!" The proletariat's agency emerges through a high-spirited slang that acknowledges the obligations of doctrine ("Sure, buddy, sure, I know / The boss has got it now—he'll have to go"), while admiring the building as an object of beauty and a source of pride:

But, say, bo, watch them clouds,
They seem to stand still while that eye-beam strouds
Across the sky.—She's pretty, ain't she, son?
That piece of work we've done.

Following Reed's lead and anticipating Hine's photos in *Men at Work* (1932), Bowen's sonnet "Skyscraper" suggests how heavy machinery exponentially magnifies the power of the ordinary worker:

One man mops his brow
And, spitting, scoops two tons of dirt up now
In one iron fist.—plain Mike or Tom or Pete.[51]

Extending the individual human frame with "fist" and "great arms," the crane incarnates the growing strength of the proletariat as a collective body. Bowen flatly refuses to interpret the skyscraper's massive scale as a shaming parable of hubris, instead appropriating the imagery of pagan idolatry for the "clear godless" nature of this human enterprise: "No god can muddle anything we try!" The building is indeed "Babel's modern tower," since it has drawn together a multiethnic workforce who "confuse the Yankee tongue," but this too becomes a source of affirmation, unifying cultural differences into class consciousness.

For other writers, the material enormity and symbolic malleability of the skyscraper give it a liminal signifying force confounding conventional spatial distinctions and promising access to new realms of experience. In "Night in State Street" (1914), Harriet Monroe notes that in many climatic conditions, skyscrapers extend past the limits of visual perception to create a sublime confusion of terrestrial and celestial: "The many-windowed walls uprear so high / They dim and quiver and float away in mist / Tangling the earth and sky."[52] Likewise, Walter Prichard Eaton in 1915 perceives the skyscraper's vastness outstripping identifiable climatic zones, transcending weather itself: "On foggy days the Singer Building and its sister peaks go up out of sight into the vapors. Again, on days of heavy atmosphere and lowering rain, . . . I have seen the lower portions of the buildings obliterated, and only their summits reared on nothing into the gray air, a dream city, unbelievable, ethereal, immense."[53] Eaton imagines skyscrapers at night as vertical thoroughfares rising into the heavens, proposing that the "upward rows of lights" give lower Manhattan "the aspect of a town of many streets running up a great dome-like hill, each little house by the roadside imagined from its square of light."[54] Similarly, Ray Stannard Baker portrays the steel-frame skyscraper as "more a bridge than a building," a sublime verticalization of horizontal structures whose supporting steel girders become "big bridges" and whose elevators convey us into the unkown heavens.[55] Such formulations remind us that in contrast to our world of routine air travel, aerial photography, and satellite imagery, at that early twentieth-century moment, with flight in its infancy, such buildings as the Woolworth and Metropolitan Towers, reaching "to an altitude where only balloons have been before," lifted people away from the earth and allowed them to survey it panoramically as almost nothing else was capable of doing.[56]

Not surprisingly, images of crossing and transformation figure often in portrayals of these buildings that made people feel themselves on the very edges of space and time, teetering "on the abyss of eternity," as Sara Teasdale put it in 1915.[57] A host of early twentieth-century poems imagine skyscrapers as thresholds to new dimensions of experience, windows into the future or the past, or harbingers of apocalyptic change. In "Skyscrapers" (1914), Horace Holley compares them to "[a] forest of strange palms" apparently not subject to natural laws: they don't sway in wind, "Nor nod sleepy at evening," nor offer "nestling birds / A warm and comfortable mossy bough."[58] Unnerved at these contraventions of the natural order, the speaker prophesies "a furious tempest" that will "tear your earth-devouring roots" and rain down "terrible fruit" of stone upon "a shore deserted."[59] William Rose Benét's "The Singing Skyscrapers" (1918) also offers an apocalyptic vision, yet his brings not catastrophe but celestial splendor. The poem's half-dreaming speaker invokes by name the city's "tall titanic towers"—Metropolitan, Flatiron, Singer, Woolworth—and imagines them "[s]inging in the air."[60] These state-of-the-art modern buildings sing of long-gone civilizations that linger "[s]pectrally" in the collective consciousness as "[m]ajestic phantom cities that move above our slumber / Hung aloft in air" and inspire us to build new cities, new towers. The poet concludes that all such towers, from Nineveh to New York, are attempts to put into material form our yearning for a "Celestial City / Blinding in the sky!"

One of the most ambitious explorations of the skyscraper as a visionary liminal space comes from a writer few would associate with urban modernity, Sara Teasdale, whose work has been unjustifiably miniaturized by high modernism's interlocking preconceptions of gender and genre. Teasdale's "From the Woolworth Tower," published in the 1915 volume *Rivers to the Sea* but eventually dropped from her collected works, adapts the idiom of the rhapsodic love lyric to an ultramodern urban setting. It consists of seventy-four lines divided into short beginning and ending sections framing a longer central meditation. The opening describes a couple enjoying the city as a space of spectacular modern amusement, who arrive "[v]ivid with love, eager for greater beauty," into the "brilliant and warm" corridors of the Woolworth Building.[61] The elevator's "sharp unswerving flight" up to the observation deck transports them through "swirling and angry" air that "[h]owls like a hundred devils" into a realm of uncanny forces in which the speaker becomes sublimely "[c]onscious of the chasm under us."[62] She has entered an unstable zone in which not even the fundamental divisions between air above and earth below can be taken for granted. The building's liminal force only intensifies as they reach the top, pass through "a door leading onto the ledge," and find themselves perched "[o]ver the edge of eternity," accompanied only by "[w]ind, night and space!" The speaker is stunned not only by the "terrible height" but by her awareness that they have actively chosen the experience, asking, "Why have we sought you?"[63] She speaks here not as a bohemian seeking esoteric urban thrills but as an American participating fully in the popular culture of her times: between 1913 and closing in 1941 due to wartime precautions, the Woolworth's observation deck attracted nearly seven million visitors.[64]

The poem's long second section, describing the view from the tower, addresses many themes of cityscape verse: the perception of the city as abstract patterns of lights and forms that rival or displace the creations of nature; the desire to balance this detached perspective with empathy for others; the anxiety that the scale and impersonality of skyscraper modernity may overwhelm the poet's communicative powers; and the uneasy attempt to orient the modern metropolis into a meaningful relationship with past and future. As she regains her bearings, the speaker perceives the abstract visual drama of the city's lights ("[a] thousand times more numerous than the stars") outlining its dark shapes:

> Oh lines and loops of light in unwound chains
> That mark for miles and miles
> The vast black mazy cobweb of the streets.[65]

As so often, the visual arts provide a point of reference for the poetic imagination: "Near us clusters and splashes of living gold / That change far off to bluish steel." The near-abstract quality of these images evokes the poet's sense of having entered a liminal realm in which vision blurs and the familiar "strident noises" of the street float up to her, now "hallowed into whispers." The stridency has been hallowed out of them, but questions remain. Does the poet's liminal sensitivity make these "whispers" comprehensible as human utterances? Or has the spectacle of the nocturnal cityscape merely aestheticized them into meaningless shapes and noises?

The anxiety created by these questions dominates the next verse paragraph, which turns toward the human element of the city conspicuously absent so far, with discouraging results:

> We feel the millions of humanity beneath us,—
> The warm millions, moving under the roofs,
> Consumed by their own desires;
> Preparing food,
> Sobbing alone in a garret,
> With burning eyes bending over a needle,
> Aimlessly reading the evening paper. . . .

Assailed by inklings of "[t]he sorrow, the torpor, the bitterness, the frail joy" that "[c]ome up to us" from the masses below "[l]ike a cold fog wrapping us round," the speaker can muster none of Whitman's hope that human connection might transcend distance between present, past, and future. She also feels unmoved by the tower as a symbol of human progress, concluding that in a hundred years, "The anguish, the torpor, the toil / Will have passed to other millions / Consumed by the same desires," and eventually "[d]arkness will blot the lights / And the tower will be laid on the earth," with only the sea and stars remaining "unchanging" and "unconcerned." Instead of, say, a somber descent from the building to contrast the exhilarating ascent, the poem's brief final section retreats from these anguishing realizations, announcing that despite the "sorrow, futility, defeat" all around, love "has crowned us / For a moment / Victors." Here Teasdale attempts to resolve the theme of liminality, implying that because the building has abstracted the lovers from the strident and chaotic textures of the city, to exist on the edge of eternity, they feel their love more intensely than they could have done below. But this wishful affirmation pales next to the bleak insight that the tower's promises of clarified vision and enhanced understanding have revealed modern life as mere clockwork acting-out of petty melodrama until the curtain rings down.

Teasdale's vision of great buildings laid low may well remind us of the "falling towers" of *The Waste Land* (1922), allowing us once more to consider the rich relation of Eliot's early poetry to the modern cityscape. In the beginning of the final section, "What the Thunder Said," when Eliot describes "mountains of rock without water," he refers directly to the quasi-biblical desert landscape that frames the entire poem, but despite its studied timelessness the desert landscape has also possessed unmistakable attributes of the modern city.[66] After all, existence in the waste land is marked not by true solitude ("There is not even solitude in the mountains") but by an alienation from others exacerbated by there being so many of them—so many "red sullen faces" sneering and snarling "[f]rom doors of mudcracked houses" that "one can neither stand nor lie nor sit."[67] Later, Eliot's speaker approaches an arid "city over the mountains" that "cracks and reforms and bursts in the violet air," leading him to a litany of human history as a succession of "[f]alling towers / Jerusalem Athens Alexandria / Vienna London / Unreal."[68] This powerful linkage of the waste land's sterile mountains of rock with the "unreal" cities of modernity is reinforced by the adjective "violet," previously used to describe the machine-age city at dusk ("the violet hour, when the eyes and back / Turn upward from the desk, when the human engine waits / Like a taxi throbbing waiting").[69] Through this connection, Eliot identifies the waste land's "hooded hordes swarming / Over endless plains, stumbling in cracked earth," with the contemporary crowd he has earlier described surging over London Bridge, eyes fixed before feet, to arrive at offices "on the final stroke of nine."[70]

This synthesis of urban and desert settings shapes the poem's concluding prophecy of a cataclysmic if entropic denouement to the human expansion into the sky. The speaker sits "upon the shore / Fishing," with the "arid plain" of desert and tower behind him, awaiting a thunderstorm equally readable as a harbinger of spiritual rejuvenation or as a cosmic coup de grace.[71] Finally, his elegantly styled phrases disintegrate into a fragmented collage of signifiers headed by the collapse of a great urban structure: "London Bridge is falling down falling down falling down."[72] Eliot's evident fascination with the industrial city even as he is repulsed by it, perhaps the most precious elements of his mixed legacy to modern poetry, largely disappears after his conversion to Christianity. Still gripped by it in *The Waste Land,* he articulates as vividly as anyone ever has the wonder and anguish of experiencing everything solid, even our most massive bulwarks, cracking, reforming, and bursting in the viole(n)t air of modernity.

Twos and Threes and Hundreds

The great building's ability to transform familiar symbolic and spatial relationships was not limited to prophecies of revolution or visions of catastrophe. Like visual artists, poets used skyscrapers to explore a central issue of modernist aesthetics: how to balance singularity and typicality, the particular instance and the synthetic inference. The two most comprehensive verse attempts to situate the great building into a modernity of marvels,

Harriet Monroe's "The Hotel" (1907) and Carl Sandburg's "Skyscraper" (1916), portray their subject as a microcosm of modern life, encompassing an entire world under a single roof. Both struggle with the problematic project of representing the vast scale of twentieth-century urban modernity, but they also discover a powerful sense of purpose for the modern poem: to make visible the essential structural elements usually obfuscated by ideology and convention.

Not surprisingly, given their enormous variety of occupants and functions, turn-of-the-century popular commentary often portrays great buildings as "cities in miniature," microcosmic compendia of modern life.[73] The Park Row Building, in 1899 the tallest and largest commercial office tower yet constructed, housing nearly one thousand office spaces and over four thousand workers, struck Ray Stannard Baker in *Munsey's* as "a city under one roof," while another *Munsey's* piece of 1899 contemplated the house phones scattered about the modern grand hotel and supposed that "one day's list of the requests transmitted over these instruments" would collect under a single roof a "marvelous catalogue" of all the "multiple wants this luxurious life has generated."[74] With each marvelous new project, these microcosmic tropes intensified, culminating with the Woolworth Building, which superseded all previous instances of what Koolhaas calls the skyscraper's "reproduction of the world."[75] The first building to possess its own power plant, the Woolworth also contained its own fire, police, detective, medical, cleaning, and repair departments, all on duty around the clock. Its permanent office occupancy was around twelve thousand people, and its average daily population was thousands more—literally a small city within a single structure.[76]

Though skyscrapers are usually thought of as commercial office buildings, Landau and Condit note the "precedent-setting role" of hotels in the emergence of tall buildings, noting that the Broadway Central Hotel (1869–70) may deserve the designation of "'early skyscraper,' if not 'first skyscraper.'"[77] The largest and best-known "skyscraper hotel"—and, in Koolhaas's view, one "of Manhattan's most definitive Skyscrapers"—was the old Waldorf-Astoria, consolidated into a 1,300-room colossus in 1897 from two adjacent Fifth Avenue properties owned by rival factions of the Astor family (on the site where three decades later the Empire State Building would be built).[78] Writing the Waldorf's history in 1925, Edward Hungerford offered an aggregation of daily statistics calculated to astound: fifteen hundred employees; seventy-five hundred meals served; six thousand eggs, fourteen thousand rolls, one thousand pounds of beef, one thousand pounds of chicken, and six hundred pounds of fish consumed; eleven thousand gallons of fuel burnt; eighty thousand pieces of linen washed. Not surprisingly, Hungerford concluded that "[t]he Waldorf-Astoria is in itself a city—and no mean city at that."[79]

According to Harriet Monroe's autobiography, "The Hotel" not only portrays the Waldorf-Astoria but was actually drafted in its English Room one day in 1907 when she was between trains.[80] Though not published until 1909, the poem was written in the same year that Henry James in *The American Scene* called the grand hotel a "synonym for civilization" and wondered whether "the hotel-spirit may not just *be* the American spirit most seeking and most finding itself."[81] James perceived the Waldorf-Astoria as "a gorgeous golden blur, a paradise peopled with unmistakable American shapes," in which "the organized and the extemporized, the element of ingenuous joy below and of consummate management above, melted together and left one uncertain which of them one was, at a given turn of the maze, most admiring."[82] The persistent imagery of visual indistinctness (*blur, melted, maze*) in this passage suggests James's susceptibility to the textures of effortless leisure that efface the great labor and expense of maintaining the luxury hotel. Given that his response to the hotel is precisely the one it seeks to create for its moneyed guests, we may find him too ingenuous in implying that "below"-stairs employees are naively delighted to serve in such a "paradise." James's will to penetrate the mystifications of the modern city turns out to be rather selective: the jagged skyline's affront to his visual pleasure merits his critical gaze, but the hotel's warm embrace proves much easier to indulge.

In contrast to James's comfortable blur, Monroe's poem anatomizes the grand hotel using sharply etched visual imagery that seeks neither to celebrate nor condemn but to comprehend it as "an epitome of modern life," as she would call the Waldorf in her autobiography.[83] "The Hotel" participates in the strain of machine-age writing traced in Cecilia Tichi's *Shifting Gears,* in which both writer and reader function, in Roland Barthes's term, as "an engineer by proxy," analyzing and demystifying the constituents of modernity as complex systems of interdependent component parts.[84] Beginning in the gilded facades of its public spaces, Monroe moves her camera-eye ever deeper into the many aesthetic, technological, demographic, gustatory, and social functions that comprise the hotel as a system. Here is the poem in full:

> The long resounding marble corridors, the shining parlors with
>   shining women in them.
> The French room, with its gilt and garlands under plump little
>   tumbling painted loves.
> The Turkish room, with its jumble of many carpets and its stiffly
>   squared un-Turkish chairs.

The English room, all heavy crimson and gold, with spreading
   palms lifted high in round green tubs.

The electric lights in twos and threes and hundreds, made into
   festoons and spirals and arabesques, a maze and magic of
   bright persistent radiance.

The people sitting in corners by twos and threes, and cooing
   together under the glare.

The long rows of silent people in chairs, watching with eyes that
   see not while the patient band tangles the air with music.

The bell-boys marching in with cards, and shouting names over
   and over into ears that do not heed.

The stout and gorgeous dowagers in lacy white and lilac,
   bedizened with many jewels, with smart little scarlet or azure
   hats on their gray-streaked hair.

The business men in trim and spotless suits, who walk in and out
   with eager steps, or sit at the desks and tables, or watch the
   shining women.

The telephone girls forever listening to far voices, with the silver
   band over their hair and the little black caps obliterating
   their ears.

The telegraph tickers sounding their perpetual *chit-chit-chit* from
   the uttermost ends of the earth.

The waiters, in black swallow-tails and white aprons, passing
   here and there with trays of bottles and glasses.

The quiet and sumptuous bar-room, with purplish men softly
   drinking in little alcoves, while the bar-keeper, mixing bright
   liquors, is rapidly plying his bottles.

The great bedecked and gilded café, with its glitter of a thousand
   mirrors, with its little white tables bearing gluttonous dishes
   whereto bright forks, held by pampered hands, flicker
   daintily back and forth.

The white-tiled, immaculate kitchen, with many little round blue
   fires, where white-clad cooks are making spiced and flavored
   dishes.

The cool cellars filled with meats and fruits, or layered with
   sealed and bottled wines mellowing softly in the darkness.

The invisible stories of furnaces and machines, burrowing deep
   down into the earth, where grimy workmen are heavily
   laboring.

The many-windowed stories of little homes and shelters and
    sleeping-places, reaching up into the night like some
    miraculous, high-piled honeycomb of wax-white cells.
The clothes inside of the cells—the stuffs, the silks, the laces; the
    elaborate delicate disguises that wait in trunks and drawers
    and closets, or bedrape and conceal human flesh.
The people inside of the clothes, the bodies white and young,
    bodies fat and bulging, bodies wrinkled and wan, all alike
    veiled by fine fabrics, sheltered by walls and roofs, shut in
    from the sun and stars.
The souls inside of the bodies—the naked souls; souls weazened
    and weak, or proud and brave; all imprisoned in flesh,
    wrapped in woven stuffs, enclosed in thick and painted
    masonry, shut away with many shadows from the shining
    truth.
God inside of the souls, God veiled and wrapped and imprisoned
    and shadowed in fold on fold of flesh and fabrics and
    mockeries; but ever alive, struggling and rising again, seeking
    the light, freeing the world.[85]

The poet begins her microcosmic figurations lightly by satirizing the tendency of hotels to evoke aesthetic or national styles by heaping up recognizably typical signifiers not integrated into coherent wholes—a feature especially notable in the old Waldorf, whose "[d]ifferent public rooms were each designed in a distinct historical style."[86] From the ersatz cosmopolitanism of the French, Turkish, and English rooms, Monroe then turns to a more serious passage troping the hotel as a *microcosmopolis,* a miniature world represented as a city. The city's arteries of transport are figured in the hotel's radiating matrix of "long resounding marble corridors," the city's intricate nocturnal lightscapes in the hotel's "electric lights in twos and threes and hundreds, made into festoons and spirals and arabesques, a maze and magic of bright persistent radiance."

As she delineates this microcosmopolis, Monroe maintains a productive tension between two distinctive modes of modern urban experience, one emphasizing hermetic disconnection among individual elements, the other emphasizing their continuous and unlimited recombination. Certainly the hotel houses in miniature a scene of modern alienation, evoked by bell-boys "shouting names over and over into ears that do not heed" and by "long rows of silent people in chairs" who "see not," reminiscent of the blank-faced rows of subway-car passengers in various poems of the era. Monroe will later mirror these arrayed rows and columns of alienated modern subjects through the "many-windowed stories" of their hotel rooms, adjacent yet isolated. Yet she also describes how the hotel makes possible new forms of interaction based not on reified social categories but on continuous intermingling and reconfiguration, evoked by "people sitting together in twos and threes," the mixing of "bright liquors" in the bar, and waiters "passing here and there" in every direction filling an unending variety of orders. Despite the bogus internationalism of its individual rooms, the hotel integrates defining technologies of modernity into a matrix of global communication. Observing "telephone girls forever listening to far voices" and "telegraph tickers" whose reach extends to "the uttermost ends of the earth," the poet apprehends the impersonal bigness of the world and the incipient interconnectedness of all its parts into a functional whole.

Monroe's anatomy of the grand hotel's spaces eventually leads her to the "great bedecked and gilded café, with its glitter of a thousand mirrors" wherein "bright forks, held by pampered hands, flicker daintily back and forth." At this key moment, as the hotel's visual opulence seems to indulge the narcissism of a modern leisure class, the poet darts through the looking-glass of these self-regarding surfaces and into the hotel that James prefers to avoid contemplating. She plunges first into the kitchen, into the cellars below, and then still further downward and inward into "[t]he invisible stories of furnaces and machines, burrowing deep down into the earth," where workmen labor to maintain the guts of the system. Monroe's strategy derives from contemporaneous images of machine-age material culture—postcards, magazine illustrations, posters—that depict in cross-section the public facades of great buildings and systems of transport and the inner mechanical workings that allow them to function.

Here she again portrays the hotel as a microcosm, this time of the socioeconomic hierarchy of capitalist modernity, to show that the luxury the hotel serves and exemplifies depends upon the labor of a strategically hidden stratum of humanity. In doing so, she asserts that the modern poet's work is to not to beautify or uplift but to *excavate*—here, to reveal components obscured from public view as integral to the system. Finally, Monroe turns her penetrating gaze toward the hotel's private rooms, where she probes beneath the "woven stuffs" and "thick and painted masonry" of furnishing, dress, and grooming to gaze upon the unclothed bodies of the occupants, and thence into their "souls." These last lines again script the modern poet as seeker after hidden truth who must look beneath surfaces that are conventionally "veiled," "sheltered," and "shut in," pursuing a poetics that acknowledges the isolation that modern mass society threatens and the visual

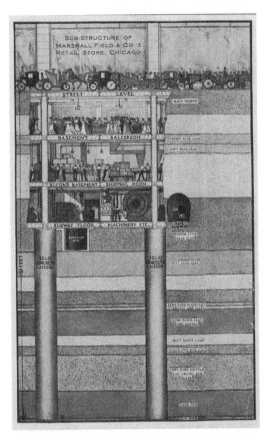

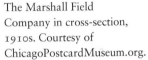

The Marshall Field
Company in cross-section,
1910s. Courtesy of
ChicagoPostcardMuseum.org.

accessibility, freedom of movement, and synthetic levels of understanding
that modernity also makes possible.

For Tichi, the paradigm of modernist artist-as-engineer is only fully realized when the artist's style matches or mirrors the engineering model
of experience, as she finds in Williams, Hemingway, and Dos Passos. But
the stylistics of minimalist efficiency she valorizes in these younger writers
is not the only possible version of machine-age experiment. "The Hotel"
represents a different but no less interesting experimental structure, one
that descends from Whitman's great descriptive catalogs, which, as Miles
Orvell has shown, themselves derive from innovative forms of visual culture prominent in the 1830s and 1840s, such as the daguerreotype gallery,
the panorama, and the exhibition hall.[87] Orvell argues that Whitman's development of "the omnibus form—a structure of variable size and shape,
containing an expandable number of particulars," outlined a new "way

of organizing experience" for a "self-consciously *modern* poet."[88] In "The Hotel," Monroe fully assimilates this formal principle but makes a further leap by using no declarative sentences at all, just an unbroken series of descriptive phrases each beginning with nouns that enumerate one after another the ingredients comprising the hotel. This grammatical model is based on a key organizing form of everyday modern life: the inventory, an ordered listing of all the components needed to comprehend a machine or system. Even at the end, when she refers rhapsodically to "God inside of the souls," Monroe eschews declarative grammar that would compromise this formal principle. "God" may be the ultimate component of this system but is no less a component than any other single part, whose meaning is only fully realized within the systemic context.

Sandburg's "Skyscraper," from *Chicago Poems* (1916), represents the great building as a complex system of interdependent technological, economic, social, and symbolic functions and also, like Whitman's ferry and Monroe's hotel, as a microcosmic nexus in which every aspect of modern experience converges:

> Prairie and valley, streets of the city, pour people into it and they
> mingle among its twenty floors and are poured out again
> back to the streets, prairies and valleys.[89]

Using long lines that emphasize continual interplay among multiple elements, the poet maintains this balance of anthropomorphic and functional elements, first announcing, "By day the skyscraper looms in the smoke and sun and has a soul," but then describing in detail the building's intricate material systems—elevator, water, garbage, electricity, phone, mail—that make it an emblem of modern urbanity:

> Elevators slide on their cables and tubes catch letters and parcels
> and iron pipes carry gas and water in and sewage out.
> Wires climb with secrets, carry light and carry words, and tell
> terrors and profits and loves—curses of men grappling plans
> of business and questions of women in plots of love.

Like Monroe, Sandburg uses the contemporary material culture of engineering as a model for his imagery, presenting a visual cross-section that demonstrates the building's structural integrity, focusing on caissons that "reach down to the rock of the earth and hold the building to a turning planet" and "girders [that] play as ribs and reach out and hold together the stone walls and floors."

And yet wonder at these mechanized marvels is not the whole story for Sandburg any more than for Monroe. He uses the skyscraper both to critique capitalism's reduction of individuals to economic counters and to maintain a sense of modernity's transformative human possibilities. The building's capacity and variety evoke a depersonalized vastness that diminishes the complex totality of many lives to "hundreds of names" arrayed "[o]n the office doors from tier to tier." Precisely because the building's design isolates and compartmentalizes, so that "the walls tell nothing from room to room," poetry must reveal the human interactions hidden by these surfaces, must remind us that "each name stand[s] for a face written across with a dead child, a passionate lover, a driving ambition for a million dollar business or a lobster's ease of life." Likewise, the building's intricate material systems cannot be ignored or dismissed into weightless abstractions—but they mean little without the human dramas played out within: "It is the men and women, boys and girls so poured in and out all day that give the building a soul of dreams and thoughts and memories." Like John Reed in "Foundations of a Skyscraper," Sandburg will only admire modernity's technological marvels while also remembering their human creators, the "[m]en who sunk the pilings and mixed the mortar," those "who strung the wires and fixed the pipes and tubes and those who saw it rise floor by floor." All those who died constructing the building, all those whose lives intersect with it after its completion: something of each has gone "into the stones of the building," comprising its soul. Sandburg presents this incarnating power as pointedly indiscriminate and egalitarian, as the "[s]miles and tears" of "[t]en-dollar-a-week stenographers" go "into the soul of the building just the same as the master-men who rule the building."

In the final two verse paragraphs, Sandburg offers a portrait of the building after hours, still murmuring with activity as "[w]atchmen walk slow from floor to floor and try the doors" and "[s]crubbers work, talking in foreign tongues," cleaning "from the floors human dust and spit, and machine grime of the day." This image of microscopic detritus, mingling the organic and mechanical, fits precisely within the portrayal of the skyscraper as a complex social system and symbol built from the most basic material components—the materials our bodies naturally exude and the foreign substances we have adapted to myriad forms and uses. The building as a symbol of an exploitative economic system also continues after hours, not only housing a nocturnal underclass of workers but serving as a giant illuminated billboard:

> Spelled in electric fire on the roof are words telling miles of
>   houses and people where to buy a thing for money. The sign
>   speaks till midnight.

If the skyscraper is to embody modern experience in microcosm, its meanings must remain irreconcilably mixed. However, in the final lines the poet affirms that such buildings, perhaps especially their contradictions, are sources of creative inspiration, presenting a self-portrait, a "young watchman" less interested in his guard duties than in the poetic activity of observation, who

> leans at a window and sees the lights of barges butting their way
>   across a harbor, nets of red and white lanterns in a railroad
>   yard, and a span of glooms splashed with lines of white and
>   blurs of crosses and clusters over the sleeping city.

This observer allows readers to see the city anew from the panoramic perspective afforded by the skyscraper, but unlike some cityscape verses, in which abstraction courts aestheticized detachment, here the poet's admiration of the city's painterly beauty has been earned by firmly grounding the building's material functions into human experience and vice versa, an integration he reiterates in the final line: "By night the skyscraper looms in the smoke and the stars and has a soul."

The Light That Never Fails

If the structure that meant the most to American visual artists of the early twentieth century was the Flatiron Building, the eyes of poets were drawn east across Madison Square to another distinctive skyscraper, the seven-hundred-foot Metropolitan Life Tower, completed in 1909. The "white tower" that dominates Giovannitti's protorevolutionary cityscape of 1916, "The Day of War: Madison Square, June 20th," is the Metropolitan in all but name. It also initiates the mystical song of William Rose Benét's "The Singing Skyscrapers" (1918) and appears in the opening lines of the exquisite lyric "Parting Gift" (from *Black Armour,* 1923) by Elinor Wylie. Gently teasing Benét (whom she married in that same year) for his fascination with these great structures, Wylie portrays the Metropolitan as an exemplary object of desire for the modern urban subject:

> I cannot give you the Metropolitan Tower.
> I cannot give you heaven;
> Nor the nine Visigoth crowns in the Cluny Museum;
> Nor happiness, even.[90]

These three poems and the ones I discuss below use the Metropolitan Tower to articulate a wide range of emotional states—love, wonder, disappointment, yearning for stability, alienation, skepticism, commitment to social change—testifying to the complexity of the skyscraper's power as a symbol of modern experience. Their references to the Metropolitan's distinctive appearance and lighting effects may strike current readers as obscure, but only because these were so familiar to the era's readers. The Metropolitan's giant clock and elaborate lighting sequences, visible from almost everywhere in the metropolis, would have been known to almost every New Yorker of the early twentieth century. The fullest description of this nocturnal spectacle is found in a 1914 guidebook to the building and its observation tower:

> As the evening darkness draws near, . . . hundreds of electric lights appear back of the dial numerals, all of which are brilliantly illuminated with splendid effect—a feature never produced by any other clock in the world. Simultaneously with the illumination of the hands and dials, an automatically actuated switch lights up a great electric octagonal lantern, eight feet in diameter, located at the top of the tower, from which powerful electric flash-lights, marking the hours in the evening, may be seen for a great distance, far beyond any possible transmission of sound, the time being signalled therefrom as follows: Each of the quarter-hours is flashed in red and the hours in white light—one red flash for the quarter, two red flashes for the half, three red flashes for three-quarters, and four red flashes for the even hour—these latter flashes followed by a number of white flashes marking the hour.[91]

The first poet to portray this iconic building was Sara Teasdale, whose lyric "The Metropolitan Tower" initiates an unofficial sequence of six poems that culminates the "Love Songs" section of *Helen of Troy and Other Poems* (1911). All six feature titles naming locations in greater New York City (Gramercy Park, the Metropolitan Museum, Coney Island, Union Square, and Central Park); collectively, they trace the unhappy progress of a modern love affair. "The Metropolitan Tower" initiates the sequence by recounting "[l]ove's birth" in the speaker's heart during an hour spent walking at dusk around the brand-new skyscraper. The first two of its three stanzas use the tower's lighting and timekeeping functions to measure the speaker's growing emotional commitment to her companion:

> We walked together in the dusk
> To watch the tower grow dimly white,
> And saw it lift against the sky
> Its flower of amber light.

The Metropolitan Life Tower by day and night, 1910s. Author's Collection.

> You talked of half a hundred things,
> I kept each hurried word you said,
> And when at last the hour was full,
> I saw the light turn red.[92]

The "amber light" that flowers on the building's clock at dusk suggests the euphoria of infinite possibility that accompanies the first feelings of love for another. This anticipation grows in the speaker as the building's illumination brightens minute by minute, culminating with lantern flashes as "at last" the hour reaches its completion. But all the while, the object of desire flits obliviously from one trivial observation to another, suggesting that the speaker must eventually be disappointed.

The final stanza foreshadows the bleak ending of the six-poem sequence, wistfully reaffirming the speaker's love despite the beloved's self-absorption:

> You did not know the time had come,
> You did not see the sudden flower,

> Nor know that in my heart Love's birth
> Was reckoned from that hour.

The syntactic and rhythmic paralleling of the phrases "the light turn red" and "the time had come" creates a strong rhetorical momentum that pulls us forward much as the speaker is pulled into deep emotional attachment— even as we note that red lights often portend danger. And yet for Teasdale, the tower is not a signifier of impersonality or alienation but one of constancy, whose steadfast presence and knowable visual sequences express the speaker's evolving emotional *durée*.

Ten years later, another young American poet turned to the Metropolitan Tower to portray love in the modern metropolis. Stephen Vincent Benét's "Chanson at Madison Square" (1920) is a striking mixture of surreal dream-vision, cityscape painting, and the intimate murmurings of lovers, which begins:

> You live in the Terminal Building, I
> In the Metropolitan Tower.
> This is what I send you every night,
> A flash of red and a flash of white,
> The red for our hearts and their pulse that is Delight,
> The white for power.[93]

Like Teasdale, Benét uses illuminated skyscrapers to evoke the ineffable sensations of love, but this time the emotions are reciprocated and celebrated. Benét establishes this reciprocity by pairing the Metropolitan Tower with another Manhattan giant three miles downtown from Madison Square, the Hudson Terminal Building (architects Clinton and Russell), which stood twenty-two stories (375 feet) high at the corner of Church and Cortlandt streets from 1908 until the early 1960s, when it was demolished to build the World Trade Center complex. Variously called the Hudson Terminal, the Terminal Tower, and the Church Street Terminal Building, it had more office space than any building in the world for many years, housing a daytime population of more than twenty thousand and containing in its bowels a major metropolitan rail terminus that ran twin tubes under the Hudson to the Pennsylvania Station in Jersey City. The image of two lovers living high in these towers is presumably fanciful, since neither was primarily residential in function, but as each gazes out at the other's adopted building, instantly recognizable in the bejewelled night sky, the poem vividly evokes the romance of space and light promised by the skyscraper metropolis.

Furthermore, the Metropolitan's lighting and timekeeping capacities trope the insistent pulse of the exhilarated lovers' hearts and their empowering identification with the nighttime cityscape. To "Moloch and his bride," those who built and rule the skyscraper city, the Metropolitan's great clock that "carries all Time like a watch on its side" may be a signifier of inexorably diminishing time, "doling out mortality," reminding them why they need life insurance and why it hardly matters in the end. But to the young lovers, the flashes become messages crossing the distance between them more instantaneously and intensely than any other form of communication could, while the clock allows them to anticipate "the clear Edens of our dream": both their sense of togetherness as they drowse "through the hot short night," and also their dreams of a future life together. In counterpoint to the Metropolitan's slender soaring shape and precise far-reaching flashes, the Hudson Terminal Building was notable for its sheer magnitude of volume and its multiple towers of equal height, while its lighting consisted of a brilliant pattern of sixteen thousand crimson lamps, continually illuminated visual symbols of the constant lover who has "hung" them as inviting signs of "home." Benét compares the Terminal Building's lights to ripe "[a]pples swinging on a tree," to rings encircling a "tall stone thumb," and to the rungs of a ladder inviting the speaker to "climb" into the lover's bower—all images variously evoking timeless love.

Meanwhile, far below, equally constant, "the motors roar like sea." This line exemplifies one side of the poem's most distinctive rhetorical feature: counterpoint between long lines of rhapsodic phrasing and strongly rhythmic pentasyllabic phrases drawn straight from the machine-age city that end each stanza ("You have crowned your hall with granite thorns, / Mine stands huge as steam"). This balancing of timeless and hypermodern imagery expresses the need of these skyscraper-age lovers, as "children lost together in a wood turned rock," to forge new expressive modes that acknowledge the unprecedented environment they find themselves in, and yet also to refuse any implication that this environment has diminished the intensity or validity of their emotional experience. The final lines reassert the Metropolitan Tower's capacity to signify their love's power: the speaker, perched high "above the clock" as if supported by it but also transcending it, finds that declarations of undying love speak most passionately when translated into the specific visual vocabulary of the tower, culminated by another driving five-syllable line:

> Shut your eyes—you are tired—let the blue bed of air
> Be your pillow through the hot short night. . . .
> Drowse into your Paradise! I say above the clock
> "*White—Red—White—Red—White!*"

The Hudson Terminal Building,
1910s. Author's Collection.

For its corporate owners, the constancy of the Metropolitan Tower's lighting was central to its meaning and value, a guarantee of the company's dependability and the basis of its self-defining slogan, "The Light That Never Fails." In 1943 the company's historian proudly described the tower's clock, chimes, and lighting beacon, which "flashed for miles over New York City and the neighboring towns."[94] Two other poems of the period, one making direct reference to the Metropolitan Tower, the other not, likewise consider the skyscraper as a measuring device, literally marking the course of modern time but also serving as a symbolic locus of enumeration and evaluation in a world where such measures have been destabilized. In "Time-Stone," from her 1920 volume *Sun-Up* (1920), Lola Ridge develops a wonderfully compressed and resonant analysis of the skyscraper's entanglement in ideologies of patriarchal capitalism. Here is the poem in full:

HALLO, Metropolitan—
Ubiquitous windows staring all ways,
Red eye notching the darkness.
No use to ogle that slip of a moon.
This midnight the moon,
Playing virgin after all her encounters,
Will break another date with you.
You fuss an awful lot,
You flight of ledger books,
Overrun with multiple ant-black figures
Dancing on spindle legs
An interminable can-can.
But I'd rather . . . like the cats in the alley . . . count time
By the silver whistle of a moonbeam
Falling between my stoop-shouldered walls,
Than all your tally of the sunsets,
Metropolitan, ticking among stars.[95]

Ridge's title portrays the tower as a gigantic sundial, a monumental and timeless device of human ingenuity. This particular time-stone, however, also possesses a specifically modern character, signified by its panoptical gaze ("Ubiquitous windows staring all ways") and its function as an enormous searchlight ("Red eye notching the darkness"). The metaphor of notching—marking a surface for the purpose of measuring, counting, or keeping a record—has important temporal and spatial functions in the poem. The red flashes of the tower's lights notch the night into a finite number of fifteen-minute temporal segments; they notch the otherwise incoherent space of the darkness into discrete units. Ridge portrays the illumination and arrangement of the night as a powerful sign of the human ability to create, reshape, and organize, but like the "[e]mblazoned zones and fiery poles" of Wallace Stevens's "The Idea of Order at Key West," written a decade later, this creative power carries substantial ambiguity.[96] Indeed, Ridge has already signaled her intent to scrutinize the tower's rationalist authority through her use of "staring"—looking without comprehension or judgment. The hypermasculine power connoted by its size and shape is then challenged by the "slip of a moon" that "at midnight," the moment of the tower's greatest aggrandizement, when even the hands of its clock point straight upward, will "break another date." Even as the tower breaks another date in human time by publicizing the arrival of midnight, it is confounded by this premodern timekeeper, which it can only "ogle" fruitlessly. With these images, Ridge begins a mischievous critique of the phallic implications of the tall thin tower, ever erect yet never satisfactorily coupled, as a symptom of patriarchal inadequacy and the compensatory powermongering that it produces.

Overcompensating for its inability to get satisfaction from the moon, the tower embraces and proclaims its own business, in two senses. The skyscraper obviously does the business of Metropolitan Life as "an enormous machine dedicated to processing insurance claims."[97] But its constant "fuss" and clutter also evokes *business* as self-important but empty activity, undermining claims to clarity and reliability. Ridge's "ant-black figures" likewise do double duty, signifying the dark-suited professionals working in the building, rendered nearly microscopic by its enormity, and the ever-multiplying numbers in the ledger books that record the business these workers do. Calling the building a "flight of ledger books" ingeniously mirrors its arrayed material components—flights of stairs, banks of elevators, rows of desks and files and shelves—with the columns of figures, human and financial, that are generated by its business. The grouping of objects into rows or flights is echoed visually in the arrayed windows of the building, as a multitude of contemporaneous photographic images of the Metropolitan make clear. That these flights are "overrun" by the ant-black figures implies the uncontrolled and irrational character of corporate capitalism despite all its claims to actuarial precision, a critique intensified by Ridge's imagery of dancing. As the ant-black human figures multiply the interminable figures in their ledgers, their "can-can," frenetic and compulsive, suggests the impaired state of modern rationality Siegfried Kracauer describes in "The Mass Ornament," in which capitalism's "processes have become ends in themselves" and its "conceptual machinery has lost sight of its goals and values beyond those which contribute to the endless growth of the system."[98] The figures, both human and numerical, are "dancing on spindle legs," offering little assurance of their ability to sustain this hectic routine. "Spindle legs" evoke the malnourishment, certainly spiritual but possibly physical as well, of the tower's human population. Equated with the numeric figures in their ledgers, these people are metaphorically reduced to stick-figures, their limbs but spindly pen-strokes.

A spindle is also a literal piece of office equipment, a spike resting on a desk on which stacks of papers are impaled. This is a suggestive shape in a poem about a very tall, very thin tower with a pointed top. But while the tower may remind us of a huge spindle, the main impact of this metaphor is to complete the ironic inversion of its phallic power, since the function of a spindle would be to skewer the paper "figures" kept within the tower, and by extension, its human figures as well. This imagery conveys a vision,

Filing office in the Metropolitan Life Insurance Company, 1910s. Author's Collection.

at once sinister and whimsical, of the spindle-tower, striving obsessively upward but failing to achieve cosmic intercourse with the moon, succeeding instead only in skewering its human creators, who may imagine themselves as partaking in its power to penetrate but who actually are penetrated by it. Already reduced to the stature of insects in their "ant-black," these movers and shakers become the moved and shaken, an ingenious gloss on Prufrock's image of the modern-subject-as-insect "pinned and wriggling on the wall."[99]

The office spindle, as a tool for assembling, organizing, and recording information, fits ingeniously into the poem's overarching metaphor of the tower as a measuring and recording device. Ridge returns to this conceit in the final five lines, unfavorably comparing the tower to the more appealing if less exact method of counting time by the moonbeams that filter between the walls of her building. Embracing the nonpatriarchal and marginal values represented by the moon, the alley cats, and the horizontal curves of her "stoop-shouldered walls," the poet playfully presents the tower as grotesque in its enormity, rigid in its stability, obsessive in its precision, ticking mechanically away among its celestial neighbors: the emblem of a narrow capitalist patriarchy whose only response to sunsets is to "tally" them. Like notch and spindle, the tally is a rich image, implying spatial shape and temporal activity: a stick on which notches are made to keep a record or count of something, particularly a debt or payment. The tower, therefore, not only keeps tallies but is itself a tally, attempting to notch the night and the sunset but instead mainly recording the interminable, hollow business of its own ledgers. In exploring this convergence of architectural hubris, patriarchal performance anxiety, and ideologies of capitalist aspiration, Ridge thoroughly ironizes the skyscraper's conventional symbolic functions. Yet the exuberance of her critique suggests that she has found the tower a source of inspiration toward a passionately engaged poetics of urban-industrial modernity.

Unlike the geographical specificity of these other poems, Robert Frost's small masterpiece of modern alienation, "Acquainted with the Night" (1928), refers to no building or city by name. But the poem's early urbanite readers might well have thought of the Metropolitan Tower upon encountering its culminating image, "One luminary clock against the sky" at an "unearthly height."[100] The Metropolitan's famous electric-powered clock, with illuminated faces three stories tall on all four sides and minute hands weighing one thousand pounds each, was the largest in the world. At more than 350 feet above the ground, it was also by far the unearthliest. Whether Frost's "luminary clock" is an actual clock or the moon has produced some fairly pedantic critical discussion; to me, the ambiguity seems intentional and one of the richest elements of the poem.[101] Where Ridge opposes clock and moon, Frost merges them into a modern cityscape all the more unsettling for being devoid of touchstones of accuracy or immutability. Natural and technological measures of value have become equally dysfunctional, even indistinguishable, and proclaim only their own lack of meaning, rendering time itself "neither wrong nor right." The ethical vacuity of modern time is reinforced by the speaker's passive response to an "interrupted cry" that punctuates his alienated wandering, a cry of unknown origins and uncertain address about which the only certainty is that it was not uttered "to call me back or say good-bye."[102] All that remains, as the poem ends precisely where it began, is the speaker's abiding acquaintance with the night, weary, wary, not notably congenial, but providing an emotional complexity that Frost clearly relishes in spite (or because) of its departure from his more typical rural persona.

That poets as divergent in style and politics as Giovannitti, Teasdale, the Benét brothers, Wylie, Ridge, and perhaps even Frost were all drawn to the Metropolitan Tower invites us to see the building as an exemplary symbol for the poetics of modernity that energized the American New Verse movement. Several of these works—many of the texts I've discussed in this chapter—belong to a category of poems largely disqualified from canonical versions of modernism. Though fascinated with the urban-industrial scene and willing to explore innovative modes of verbal representation, they reject the referential opacity and emotional reserve of conventional high modernism and instead adapt the rhapsodic tonalities of nineteenth-century romanticism to twentieth-century uses. These metropolitan rhapsodies are central to the hidden history of modern American poetry. Recovering and reevaluating them will furnish us with richer accounts of poetry's response to the challenges of twentieth-century experience and help us to integrate the genre more productively into the ongoing historicist project of the twenty-first-century literary academy.

CHAPTER 8

Subway Fare

Toward a Poetics of Rapid Transit

Wishful civic boosters of the early twentieth century discerned signs of financial utopia in the "symbiotic relation" between the skyscraper and the urban railway, which they saw as the source not only of the American city's spectacular skyline but of "its constantly rising real estate values."[1] More than one early commentator imagined this symbiosis through an axis of unlimited spatial accessibility and freedom of movement, interchangeably horizontal and vertical. In this view, skyscrapers were understood as "street railways running perpendicularly," turning the air into new capital just as expanding networks of rapid transit were modernizing the regions surrounding the city, creating the far-flung commuter metropolis.[2] Others saw the relationship between these two quite differently, as a "vicious interbreeding" in which the expansion of transit systems, driven by the increasing density of the centralized skyscraper city, brought greater congestion and exacerbated the need for more tall buildings, which required yet more transportation infrastructure, and so on.[3] But most saw these interdependent social forms as defining the character of twentieth-century urban modernity—not least the American poets who discovered rapid transit as they discovered the skyscraper, beginning with isolated poems soon after 1905, peaking in the mid-1910s, and continuing well into the next decade.

Yet skyscraper verses and rapid-transit verses engaged the modern urban landscape in strikingly different fashion. In many respects, the latter subject was the more radical departure from existing poetic traditions. Skyscraper and skyline could be more readily imported into existing symbol-making practices, as modern urban versions of the monumental natural objects, the mountains or bodies of water, through which so many poems of the romantic sublime had posited divine immanence or a grand cosmic design. Great buildings, however overwhelming, were primarily experienced in this symbolic sense, as discrete *objects* that could be observed from outside themselves. The skyline may have been "ever-changing," in the lexicon of the era, but its changes could be charted from a distance, while individual buildings impressed observers as monolithic and otherworldly, virtually the only compelling symbols of the eternal that the modern city had to offer.

In contrast, rapid transit was experienced not as an externalized symbolic object but as an immersive, unstable *environment* that was felt all around and even within the observing body. The designs of conveyances, the labyrinthine networks of tracks they moved on, and the liminal transfer points among them all worked to transform the modern urban subject's experience of space, altering the relations between work-spaces and home-spaces, public and private experience, city and countryside, the observing consciousness and the surrounding objects of observation. In this rapid-transit environment, perceptual categories such as *space* and *distance* were fragmented into inversely related dyads: the city space one moved past or through and the containing space within which one was carried; the expanding distance one could traverse and the contracting distance between one's own body and those of others. American rapid-transit verses often register this reconfiguration of spatial categories by emphasizing tensions between hurtling motion and enforced stasis, between unprecedented personal mobility and uncanny confinement in an enclosure traveling at the same speed as the passenger's body while a landscape unspools cinematically outside the window, vividly accessible to the sight but uninhabitable by the body.

The poetics that emerges from this rapid-transit environment emphasizes unpredictable and omnidirectional shifts in narrative and visual perspective. Few American verses about rapid transit sustain the sweeping panoramic views prevalent in the cityscape and skyscraper verses I discussed in earlier chapters. Nor do many attain the spectatorial detachment of Basil and Isabel March of William Dean Howells's *A Hazard of New Fortunes* (1890), who, upon returning to New York, use the new elevated cars to explore the city's changed spaces but also finally to preserve comfortable distance from its intrusive forces by translating them into the "harmonizing vision" of the picturesque.[4] Instead, rapid-transit poems of the early twentieth century feature close-up encounters mingling people of different classes, races, and genders with unprecedented frequency, unfathomable swiftness, and sometimes uncontrollable force. In other words, the rapid-transit aesthetic is inevitably a *social aesthetic*. The observers of previous chapters, surveying skylines much as a painter or photographer ponders a landscape, give way to more active, mobile participants in what Marshall Berman calls "primal scenes" of modernity.[5] These rapid-transit observers consitute a vivid twentieth-

New York City Elevated Train, 1910s. Author's Collection.

century gloss on *flânerie* as a paradigm of modern urban experience. Though most often used in reference to an earlier modern moment, the discourse of *flânerie,* descending from Charles Baudelaire through Walter Benjamin down to Marshall Berman, Janet Wolff, Deborah Parsons, and many others, remains a valuable model for describing twentieth-century metropolitan experience. *Flânerie* in the rapid-transit city still possesses unpredictability and hybridity of form, the surprise and exhilaration and incipient menace generated by encounters with social otherness. But the experience loses its earlier connotations of leisurely wandering by a bemused and detached observer, becoming instead an intensely felt activity somewhere between a search for personal enlightenment and a form of social investigation.

The body of work I designate here as "rapid-transit verse" is larger and more significant than simply the numerous works that describe actual rail journeys. In many poems of the period, as in John Dos Passos's monumental study of the machine-age metropolis, *Manhattan Transfer* (1925), rapid transit becomes an overarching condition and metaphor for all of twentieth-century urban experience. Travel in all forms of conveyance, entering and leaving public spaces, even just traversing the city street and sidewalk on foot, take on the experiential qualities of high-speed mechanized travel: exhilaration and danger; constant novelty and lurking routinization; unrelenting bodily proximity to, and emotional detachment from, innumerable strangers. As they move from ferry and street into streetcar and subway, these twentieth-century rapid-transit verses dramatize a productive tension between two quintessential modern experiences: the promiscuous mingling of bodies in confined conveyances, which creates a powerful sense of alienation among any given individuals; and the often liberating corollaries of this alienation, the disruption of reified boundaries and the emergence of new forms of sociality.

Modernity by Rail

Perhaps more than any other invention, machine-aided transportation made life modern. The beginning of *modernity,* as I have used the term throughout this book, can be plausibly dated to the first appearance of railroads in the late 1820s. Until then, the velocity with which the embodied consciousness could move had changed little, at least on land, since the invention of the wheel and the domestication of the horse. Splendid scholarship by Wolfgang Schivelbusch, Stephen Kern, John Stilgoe, and others has elaborated the many ways in which early rail travel ruptured existing perceptual categories of time, space, and the relations between them. But while the intercity railroads of the mid-nineteenth century initiated this acceleration of consciousness, the vast metropolitan transit systems developed between 1870 and 1920 were perhaps even more transformative to the modern subject's spatio-temporal experience. After all, nineteenth-century intercity rail travel remained a controlled experience of motion and distance that we can call diachronic and linear: a single train proceeding on a single line from a fixed point of departure to a predictable destination. Such long-distance train travel, then as now, was defined as much by longueurs of uneventful waiting as by the sensation of breakneck speed. The experience of social otherness on early railways, while certainly remarked upon by many, was managed and to some degree muted by the quasi-domesticity of the enclosures in which people rode.[6] On a given journey, passengers, especially in European compartment carriages, encountered only a few fellow travelers and, according to Schivelbusch, seldom interacted with them meaningfully.[7] Even in the larger, more public, and at first "classless" American cars, where travelers typically generated sociable conversation, most of those encountered would be roughly kindred in class and regional identity.[8] No doubt early train journeys were felt by many as landmark moments in their lives, but that very momentousness meant that the sensation of high-speed motion was not yet the ground of everyday experience.

Furthermore, although railroads had an immediate global impact, the sheer number of people traveling by train at any given moment during the middle of the nineteenth century was minuscule compared to the tens of millions for whom short repetitive journeys through urban space had become the basis of everyday life by 1910.[9] The experience of interurban rapid transit differed in fundamental ways from long-distance rail travel. As people and conveyances swarmed in all directions through ever more sprawling and complex expanses of metropolitan space, the cast of characters surrounding the traveler, now completely unrestricted by social status, changed at every intersection or station. Rather than encountering other people in the dozens, the traveler could expect to intersect the paths of hundreds, possibly thousands of others within a single day's journeying. In contrast to long-distance rail travel, the option of an impulsive change of route or destination remained always at hand. The traveler's experience of space inside the conveyance no longer consisted of occupying an assigned seat while gazing upon fellow passengers or passing scenery but a scramble for any seat or standing place, followed by an interval of studied staring at nothing and no one, culminated by a darting sideways exit, dodging those waiting to enter. The imperative for quick, continuous egress and ingress was facilitated by seats facing the car's center rather than its front, which reoriented the traveler's experience away from linear forward motion in relative privacy toward sidelong observation and intimate bodily proximity to many other people—but not usually meaningful conversation with any of them.

These experiential conditions of rapid transit—continual perceptual dissonance combined with constant physical and social flux—were readily assimilated into various dystopian portrayals of urban modernity. Indeed, subway travel eventually became the quintessential modern site of urban alienation and even terror in such late twentieth-century cultural touchstones as LeRoi Jones's incendiary 1964 play *Dutchman* and the bleak saga of the vigilante Bernhard Goetz in 1984.[10] But it is equally important to realize that in the 1910s and 1920s, when El and subway rides in New York and other cities were not only quick but cheap and generally quite safe, American poets, no less than the novelists, playwrights, and visual artists discussed by Michael W. Brooks in *Subway City,* attached a much wider range of meanings to the experience, including not only the expected revulsion and despair but physical exhilaration, social solidarity, and even utopian possibility. The poets of those years seek out trolleys, streetcars, suburban trains, and subways to dramatize the impossibility of maintaining Olympian detachment when thrown into close quarters with crowds of strangers. In other words, they use these conveyances, particularly the subway, to challenge their own reluctance, and poetry's, to address the pressing and troubling dynamics that define social life in the modern metropolis. Some of their verses merely conclude that the new spaces and forms of the twentieth-century rapid-transit city vex all dreams of commonality, threatening to impose instead what Georg Simmel called in 1903 the disquieting "attitude of the people of the metropolis to one another," a "reserve" that goes beyond indifference to "slight aversion, a mutual strangeness and repulsion."[11] At other times, however, encounters across class, ethnic, or gender lines, often ambiguously sexualized, generate moments of solidarity and liberation from stifling social norms. But whether they end happily or unhappily, verses using rapid-transit settings address questions of social otherness at an unusually immediate level and reveal an urban modernity far richer than the "hell" portrayed by Monroe K. Spears and other literary historians writing in the ambit of postwar high modernism.[12]

The Modern Commuting Poem

In contrast to the many long-distance epics of nineteenth-century verse—*The Prelude, Don Juan, Evangeline*—American poems after 1910 favor brief, reproducible journeys through urban and suburban terrain that do not culminate in any momentous destination or denouement. In other words, they are commuting journeys. Though overall my argument has emphasized the paucity of useful precursor texts for the New Verse, the modern commuting poem has one richly generative source. In "Crossing Brooklyn Ferry" (first published in 1856 as "Sun-Down Poem"), Walt Whitman builds a modern poetics from the experience of masses of people moving in workaday fashion through urban-industrial space. Unlike, say, *The Prelude* of Wordsworth, in which the sublimity of Mount Snowdon provides a compelling symbol of cosmic immanence, "Crossing Brooklyn Ferry" eschews monumental symbolism and epic structure for the climate of everyday experience: the sea, sky, and weather during a typical, reproducible journey through urban terrain to no destination other than work or home. For Whitman, ferry, city skyline and shoreline, flood-tide and clouds do not symbolize the transcendence of spatial and temporal limitations so much as comprise the physical and experiential conditions in which such transcendence might be sought.

In Whitman's rapidly industrializing city, Wordsworth's anti-urban version of transcendence through the measured contemplation of natural grandeur has given way to radical contingency and mutability. The shared presence on the Brooklyn ferry of any particular collection of individuals is not preordained or even significant but the product of countless contingencies: the uncertain accuracy of clocks in a world before standardized time; the angle of early morning sunlight coming through windows; impulsive decisions to do errands in a certain order or take one route rather than another; the press of foot traffic approaching the ferry slip. In the few minutes on the ferry, the poet can glimpse the merest slice of other peoples' lives, can make only tenuous surmises about them. Yet the same contradictory factors that make Whitman's ferry journey an unconvincing symbol of sublimity and immanence—its simultaneous ephemerality and repetitiousness, its radically contingent yet relatively unchanging particulars—make it a rich emblem of experience in the modern city. For the travelers, repeated intervals on the ferry serve as markers punctuating their days but also as temporary suspensions of work-time, affording some familiarity and stability within a constantly changing milieu, and moments of closeness to the natural world that the city's density of construction threatens to crowd out altogether. For the poet, the ferry carries a liminal force that is figured by the action of crossing—literally traversing shore to shore, but also bridging seemingly insurmountable distances. Whitman explores these concerns by balancing images of time and distance at opposite extremes of scale: the tiny passing moments, measured by transportation timetables and work clocks, that drive the metropolitan consciousness through its daily paces; and the momentous spans that will see him and his fellow passengers gone long before future readers are born.

By seeking continuity and community from the daily textures of millions of anonymous urban lives, "Crossing Brooklyn Ferry" instigates a poetics of urban encounter that anticipates by several years Charles Baudelaire's foundational modernist proposition in "The Painter of Modern Life" (1863) that contingent, even random intersections are the material from which modern art must be created. Baudelaire describes the immersion of his exemplary painter (Constantin Guys) in a metropolitan condition that, he insists, "you must allow me to call 'modernity'": a condition "whose metamorphoses are so rapid" that they require a painter willing to ignore the convention that demands artists pursue the eternal and instead to seek art only in "the passing moment."[13] Even more than Baudelaire's artist-*flâneur*, Whitman's ferry-going poet confronts experiential conditions that seem to leave no psychic room for those we find right next to us, nor much hope that traces of our existence might outlast us. Yet by burrowing into the contradictory demands that mass-transit environments make on our experience of distance and time—to be "one of a crowd," to stand still and yet be hurried, to share with others the experience of constant flux—Whitman converts the limitations and discomfitures of mass-transit time and space into a basis for commonality between self and other, which he terms "similitudes of the past and those of the future."[14]

Whitman's "similitudes" are neither symbols of Wordsworthian immanence nor the analogical correspondences between human experience and
the natural world that shape the verse of Bryant and Emerson. They are
nothing more or less than the bodily experiences shared by those who surround him on the ferry day after day, and equally by "[t]he others that are
to follow me": by everyone who has occupied or will occupy that space.
Although the ferry only goes from this specific place to that one, and only at
certain times, these very restrictions intensify the resemblances between his
experience and those of others. These communitarian aspirations coalesce
as a bold thesis beginning section three—

> It avails not, neither time or place—distance avails not;
> I am with you, you men and women of a generation, or ever so
>   many generations hence,
> [I project myself—also I return—I am with you, and know how
>   it is.]
> Just as you feel when you look on the river and sky, so I felt;
> Just as any of you is one of a living crowd, I was one of a crowd;
> Just as you are refresh'd by the gladness of the river and the
>   bright flow, I was refresh'd;
> Just as you stand and lean on the rail, yet hurry with the swift
>   current, I stood, yet was hurried;
> Just as you look on the numberless masts of ships, and the thick-
>   stem'd pipes of steamboats, I look'd

—and on for hundreds of lines, since Whitman's materialism rules out the
shortcuts of symbolism and requires reproducing the scene with enough
detail and intensity that others distant in time and space might feel that they
have experienced it as the poet did on those particular days of the mid-1850s.

Until 1882, the poem included the line enclosed in brackets in the passage
above: "I project myself—also I return—I am with you, and know how it
is."[15] Whitman's excision was unfortunate because *project* is a brilliantly
layered verb. This poet of modern life, a ferry-going *flâneur* who *projects
himself* into contact with others, is strikingly like the painter Baudelaire
describes using three vivid visual metaphors: "[H]e enters into the crowd
as though it were an immense field of electrical energy. Or we might liken
him to a mirror as vast as the crowd itself; or to a kaleidoscope gifted with
consciousness, responding to each one of its movements and reproducing
the multiplicity of life and the flickering grace of all the elements of life."[16]
Projected physically into collision with innumerable anonymous others,
Whitman's poet draws energy from the electrifying friction of bodies in mo-

tion and contact. Projecting himself emotionally, he mirrors the experience of others with empathy and solidarity ("I . . . know how it is"). Projected imaginatively among the kaleidoscopically shifting crowd, his consciousness refracts the fragments of each momentary encounter into a distinctive design that can then be projected onto the page and into the reader's mind's eye in a process reminiscent of the moving panoramas of mid-nineteenth-century New York that fascinated Whitman—ingenious optical technologies either mounted on walls or unrolling pictorial tableaux from drums, the pre-electronic ancestors of movie projectors.[17]

To portray these new experiences of space and time, Whitman creates a formal structure that embodies precisely the sort of modern journey he writes about: rhapsodic unmetered lines using simple yet infinitely expandable syntactic parallelisms. Starting with a potent anaphoric construction expressing commonality of self and other, "Just as you, I," he soon moves to the even more compressed syntax "I too."[18] That simple subject and modifier open a universe of syntactic space that he furnishes with one parallel verb phrase after another, resulting in a sprawling yet coherent sentence of 249 words that unfolds to the end of the section and implicitly continues forever. Each line of this enormous sentence might be imagined as a daily journey, all beginning in the same place, but each taking varying lengths of time, involving different routes, featuring some newly observed element of the metropolitan environment. Or each "I too" might be imagined as an encounter with another person moving through the city, inevitably a different individual each time, yet containing enough commonality of experience and desire that Whitman can begin the next section by reaffirming, "These, and all else, were to me the same as they are to you." For him, these finite and yet infinitely reproducible journeys of mass transit, shared as are few other experiences of modern life, render others not only coincidentally proximate but *close* in a powerfully communitarian sense, an apprehension he states with affecting simplicity: "The men and women I saw were all near to me."

In the poem's final section, Whitman theorizes this urban-materialist paradigm of experience by addressing the things of the city as "objects than which none else is more lasting" and as "dumb, beautiful ministers" that "great or small, furnish your parts toward the soul." He proposes here an idea we can still find radical 150 years later: that the modern "soul" is composed of the body's movements and sensations, and the objects that surround it. This investiture of spiritual experience into the material and mutable again corresponds strikingly to a claim of Baudelaire's: that the modern artist must be "the painter of the passing moment and of all the suggestions of eternity that it contains."[19] For these men, born only two years apart, attuned to the modernizing city as few before them had been, the poet of modern life must be a poet of body and object and moment, observing contemporary manners, fashions, physiognomies, machines, "men and women near to me," "objects than which none else is more lasting"—all preserved in their spatio-temporal particularity, not lumped by the force of tradition into what Baudelaire derisively calls "the abyss of . . . abstract and indeterminate beauty."[20] Even if we suspect that Whitman posits this communion in verse to address the felt lack of it in his urban environment, the intensity and integrity of his commitment to the social forms of his times demands that we include him with Baudelaire among the great nineteenth-century realists who created the socially engaged modernism Raymond Williams urges us to investigate.

Among poets, Whitman's ability to live imaginatively in the material conditions of industrial modernity was matched by none of his American contemporaries, nor by several generations of successors. But between 1905 and 1920, during the same years in which he became fully canonical in the United States, rapid-transit verses began appearing across the entire stylistic spectrum of American verse, from the archaic-rhapsodic idiom of Joyce Kilmer's "The Twelve-Forty-Five" to William Carlos Williams's futurist "Overture to a Dance of Locomotives." These verses reflect an intervening half century of headlong growth and mechanization that had accelerated the pace and exacerbated the spatial chaos of urban life. Whitman's open-air horse-cars and ferries have become electrified trolleys, elevated trains, automobiles, and subways.[21] These changed material conditions make twentieth-century poets less idealistic than their great predecessor, but no less passionate in their address to the city. As they explore what happens to Baudelaire's "perfect *flâneur*" of streets and carriages in an accelerated environment of transportation without nature, many revisit "Crossing Brooklyn Ferry" for the twentieth-century city, asking whether, in the vast stretches of metropolitan space, the time and distance that separate people can still be found not to avail.

The effort to portray modern spaces of transit in verse was not a simple matter of choice or will. It required representational tools that prevailing romantic-genteel poetics had failed to provide. The difficulty of using inherited poetic convention, and the benefits of looking to the contemporary visual arts instead, can be measured by examining two commuting poems of the mid-1910s that depict emblematic train journeys, Joyce Kilmer's "The Twelve-Forty-Five" (1914) and Carl Sandburg's "Halsted Street Car" (1916). We have largely forgotten that Kilmer, the author of the famous and fatuous "Trees," addressed the twentieth-century urban scene in many verses such as "The Apartment," "Delicatessen," "The Alarm Clock," and "Servant Girl and Grocer's Boy"; in 1910 he had even aroused the particular ire of traditionalists with his "gutter verse" sonnet "The Subway (96th Street to 137th Street)." "The Twelve-Forty-Five" employs a mock-epic mode to depict a late-night train journey from Manhattan to the poet's cottage in Mahwah in the outer suburbs of northern New Jersey.[22] Kilmer's far-fetched personifications, hackneyed adjectives, and too-insistent iambic tetrameter will doubtless never be considered the stuff of modernist greatness, but any poem of early 1914 that begins with the line, "Within the Jersey City shed," is noteworthy at least for its aggressive departure from genteel convention and its intention to engage urban-industrial modernity.[23]

As his train chugs through quiet suburban towns, seeming to "[p]ollute the still nocturnal air" with light, smoke, and noise, Kilmer's speaker rationalizes this "blasphemy" with idealizations that strike us now as preposterous: "What precious secret is our freight? / What king must be abroad so late? / Perhaps Death roams the hills to-night / And we rush forth to give him fight." But no matter how high-flown his rhetoric becomes, Kilmer remains aware of the specific geography of the journey, punctuating the poem with the names of localities the train passes through—Rutherford, Carlton Hill, Passaic, Clifton, Lake View, Paterson—much as a train conductor would call them out one by one. At the moment of greatest rhetorical excess, this structural principle becomes explicit:

> The train, that like an angel sings,
> The train, with healing on its wings,
> Now "Hawthorne!" the conductor cries.
> My neighbor starts and rubs his eyes.

This interruption of the speaker's reverie and the departure of his neighbor precipitate the realization that the workaday "reason of our quest," to "carry people home," is no less valuable than all his idealized fantasies:

> In Ramsey, Mahwah, Suffern stand
> Houses that wistfully demand
> A father—son—some human thing
> That this, the midnight train, may bring.

The final lines ("My cottage lamp shines white and clear. / God bless the train that brought me here") still cling to a genteel, if now thoroughly suburbanized, idyll of Christian domesticity. But applying this elevated rhetoric to something so mundane and modern as a suburban train creates a productive incongruity that undermines the compartmentalizations of work and home, urban and pastoral, profane and sacred, ephemeral and eternal, upon which American genteel poetics had been built.

I set "The Twelve-Forty-Five" in a mildly positive light, presuming that if you can't now say something nice about Joyce Kilmer, there's no reason to say anything at all. Clearly Kilmer's desire to portray urban modernity was stunted by his lingering investment in an intransigent antimodern poetics that offered him only mushy descriptors and rhetorical excess. Seeking a way out of this stifling epic-romantic tradition, other poets looked to the more compressed and unadorned aesthetic of modern life that had recently emerged in the visual arts. Along with William Carlos Williams, discussed in detail later in the chapter, the most consistently successful in doing so was Carl Sandburg, whose "Halsted Street Car," an empathetic portrayal of spatially segregated working-class experience, wastes no time in announcing an affinity with such urban realists as Constantin Guys and Honoré Daumier. It begins,

> Come you, cartoonists,
> Hang on a strap with me here
> At seven o'clock in the morning
> On a Halsted Street car.
>
> Take your pencils
> And draw these faces.[24]

Moved by the visages of surrounding riders, who are "[t]ired of wishes, / Empty of dreams" even at "cool daybreak," the poet urges cartoonists to "[f]ind for your pencils / A way to mark your memory" of these faces.[25] Here Sandburg calls for realist artists of his own day and milieu, Chicago descendants of Daumier or siblings to John Sloan, who will strive to record honestly and intensely the industrial city's effects on its populace. Of course, this pencil-wielding artist tropes poet and reader as well, making this little verse into a manifesto for modern poetry's reponsibility to challenge the voicelessness that capitalist modernity enforces upon most of its inhabitants.

The "way" that Sandburg's artist-poet seeks to preserve these faces, the method of portrayal, comes not through adherence to any particular style but through a willingness to inhabit the same physical spaces as those he writes about, to get to that grimy streetcar early enough to observe the morning commute. This materialist-modernist poetics is embodied by his fanciful proposition that the poet-cartoonists of modern life so thoroughly internalize the experience of rapid transit that they might learn to write or draw while hanging from a trolley strap. This startling posture echoes Baudelaire's portrayal of Guys as artist-*flâneur*, composing while bent awkwardly over a table—"darting on to a sheet of paper the same glance that a moment ago he was directing towards external things, in a ferment of violent activity, . . . elbowing himself on"—so fully identified with the crowd that its jostling elbows are incarnated in his own body even as he works alone in his studio.[26] In likewise connecting bodily discomfort to authenticity of observation and representation, Sandburg proposes the modern poet as one who struggles against the prevailing ideological grain and articulates a distinctive version of Whitman's "projection" into the crowd for his own twentieth-century moment.

Subterranean Selves and Others

Though ferries, trolleys, suburban railways, streetcars, taxis, and autos all make their share of appearances, the mode of modern transport most compelling to the New Verse of the 1910s was the subway, which combined the physical excitement of high-speed travel with the Promethean feats of tunneling and lighting the earth's interior. Verses written in the first decade after the opening of the New York City subway system in 1904 tend to treat the experience as an exhilarating amusement-park ride as they describe plunging on a narrow rail through darkness relieved only by dangerous charges of electricity. Chester Firkins's "On a Subway Express" and verses by Louis Untermeyer and Louis Ginsberg both entitled "In the Subway" portray the ride as a paradigmatic experience of modern life by comparing the train's path through subterranean blackness to a meteor hurtling through space.

The obscure Firkins was exploring modern subject matter in magazine verse by 1907, though in much more homiletic fashion than Harriet Monroe. But in "On a Subway Express" (*The Atlantic,* February 1908), he broke through to more immediate engagement with the modern urban environment. His speaker is a "city clod" who has "lost the stars, the sod, / For chilling pave and cheerless light," yet who (despite these nostalgic phrasings) finds that the subway experience fully compensates this loss because the flashing lights of the tunnels and trains supply a constructed cosmos of breathtaking immediacy:

> In this dim firmament, the stars
> Whirl by in blazing files and tiers;
> Kin meteors graze our flying bars,
> Amid the spinning spheres.[27]

The poet acknowledges the subway's alienating aspects, noting that passengers "sit muted by the roar," each feeling but "a figment in the crowded dark." But this sense of insignificance, combined with perceptual vertigo and actual bodily danger ("Death rides about me, on either hand"), generates a sublimity that exemplifies and justifies modern experience. The subway's "new and nether Night" has become his "meeting-place with God," his "wild ride" the "only respite of the Day" in an otherwise mundane life. *Respite* is a notable usage here, implying a lingering valorization of the imagery of shelter and escape from chaotic modernity so prevalent in nineteenth-century American genteel verse. But Firkins's modern straphanger feels no desire to turn away from the subway world of "Speed! Speed!" instead perceiving acceleration and flux as forms of respite from the worse danger of deadening routinization.

"In the Subway" (1910s) by Louis Ginsberg (Allen's father) advances an even more exuberant accommodation to the vertiginous textures of twentieth-century experience. Working through his initial disorientation and distress (the car, "screeching and mad with speed," "lurches in the roar and veers" alarmingly), the poet accepts these discomforts as emblems of

Subway Train in Tube—
Battery Tunnel, 1905.
Author's Collection.

human progress, turning to space travel as the only metaphor adequate to his idealistic hopes:

> And who can tell in years to come,
> What speed will whirl us through the sky?
> What lights of stars our cars will graze?
> What worlds will flash and flutter by?[28]

Likewise, Untermeyer's "In the Subway" (1914) portrays the underground train as a triumph of rationality: "Chaos is tamed and ordered as we ride; / The rock is rent, the darkness is flung aside / And all the horrors of the deep defied."[29] Riding underground on "a screaming meteor" while "[t]he ancient elements become our slaves," the poet senses that no chimera of the past, no limitation of the present, is now insurmountable. In the final couplet, however, he turns from rhapsody toward irony, finding that the "wildest glimpse of all" is to see how nonchalantly the ride through the earth is treated by fellow passengers, "The score of men and women facing me / Reading their papers calmly, leisurely."

In Untermeyer's poem, the twentieth-century urbanite's quick acclimation to remarkable technological change remains whimsical rather than sinister, but it anticipates a second phase of verses that turn toward the social implications of the rapid-transit environment. As sheer vertiginous novelty diminished, subway or trolley poems became sites exploring anxieties over the atomized and routinized conditions of modern urban life, often by foregrounding the experience of intimate confinement with a group of strangers in public enclosures that lack the emotional comfort that more domestic communal enclosures provided such nineteenth-century poets as Longfellow in *Tales of a Wayside Inn*. Louis Ginsberg's "In a Street-Car" (1910s) is a typical example, drawing a fundamental irony of urban life from "rows of people" staring past each other, lined up like objects on shelves: "Though huddled together they journey alone."[30] For poets in this mood, fellow riders offer not spiritual communion but unwanted physical intimacy and claustrophobic alienation. In "Summer Evening: New York Subway Station" (1922), Maxwell Bodenheim portrays the subway experience as a furtive, fleeting, yet somehow still mundane form of sexual predation: "People savagely tamper with each other's bodies, / Scampering in and out of doorways."[31] The loss of control over one's own body—where it can move, what it touches and smells, how it intersects with the similarly uncontrolled bodies of others—can turn even socially progressive writers misanthropic. The speaker of Louis Untermeyer's "Lenox Avenue Express" (1923), for example, sees his fellow subway passengers as "[f]aces gone blank except for groveling lusts; / Trace of the beast caught in some black abyss," finally exclaiming in disgust, "God! Am I dying for these?"[32]

"Lenox Avenue Express" never recovers from this corrosive initial perception and reveals little about the problems of social class except to dramatize Simmel's description of the characteristic relations between metropolitan subjects as mutual reserve tending toward aversion.[33] But the poem's familiar rhetoric of physical revulsion and interpersonal alienation hardly exhausts the complex implications of millions of people interacting in common carriages that, unlike most intercity railroads of that era, did not distinguish passengers by economic status but offered equal access and (dis)comfort to everyone with the nickel fare. Do those facts make mass-transit systems into social levelers? Or, given that all classes might ride the same trains but not to the same destinations or for the same reasons, does the rapid-transit environment merely reinforce existing class divisions and segregations?

By foregrounding such questions, however troubling or unanswerable, poets made the subway and other settings of transit into sites of ideological critique against the forces obfuscating the impact of class divisions upon the life of modern America. As early as 1910, in Kilmer's sonnet "The Subway (96th Street to 137th Street)" (1910), the roller-coaster response has given way to an emphasis on the train's indiscriminate mingling of all classes and stations of modern city life: "Tired clerks, pale girls, street-cleaners, business men, / Boys, priests and harlots, drunkards, students, thieves."[34] The experience of modernity as one of continual and largely untrammeled encounters with social difference, which Baudelaire's *flâneur* had experienced in the open air of streets and boulevards, is now confined to a "stifling, loud-wheeled pen" surrounded by perpetual darkness, in which people are made to feel like caged animals, or like "human parcels who dispatched themselves to their destination," as Schivelbusch puts it, following John Ruskin's critique of railway experience.[35] Yet although noting that he and his fellows glimpse only "transitory gleams" of "God's day," Kilmer's observer discerns no qualitative difference between himself and these others, concluding, "That is our life, it seems."[36] Employing first-person plural to the end of the poem, he finds solidarity with this motley assortment of strangers through their shared physical discomfiture—another ironic updating of Whitman's emphasis on the commonality of bodily experience as the basis of modern sociality.

Kilmer's sonnet seems to suggest that by removing the modern urban subject from nature, and by enforcing continual encounters with social otherness and the technological sublime, the subway environment might disrupt old social relations not despite but because of its alienating force. A similar trajectory appears in the sonnet "In the Subway," published in *The Masses* in August 1916 by the Barnard alumna Florence Ripley Mastin, who satirically reverses a conventional dynamic of compassion and class distinction in which the earnest bourgeois reformer patronizes or pities the underprivileged masses. The poem features an implicitly middle-class observer confronted by alienating class otherness, but ironically this happens as she surveys a car full of vapid bourgeois pleasure-seekers and finds herself *self*-alienated, unable to identify with the class she was born into. The objects of her pity are not "[t]he pale lipped workers" she usually sees in the subway but these "[w]arm furred and decent" ones "smiling so dreamlessly" with "eyes, so unafraid," "complacent seekers after joy" who "never come to grips with anything."[37] They are "earth's most wistful," since they cannot even imagine a different plane of experience. Better, Mastin concludes, to be "burned as though with fire, / Swaying in pallid sleep and pinched with want," if the alternative is this life of cosseted inauthenticity.

For Mastin, the estranging subway setting enables the traversal of social boundaries, but still she experiences alienation from her own class much more palpably than identification with a deprived laboring class. The struggle of middle-class poets toward identification with class otherness advances further in "The Subway," an ambitious rapid-transit verse Edgar Lee Masters published in *Others* in the summer of 1916. "The Subway" begins as a Robinsonian study in romantic melancholy but turns unpredictably into a meditation on the emotional costs of technological progress and the surprising malleability of class allegiance. In the first half, the speaker, who resembles Masters in his penchant for sexual intrigue, addresses a lover who has fled their extramarital liaison to escape the scorn of repressive middle-class morality, leaving with no proper farewell. After forty-five lines of recrimination and self-pity, the work abruptly shifts to narrate the speaker's dream of the future in which he, and later his beloved, are buried in the same suburban cemetery:

> Well, I had a dream one night
> That a dead man well could dream.
>
> They had buried me in Rosehill.
> And after twenty years from France they brought you
> And put you just across the walk from me.[38]

Here is a valedictory image for separated lovers of the sort poets have offered from time immemorial. In modern times, however, such commemorations become no less transitory than anything else:

> . . . the crowding city grew
> To a vast six millions, and they were building
> A sub-way to Lake Forest.
> And we were forgotten of every-one,
> And almost our family names were lost.

At this moment of their ultimate oblivion, the lovers achieve decidedly ironic togetherness as Polish and Italian workmen, digging up graveyards to make way for the Lake Forest line, "dump our bones in a careless heap, / The ribs of me by the ribs of you."

Then, in the poem's most distinctive stroke, the lovers are indeed forgotten, as Masters makes another narrative shift, entering the emotional life of one of these future workmen, who complains to his companion of a beguiling but inaccessible girl who "bothers [him] almost to death" and concludes that "as soon as this sub-way job is over," he will "beat it back to Poland." In the poem's final line, the other digger, evidently commenting on their shared disgust with the times, mutters simply, "1976." America in its bicentennial year is still a place of economic opportunity for people of other nations, but the emotional costs of its alienating textures have grown too high, sending them back to the more integrated societies from which they came. The poem ends with no further reference to the angst-ridden lovers. Its jagged refusal of narrative unity captures in structural terms the material impermanence and emotional dispossession punctuating life in the rapid-transit city. The poem's emphasis on disjuncture is reinforced by its title. The subway plays only a peripheral role in the narrative, yet by rending the settled order of the earth to enable the city's perpetual expansion, it emblematizes a modernity in which all that is apparently solid will end pulverized into dust, in which "everything we said, or thought, or felt" will be "forgotten / With the whispers of boys and girls / In a temple's shadow in Babylon." Yet the insight that "the subway" dominates all modern lives, even those who don't travel on it, has carried sufficient defamiliarizing force to wrench Masters out of his customary self-involvement into sympathetic identification with one of another era, nationality, and class.

The tentative proposition advanced by these three poems—that the alienations of subway modernity might propel poet-observers and their readers toward more genuine identification with social otherness—is realized wholeheartedly by "Crayon," another of Carl Sandburg's many mass-transit vignettes of the 1910s. Beginning with a title that defines the modern poem as a quick sketch captured from everyday urban life (as in "Halsted Street Car"), Sandburg depicts a "sewer digger's daughter" who hears her mother announce that they can't afford eggs for breakfast, then takes a trolley to her work in a corset factory, and while straphanging, "Reads a morning newspaper society page twice and is teased all day by thought of what a 'dog collar of pearls' might be."[39] Two of the qualities Raymond Williams identifies as central to the realist-modernist aesthetic—"metaphoric control" and "economy of seeing"—are on full display here, as Sandburg's spare but telling details metonymize a society founded on exploitation, punctuated by wasteful consumption and empty celebrity, and maintained through spatial segregation and ideological false consciousness.[40]

As a matter of course, the daughter of a lowly worker in such a socio-economic system becomes a worker herself. She moves about the city in a transit network that seems to allegorize class separation, since her only contact with those who don't ride crowded early-morning trains through factory districts comes through the newspaper, a mass medium with its own questionable democratizing claims that tantalizes those who have risen just far enough above their parents' sewers to work above ground, and to read about what they will never possess. The content of Sandburg's analysis of capitalist social relations may seem bleak, but the poem's action on the reader is exhilarating, one of those "moments in which the deep structures and processes that configure and are configured by economic forces surface" into visibility, as Eric Schocket puts it.[41] Something else emerges into view as we read "Crayon": a poetry of modern American life that rejects genteel disdain toward class otherness and instead adopts the othered perspective of the unspoiled working-class girl whose incomprehension exposes the incomprehensibility of a leisure class that will drape itself (or its pets) in pearls rather than ensure that its fellow citizens are minimally fed and housed.[42] Sandburg's artist-*flâneur* here is no detached dandy picking his way fastidiously through the city, "display[ing] himself for observation" through his perfect apparel and demeanor of bemused boredom.[43] Instead he is a rapid-transit version of Baudelaire's "passionate spectator," a deeply engaged figure who "set[s] up house in the heart of the multitude, amid the ebb and flow of movement, in the midst of the fugitive and infinite," commemorating urban life without sentimentality but with great empathy.[44]

The Mobile City as "Woman's World"

So far I have discussed poets' encounters with social otherness mostly in terms of class rather than gender, but in "Crayon" a male writer observes a woman in the city and wholeheartedly identifies his subjectivity with hers, suggesting how urban transit environments could propel American poets

toward new and more flexibly gendered subject positions. Various participants in the American New Verse scrutinized existing gender boundaries
through a distinctively modernist textual figure who carries narratological
and social meanings: the woman who moves through the city, claiming the
authority to comment upon and use whatever she encounters. Whether or
not we term that artist-observer figure a *flâneuse,* she is a welcome and
salutary sign of the progressive force of the movement.[45]

Along with enclosed shopping spaces such as arcades and department
stores, modern mass transit was a powerful factor in the erosion of long-
standing taboos against "respectable" women moving alone through the city
detached from obvious destination or purpose. Poems of the 1910s exploring
the breakdown of these restrictions often draw upon the Baudelairean figure
of "*la passante,*" "the unknown woman who cannot be easily defined and
thus controlled" whose path intersects the observer's.[46] Deborah Parsons
argues that the growing accessibility of the city to women led to their being
"characterized, examined, and theorized into one or more male-authored
stereotyped pathologized states."[47] Certainly one finds plenty of portrayals
of *passantes* by male participants in the New Verse, usually featuring explicitly or implicitly male narrators who are tinged by this dynamic as they
employ such familiar categories of female social identity as the prostitute or
courtesan (as in Ficke's "The Dancer," discussed in chapter 4), or the hapless
victim of class exploitation, as in a series of verses by Maxwell Bodenheim
with titles like "Factory Girl," "Shop-Girl," "Chorus-Girl," "Manicurist,"
"Waitress," and "The Scrubwoman," which type their characters by the
menial or demeaning labor they perform.[48] Generally such poems treat their
subjects with empathy, but their reliance upon these patriarchal typologies
tends to deprive their female characters of full interiority and to estrange
them from the reader's identificatory powers. "Crayon" is a notable exception in which Sandburg's trolley-riding girl is clearly working-class but is
otherwise not reducible to any familiar pathologizing label, leaving her free
to become identified with the observing consciousness of poet and reader.

More interesting still are verses by women that merge the disconcerting,
often alluring unreadability of the *passante* with the observational capacities of the classic *flâneur.* Parsons argues convincingly for greater fluidity
between the female urban observer and the objects of her observation, since
in a "modern city of multiplicity, reflection, and indistinction, *la femme
passante* is herself a *flâneuse,*" or at least can become one.[49] In American
poems of the 1910s that portray women in metropolitan settings, either the
woman observed or the observing woman can assume the role of *passante* or
flâneuse, at times combining these roles. The narrators or implied authors of

such poems can either maintain conspicuous and judgmental distance from class otherness, or they can imaginatively inhabit the subject positions these women are shown to occupy. The attitude of these narratological figures toward those they observe often determines a poem's progressive force.

The former result is typified by "The Night Court" (1916) by Ruth Comfort Mitchell, which turns upon the intersection of an implicitly bourgeois narrator-observer and an abject *passante,* a woman named Rose Costara who is hauled up before the court for solicitation, not for the first time. A group of bored, purposeless people, would-be *flâneurs* but too indolent even to wander the streets, have turned her misfortune and the mundane business of the law into an occasion for cheap spectatorship and supercilious moralism: "The watchers, practised, keen, turn down their thumbs. / The walk, the talk, the face . . . / It is old stuff; they read her like coarse print."[50] The author figures herself too as a spectator of ambiguous motives, a "lady novelist in search of types" who is inclined to join in this ritual humiliation as she deduces from Costara's demeanor that "[h]ere is no hapless innocence waylaid" but instead "a stolid worker at her trade." But this initially complacent observer "turns pale" when she hears the words "*eighth conviction.*" Pondering the life of empty misery implied by those two words, she embarks upon an extended meditation on the forces that have made Costara into the "bitter fruit" of modern urban life, using the courtroom command "*Call Rose Costara*" as a rhetorical linchpin. Before we can fairly call Costara to account as a dissolute and "loathsome" character, the poet proposes, we must first "call the cop," "the court," "the city," and "the code" through which this role has been forced upon her. The narrator ends by chiding herself as "lady novelist" to "[r]ub biting acid on your little pen," "Reverse the scheme," "Summon the system," and "Call us!" before simply blaming the victim. And yet, however sincere her sympathy with such blighted lives, Mitchell still confidently reads Costara's character from surface signifiers and classifies her as one of the types the observer-author went to night court to find. The bourgeois narrator remains notably "chaste" in the transaction, and this unbridgeable separation between observer and object, *flâneuse* and *passante,* limits the poem's range of critique to some fairly obvious targets.

Perhaps the New Verse's most penetrating meditation on how to represent women in the modern American city came in five vividly observed and sexually frank *vers libre* poems by Mary Aldis, collected into a section called "City Sketches" in her 1916 volume *Flashlights.*[51] All five are built around ambiguously sexualized encounters in metropolitan Chicago settings between a bourgeois narrator or implied author and women of a lower socioeconomic class. "The Barber Shop" is set apart by its satirically treated male narrator, but the other four poems feature leisured bourgeois women engaged in various errands of personal grooming or enjoyment: having hair styled, bathing in a Turkish bath, sitting in a café.[52] Though not featuring frenetic movement or strenuous acts of travel, these poems are strongly inflected by the modern transit environment because the female urban subject is presumed to move freely through the city pursuing her leisure, never having to worry about logistics or social propriety. At the same time, the excess of free time and money Aldis's women enjoy implies the author's skepticism toward *flânerie*—and poetry—as leisure-class pursuits that may be impossible to justify unless placed into encounters with social otherness. In other words, although the narrators of "Love in the Loop," "A Little Old Woman," and "Window-Wishing" function as full-fledged poetic *flâneuses,* observing and recording serendipitous encounters with the heterogeneous life of the city, they are also positioned as pampered, even parasitic, members of a sheltered class who need to be taught, or teach themselves, how people really live and love. The effect is somewhat as if the grand lady with the pearl dog collar suddenly felt compelled to investigate the life of the factory girl on the trolley.

Each of these three poems takes a different approach to a common scenario: the haute-bourgeois woman discovering gender solidarity through her discomfiting encounters with class otherness. "Love in the Loop" features the narrator closest to the classic notion of *flânerie* as free wandering and observation of social dynamics upon the urban boulevard. The narrator is an implicitly solitary female figure sitting at a café table watching a nearby couple: "An awkward, ill-dressed girl / With a lovely skin and a country smile" and a much older man, portly and florid-faced, "who was paying for her dinner."[53] Despite their obvious mismatch of age, beauty, and finances, the sardonic narrator calls them "[t]he traditional couple," "Exploiter and Exploited," confidently assigning the episode to a well-worn genre: the seduction of the naive, powerless female by the predatory male. For several verse paragraphs the narrator closely observes and describes the girl's lamentable clothing in contrast to her radiant looks, the man's ostentatious displays of wealth ("fat and white" hands glinting with "shiny nails and diamond rings"), and the sequence of dishes brought to them: oysters the girl gawks at, "'country sausages'" she wolfs down, and champagne she imbibes, apparently oblivious of its likely consequences to her virtue. In short, Aldis's speaker seems very much the acute Baudelairean chronicler of the passing moment, of fashions, manners, and physiognomies, engaged and empathetic with the objects of observation up to a point, yet also notably protective of her own freedom to remain or depart at will:

I watched it all,
Wondering miserably if it was my duty
To warn the girl,
And whether she would prove clinging if I did.

But as the girl pleads for a momentary breath of air to clear her head of "that fuzzy stuff you made me drink," the poem takes a surprising (though not entirely unexpected) twist. After twenty minutes of "troubled scrutiny" of a newspaper's "stock reports," the man finally gets up to leave and discovers she has absconded with eight hundred dollars from his wallet, bellowing, "'Hi! get that girl, I tell you, GET THAT GIRL!'" Aldis offers only one laconic comment on this denouement and his impotent rage: "But nobody stirred." Externally, her speaker still enjoys untethered detachment from the event, with no clinging vine to obstruct her subsequent movement through the city; yet those three words imply that she has been affected by her experience as observer. The girl's nuanced mastery of what Schocket calls "class performativity"—naive, coy, tipsy, sincere—has fooled the narrator no less than the would-be seducer.[54] Yet instead of outrage at having her observational powers destabilized, the narrator seems to savor a transgressive gender solidarity, even to the extent of condoning criminality as poetic justice. At a moment when patriarchal institutions were adapting to the growing physical mobility of the urban population by devising increasingly invasive and precise methods of rendering bodies (of both genders) criminally identifiable, the female writer experiences the girl's transgressive illegibility as a form of resistance. The poem thus liberates *flânerie* from the exercise in male observational mastery it has sometimes seemed ever since Poe's narrator in "The Man of the Crowd" (1840) claimed the power to assign a social and moral station to any passerby from the briefest of glances at his or her gait, physiognomy, or apparel (an attitude which, to his credit, Poe himself satirizes).

The observer of "Love in the Loop," content at her café table yet perfectly free to depart at any moment, is a female version of the *flâneur* who strolls with no ties or responsibilities through an urban landscape that at times seems to exist merely for his own pleasure. But in the other two poems, Aldis begins to rethink the function of this overprivileged and perhaps rather fantastical figure of urban modernity. The *flâneuse*-narrator of "A Little Old Woman," set in a Turkish bath, also craves the freedom to indulge in the city's amusements but is now placed in a position perhaps more representative of everyday bourgeois urban experience. She is a client required, at least if she wishes to continue patronizing this bathhouse, to encounter a particular class other repeatedly, and even to engage her on a personal basis to some extent. The narrator initially presents the "twinkling little old woman" who "[b]rings me sandwiches after my Turkish bath" as the ideal type of the self-effacing servant, whose invisibility is figured by her disembodied voice murmuring, "Don't worry honey, I'll take care of it," while the narrator drowses in the "languid" pleasure of urban privilege.[55]

But the "little old woman" is neither as self-effacing (nor perhaps as old) as the narrator assumes, and in the gradual disclosure of her agency, Aldis dramatizes the bourgeois *flâneuse* learning about class otherness as the male *flâneur* can perhaps never do from his desirous and yet contemptuous glimpses of demi-monde *passantes*. Though her privileged clients may know or think nothing of her, the bath attendant gains intimate knowledge of them from observing their *deshabille*. She uses this knowledge not to steal or blackmail, as the girl in the Loop might do, but to claim self-affirmation from those who consider themselves her social betters:

> One day after she had hooked me up
> She raised her sober dress
> To show me that she too could wear a lace-trimmed petticoat;
> And a dainty thing it was, with tiny rosebuds
> Festooned all around.
> She dropped her skirt and laughed.
> "I've got one . . . too," she said.
> This was uncanny, so I said Good-day.

The narrator initially recoils at unwanted confidences from one she had comfortably typed as her social inferior. Yet she grows intrigued after observing a younger man of comical clothing ("a black frock coat too big for him") and unpromising physiognomy ("A delicate, chiselled face with soft blue eyes, / Under his chin from ear to ear a fringe of yellow down / Around a bald spot, curls of whity-gold"), who she gradually realizes is the bath attendant's lover. Her response to discomfiting intimacy with class otherness then becomes more multifaceted, mingling surprise, self-knowledge, and empathy with a frank acknowledgment of female desire:

> So that was why she wore the petticoat
> And smiled so knowingly—
> But how she worked!
> I wouldn't work like that.
> Perhaps she kept that little thing for pleasuring.
> Well, this is a woman's world, why not,
> If so be that he pleased her?

Here in the "steamy," sensuous "woman's world" of the baths, the gender solidarity felt by the *flâneuse*-narrator extends to the startling sexual objectification of the male as a "little thing for pleasuring." This comic objectification is extended through the second half of the poem as the narrator initiates further intimacies, asking the woman how she "got a lover, / And how she kept him." She is astonished to hear that the attendant considers herself to have bought this man by extricating him from a breach-of-promise judgment he was unable to pay—"I paid for him five hundred dollars cool, / And now he likes me!" This attitude so stuns the narrator's bourgeois sensibility that she is reduced to numb acknowledgment of the infinitude of possible approaches to love and sex, no longer feeling that she can judge any of them: "Well, anything may be." Aldis's final satirical assault on bourgeois decorum is the narrator's discovery that this kept man is a poet who "writes verses all day long for the Sunday papers; / Mostly they don't get in, / But every now and then he gets two dollars." The old woman's latest act of love, as she and the man define it, has been to give him a brand-new Underwood typewriter that cost her "a hundred and twenty-five"—a staggering amount for the day, and fully one-quarter of what she "paid" for him! The old woman's rueful acknowledgment of the typewriter's imperfect functionality ("He was so pleased, / Only the punctuation isn't right") aligns the male's function of poet with the previous enumeration of his physical shortcomings, comically culminating his reduction to the status of object (for female pleasuring) and machine (for composing poems).

Mary Aldis's inquiry into the ways of representing female subjectivity across class lines in the accelerated twentieth-century metropolis reaches its most insightful level in "Window-Wishing," an account of the lives of a young beautician and her sister, as heard by a bourgeois listener having her hair done. The poem is a challenging critique of the relations between social class, ideology, mass culture, and consumer desire, anticipating William Carlos Williams's "To Elsie"—but as narrated by Elsie herself. For Williams, the extremity of Elsie's cultural deprivation renders her broken-brained and almost altogether voiceless. In contrast, Aldis is intent upon affirming that her female "other" not only possesses a voice but also substantial insight into the pervasive frustrations and fleeting satisfactions of her own life. Here is the poem in full:

Oh yes, we get off regular
By half past six,
And six on Saturdays.
Sister an' I go marketing on Saturday nights,
Everything's down.

Besides there's Sunday comin';
You can sleep.
Oh my, how you can sleep!
No mother shakin' you
To "get up now,"
No coffee smell
Hurryin' you while you dress,
No Beauty Shop to get to on the tick of the minute
Or pony up a fine.
Sister an' I go window-wishin'
Sunday afternoon, all over the Loop.
It's lots of fun.
First she'll choose what she thinks is the prettiest
Then my turn comes.
You mustn't ever choose a thing
The other's lookin' at,
And when a window's done
The one that beats
Can choose the first time when we start the next.
The hats are hardest.
'Specially when they're turnin' round and round.
But window-wishin's great!

Then there's the pictures,
Bully ones sometimes,
Sometimes they're queer.
Sister an' I go 'most every Sunday.
We took Mother 'long last week,
But she didn't like 'em any too well.
Mother's old, you know,
We have to kinda humour her.
Next day she couldn't remember a single thing
But the lions on the steps.

You know what happened the other night?
Sister and I didn't know just what to do.—
A gentleman came to see us.
He said Jim asked him to
Sometime when he was near.
Jim's my brother, you know.
He lives down state.

We have to send him part of our wages regular,
Sister an' I;
He doesn't seem to get a steady place,
And Mother likes us to.
She's dotty on Jim.
Sometimes I get real nasty—
A great big man like that!

Anyway his friend came walkin' in
And said Jim sent his love.
Sister an' I didn't exactly know what to do.
And Mother looked so queer!
Her dress was awful dirty.
He said he was livin' in Chicago,
And Sister said she hoped
He had a place he liked.
He only stayed a little while,
Till half past eight,
And then he took his hat
From under the chair he was sittin' on
And went away.
I said just now it happened the other night,
But it was seven weeks ago last Friday evening.
He said he'd come again.
I dunno as he will.
Sister an' I keep wonderin.'
We dressed up every night for quite a while
And stayed in Sundays.
Yesterday we thought
We'd go down window-wishin',
And what do you think?
Just as she'd picked a lovely silver dress
Sister jerked my arm.
Then all of a sudden there she was
Cryin' and snifflin' in her handkerchief
Standin' there on the sidewalk.
And what do you think she said?
"I'd like to kill the woman that wears that gown!"
I tell you I was scared,
She looked so queer,

But she's all right today.
Oh thank you, two o'clock next Saturday the tenth?
I'll put it down.
A shampoo and a wave, you said?
I'll keep the time,
Good-morning.[56]

Unlike Aldis's other city sketches, here the leisured *flâneuse*-narrator goes altogether unheard. Her presence is signaled by the structure of the opening sentence, which responds to a question, suggesting that the narrator-*flâneuse's* curiosity toward the women of "Love in the Loop" and "A Little Old Woman" has now become active investigation into the lives of working-class service providers. And yet this implied author is pointedly not the poem's narrator. The effacement of an educated bourgeois vocabulary and tone of voice, coupled with the lack of distancing quotation marks around the beautician's words, indicate that the poet no longer understands the subjectivity of the class other as external to herself, a merely exotic or entertaining ornament to her *flânerie.* Instead, very simply, she allows that working-class voice to become the voice of her poem. The beautician-speaker thus assumes a dual narratological role as observing subject and observed object. She is both the *passante,* the uncanny or othered woman whom the implied author encounters (once a week for an hour), and the *flâneuse* herself, wandering through the city space, responding aesthetically and critically to its objects and texts. That she is the sole narrator of her own life-story is in itself significant; but she also takes on the authority to narrate the life of another woman, her sister, who shares much with her but reacts to situations in distinct ways.

As an ill-educated working girl, the beautician doesn't have elaborate words for the intertwining meanings of the disparate events she recounts from her life and her sister's. But as she speaks in her own voice with the words she does have, she clearly discerns ideological connections among these events and habits: the thoroughgoing and onerous regulation of their time and movements, the resentment they repress toward their ne'er-do-well brother, the unimpressive suitor's single ambiguous appearance, the frustrating self-denial of their Sunday pleasures as they wait hopelessly for his return, and the desires poignantly evoked, tantalized, and commodified by their spectatorial fetish-activities of window-shopping and cinema-going. These experiences are culminated and critiqued by the sister's outburst of rage at those women who by accident of birth actually possess the commodities and lives the two beauticians can only gaze at from outside (and yet must encounter every day in their job). Obviously Aldis is the one forging these connections, since the beautician is her creation, but her assumption that such a person would be capable of discerning them herself expresses powerful solidarity with women of other classes and ways of life. Straddling these various narrative functions, the beautician thus becomes the embodiment and voice of a feminist poetics that balances analytical social critique with empathetic respect for the objects of observation.

The poem's final rhetorical shift, a reply to another unheard question about a future hair appointment, breaks the mood of intense contemplation and returns us to a realm of quotidian reality—just more daily labor for the beautician, and one more in an unending round of leisure activities for the client. The disruptive effect of this ending perhaps implies the abrupt departure of the client unnerved by hearing an expression of murderous envy directed toward her own class. But Aldis does not force her beautician to apologize or register any distress at having made this discomfiting juxtaposition between the events she narrates and her narratee. Indeed, given that the author's imagining of a feminism transcending class barriers is always balanced by a commitment to social realism, the coming back to earth is perhaps a necessary step and hardly dilutes the progressive work done by this fine poem.

A similar scenario of gendered intersection across class lines, and precisely the same final tonal shift that descends from an interlude of visionary fantasy back into the realist everyday, shape one of the most resonant city verses by any American writer of the period. Edna St. Vincent Millay's "Recuerdo" (from *A Few Figs from Thistles,* 1921) combines the theme of cross-class encounter with a compressed portrayal of the varied spaces and modes of experiencing the modern city: street and park, ferry and pushcart and subway. Here is the poem in full:

> We were very tired, we were very merry—
> We had gone back and forth all night on the ferry.
> It was bare and bright, and smelled like a stable—
> But we looked into a fire, we leaned across a table,
> We lay on a hill-top underneath the moon;
> And the whistles kept blowing, and the dawn came soon.
>
> We were very tired, we were very merry—
> We had gone back and forth all night on the ferry;
> And you ate an apple, and I ate a pear,
> From a dozen of each we had bought somewhere;
> And the sky went wan, and the wind came cold,
> And the sun rose dripping, a bucketful of gold.

We were very tired, we were very merry—
We had gone back and forth all night on the ferry.
We hailed "Good morrow, mother!" to a shawl-covered head,
And bought a morning paper, which neither of us read;
And she wept, "God bless you!" for the apples and pears,
And we gave her all our money but our subway fares.[57]

The first stanza presents a couple, marked as bourgeois by their consumption of excess transportation as a form of leisure, who have made the city into their giant pleasure ground, enacting a primal scene of the modern boulevard in which new forms of urban space allow people to "be private in public, intimately together without being physically alone. Moving along the boulevard, caught up in its immense and endless flux, they could feel their love more vividly as the still point of a turning world."[58] Millay cultivates two ingenious aporias concerning this couple. The first of these is the indefiniteness of their relationship; although their emotional intimacy is not in question, they could be sexual partners or platonic friends, an ambiguity that defuses the familiar gender dependencies and exploitations termed "traditional" by Mary Aldis in "Love in the Loop." Whether or not their relationship is physical, their actions and movements are sexualized by the poet's imagery. Their ride on the ferry, whose olfactory redolence generates not revulsion but the savoring of the earthy and sensuous, leads first to a fireside supper and then to their use of the earth itself as bed or couch. These intimacies, though still open-ended, are sexualized further by the imagery of the stanza's final line, in which ferry whistles evoke the explosive release of pent-up physical energies followed by the repetition of the verb "came" to describe the all-too-quick arrival of the dawn. The second indeterminacy surrounding the couple, which may strike the reader only gradually, concerns their gender. If Aldis pursues a feminist poetics by assertively inhabiting a "woman's world," Millay does so by taking the opposite approach: destabilizing patriarchy—and heteronormativity—by eradicating all gender pronouns and cues. Her refusal to identify speaker or companion as either male or female is a utopian gesture, a way of imagining a world beyond present gender conventions and stereotypes.

The construction of the second stanza pursues a vision of what might lie beyond: a mode of modern life at once emotionally genuine and sexually liberated. Powerful caesuras dominate the center of four of the six lines, balancing them between two elements joined together, neither one dominant, neither subordinate. These caesuras, the persistent syntactic parallelisms ("And you . . . and I . . ."; "And the sky . . . and the wind . . ."), and the initial assertive use of *we* followed by the evenhanded employment of *you* and *I*, suggest a total sharing of resources, decisions, and desires. Neither person tells the other what to do or where to move; neither is in charge of money; they do everything with complete independence and complete togetherness. Also in these lines the poet playfully uses ordinary market fruit to alter the Eden story, revising its misogynistic implication of female sexual knowledge as the origin of human corruption with a forthright celebration of sensuous, and implicitly sexual, experience that again reaches beyond patriarchal gender norms.

Such life experiences as this are inevitably interludes rather than permanent conditions. And yet, however "romantic" her public persona may have been, Millay's art has a strong realist streak, and as "Recuerdo" draws toward a close, she returns to the everyday world in a complex and thoughtful way. Even before the second stanza ends, she presents an ambiguous image of the rising sun as a bucket of gold coins. In that stanza, the image may suggest that all quotidian material concerns have been transfigured by the couple's emotional plenitude. But the gold also looks forward to the final stanza, which along with daybreak brings poverty, class inequity, gender victimization, cultural deprivation, and bourgeois self-protectiveness.

In the last six lines, the poem's social-realist goals are embodied by the old woman the companions encounter as they return to the city streets. The newspaper-seller is marked by her age, her old-world dress, and her desperate gratitude as one deprived of everything they enjoy about the modern city, one who doesn't have the luxury of riding back and forth for fun, or treating food as symbol instead of sustenance. They buy a paper from her but are disinclined to read it, still clinging to that magical moment in which nothing mattered but their togetherness. Until now they have kept and carried all that excess fruit—twenty-two pieces!—but the notion that their joy might be transferable to others impels them toward the culminating phase of Berman's primal scene of the modern boulevard, in which urban bourgeoisie display their love (and their wealth) to someone less fortunate, hoping that "the more they saw of others and showed themselves to others—the more they participated in the extended 'family of eyes'—the richer . . . their vision of themselves" would become.[59]

But if this is a moment of self-display, the poet is generous enough to make it one of insight and empathy as well. The old woman's seeming overreaction to the couple's casual largesse startles them, and they impulsively give her "all our money but our subway fares." The extraordinary final line compresses into eleven words a complex bourgeois response to the modern world. Millay is fully in control of the contradictions she is evoking: the couple's final gesture is both sincerely generous and resolutely self-protective. Their naive hope that their own joy could be transmittable to the world at large darkens to the liberal guilt of people who are acutely aware of their difference from the class otherness they routinely encounter, and who are bent on maintaining those differences despite their benevolent intentions. That bare nickel each has kept, which, courtesy of a cheap and efficient urban transit system, will quickly return them to domiciles with heat, food, and security, might as well be a bucketful of gold in terms of what it signifies about the divisions between classes in the early twentieth-century city. This liberal ambivalence outlasts the poem, as intractable a problem to Millay in 1920 as to any middle-class citydweller nearly a century later. But by confronting it with such honesty, by imagining a utopian version of modernity and then demonstrating an acute yet empathetic understanding of the real thing, Millay created one of the richest social texts of the American New Verse.

Transfer, Intersection, Collision

Georg Simmel asserted in 1903 that "[t]he most significant aspect of the metropolis" is its functional extension "beyond its actual physical boundaries."[60] If so, then the spaces most representative of metropolitan life are not self-contained wholes but interdependent components of a larger network that exist only for people to pass through to somewhere else—the structures that Schivelbusch calls "traffic buildings."[61] In the urban verse of the 1910s, such liminal places serve as specific material spaces that can be closely described in a social-realist context and as potent emblems of the metropolis as a complex functioning system. Often these traffic buildings epitomize the modern city's paradoxical yet pervasive regulation and fragmentation of experience, as in paired verses from Sara Teasdale's 1915 volume *Rivers to the Sea,* where terminal settings measure the city's disruptive effects on romantic love. In the first, "In a Railroad Station," the extreme spatial disorientation and rigid temporal regulation of the terminal environment prevent lovers from articulating their deepest feelings:

> We stood in the shrill electric light,
> Dumb and sick in the whirling din—
> We who had all of love to say
> And a single second to say it in.[62]

The companion poem, "In a Subway Station," features a speaker who remembers being in the same space a year earlier, unable or unwilling to confess her feelings to a man who loved her. Instead of looking into his eyes, she had gazed at "[t]he gleaming curve of tracks, the bridge above," and then answered his entreaties "with a lie," as if genuine emotional expression has been displaced by the impersonal visual spectacle of the curving tracks and the looming bridge. Now the setting is exactly as before, full of "hunted hurrying people," but she is beside another man, aching for the one she had refused. Why had she stayed silent if she "would have died to say the truth"?[63] The lack of any explanation for this failure implies that emotional and physical disarticulation are not only endemic to modern experience but are ironically exacerbated by spaces designed to facilitate movement and interchange.[64]

And yet like the subway ride, settings of terminal and intersection lead not only to disconnection and inexpressiveness but also to moments in which the forms of modern life recombine into refreshed forms. That microscopic monument of modern verse, Ezra Pound's "In a Station of the Metro" (1913), depends on this aspect of the rapid-transit environment for its force. The poem's metaphoric leap, faces compared to "petals on a wet, black bough," is memorable mostly because it comes from such an unlikely source: the dark interior of a metro station among an anonymous and ever-changing crowd.[65] Pound's startling formal innovation, limiting the poem to this single metaphor, is usually attributed to his intimacy with Asian traditions that cultivate economy and precision. But by paring down the act of poetic observation to a fragmentary glimpse within a rapid-transit world of fleeting, kaleidoscopic perception, he produced a poem whose modernist structure corresponds to its modern setting as few others.

"In a Station of the Metro" effaces social relationships and geographical specificity from the rapid-transit metropolis to foreground one striking visual correspondence. That's fair enough in a poem consisting of a title and two lines. But to aestheticize and depoliticize the rapid-transit environment in this way is not the only valid "modernist" response to it. Other poets find intersections and termini productive sites of encounter with social otherness, none more so than Sandburg, whose poems of transfer, crossing, and collision use the spatial dislocations of the metropolis to trope the effects of class upon twentieth-century life. If Pound's descriptive strategies in his metro poem are analogous to those of the cubist or abstract painter, Sandburg's are closer to those of the realist photographer chronicling the city as a hyperspecific geographical, material, and social terrain. Through Sandburg wrote about many parts of Chicago, the industrial and working-class regions south and west of the Loop provided him particularly fertile material. "Blue Island Intersection" (1920) offers two sections of nine lines each, contrasting pictures of a busy intersection of six radii created by the diagonal-running

Blue Island Avenue. This bipartite structure, drawn from a contemporaneous genre of postcard that pictures the same space by day and night, tropes alternative paths toward a poetics of modernist representation. The daylight scene, packed with people, wagons, horses, trolley cars, and baby buggies spilling into the intersection, offers a Whitmanesque plenitude that aspires to portray everything, every *thing,* in that space. The second, taken just before dawn, is empty and quiet—but for "one milk wagon" that anticipates the cacophony of the sunrise.[66] The visual framework of the scene, its architecture and infrastructure, are exactly the same, but the lone vehicle now metonymically represents every other object that day will bring.

A rapid-transit poem of a very different sort is the satirical "Speed Bug" (1910s), in which Sandburg uses the uncontrolled intersection of urban traffic to measure how far American poetry had traveled from the ideology of genteel domesticity prevalent only a decade earlier. "Speed Bug" describes the horrific driving record of Edward Singleton, a middle-class building contractor who "at various times in his career of rushing from job to job" runs "his motor car into four people, two of them children," but manages to defer damages indefinitely by employing lawyers "to keep the litigants busy spending money carrying the cases to higher courts."[67] Sandburg uses the multiple meanings of "career" to position Singleton, whose very name evokes isolation, as an exemplary figure of alienated capitalist modernity. To maintain his tenuous career in a hypercompetitive economic system, he must career so heedlessly through urban space that he endangers the life of anyone whose path intersects with his, becoming a nightmarish inversion of Whitman's *flâneur*-poet who wanders through the city seeking serendipitous connection with others.

But the same technopathology that makes Singleton a menace eradicates him from the scene when an "Aurora and Elgin interurban car" smashes into his auto and "disembowel[s] him forty feet along the tracks" for good measure. Singleton is a "speed bug," as is the motorman whose train collides with him; more generally, the term describes not a person but a condition afflicting the entire age. The poem ends by pondering two interpretations of his demise:

> There were some good church folks said it was retribution and an
>   act of God.
> Others left God out of the case and said they were glad the
>   Aurora and Elgin motorman on that interurban car felt like
>   making high speed that morning.

The first lampoons the bankrupt piety of bourgeois-genteel Christianity, revealing "good church folk" to be bitten by the speed bug of the modern age as fatally as Singleton and hinting at a mordant system of cosmic justice dispensed by an avenging God of the working classes. The second, more honestly hard-hearted, diminishes modern ethical understanding into a search for ironic incidental benefit from disasters caused by intersecting yet essentially random actions and impulses. Sandburg's geographical specificity again enhances his poem's social resonance. The exurban area between Aurora and Elgin, implicitly Singleton's habitual zone of movement, is a good forty miles west of the crush of the Loop and the factory districts of central Chicago. Applying the exemplary urban dynamics of speed, density, danger, and the continual transformation of space to this far-flung region of small towns becoming the newest metropolitan suburbs, Sandburg proposes the inexorable incursion of the rapid-transit paradigm into all aspects and spaces of American life.

Sandburg's most ambitious study of urban bodies in transit and collision, and perhaps the most prodigious unknown monument to the New Verse as a social movement as well as a literary one, is "The *Eastland*," his furious response to the capsizing of an overcrowded Great Lakes steamer in the Chicago River just west of the Clark Street Bridge, where on every fine day dozens of cruises now embark to carry tourists around the city's storied waterways (without mentioning the *Eastland*). Sandburg's poem, written soon after the disaster of July 24, 1915, but not published until 1993, is a portrayal of a modernity on a horrific collision course with itself. If "Speed Bug" depicts the appalling but easily comprehensible physics of colliding bodies, "The *Eastland*" suggests that in the scene of modern urban capitalism, nothing more than the dense clustering of human desires is needed to produce catastrophic results.

The ironies of time, space, depth, motion, and symbolism that accumulate around the *Eastland* disaster are so pervasive that they seem to cast modern mass society itself in an ironic mode. The occasion was to be a happy one, the annual summer excursion across the lake to Michigan City, Indiana, for employees of the giant Hawthorne plant of the Western Electric Corporation based in the working-class inner suburb of Cicero. The 2,500 people on board were among seven thousand who had bought tickets, the *Eastland* but one of several large vessels chartered for the outing. Most of the bodies pulled from the river were in weekend finery, summer suits and white dresses and fancy hats, dressed to celebrate a precious opportunity for leisure. When it rolled them into the water, the *Eastland* was still at the dock, only just beginning to move. The immediate cause was not velocity, collision, or weather but simply the accumulated weight and trivial motion of too many bodies in a top-heavy confined space. The capsizing happened not in a violent instant, as Singleton's death had, but over fifty minutes of sickening slow motion in which the ship listed toward the land (starboard) as passengers piled on and was then seemingly righted by water ballast added to the portside tanks. But these corrective measures gradually overbalanced the ship to port, and finally at 7:28 A.M. it capsized with almost no splash, yet so abruptly that people in deck chairs slid into the water before they could even stand up.[68] Onlookers on riverside streets and nearby vessels, many of them knowing family members or friends had been submerged, had to witness the whole thing unfold like a horrifying newsreel. That so many could drown in perhaps ten minutes and twenty feet of calm water beggars thought, as does the later finding that the *Eastland,* an already top-heavy design, had been further destabilized by new safety measures: three dozen lifeboats and rafts and 2,500 life-preservers installed on the upper decks after the *Titanic* disaster three years earlier.[69] When it capsized, the ship was at but not beyond its legal passenger capacity of 2,500. Legal or not, that vast figure meant fatal consequences for people of a social class whose experience of space and time, even in leisure, was tightly regulated by exploitative economies of scale. Despite Western Electric's generally superior reputation for workplace safety and employee morale, the event suggests that paternalistic corporate capitalism fails to protect its employees, in this case by complacently assuming the competence of the steamship line and the appropriateness of regulatory guidelines for passenger capacities and vessel weights.[70]

Yet Sandburg's *Eastland* poem touches on the specific circumstances of the disaster only slightly, and this reticence makes the poem distinctively modernist. The subject matter is one of epic suffering, as nearly 850 people died in the river that day, many of them immigrants, young women, and infants. In the previous century such an event would have led poets toward epic narrative, as the wreck of the *Hesperus* had for Longfellow and the charge of the Light Brigade for Tennyson. But Sandburg makes his poem as much about the need to resist familiar tragic and epic modes of narrative as about the disaster itself. Of the capsizing and its aftermath he offers but two sentences of bare outline:

> It was a hell of a job, of course
> To dump 2,500 people in their clean picnic clothes
> All ready for a whole lot of real fun
> Down into the dirty Chicago river without any warning.
>
> Women and kids, wet hair and scared faces,
> The coroner hauling truckloads of the dripping dead
> To the Second Regiment armory where doctors waited
> With useless pulmotors and eight hundred motionless stiff

The *S.S. Eastland* in the Chicago River, 1915. Author's Collection.

Lay ready for their relatives to pick them out on the floor
And take them home and call up an undertaker.[71]

The remainder of the poem's thirty-eight long lines develop a sophisticated analysis of the *Eastland* as emblematic of the structural logic of capitalism, which the poet proposes will inevitably produce massive suffering that can never be adequately represented by or understood through a capitalist-controlled media. By calling the poem "The *Eastland*" and then refusing to narrate the events of July 24 as spectacle or tragedy, Sandburg proposes that modern verse must directly engage the most urgent events of current American life, yet can no longer do this through the old distancing forms and consoling conventions. Instead,

If you want to see excitement, more noise and crying than you
    ever heard in one of these big disasters the newsboys clean
    up on,
Go and stack in a high pile all the babies that die in Christian
    Philadelphia, New York, Boston and Chicago in one year
    because aforesaid babies haven't had enough good milk;
On top the pile put all the little early babies pulled from mothers
    willing to be torn with abortions rather than bring more
    children into the world—

Jesus! that would make a front page picture for the Sunday
    papers.

And you could write under it:
Morning glories
Born from the soil of love,
Yet now perished.

These ferocious lines align the practices of sentimental poetry with capitalism's control of the flow of information, and in particular with its structural obfuscation of political realities, strategically punctuated by eruptions
of spectacular oversaturated coverage. Most often the suffering generated
by capitalism is concealed and diffused through vast spatial and temporal
reaches, atomized into isolated cases and individual aberrancy, routinized into
the mundane textures of everyday business. When such suffering becomes
so concentrated in space and time that it cannot be hidden, as the *Eastland*
cannot, it is converted into a media extravaganza of mourning and breast-
beating—itself a lucrative commodity that diverts and then exhausts public
attention rather than spurring any real impulse toward change. As Sandburg
gathers all the bodies of those who have died of consumption or abortion or
malnutrition across the vast space of the nation and stuffs them into bulging
lines that far exceed formal decorum, he proposes that the modern poet's
job is to reconcentrate the diffused catastrophes of capitalism and to draw
from them collective meanings about its effects on our lives. But this urgent
purpose can't be achieved through the old euphemistic modes that populate
the nation's newspapers and other mass media, softening front-page horrors
with consoling bromides. Instead, Sandburg suggests, we must create and
endure a poetry that "ain't ticklish" about the "big disasters," and even less
so about the everyday *Eastlands,* which he ends the poem by foregrounding
once again:

Yes, the *Eastland* was a dirty bloody job—bah!
    I see a dozen *Eastlands*
    Every morning on my way to work
    And a dozen more going home at night.

The Young Doctor: At the Prow, on the Train

Of all those involved with the New Verse of the 1910s, the career of William
Carlos Williams best demonstrates the impact of the movement's passionate
engagement with urban-industrial space as the site of modern experience.
Williams is exemplary not least because of how far he had to come, how

much obsolete tradition he had to unlearn. He began by trying to write about the city as a fervent Keatsian and ended as one of American poetry's boldest experimentalists. His struggle toward a viable poetics of modernity can be charted with particular clarity through his evolving treatments of urban mass transit between 1914 and 1927. As he learned, year by year, poem by poem, to use the rapid-transit environment to articulate the distinctive demands of metropolitan space and time, Williams modeled the immense collective struggle of American poets after 1910 to address the conditions of machine-age life that surrounded them.

In his earliest significant urban poem, "The Wanderer: A Rococo Study," published in *The Egoist* in 1914, Williams portrays the city in rhapsodic tonalities that were retrograde by Whitman's standards, not to mention those of contemporaries like Sandburg, Bodenheim, and Eliot. The result is an almost unreadable work of ponderously elevated tone and superheated rhetoric punctuated by a forest of exclamation points—I stopped counting at fifty—which are the last qualities one would associate with Williams's mature work. The first section unmistakably evokes Whitman and modern urban travel with a ferry crossing to Manhattan but soon turns toward a romanticized female muse that his predecessor would never have used: "Suddenly I saw her! And she waved me / From the white wet in midst of her playing!"[72] This mythical entity guides the poet on an extended tour of the industrial netherworld of northern New Jersey, leading to a riverbank wilderness where he tries to enact his immersion in the modern scene by baptizing himself the progeny of the muse-mother and the "filthy" Passaic River. But despite its aspiration to be "a mirror to this modernity," "The Wanderer," whose title evokes the innumerable poetic vagabonds of nineteenth-century verse, remains firmly within the emotional and formal frameworks of romanticism, treating the poetic journey and its denouement in grand agonistic terms. Williams's awareness of its failure is perhaps suggested by the subtitle he attached, which David Frail argues is a distancing strategy through which the "embarrassed" poet "tried to imply that he intended its Keatsian anachronisms as self-parody."[73]

Even as his poetics shifted toward much sparer textures, Williams nursed a lingering attachment to this histrionic romanticism, revising "The Wanderer" for the 1917 volume *Al Que Quiere!* But a new urban-transit poem in that volume dramatically advanced him toward the modernity he sought. "January Morning: Suite" uses the nonlinear sequence form developed in the pages of *Others*—fitting for a major poem in a book whose title pays homage to its editor, Al K—to depict another ferry journey toward Manhattan.[74] Here Williams exchanges the sprawling rhetoric of "The Wanderer" for fifteen compressed fragments evoking the accelerated rhythms of the rapid-transit city.

II

Though the operation was postponed
I saw the tall probationers
in their tan uniforms
                    hurrying to breakfast!

III

—and from basement entries
neatly coiffed, middle aged gentlemen
with orderly mustaches and
well-brushed coats[75]

The second through the eighth of these fragments trace back to the verb phrase "I saw," forming an expandable parallel grammar that echoes Whitman's "just as you look, . . . I look'd" in "Crossing Brooklyn Ferry." Each of these glimpses of the urban scene portrays or implies motion—interns striding to breakfast, unaccountably dapper men exiting basement apartments, a horse baring its teeth, "worn, / blue car rails" glinting among the cobblestones—suggesting that Williams's method is not so much painterly or even photographic as cinematic, each section functioning like a shot in a cinematic montage sequence, the cuts signified by "—and."[76]

Williams's adaptation of cinematic montage demonstrates how an emerging visual technology can represent forms of motion that define the urban conditions of his own moment, much as Whitman had used the moving panoramas and dioramas of the 1830s and 1840s to build his poetics.[77] Defining reality as fragments that can and must be constructed into larger units of meaning through acts of creative bricolage, montage provides a representational mode powerfully appropriate to a fragmented metropolitan environment that consists, as Simmel put it in 1903, of "the rapid telescoping of changing images, pronounced differences within what is grasped at a single glance, and the unexpectedness of violent stimuli."[78] Within three years of "January Morning," the structuring possibilities of montage would generate a seminal urban text of visual modernism from among Williams's circle of artist friends. In *Manhatta* (1920–21), the cinematic poem to machine-age New York by Paul Strand and Charles Sheeler, "Crossing Brooklyn Ferry" provides the literary inspiration and nonnarrative montage the structural method for what Juan A. Suárez calls "a decomposition, a dissemination, of the cityscape"—terms I find equally applicable to "January Morning."[79]

The poem's montage of movement culminates in the tenth section, a self-portrait of the artist as young commuting professional:

> The young doctor is dancing with happiness
> in the sparkling wind, alone
> at the prow of the ferry![80]

Like Whitman's, Williams's ferry journey contains no grand denouement but possesses the enormous virtue of being indefinitely repeatable. He now has no need of the symbolic muse that had guided the Wanderer. For him, as for Whitman, physical immersion in the scene has become the necessary and sufficient ground of experience, liberating the poetic imagination immersed in winter to remember or anticipate its distant opposite, a summery seascape of bright greens:

> He notices
> the curdy barnacles and broken ice crusts
> left at the ship's base by the low tide
> and thinks of summer and green
> shell-crusted ledges among
> the emerald eel-grass.

Williams uses the final third of "January Morning" to theorize a poetics from the fragmented forms and experiences of the modern city. He evokes another "old woman," this one not mythical but flesh-and-blood—his mother, according to annotations the poet later made in a copy of his collected works—who becomes his comic muse by nagging him to write a poem she can understand.[81] But before long, his earnest attempt to affirm the virtues of poetic accessibility breaks down into celebration of a disjunctive aesthetic of piecemeal perceptions:

> But you got to try hard—
> But—
> Well, you know how
> the young girls run giggling
> on Park Avenue after dark
> when they ought to be home in bed?
> Well,
> that's the way it is with me somehow.[82]

Comparing himself to young girls dashing randomly about with the giddy energy of youth, the poet cheerfully deflates the agonistic romanticism of *The Wanderer* and once again embraces a fragmentary formal method whose meaning emerges out of the experience of one's own body moving through finite physical space. No wonder he placed "January Morning" near the head of his *Selected Poems*. In its time of year, time of day, and sensitivity to the material environment of the city, the poem captures the exhilaration of inhabiting a modern world made once again young.

Within months of publishing "January Morning," Williams was again working to address the rapid-transit city in "Overture to a Dance of Locomotives," drafted by April 1917 and published in *Sour Grapes* in 1921.[83] Here he sets himself the challenge of representing a transcontinental rail network, exactly the sort of powerfully impersonal social form Simmel has in mind when he remarks that "the technique of metropolitan life . . . is not conceivable without all of its activities and reciprocal relationships being organized and coordinated in the most punctual way into a firmly fixed framework of time which transcends all subjective elements."[84] The qualities of punctuality and integration evoke the modernist fascination with simultaneity that was then at its height, extending across many generic boundaries: the cubist and futurist depictions of moving objects from multiple perspectives, the emerging grammars of montage and parallel editing in cinema, the experimental spatial verse of Apollinaire and Cendrars. Yet as Stephen Kern notes, the most compelling formal models for simultaneity came from that most sequential of art forms, music.[85] The landmarks of early twentieth-century music can be read as a series of experiments in simultaneity: the vast contrapuntal landscapes of late Mahler, the coruscating polytonalities of Debussy, the clashing polyrhythms of Stravinsky and Ives, even perhaps the equal harmonic weight carried by each note in the twelve-tone scale.

Williams's poem evokes simultaneity in several senses, first through "the names / of cities in a huge gallery" chanted by the announcers, which are heard as "promises / that pull through descending stairways."[86] Much as Schivelbusch describes the modern traveler's "identification of the railroad station with the . . . destination" rather than the point of embarkation, these chanted names tantalize the urban subject with the promise of simultaneous access to every distant and exotic place.[87] Since Williams identifies the poem as an overture, this chanting must be heard also as music, specifically music designed to fill listeners with anticipation of an imminent experience. A station is, after all, a place for overtures rather than main events. Yet unlike many who wrote terminus poems in the 1910s, Williams discovers not vacuity or alienation in this traffic building but a sense of simultaneity and interconnectedness so palpable that even its most nondescript surfaces seem alive and dancing: "grey pavement" "quickened" by the eager "feet /

of those coming to be carried" and "earthcolored walls of bare limestone" enlivened by the intricate play of light and shadow produced by figures in constantly varying motion.[88]

As in "To a Solitary Disciple," Williams draws inspiration from the contemporary visual arts, building a geometric composition of scintillating complexity. The "hands of a great clock / go round and round," counterpointed by a "pyramid of sunlight" creeping past the clock, by lights hanging slightly crooked from the ceiling, and finally by the "dingy cylinders" of the train cars themselves, "Poised horizontal / on glittering parallels." Yet the "Overture" is no static abstract. Indeed, Williams called it a "futurist" poem, and certainly it expresses "our whirling life of steel, of pride, of fever and of speed," as Umberto Boccioni described the goals of futurist painting in 1910.[89] The overall impression it creates is of enormous potential energy. Forces of space and time "pull" against one another, as the observer is drawn toward the tracks by the promise of distant destinations; as porters dart to and fro directing people to trains; as the cylindrical cars, dingy yet inviting, are "packed with a warm glow" of vitality and plenitude.[90] This scene's full kinetic power is temporarily held in check—the locomotive's "brakes / can hold a fixed posture till" the complex network of integrated forces dictates otherwise, and the great clock's moving hands reach a certain alignment, triggering "[t]he whistle!" at which point the whole scene springs into motion "[i]n time."

This motion-in-time is clearly railway time, ordering our lives in ways we sometimes resist or deplore yet also offering access to speeds, distances, spaces, and experiences unimaginable a few decades earlier. It is also emotional durée, since railroads pull lives apart forever and equally, throw them randomly together for fleeting moments of shared travel. Finally, the poem's time is musical and dance time, as Williams's verbal experiments parallel those of composers (Erik Satie, Henry Cowell, Leo Ornstein, George Antheil, Edgard Varèse) who were then seeking to make music inspired or even created by industrial machines like turbines, sirens, and train whistles. As each element of his mechanical ballet works together "in time," simultaneously avant-garde orchestra, dance troupe, futurist abstract, and well-oiled machine, Williams traces an exuberant modernism of intergeneric synaesthesia—poetry into painting, machines into music, locomotives into dancers, matter into energy, and back again. However futurist in style, the poem celebrates not the heedless destruction urged by the rantings of Marinetti and realized on the landscapes of northern France but rather the creative, constitutive power of system building. The final lines sweep us away from the station into distant landscapes made accessible by railroads tunneling under rivers and crossing otherwise impassable "oozy swampland" on trestles. Distances of time and space avail not, in this case, because of the tightly ordered physical logic behind these modern technologies, again expressed in repeated patterns of kinetic geometry:

> wheels repeating
> the same gesture remain relatively
> stationery: rails forever parallel
> Return on themselves infinitely.

Williams thus draws from the railway system an incipiently utopian view of industrial modernity, discerning in the indifferent laws of physics and in the specific uses extrapolated from them an integrated design marrying the freedom of art and the precision of technology, a balance he articulates in the poem's final line: "The dance is sure."

Though Williams never completely stopped pursuing settings of urban transport, my pursuit of them here will terminate with the untitled work of 1923 that he would begin calling "Rapid Transit" in *Collected Poems 1921–1931*. Cecilia Tichi describes how this poem fits into an aesthetic of machine-age efficiency, and Peter Schmidt links it to Williams's experiments with "cubist" polyphony, but neither situates it within its original site of publication, the experimental collage volume *Spring and All* (1923).[91] Alternating untitled poems headed by Roman numerals with brief prose pieces expounding a fractured form of aesthetic theory, *Spring and All* exemplifies Williams's most extravagantly avant-garde mode from its first sentences: "If anything of moment results—so much the better. And so much the more likely will it be that no one will want to see it."[92] The volume's structure evokes a modernity of kaleidoscopic incoherence, foregrounded by a madcap sequence of chapter headings—chapter 19 is followed by "Chapter XIII" printed upside-down and backwards, then by "Chapter VI," "Chapter 2," and another nineteen, this time printed "Chapter XIX," after which Williams offers a deadpan gloss: "I realize that the chapters are rather quick in their sequence and that nothing much is contained in any one of them but no one should be surprised at this today."[93] In other words, if his work produces anything of moment, it will be both in spite and because of the convulsive incoherence of twentieth-century experience that may, merely may, comprise more than its fragments.

"Chapter XXV," not yet bearing a title, uses the experience of rapid transit to articulate a structural manifesto for the fragmented hypermodernist form of *Spring and All*. Consisting of roughly fifteen utterances, most derived from advertising materials on subway walls, the poem generates collisions among seemingly random and incongruous discourses, including the news factoid, the public-service message, and the cranky interior commentary of a self-doubting poet:

> Somebody dies every four minutes
> in New York state—
>
> To hell with you and your poetry—
> You will rot and be blown
> through the next solar system
> with the rest of the gases—
>
> What the hell do you know about it?[94]

From this comically caustic self-examination, the poet leaps to didactic "AXIOMS" of notably obvious and redundant character ("Don't get killed," "Careful Crossing Campaign / Cross Crossings Cautiously") before indulging in one nostalgic glance at preindustrial horse transit that is so playfully modern in form that we can't be sure how to read it aloud:

> THE HORSES   black
>   &
> PRANCED   white

Still dissatisfied with the train of his perceptions, he next plunges into a series of phrases derived from a specific advertisement for the subway company, which offers "Outings" in New York City's "Great Parks," enumerates their attractions for overheated citydwellers, gives specific directions for which branch line to take to Pelham Bay Park, and concludes with the legend "Interborough Rapid Transit Co." The poet has enacted a dizzying rapid transit among various discourses of urban modernity, switching away from unpromising lines of thought until he finds a branch that will carry him to the end of this fairly arbitrary segment. Having earlier mined film, painting, music, and dance, here Williams makes his most radical generic adaptations yet, from advertising and from the rapid-transit map itself, a mundane form of metropolitan material culture with a curiously utopian goal: to show people how, if they switch lines enough times and keep on riding, they can get anywhere in the city they want to go.

I won't claim that nothing is lost in the transformation of Whitman's industrializing city into Williams's rapid-transit megalopolis. Clearly Williams has resisted going underground; "The Wanderer" and "January Morning" are entirely poems of the open (if not necessarily clean) New Jersey air. The "Overture" begins inside but emerges into the air in its final lines, as if "the dance" of art and technology can only be culminated outside. This dynamic also inflects XXV/"Rapid Transit," whose subterranean movement swerves upward and outward toward the "great parks," although here the emergence from the dark subway is anticipated rather than portrayed. Nor in any of these poems does Williams project the powerful emotional connection that Whitman made with fellow passengers. The "Overture" perceives people as disembodied voices, feet, and shadows, while in XXV/"Rapid Transit," empathy for the suffering of others is confined to statistics, communication to advertising messages, conversation to self-alienated interior dialogue.

Even so, reading Williams's rapid-transit poems in sequence powerfully affirms Raymond Williams's proposition in "When Was Modernism?" that modernist stylistic innovations might be viewed not as mere displays of individual authority but as complex and deeply engaged responses to the defining "social forms" of the modern metropolis.[95] For his part, William Carlos Williams drily acknowledges the claims of these impersonal social forms upon the modern poet by ceding ownership of XXV/"Rapid Transit" to the IRT, whose corporate name he positions on the page like an authorial signature. Just as Whitman had become a great modernist by immersing his forms in the city that surrounded him, and the city in his forms, Williams becomes one by meeting the different experiential conditions of his own day with structural adaptations that those conditions make available: cinematic montage, abstract and futurist painting, machine-age music, subway maps and ads. By populating XXV/"Rapid Transit" with a collection of found objects from American material culture, Williams adumbrates the structure of his great collage epic *Paterson,* the first version of which he would publish in *The Dial* in early 1927. We can see his arrival at the method of *Paterson,* just a dozen years removed from the rococo anachronisms of *The Wanderer,* as culminating the collective achievement of American poets after 1910 to create prosodic, tonal, and representational strategies that would speak to the unprecedented challenges of the twentieth-century urban landscape. It is a particularly satisfying modernist irony that their momentous journey was made navigable through the small everyday journeys of modern city life.

NOTES

INTRODUCTION

1. Greenslet, "Propaganda," 52. American poetry's declining cultural status after 1850, and the interval of crisis between 1890 and 1910, are treated in my 2004 book, *Would Poetry Disappear? American Verse and the Crisis of Modernity*, which argues that the aspiring poets of these years, despairing that their work would be appreciated or even seen, produced a poignant body of verse marked by anxieties of belatedness and uselessness.

2. Monroe, "At Twilight," 120–21.

3. To consider how these terms were used and varied, note the titles of several works competing to summarize the developments of the 1910s: the three volumes entitled *Others: An Anthology of the New Verse*, edited by Alfred Kreymborg (1916, 1917, 1920); the 1917 anthology *The New Poetry*, edited by Harriet Monroe and Alice Corbin Henderson; Louis Untermeyer's critical survey *The New Era in American Poetry* (1919); and Marguerite Wilkinson's anthology *New Voices: An Introduction to Contemporary Poetry* (1919).

4. Lowell, *Tendencies*, 1.

5. I use the terms *vers libre* or *unmetered verse* rather than *free verse* because the latter so easily slips from a neutral description of prosody into an implicit claim of liberation from the shackles of tradition, faction, or ideology.

6. R. Williams, *Politics of Modernism*, 32.

7. Ibid., 33.

8. Ibid.

9. The devaluation of poetic subject matter was a central tenet of the high-modernist project. To organize the verse of a given period by subject—city streets or skyscrapers or advertisements or farm implements—means tolerating a jumble of forms and rhetorical styles, including many verses that don't seek to forge their own forms but willingly situate themselves within some anterior stylistic tradition. Attending to the subject matter of poems also means treating them as statements about the

world, which in high-modernist dogma led inevitably to propaganda or didacticism. This anxiety produced such defensive formulations as the "fallacy of communication" from Allen Tate's seminal New Critical essay "Tension in Poetry" (1938). For Tate, because "communication" had "tainted" all forms of "public speech" in the twentieth century, poetry written to communicate to a reader became just another form of "mass language," devoid of artistic integrity (58, 57).

10. Spears, *Dionysus*, 74.

11. Harrington, "Why American Poetry"; see also Harrington, *Poetry and the Public*, 160–69.

12. The high-modernist campaign against popular female poets was exemplified by John Crowe Ransom's 1937 essay "The Woman as Poet," in which he circumscribed verse by Millay and all women to the expression of "personal moods" and "natural objects which call up love and pity" (104). The ostensible closeness of "woman" to "the world of the simple senses" (77) meant that she must remain "fixed in her famous attitudes, . . . indifferent to intellectuality" (78); her mind, untempered by scientific training, was "not strict enough or expert enough to manage" complex poetic forms (103). For Ransom, such failures of intellect had feminized and disfigured late Victorian verse and threatened, particularly through the enormous popularity of Millay, to mire twentieth-century poetry in immature emotionalism and obsolete formalism. For detailed discussion of New Critical attacks on Millay, see Newcomb, "Woman as Political Poet."

13. Waggoner, *American Poets*, 456.

14. Among the valuable exceptions to this pattern are Susan Schweik's *A Gulf So Deeply Cut* (esp. 67–77) and articles by Artemis Michailidou, Elizabeth Willis, and Walter Kalaidjian.

15. R. Williams, *Politics of Modernism*, 35.

Chapter I. American Poetry on the Brink

1. Newcomb, *Would Poetry Disappear?* 104–39.

2. The motley assortment of poetry anthologies that were published between 1901 and 1912 vividly reveals poetry's low estate. Apparently the only markets for anthologies consisted of seekers after local civic pride (*The Evanston Poets* [ed. William C. Levere, 1903]); pupils in recitation classes (*Days and Deeds: A Book of Verse for Children's Reading and Speaking* [ed. Burton E. Stevenson and Elizabeth B. Stevenson, 1906], *Poems of American History* [ed. Burton E. Stevenson, 1908], and others); and people seeking undemanding light verse, who were served by compilations with such titles as *The Golden Treasury of American Songs and Lyrics* (ed. Frederic Lawrence Knowles, 1901), *A Book of American Humorous Verse* (ed. Wallace Rice, 1904), *American Familiar Verse* (ed. Brander Matthews, 1904), *Heart Throbs in Prose and Verse Dear to the American People* (ed. Joseph Mitchell Chapple, 1905), and, most revealing of all, *The Humbler Poets* (ed. Wallace Rice and Frances Rice, 1911). As far as I can determine, only two anthologies of American verse with

a serious literary emphasis appeared during these years, and neither admitted the existence of contemporary verse. *American Poets, 1776–1900* (ed. Augustus White Long, 1905) was a textbook for classroom instruction and contained nothing written after 1900; *The Chief American Poets* (ed. Curtis Hidden Page, 1905) was a high-toned volume offering an exclusive canon of nine poets, all dead and male (the six Fireside writers, Whitman, Poe, and Sidney Lanier).

3. For a discussion of the impact of the Fireside canon (William Cullen Bryant, Ralph Waldo Emerson, Oliver Wendell Holmes, Henry Wadsworth Longfellow, James Russell Lowell, and John Greenleaf Whittier) on American poetry, see Newcomb, *Would Poetry Disappear?* 106–11, 146–50.

4. In a typical pattern, the July 1907 publication of E. M. Calder's "Personal Recollections of Walt Whitman" in *The Atlantic* was countered by *The Century's* publication of Horace Traubel's "Whitman in Old Age" that same September, and then by E. L. Keller's "The Last Days of Walt Whitman" (in *Putnam's* for June 1909). Note also these paired titles: "Reminiscences of Walt Whitman" (*The Atlantic*, February 1902) and "Leaves from Walt Whitman's Later Life" (*The Critic*, October 1902); L. C. Willcox, "The Personality and Power of Whitman" (*North American Review*, August 1906) and M. A. D. Howe, "The Spell of Whitman" (*The Atlantic*, December 1906); "Whitman's Table Talk" (*Current Literature*, July 1905) and "Talks with Whitman" (*American Magazine*, July 1907); "A Frenchman's Fervid Tribute" (*Current Literature*, September 1908); and "An Englishman's View of Whitman" (*Living Age*, May 1909).

5. For an account of the famous series of canonizing articles and illustrations on the Fireside poets in the 1870s, when *The Century* was called *Scribner's*, see Newcomb, *Would Poetry Disappear?* 33–34.

6. "Some Portraits and Autographs," 531.

7. Lee, "Order for the Next Poet," 703.

8. Ibid., 698.

9. Ibid., 700, 699.

10. Ibid., 698.

11. Aside from the lengthy excepts in *The Century*, pieces by Traubel included "Walt Whitman at Fifty Dollars a Volume" (*Era*, June 1903); "Talks with Walt Whitman" (*American Magazine*, July 1907); "Walt Whitman's Views" (*Appleton's*, October 1907); and "With Walt Whitman in Camden" (*The Forum*, October 1911, November 1912, and January 1913).

12. Traubel, "Sermon to Poets," 133.

13. Ibid., 134.

14. Ibid., 135–36.

15. See John L. Hervey's 1915 attack on *Poetry* for its sponsorship of new and radical poets ("Bryant and the 'New Poetry'"); and Alice Corbin Henderson's rebuttal, "What Would Walt Think?" This dispute is discussed in more detail in chapter 2.

16. Scholars have made widely divergent claims for Braithwaite's importance in the emergence of modern American poetry. William H. Robinson's assertion that he

was instrumental in "bullying and cajoling American readers into accepting modern and unconventional writings" ("William Stanley Braithwaite," 4) is questionable, as is Kenny J. Williams's view of him as "maker of poetic reputations" ("Invisible Partnership," 520), since to an important contingent of writers, especially after 1917, an imprimatur from Braithwaite functioned as a negative recommendation. Citing many of their harsh remarks, Craig S. Abbott's article "Magazine Verse and Modernism: Braithwaite's Anthologies" provides a corrective to the inflated claims of others but also obscures the real importance of Braithwaite's pioneering efforts by emphasizing only his shortcomings as editor and critic. Objectionable comments from contemporaries—an example is Ezra Pound's virulent letter of January 16, 1913—reveal that some of the animosity toward Braithwaite derived from racist discomfort that an African American had claimed the authority to evaluate the work of white poets (Pound, *Letters of Ezra Pound*, 15). See also Marek, *Women Editing Modernism*, 41, and Benstock and Benstock, "Role of Little Magazines," 78, for brief discussions of this issue.

17. Burton J. Bledstein argues that after 1870, "the professionalization of American lives" became manifest "everywhere, in popular culture, the academy, and spectator sports, indeed in the ordinary habits of middle-class life" (*Culture of Professionalism*, 80). Bledstein notes that in the 1870s and 1880s alone, "at least two hundred learned societies" of ever-increasing subspecialization were founded in the United States (86).

18. Rittenhouse, *My House of Life*, 222.

19. Ibid., 223–24.

20. Ibid., 225.

21. Ibid.

22. Ibid.

23. Ibid., 226. The widely admired William Vaughn Moody, almost the last survivor among the younger American poets who had come to prominence in the 1890s, died in the same month as the society's first meeting, October 1910. In syntax and tone, Torrence's comment about Moody suggests that he was recently dead, yet Rittenhouse dates this conversation to the spring of that year. Writing decades later, she has evidently misremembered the exact order of events, but her point remains revealing.

24. The forty-two charter members of the Poetry Society included a few bright young writers such as Witter Bynner and maverick westerners such as Edwin Markham, George Sterling, and Joaquin Miller, but the majority were in the mainstream of late genteel poetry. Among the better-known were Richard Burton, Bliss Carman, Madison Cawein, Richard Le Gallienne, Percy MacKaye, Josephine Preston Peabody, Lizette Woodworth Reese, Clinton Scollard, Charles Hanson Towne, Henry van Dyke, Ella Wheeler Wilcox, and George Woodberry.

25. Rittenhouse, *My House of Life*, 240. She also describes the role played by the Poetry Society and its president, Wheeler, in rectifying the omission of poetry from the original endowment of the Pulitzer Prizes, which were based at Columbia

University beginning in 1917. Dissatisfied with the Pulitzer organization's response to his inquiries about the lack of a poetry prize, Wheeler found a patron who agreed to supply five hundred dollars to Columbia for a Poetry Society Award. After two years, the society decided to administer the award itself rather than through the university, at which point the Pulitzer family finally endowed an official poetry prize (243–44).

26. Vale, "Lyric Year," 91.

27. Earle, *Lyric Year*, vii.

28. Ibid., viii.

29. Tanselle, "*Lyric Year*," 469.

30. Ibid., 466–67.

31. "Case of Poetry," 479.

32. As Max Putzel suggests, the award to Johns was something of an inside job, since he was a protégé and erstwhile employee of the St. Louis publisher William Marion Reedy, who was a close friend of the publisher Mitchell Kennerley, who had urged the young poet, recently arrived in New York, to enter his poem (*Man in the Mirror*, 174–76). That out of ten thousand entries the winning submission was scouted by the contest's publisher can hardly be pure coincidence.

33. Johns, "Second Avenue," 133–34, 135.

34. Ibid., 136–37.

35. Earle, *Lyric Year*, viii.

36. Monroe, Rev. of *The Lyric Year*, 130.

37. W. Williams, "On First Opening," 114–15. Williams had personal reason to be ambivalent, even malicious, about *The Lyric Year*. In the summer of 1912, he had met Ferdinand Earle at the family home of his fiancée, Flossie Herman, where Earle, although already married, was falling in love with (and would later wed) Flossie's sister Charlotte—whom Williams had long loved himself. Taking a "paternalistic sort" of liking to the younger poet, according to Paul Mariani, Earle had offered to get Williams into the anthology but eventually told him that the other judges had objected, and he was out (Mariani, *New World Naked*, 100–101). Mariani asserts that after these various outrages, Williams "came to hate the man with a stone-cold intensity" and "felt heartsick at his failure to appear, miserable that he could find absolutely no outlet" for his work as his thirtieth birthday approached (101).

38. W. Williams, "On First Opening," 114.

39. Vale, "Lyric Year," 91–106; Tanselle, "*Lyric Year*," 457–60. Kennerley blamed these unfavorable responses for the editor's departure for Europe, needling Wallace Rice only half-facetiously, "I should not be surprised if [Earle] was prompted to this decision by your review in the Chicago Evening Post" (Kennerley to Rice, March 5, 1913, Wallace Rice Papers).

40. "Case of Poetry," 477.

41. Ibid.

42. Ibid., 478.

43. Qtd. in Tebbel, *History of Book Publishing*, 700. The utility of this yearly

data from *Publishers Weekly* (reproduced in Tebbel's book) is limited because the compilers relied on voluntary reporting from sometimes disorganized or indifferent publishers, and because poetry and drama books were lumped together. At any rate, the number of published books classified as "Poetry and Drama" leapt from 250 in 1902 to 421 in 1903 and never again fell below four hundred per year. Between 1900 and 1904, the number of books in this category increased 52 percent over the corresponding total between 1895 and 1899; the figures would increase another 30 percent between 1905 and 1909 before peaking in 1910 at 721 books. Thereafter the numbers leveled off, staying largely between six and seven hundred from 1911 through 1917.

44. Monroe's pamphlet is held in the Eunice Tietjens Papers at the Newberry Library; Bradley, "Lyres and Laureates," 197. Monroe had ample personal experience with this issue of author subventions. In early 1910 she had written to Houghton Mifflin about issuing a book of her verse, which they firmly declined on "any other basis than the commission one," citing "the present state of public inattention to anything in verse form." Monroe to Houghton Mifflin, March 8, 1910, Harriet Monroe Personal Papers (hereafter cited as Monroe Papers).

45. H. Russell, *Edgar Lee Masters,* 58–59.

46. Masters qtd. in ibid., 60. Masters's only books of verse during these years appeared through Rooks under pseudonyms (*Blood of the Prophets* by "Dexter Wallace" in 1905, and two series of *Songs and Sonnets* in 1910 and 1912 by "Webster Ford").

47. Greiner, "Robert Frost," 93–94.

48. Drake, "Sara Teasdale," 397. After 1910, a few inklings of change began to appear. After a year of circulating the manuscript, Teasdale managed to get Putnam's to issue *Helen of Troy* without subvention in 1911 (398). Amy Lowell's *A Dome of Many-Colored Glass,* her first book apart from a teenage pamphlet in 1887, was published unsubsidized in 1912 by Houghton Mifflin, although the firm's long-standing business relationship with her illustrious older relatives may have played a part.

49. Kennerley to Monroe, October 18, 1911, Monroe Papers.

50. Ibid.

51. Kennerley had announced his intention to issue "a new volume of original poetry each month of the year" in *The Forum* in the spring of 1912 ("Announcement by Mitchell Kennerley"). But he was also notably wary of overcommitting himself, writing Wallace Rice in April that, although he would look at Rice's manuscript, "I have so many offers of verse manuscripts that I feel obliged to confine myself to those by entirely unknown authors" (Kennerley to Rice, April 3, 1912, Wallace Rice Papers). Yet Kennerley's ostensible commitment to unknowns was not borne out by his poetry list, which featured a large proportion of familiar names such as Bliss Carman, Algernon Swinburne, A. E. Housman, Richard Le Gallienne, and Theodosia Garrison. Assuming, like nearly everyone else, the economic marginality of poetry, the publisher aspired to have it both ways: to preen himself for his adventurousness while incurring little risk in the poetry he actually published.

52. "A Boom in Poetry," 19.

53. Qtd. in ibid., 20.

54. Ficke to C. J. Hambleton, August 12, 1913, correspondence of Arthur Davison Ficke. Ficke would be disillusioned soon enough, grumbling in March 1914 that Kennerley's finances were "not wholly reliable. He pays only after repeated and insistent duns." Ficke to Eunice Tietjens, March 13, 1914, Eunice Tietjens Papers.

55. Rittenhouse to Louis Untermeyer, November 25, 1913, Louis Untermeyer Papers (hereafter cited as Untermeyer Papers).

56. Qtd. in "Poets Again Best Sellers," 987.

57. Russell, *Edgar Lee Masters*, 78.

58. Huebsch to Untermeyer, April 1918, Untermeyer Papers.

59. Abbott, "Publishing the New Poetry," 100.

60. Wilkinson to Eunice Tietjens, October 29, 1919, Eunice Tietjens Papers.

61. Abbott, "Publishing the New Poetry," 100–101.

62. Monroe, "Down East," 85.

63. Ibid.

64. Ibid.

65. Monroe, "Various Views," 140.

66. Kaestle and Radway, *Print in Motion*, 2–3.

67. Hoffman, "Research Value," 314. This strongly authorial emphasis in little-magazine studies was exemplified by the organization of William Wasserstrom's 1963 study, *The Time of "The Dial,"* in which six of seven chapter titles refer to "leading figures in American prose and verse"—such as "The Mark of a Poet: Marianne Moore"—in order "to connote some of the ways my subject might be exploited by students of, say, Ezra Pound's career or Henry Miller's" (3). For Wasserstrom and most of his contemporaries, histories of magazines existed only to throw more light upon already canonical authors.

68. Churchill and McKible, Introduction, 4.

69. Nelson, *Repression*, 230.

70. Morrisson, *Public Face of Modernism*, 5.

71. Churchill and McKible, Introduction, 5.

72. I considered discussing several other American magazines of the 1910s but concluded that they were markedly less important to the success and character of the New Poetry. *The Crisis*, appearing from 1910 under the auspices of the NAACP, became an important agent of modern African American literature under the literary editorship of Jessie Fauset (1919–26), but earlier it played relatively little role in the emergence of the New Verse. The *Poetry Journal* appeared from Boston intermittently between late 1912 and 1918 and published verses by many familiar names, but it left remarkably little impression on participants or later historians. Alfred Kreymborg's *The Glebe* (1913–14) published some significant imagist verse, but as an institutional intervention it seems a trial run for *Others*. Likewise, *Rogue,* issued by Allen and Louise Norton in 1915–16 along whimsical symbolist-decadent lines, is mainly important for a few individual poems by

key figures such as Wallace Stevens, Mina Loy, and Gertrude Stein. Produced by the New York art dealer Robert Coady, *The Soil* (1916–17) lasted only five issues but marshaled verse by Stevens, Loy, Maxwell Bodenheim, and others into an intriguing synthesis of experimental artsiness and open-hearted enthusiasm for modern mass culture. For discussions of *The Soil* primarily in relation to the visual arts, see Bochner, "Marriage," 49–66; Suárez, "City Space," 90–96; Munson, *Awakening Twenties*, 39–46; Bohan, *Looking into Walt Whitman*, 165–88; Schleier, *Skyscraper in American Art*, 67–68; Gorman, *Left Intellectuals*, 68–70; and Zilczer, "Robert J. Coady," 77–89. The *Little Review*, begun by Margaret Anderson in Chicago in March 1914, at first featured many of those also involved with *Poetry*, such as Vachel Lindsay, Arthur Davison Ficke, and Eunice Tietjens, but after moving to New York in 1917 and Paris in 1922 it became an important impresario of European experimental modernism. Ultimately I judged the *Little Review* too similar to *Poetry* in its earliest years, and too marginal to the American New Verse movement later on, to warrant a chapter in the present study.

CHAPTER 2. *POETRY'S* OPENING DOOR

1. Advance announcement for *Poetry: A Magazine of Verse*, Untermeyer Papers.

2. Marek, *Women Editing Modernism*, 176.

3. For an example of this condescension among historians, consider a decidedly odd sentence from David Perkins's *History of Modern Poetry*, which uses Pound's slighting characterization of Monroe (detailed below) to define not only her publication but the entire field of twentieth-century little magazines: "Most of the little magazines have been, *mutatis mutandis*, what Pound said of *Others* in 1916: 'a harum scarum vers libre American product,' which 'keeps' Arriet . . . from relapsing into the nineties'" (vol. 1, 322). See also Waggoner, *American Poets*, 444.

4. Pound, "Small Magazines," 690.

5. Ibid., 692.

6. This attitude of sexist condescension toward Monroe (and the sloppy history it requires) is perhaps most egregious in the 1976 study *The Little Magazine: A Study of Six Editors*, where Ian Hamilton even denies Monroe the credit for the magazine's founding, insisting that "if *Poetry*'s success can be attributed to any single figure, that figure must be" Hobart C. Chatfield-Taylor, who suggested to Monroe that they "get one hundred of his Chicago friends and contacts" to donate money (45). Implying that this assertive woman, active in Chicago culture her entire adult life, had developed no "friends and contacts" of her own, Hamilton remarks flatly that Chatfield-Taylor "undertook to make the approaches himself and it took him less than a year to raise the cash" (45), simply ignoring Monroe's autobiography *A Poet's Life*, where she supplies pages of detailed and unequivocal memories of making these visits herself (244–48).

7. Marek, *Women Editing Modernism*, 167.

8. Hine, Introduction, xxxv–xxxvii. The continuing tenacity of these assumptions

is revealed by the portrayal of Monroe in the 1993 volume of Pound's letters to Alice Corbin Henderson (Nadel, *Letters of Ezra Pound*, xiv, xxii, xxv, 194).

9. Monroe, "Cantata," 214–15; Monroe, "Chicago," qtd. in Ann Massa, "'Columbian Ode,'" 62.

10. The phrase comes from the frontispiece to Monroe's *Chosen Poems*; see Massa, "Form Follows Function," 122–24.

11. Massa, "Form Follows Function," 117–18.

12. Monroe's interest in Sullivan's eccentric progressivism led her in 1916 to excerpt in *Poetry* his unpublished essay "Democracy," whose Whitmanesque cadences and diction portrayed "the poet" not as a "trifler" who merely makes words rhyme but as a locus of creativity who "sees things rhyme" and understands "the superb moving equilibrium of all things" (Sullivan, "Wherefore," 306). On the activist women who powerfully influenced the city's culture and politics during these decades, see D. Miller, *City of the Century*, 413–23.

13. Massa, "Form Follows Function," 120, 127. Massa also details Monroe's contributions to a variety of progressive social causes, including work at Hull-House and "journalistic campaigns for the city beautiful" (118).

14. Biggs, "From Harriet Monroe," 184, 185.

15. Ibid., 190–91.

16. For a discussion of the Columbian Ode and Monroe's copyright suit as key events of American poetry in the 1890s, see Newcomb, *Would Poetry Disappear?* 203–4.

17. Monroe to Kennerley, October 16, 1911, Monroe Papers.

18. These poems can be found in Monroe's 1914 volume *You and I* and her 1935 collection *Chosen Poems*.

19. Perry to Monroe, November 13, 1905, Monroe Papers.

20. Perry to Monroe, December 15, 1908, Monroe Papers.

21. Monroe, *Chosen Poems*, ix–x; Monroe, *Poet's Life*, 190–91.

22. Monroe, "Bigness," 373.

23. Ibid., 374.

24. Undated handwritten draft of a letter addressed to Howard Elting, Monroe Papers.

25. Monroe to C. L. Hutchinson, September 8, 1912, C. L. Hutchinson Papers.

26. Kreymborg began with *The Glebe*, which lasted little more than a year in 1913–14 before the editor resigned under pressure from his backers, Albert and Charles Boni, who favored European writers over the Americans Kreymborg preferred. In 1915, Kreymborg was back with *Others*, but again the editor and his financial backer, the art collector and sometime poet Walter Arensberg, could not agree on an aesthetic policy, and soon the magazine's finances became chronically precarious (Hoffman, Allen, and Ulrich, *Little Magazine*, 45–46, 49–50).

27. Arthur Aldis to Monroe, July 28, 1912, Monroe Papers.

28. O'Brien, *New Men*, 98, 188.

29. Ibid., 188–89.

30. Ibid., 190; Monroe, *Chosen Poems*, 234–35. In 1916 Monroe published an essay by the architect Louis Sullivan proposing that comparisons of building and poetry need not produce the complacency of O'Brien's magnate. Sullivan defined the poet as one who does pioneering creative work in any form and specifically opposed this figure to the "sensible and practical" ones who lack that dimension of creativity: "[S]ome great poets have made verses . . . instead of doing something else," but poetry in its essence "is the very soul of adventure—the going forth, the daring to do, the vision of doing and the how to do," and is thus "the highest of practical powers" ("Wherefore," 306–7). The fact that some moderns built rather than wrote their poetry did not mean to Sullivan that writing had become obsolete. On the contrary, his reliance on poetry as a metaphor for this creative impulse suggests that he saw writing as the model of imaginative activity to which the builder must aspire.

31. Monroe, *Poet's Life,* 285; Susan Albertine, "Cakes and Poetry," 99.

32. Monroe to O'Brien, September 28, 1912, Monroe Papers.

33. The traces of this contretemps are evident in a footnote in *Poetry*'s first issue: "Eight months after the first general newspaper announcement of our efforts to secure a fund for a magazine of verse, and three or four months after our first use of the title *Poetry*, a Boston firm of publishers announced a forthcoming periodical of the same kind, to be issued under the same name." The note concludes haughtily: "The two are not to be confused" ("Notes and Announcements," 32). The Bostonians would change their publication's name to the *Poetry Journal*, which appeared intermittently into 1918 but lacked the adventurousness and the financial stability to become a serious competitor to *Poetry*.

34. Ficke, "Poetry," 1.

35. Monroe, "Motive of the Magazine," 26.

36. Ibid.

37. Ibid.

38. "Poet's Bread and Butter," 117.

39. Ibid.

40. Ibid. The most insistent defender of this position was *Poetry*'s Chicago neighbor *The Dial*, which in February 1912 referred dismissively to the recently announced *Lyric Year* contest as "a pecuniary inducement to poets" ("Pecuniary Inducement," 118). About once a year thereafter, *The Dial* issued ritual denials of any legitimate relationship between poetry and economics. A commentary of May 1, 1913, claimed that notoriously "improvident poets" such as Poe or Shelley "not only escape the serious censure of posterity for their unthrifty habits, but even have a way of winning added favor by reason of this very lack of worldly foresight" ("Improvident Poets," 368). In contrast to their endearing unworldliness, the well-heeled or financially canny poet aroused suspicion and even contempt: "Browning's sleek and prosperous appearance moves the observer to question whether that can indeed be the author of 'The Ring and the Book'" ("Improvident Poets," 368). On November 1, 1914, *The Dial* asserted "the indisputable fact . . . that soul-stirring song has seldom been

the product of luxurious living" ("Poetry and Prosperity," 328) and returned to the theme yet again the following February, objecting to the industrialist and would-be literary critic Hudson Maxim's "scientific" approach to poetry, remarking, "Poetry and Efficiency—dare we name the two in the same breath, or even on the same day?" ("Poetry and Efficiency," 103).

41. Monroe, "Poet's Bread and Butter," 196.

42. Pound, "To Whistler," 7.

43. "Notes and Announcements," 29–30.

44. Monroe, "'That Mass of Dolts,'" 168.

45. Ibid., 169.

46. Fogelman, "Evolution," 99.

47. Pound, "Contemporania," 1.

48. Ibid., 11–12. Pound's equivocal attraction to Whitman, which "A Pact" presents in tightly controlled fashion, emerged more spasmodically in letters of the period. In January 1911, Pound grumbled, "I have never owned a copy of Whitman, I have to all purposes never read him. What you and every one take for Whitman is America." Pound to Floyd Dell, January 20, 1911, Floyd Dell Papers. But his sense that "everyone" was recognizing a connection between them suggests that Pound was not telling the whole story. And he immediately went on to acknowledge that "Whitman is the only American poet of his day who matters." In October 1912, in one of his earliest letters to Monroe, Pound would effuse more directly: "Whistler and Walt Whitman, I abide by their judgment." Pound to Monroe, dated by her October 22, 1912, *Poetry* Magazine Papers. Pound's letter of January 31, 1915, again acknowledged Whitman as "the best America has produced" (*Selected Letters,* 50).

49. Pound, "Contemporania," 3–4, 6.

50. Monroe to Floyd Dell, March 30, 1913, Floyd Dell Papers.

51. "Major and Minor," 555. For responses portraying Whitman in animalistic or subhuman terms, see Newcomb, *Would Poetry Disappear?* 9. For more discussion of the controversies generated by "Contemporania" and other poems of *Poetry*'s first year, see Monroe, *Poet's Life,* 302–11; and E. Williams, *Harriet Monroe,* 48–53.

52. Bynner to Monroe, April 12, 1913, *Poetry* Magazine Papers.

53. Qtd. in Monroe, *Poet's Life,* 310.

54. Ficke to Dell, April 6, 1913, Floyd Dell Papers.

55. In 1904, Monroe had written Payne in the style of a young aspirant grateful for the attention of her elders: "[T]hank you for your very kind word about my book in the Dial. . . . I am glad you think I am improving since the last time" (Monroe to Payne, April 5, 1904, William Morton Payne Papers). This tone of supplication is quite different from the commanding voice that emerges from her correspondence and editorials after 1912.

56. "Case of Poetry," 478.

57. Rice, "Mr. Ezra Pound," 370.

58. Ibid., 371.

59. Ibid.

60. No doubt the animosity of such attackers was exacerbated by *Poetry*'s immediate success in garnering more attention than their own efforts had ever achieved. Though also a poet (and charter member of the Poetry Society of America), Wallace Rice was best known as a prolific anthologist of more than sixty books. As an experienced editor based in Chicago, he may have felt slighted not to be asked for more guidance. In January 1912 Monroe wrote to him, offering rather curt thanks "for your wish to be of service to the magazine project" and proposing that he find some financial guarantors—probably not the sort of help he had in mind (Monroe to Rice, January 9, 1912, Wallace Rice Papers). A year later, Rice's pointed criticisms of "compilers of verse without judgment" and "editors who have never before edited" were clearly aimed at Monroe's lack of editorial experience (Rice, "Mr. Ezra Pound," 370). She retorted with disingenuous but understandable pride, "Others could doubtless do the work better; but no one else attempted it" (Monroe, "Poetry and the Other Fine Arts," 497).

61. Monroe, "In Defense," 409.

62. Monroe, "Poetry and the Other Fine Arts," 497.

63. Ibid.

64. Alden, "New Poetry," 387.

65. Monroe, "New Beauty," 22.

66. "Muse in a Pet," 245–46.

67. The common prominence of Pound and Sandburg in *Poetry*'s early history suggests an overlooked aesthetic and ideological affinity between them during the 1910s. In 1916, Sandburg wrote a spirited appreciation and defense of Pound, remarking, "If I were to name one individual who, in the English language, . . . has done most of living men to incite new impulses in poetry, the chances are I would name Ezra Pound," "the best man writing today" ("Work of Ezra Pound," 249–50). Pound's respect for Sandburg during these years, though characteristically more grudging, emerges from various references acknowledging him as the best of the "American" school of the New Verse (See *Selected Letters*, 55, 57, 124, 158, 159, 209).

68. Sandburg, "Chicago Poems," 191.

69. "New Lamps," 231–32.

70. Ibid., 232.

71. Ibid.

72. Ibid., 232, 231.

73. Wyatt, "Old and the New Poetry," 375.

74. Monroe, "Enemies," 63–64.

75. Sandburg, "Chicago Poems," 192.

76. V. Brooks, "On Creating," 337.

77. Henderson, "Contemporary Poetry," 176.

78. Ibid., 177.

79. Ibid.

80. Monroe, "Sobriety," 140, 142.

81. Ibid., 142.

82. Ibid.

83. Ibid., 144.

84. Ibid.

85. David Frail terms Pound's social and political judgments "aestheticocentric"—that is, "determined almost exclusively by his interests as one of the complete Individuals who kept true intelligence alive for the good of society" (*Early Politics and Poetics,* 71).

86. Monroe, "Motive of the Magazine," 27.

87. Pound, "To Whistler," 7.

88. "Poet's Bread and Butter," 117. Many commentators between 1890 and 1915 drew upon the tragic legend of the English "boy-poet" Thomas Chatterton to express the anxiety that poetic genius in the unkind environment of modern America might be unrecognized and wasted. For further discussion of the Chatterton phenomenon, see Newcomb, *Would Poetry Disappear?* 131–35.

89. Monroe, "Poet's Bread and Butter," 197.

90. Ibid.

91. Ibid., 197–98.

92. Ibid., 198.

93. Monroe, "Question of Prizes," 246.

94. Ibid.

95. Ibid., 248, 249. Aiken's comment is found in "Prizes and Anthologies," 98.

96. Aiken, "Prizes and Anthologies," 99.

97. Ibid.; Monroe, "Question of Prizes," 249.

98. Monroe, "Question of Prizes," 246–48.

99. E. Williams, *Harriet Monroe,* 77–78.

100. Aiken, "Prizes and Anthologies," 98.

101. Monroe, "Word to Our Readers," 247.

102. Ibid.

103. Monroe, "Open Door," 64.

104. This model of the canon as continually evolving and possessing no preordained form or end was pursued further by Henderson in an October 1915 commentary, in response to yet another attack on Sandburg and *Poetry* that had appeared in *The Dial* in August. In this case, John L. Hervey had demanded: "And, by the way, what, oh, what, do you suppose Walt would have thought of Miss Monroe's magazine if he had lived to see it?" (Hervey, "Bryant and the 'New Poetry,'" 93). Pointing out that Whitman was "very tolerant", Henderson proposed an ingenious two-pronged relativist account of canonicity ("What Would Walt Think?" 48). First, she rejected the notion of canons as unalterable Platonic ideals of aesthetic value by pointing out that they always reflect present attitudes: "Undoubtedly, [Walt] would have thought about it just as each of you, whoever you are, now reading this magazine, think about it. For the great dead, curiously enough, always mold their opinions to suit their admirers" (49). Second, she drew a compelling analogy between the present uncertainty of Sandburg's ultimate significance and Whitman's

history as a long-dismissed, even reviled figure only recently canonized: "Fortunately there were people intelligent and courageous enough to risk an opinion on Whitman fifty years ago" (49).

105. Wyatt, "On the Reading," 24.

106. Ibid.

107. Monroe, "New Beauty," 23.

108. Ibid.

109. Ibid., 23–24.

110. Ibid., 22.

111. Monroe, "Tradition," 67.

112. Brooks, "On Creating," 339.

113. Whitman, "Notes Left Over," 1056–58.

114. Contrary to Pound's assertions, *Poetry* drew widespread criticism in the early 1910s for its harsh treatment of poets who did cater to traditional and popular tastes, such as Monroe's cruel dismissal of Ella Wheeler Wilcox in 1913. In an article about the failure of the British antiquarian poet Stephen Phillips despite his initial popularity, Monroe dismissed popular versifiers such as Phillips, Wilcox, and Martin Tupper by saying that they "have no souls to save" (Monroe, "In Danger," 68). A year later, noting Wilcox's understandably wounded reply printed in another magazine, Monroe used her ostensible apology to take more potshots, quoting her earlier remark "that it is hard for a popular poet to save his soul, and that some of them [here naming Wilcox again] . . . have no souls to save" (Monroe, "Enemies," 63). Disingenuously withdrawing this "rash statement," since "no doubt" Wilcox was "richly endowed" with a soul, Monroe could not resist crowing that Wilcox "herself sang long ago with singular precision, 'My soul soars not as it ought to soar'" (63). In early 1915, the editor's dismissal of Louis Untermeyer's volume *Challenge* as "the conventional trappings and claptrap utterances of the god of war" (Monroe, Rev. of *Challenge,* 204) drew the ire of Untermeyer's friend Clement Wood, who claimed that because Untermeyer's poems "have been reprinted from Maine to Miami, from Hackensack to Nome," Monroe's criticisms showed "a surprising lapse of critical ability" (Wood, "Lyrical Challenge," 142), as if popularity were a self-sufficient criterion of value. With such antagonists, Monroe and *Poetry* can't be convicted of merely courting a popular audience.

115. Pound, "Audience," 29–30.

116. Ibid., 30. This editorial anticipated Pound's imminent shift of loyalty from *Poetry* toward another avant-garde magazine, the *Little Review,* whose motto (from 1917) would express Olympian antagonism toward a populace assumed to be hopelessly benighted: "Making no compromise with the public taste." At another level, in their authoritarian elitism, in which the intelligent few "manage" the multitudes, these sentences seem to prefigure Pound's attraction to Fascism.

117. Pound, "Audience," 29–30.

118. Monroe, "Audience," 31.

119. Ibid., 32.

120. Monroe, "Fight for the Crowd," 281.

121. Ibid.

122. Ibid., 281–82.

123. Ibid., 282.

124. Ibid.

125. Monroe, "This Southern Number," 31.

126. Monroe, "New Beauty," 25.

127. Monroe, "Incarnations," 102.

128. Monroe, "New Beauty," 25.

129. A recent *PMLA* article by David Ben-Merre and Robert Scholes reproduces and contextualizes some of *Poetry*'s many verses about the war, but a full-scale study of this rich body of material remains to be published.

CHAPTER 3. YOUNG, BLITHE, AND WHIMSICAL

1. Churchill, *Little Magazine* Others, 5.

2. *The Masses* goes unnoticed in major postwar histories of American poetry by Roy Harvey Pearce, Hyatt Waggoner, David Perkins, Bernard Duffey, and Albert Gelpi, most of which do mention *Poetry* and *Others*. The most comprehensive recent study of the American avant-garde movements of the 1910s, Steven Watson's *Strange Bedfellows*, follows earlier scholarship by framing discussion of *The Masses* entirely around its artwork and prose articles sponsoring radical causes (159–65). Watson acknowledges in passing the editors' interest in poetry (161) but does not discuss any specific poems. Since his book does contain extensive discussions of *Poetry* and *Others*, the decision not to contextualize *The Masses* within his account of the New Poetry movement seems a missed opportunity. Mark S. Morrisson, in *The Public Face of Modernism*, is virtually the only scholar to treat *The Masses* as an important participant in the history of literary modernism, though his primary focus is not on its verse (see esp. 171).

3. Hoffman, Allen, and Ulrich, *Little Magazine*, 149.

4. Eastman, "Editorial Notice," 3. For valuable accounts of *The Masses* in the radical culture of the 1910s, see William L. O'Neill's biography of Max Eastman, *The Last Romantic*; O'Neill's compilation *Echoes of Revolt*, a wide-ranging anthology of material from the magazine; Rebecca Zurier's monograph *Art for the Masses*, which reproduces many examples of its lively artwork; Margaret C. Jones's study *Heretics and Hellraisers*, which quotes extensively from the magazine's verse and addresses the gender imbalances seen in some earlier works; and Sandra Adickes's *To Be Young Was Very Heaven*, which briefly surveys verse and prose contributions to *The Masses* made by women. But no scholarship has read the verse of *The Masses* in the context of other developments in the New Poetry during those years.

5. *The Masses* accused the Associated Press of having "suppressed and colored" the coverage of the West Virginia strike in favor of the employers. The A.P. brought suit, and the editors were indicted in December (Dell, "Indicted for Criminal Libel,"

33). When they resolutely met this attempt at intimidation by holding public rallies and writing open letters to the mainstream New York press, the A.P. dropped the suit, perhaps reluctant to expose its strike coverage to the scrutiny of a court case (O'Neill, *Echoes*, 37–38; Zurier, *Art for the Masses*, 44–45).

6. Eastman, "Editorial Notice," 3.

7. O'Neill, *Echoes*, 53.

8. Fishbein, Introduction, 4; P. Douglas, "Letter," 32–33. For responses of other outraged readers to the magazine's promiscuous mixing of topics and tones, see Stansell, *American Moderns*, 173–74.

9. Instances of satiric irreverence toward conservatives are found in every issue, but *The Masses* also carried on a good-humored lampoon of bohemian trends and fads, such as John Sloan's witty parody of cubism in the April 1913 issue, "A Slight Attack of Third Dimentia Brought on by Excessive Study of the Much-Talked-of Cubist Pictures in the International Exhibition at New York" (Zurier, *Art for the Masses*, 159). See also Sloan's February 1914 drawing "Orango-Tango" (Zurier, *Art for the Masses*, 104), parodying the tango craze of 1913–14 with a massive yet soulful ape dancing with a young creature of fashion. The magazine's willingness to poke fun at its own bohemian-radical readership was typified by Henry Glintenkamp's sketch in the December 1915 issue depicting a couple dining in a slightly seamy café. The man, attired in the trademark floppy bow tie of the Greenwich Village radical, earnestly informs his companion that he is "an anarchist and a Free-lover." Evidently familiar with this sexual gambit, she parries, "Oh, indeed!—I thought you were a Boy Scout" (Zurier, *Art for the Masses*, 103).

10. Qtd. in Zurier, *Art for the Masses*, 37.

11. Ibid.

12. Eastman's final version reads: "A revolutionary and not a reform magazine; a magazine with no dividends to pay; a free magazine; frank, arrogant, impertinent, searching for the true causes; a magazine directed against rigidity and dogma wherever it is found; printing what is too naked or true for a moneymaking press; a magazine whose final policy is to do as it pleases and conciliate nobody, not even its readers—there is room for this publication in America." As Morrisson notes, this "rhetorical scorn for audiences" links *The Masses* to "modernist magazines" such as the *Little Review,* whose famous avant-garde motto, "Making no compromise with the public taste," was adopted only in 1917, almost five years after *The Masses* began refusing to conciliate its readers (*Public Face*, 172).

13. Zurier, *Art for the Masses*, 30; O'Neill, *Last Romantic*, 32–33.

14. Eastman, "Policy," 302.

15. Zurier, *Art for the Masses*, 30–31.

16. As often with little magazines, one finds widely varying circulation figures for *The Masses*. O'Neill puts circulation at around twelve thousand on the average (*Echoes of Revolt*, 18), while Hoffman, Allen, and Ulrich propose fourteen thousand (*Little Magazine*, 29), and Zurier estimates between twenty and forty thousand (*Art for the Masses*, 51).

17. Morrisson, *Public Face,* 176, 178–79.

18. Wheeler to Untermeyer, August 6, 1913, Untermeyer Papers.

19. Peckham to Untermeyer, August 10, 1913, Untermeyer Papers.

20. Braithwaite to Untermeyer, January 2, 1914, Untermeyer Papers.

21. Morrisson, *Public Face,* 176.

22. Advertisement for *The Masses,* 44.

23. "Are You a Poet?" 11.

24. Monroe, "Newspaper Verse," 325.

25. The laudatory review of *Enjoyment of Poetry* in *Current Opinion* noted that "Max Eastman's new book on poetry is ranked by one critic with the essays of Shelley" and included a profile portrait of the strikingly handsome young author captioned, "The Latest Protagonist of the Romantic Spirit" ("Practical Value of Poetry," 126, 127). Most responses, such as that in the *North American Review,* ignored the paradox that this arch-romantic was also the radical editor of *The Masses,* concentrating instead on his background in philosophy (Rev. of *Enjoyment,* 858–59). However, the book's most perceptive reviewer, Harriet Monroe in *Poetry,* did find continuity between Eastman's aesthetics and his politics, describing the book's effort "to combat the popular heresy that poetry is a bookish art" and to show instead that "'[p]oetry ushers us out of the library; it is a gesture toward the world'" (Monroe, "Poetry a Zest for Life," 142).

26. Eastman, "Lazy Verse," 138.

27. Ibid. See also Eastman's 1917 essay "Science and Free Verse" in the *Seven Arts.* His polemics drew return fire from such champions of *vers libre* as Alice Corbin Henderson and James Oppenheim. Henderson's response in *Poetry* argued that Eastman's position "put a halo around the head of anyone who writes metrical verse, however poor," by implying that "all *vers libre* is journalism, all metrical verse literature—a conclusion hard to accept" (Henderson, "Lazy Criticism," 145). In the first issue of his magazine the *Seven Arts,* Oppenheim pointed out the "lazy thinking" of anti–*vers libre* critics such as Eastman, who mistook inevitably uneven experiments in new forms for inherent limitations of the forms themselves: "Because free verse is a new form, and because much of it is bad, they attack, not the bad poets, but the form itself" (Oppenheim, "'Lazy' Verse," 72).

28. Kreymborg to Louis Untermeyer, July 1920, Untermeyer Papers.

29. Dell to Arthur Davison Ficke, December 17, 1915, Floyd Dell Papers.

30. Ibid.

31. O'Neill, *Echoes,* 19.

32. Dell to Ficke, December 17, 1915, Floyd Dell Papers. One of the Aldis submissions, "The Barber Shop," would appear in *The Masses* the following April, and another, "Words," in October.

33. Nelson, *Repression,* 89.

34. Ibid.

35. Untermeyer, "God's Youth," 12.

36. Santayana, *Sonnets,* 6.

37. Untermeyer, "God's Youth," 12.

38. A similar repudiation of genteel piety appears in Gelett Burgess's "Darkness before Dawn: A Revolutionary Hymn to the Anthropomorphic God" (*The Masses,* June 1913), which ends by addressing the deity, "Lo, thou has failed, but Man, divinely glorified / He shall achieve alone the Brotherhood of Man" (Burgess, "Darkness," 3). Less ponderously, Arthur Davison Ficke's *vers libre* poem "Tables" (December 1916) proposes a modernized iconography of spiritual experience that substitutes café for church, human for God:

> Once the altar was sacred;
> But now, I think, it is the table.
> For across tables
> Go the words, the looks, the blinding flashes of thought
> That are truly the race's history. (11)

See also Clement Wood's "God's Blunder" (June 1914), an obvious imitation of "God's Youth."

39. Untermeyer, "God's Youth," 12.

40. For contextualizing discussions of "The Man with the Hoe," see Nelson, *Revolutionary Memory,* 17; Newcomb, *Would Poetry Disappear?* 77–79.

41. O'Neill's anthology *Echoes of Revolt* reprints much of the coverage *The Masses* devoted in 1913 and 1914 to labor strife in New Jersey, West Virginia, Colorado, and elsewhere. See especially John Reed's "War in Paterson" (June 1913) and two articles by Eastman, "Class War in Colorado" (June 1914) and "The Nice People of Trinidad" (July 1914). For a detailed study of the Paterson strike, see Tripp, *IWW and the Paterson Silk Strike.* For a poetic response to the strike at an earlier stage, see Untermeyer, "Sunday."

42. Stokes, "Paterson," 11.

43. Wilkinson, "Food Riots," 23. Although one labor historian describes such food riots unempathetically as a "reactionary form of collective action, . . . purely local in focus, apolitical and communally based," Wilkinson and *The Masses* were bound to take them as confirmation of their own critique of a needless and cruel war and possibly as harbingers of broader rebellions against capitalist oppression (L. Taylor, "Food Riots Revisited," 483). See also D. Frank, "Housewives," 255–85; Freiburger, "War Prosperity," 217–39.

44. Wilkinson, "Food Riots," 23.

45. Van Wienen, *Partisans,* 152–53.

46. Wilkinson, "Food Riots," 23.

47. In the 1997 monograph *Partisans and Poets* and the 2002 anthology *Rendezvous with Death,* Mark Van Wienen has exhaustively demonstrated that American verse took many positions on the morality of war, the proper global role of the United States, the long-range consequences of the cataclysm, and the relation of foreign wars to conflicts of race, class, and gender within the nation's borders. Van Wienen makes a compelling case for remembering and learning from this diversity of response, both dissident and bellicose.

48. Brooke, "Peace," 111.

49. Ibid.; Fussell, *Great War,* 22–23, 301.

50. Hale, *Friends,* 285; see also Read, *Forever England,* 246–60.

51. To chart the near-obsession of the *Little Review* with Brooke in 1914–15, see M. H. Partridge's "The Case of Rupert Brooke" (March 1914), George Soule's "Rupert Brooke and Whitman" (April 1914), "Rupert Brooke's Visit" (June 1914), Arthur Davison Ficke's "Of Rupert Brooke and Other Matters" (July 1914), "Rupert Brooke on the War" (December 1914), and the elegiac photograph of the poet in the June 1915 issue.

52. "Murder of a Poet," 36.

53. Monroe, "Death of Rupert Brooke," 137–38.

54. Dell to Ficke, September 16, 1915, Floyd Dell Papers.

55. Ibid.

56. Wood, "Breath," 6.

57. Untermeyer, "To a War Poet," 3.

58. Ibid.; Owen, "Dulce," 15.

59. Untermeyer, "To a War Poet," 3.

60. Sandburg, "Buttons," 10.

61. From the beginning of the war, influential American proponents of preparedness such as Theodore Roosevelt and former army chief of staff General Leonard Wood had advocated recruitment campaigns, increases in armament strength, even universal military service. The latter position inspired a sonnet published in *The Masses* the same month that America declared war, April 1917, by Robert Hillyer, whose "To Congress Concerning the Bill for Universal Military Service" indicted those advocating conscription as "[i]gnorant tyrants" forcing "a sword into the hand of Youth," who would eventually cause a revolt among young people willing to "[b]etray . . . nations for the cause of Man" (14). Thirty years later, no longer of draft age, Hillyer would take a drastically different position as an anticommunist cold warrior.

62. Jones, *Heretics,* 97.

63. For accounts of the antipreparedness argument as it extended across various genres in *The Masses,* see ibid., 78–98; and O'Neill, *Echoes,* 275–84.

64. Giovannitti, "Day of War," 20.

65. Another *Masses* poem not directly about the war yet closely related in setting and theme is Freda Kirchwey's "To a Soap-Box Orator" (February 1915), where a young man offers a distracted crowd the communist premise that "the world and all's our share" (8). The poet questions whether the people can "hate enough to fight" and "think enough to win," given all "the noises and smells" and "the pressing crowds and beckoning eyes" of "a reeling summer night." Despite realizing that the young man's words are "urgent and wise," the poem trails off, "But . . . it's Saturday night—and a dime to spare!" Its publication in *The Masses* suggests the magazine's thoughtful exploration of the difficulties of revolutionism, as opposed to some of its successors, which had little use for literature not offering party-line affirmations.

66. Giovannitti, "Day of War," 20.

67. Rogers, "Insolence," 298.

68. Reed, "One Solid Month," 294.

69. Fortunately, Stokes's wealthy husband was able to keep her free on bail until her conviction was overturned by the U.S. Court of Appeals in March 1920.

70. Compare the mission statement of *The Masses* (discussed above) to the grimly serious one of *The Liberator,* which "will be distinguished by a complete freedom in art and poetry and fiction and criticism. It will be candid. It will be experimental. It will be hospitable to new thoughts and feelings. It will direct its attack against dogma and rigidity of mind upon what-ever side they are found" ("Editorials," 5). Most of the assertions are the same in substance, yet the tone of *The Liberator*'s is drained of all vitality, nearly all hope.

71. O'Neill, *Last Romantic,* 90–96.

72. Nelson, *Repression,* 140.

73. O'Neill, *Last Romantic,* 98.

74. Untermeyer, "Ivory Tower," 60.

75. The "Ivory Tower" exchange has been cited by dozens of Wallace Stevens scholars over the past five decades, usually serving to frame a "long-continuing debate" (Doyle, Introduction, 1) between "two essential—and essentially antagonistic—ideologies in early twentieth-century American criticism" (Schaum, *Wallace Stevens,* 35). For representative references, see Willard, *Wallace Stevens,* 54; Lentricchia, *Modernist,* 225; Pearce, *Act of the Mind,* 246–47; and Schaum, *Wallace Stevens,* 35–41.

The evolving personal relationship between Untermeyer and Aiken provides an intriguing gloss on the emergence of this binary framework. After frosty exchanges following the "Ivory Tower" debate in mid-1919, they became good friends over the next two years, complete with weekend visits and shared confidences about mutual literary acquaintances. In a letter written sometime in 1920, Aiken spun their differences into a fantasy of mutual withdrawal to a realm of pure aesthetic contemplation, figured as a "coral atoll in the south seas": "One tip of the atoll is yours, the other is mine, and we will contemplate each other across the little strait of blue water, marveling at the imaginativeness of the god who created us. Bolshevize the bananas if you wish: I shall have no further need of the ivory tower" (Aiken to Untermeyer, n.d., Untermeyer Papers).

This narrative of onetime opponents bonding over a shared love of poetry would be more uplifting if it didn't presage the American left's nearly complete withdrawal from the literary field under the escapist pressure of the 1920s, epitomized by Untermeyer's discarding of his early radical associations to become merely a prolific anthologist of mildly populist inclinations.

76. Taggard, *May Days,* 13.

77. Ibid., 13, 14.

CHAPTER 4. THERE IS ALWAYS *OTHERS*

1. The circulation figure of five hundred is reported by David Perkins (*History of Modern Poetry,* 323), although Kreymborg claimed it never reached three hundred ("Early Impression," 12).

2. Churchill and McKible, Introduction, 4.

3. Hoffman, Allen, and Ulrich, *Little Magazine,* 51.

4. Ibid., 247–48.

5. The intermittent gestures *Others* made toward critical commentary invariably proved abortive. The April 1916 issue, for example, announced the beginning of "a Review Department in charge of Maxwell Bodenheim" and contained two reviews by him (Untitled Announcement, 210–13). But in the very next issue, this "Review Department" was no more. In the magazine's final phase, beginning in December 1918, a critical impulse emerged again, and each of the next four issues featured one prose piece, but with the partial exception of Emanuel Carnevali's essay on Rimbaud in March 1919, this prose had little to do with contemporary verse.

6. During the crisis of the previous two decades, many worried that poetry no longer possessed any distinct generic identity. Thus in 1910, Brian Hooker concluded that "[t]here is something wrong with an art of which people commonly speak with allowance and condescension," citing as evidence the fact that "in lists of new books the poetry is grouped under a miscellaneous heading with closet-dramas and works on Travel and Art" ("Recent Volumes," 465).

7. Kreymborg, "Vers Libre," 1.

8. W. Williams, "Gloria!" 3; "Belly Music," 29.

9. Brownell, "Irrational Verse," 22.

10. Ibid.

11. Ibid., 23. Brogan discusses Brownell's essay as a precursor to what she calls "the 'Revolution' of the Early 1920s," in which the language of radical social change, so prevalent in the 1910s, was increasingly applied to the realm of literary form (*Part of the Climate,* 318). Brogan claims that this artistic "revolution" was still "deeply aligned with sociopolitical revolutions" (62), but I see the relationship of the aesthetic and political in the 1920s less as an alignment than a displacement, in which experimentalism divorced from activism became a way of repressing "the threat of total social chaos" that the war and its aftermath had raised (63).

12. Churchill, *Little Magazine* Others, 61–62.

13. Brownell, "Irrational Verse," 22, 25.

14. Ibid., 25.

15. Untitled Statement, 1.

16. Ibid.

17. Churchill, *Little Magazine* Others, 25.

18. Davies, "Songs of a Girl," 3. In the third issue of *Others,* the tendency to combine first-person writing with the personification of intangibles achieved self-parodic quintessence in Maxwell Bodenheim's "After Writing Poetry," which earnestly in-

formed readers, "My mind is a naked child / Living in the little half-crimson garden of my soul" (52). Early issues of *Others* featured this distinctive form of first-person address so often that it became an object of mirth to skeptical critics, particularly *Poetry*'s Alice Corbin Henderson, whose review of the first *Others* anthology poked fun at the "I-am-it school" by assembling snippets from various self-involved poems, including Davies's (Henderson, "New School," 103–5).

19. Loy, "Love Songs," 6. Loy expanded the "Love Songs" sequence into "Songs to Joannes," a much larger work of thirty-four units, to which the April 1917 issue of *Others* was entirely devoted.

20. Churchill, *Little Magazine* Others, 73.

21. Loy, "Love Songs," 7.

22. Helen Hoyt's preface to the "Woman's Number" of *Others* (September 1916) emphasizes the exploration of female consciousness as a governing premise: "At present most of what we know, or think we know, of women has been found out by men. We have yet to hear what woman will tell of herself, and where can she tell more intimately, more immediately, than in poetry?" (Hoyt, Editorial Comment, 54). The "special number" can, of course, be seen as an ambiguous benefit, but in this case it was not an insincere ploy to contain female poets within their own expressive ghetto. Women appeared in almost every issue of *Others* and comprised about 40 percent of its total roster of contributors.

23. Ransom, "Woman as Poet," 91.

24. Churchill, *Little Magazine* Others, 16.

25. By mid-1915 *Poetry* had published a few sequences structured along similar juxtapositional principles, such as A. J. Russell's "The House of Takumi," a "Poem-Sequence from the Japanese" (April 1914), John Gould Fletcher's "Blue Symphony" (September 1914), and John Rodker's "London Night" (December 1914). But sequence poems never played the central role there that they did in *Others,* and the innovative force of those that did appear was diluted by *Poetry*'s many faux-sequences.

26. Johns, "Olives," 12.

27. Churchill, *Little Magazine* Others, 75.

28. Johns, "Olives," 9–12.

29. Kreymborg, "Variations," 16.

30. Kreymborg, "Overheard," 18.

31. Kreymborg, "Variations," 17.

32. Stevens, "Thirteen Ways," 25.

33. C. Miller, "Tongues," 456.

34. Churchill, *Little Magazine* Others, 7.

35. Johnson, "Tired," 8.

36. Johnson, "Aunt Hannah Jackson," 17.

37. C. Miller, "Tongues," 456.

38. Woolley, "From Chicago Renaissance," 46.

39. Kreymborg, *Our Singing Strength,* 573; Hutchinson, "Fenton Johnson," 14.

40. C. Miller, "Tongues," 468.

41. Ibid., 467.

42. Ficke, "The Dancer," 178, 179.

43. For discussion of the frequent treatments of prostitution in *The Masses,* see O'Neill, *Echoes of Revolt,* 182–95; Fishbein, Introduction, 13; Zurier, *Art for the Masses,* 100; and Jones, *Heretics,* 41–42. *Poetry* took up the theme as well: see Untermeyer's "Any City" (July 1913), Lydia Gibson's "Lies" (October 1913), William Rose Benét's "Poor Girl," and Edmond McKenna's "Another Poem" (both April 1914). Besides Ficke's, at least three *Others* poems—Conrad Aiken's "Meretrix: Ironic" (June 1916), Eunice Tietjens's "The Lady of Easy Virtue: An American" (June 1917), and Mark Turbyfill's "Reality" (June 1917)—explore the figure of the prostitute with varying degrees of empathy and acuity.

44. Ficke, "The Dancer," 178.

45. This portrayal of the modern poet as incarcerated agitator-derelict links *Others* to *The Masses,* which in Max Eastman's second issue (January 1913) had printed Arturo Giovannitti's "The Bum," a self-portrait of the artist captioned, "Salem Jail, Nov. 20, 1912" (15).

46. Biographical information on Wolff is provided by Naumann and Avrich, "Adolf Wolff," 496.

47. A. Wolff, "Prison Weeds," 86.

48. Kreymborg's reminiscence of the Allen Norton–Walter Arensberg circle has been widely cited as an early account of Wallace Stevens in the New York avantgarde. But the anecdote (narrated in third person) is equally revealing of "Krimmie's" sense of social otherness amid a gaggle of Ivy League bohemians: "So as not to appear outside the circle, he tried to hold his tea cup nonchalantly and assumed a casual air whenever he was addressed. . . . As his ear soon detected that what sounded natural in the other men about the room was affected in his case, he dropped the drawl" (*Troubador,* 219).

49. Kreymborg, "New York," 43.

50. C. Miller, "Tongues," 466.

51. Crunden, *American Salons,* 413.

52. Williams's phrase comes from a letter to Harriet Monroe, March 5, 1913, in W. Williams, *Selected Letters,* 24.

53. Swasey, "City in Summer," 134; Trachtenberg, *Reading,* 170–71, 190–92. Orvell describes Jacob Riis's famous compositions in *How the Other Half Lives* as "a metonymic typology of urban slums, representing for us 'the poor,' 'the miserable,' 'the other half.' He is after the general truth of a general category, and the finer truths of individuals necessarily escape him" (*Real Thing,* 97). In contrast, the modern documentary ideal developed by Alfred Stieglitz after 1905 and later taken by Hine to its highest pitch of social engagement relied on the camera's status as an exalted machine, which for its adherents guaranteed the "authenticity of its productions" and made it "a model for the synthesis of science and art" (198).

54. Bodenheim, "East Side Children," 7.

55. W. Williams, "Young Housewife," 18.

56. W. Williams, *Collected Poems,* vol. 1, 217–19, 87–88, 106–7.

57. Endicoff, "New York Etchings," 137–38.

58. See also Lola Ridge's "Blossoms" (December 1918), written in the wake of the Russian Revolution, which combines the futurist-industrial vocabulary of Endicoff with her idiosyncratic Christian Marxism, portraying machine-age labor as an ennobling "flame of sacrifice, / Like a lily swaying," portending "[d]ay . . . at the gates / And a young wind" of coming revolutionary change (Ridge, "Blossoms," 5). Ridge controls the oracular tendencies of this theme by grounding her imagery in the concrete functions of the metallurgical converter.

59. A. Wolff, "Mending," 22.

60. L. Pearce, "Machine Made," 170.

61. W. Williams, *Collected Poems,* vol. 1, 405–6.

62. Saphier, "Machine Shop," 18.

63. Lewis Hine's photos of skilled industrial workers during the 1920s, culminating in the famous series he took hundreds of feet in the air during the construction of the Empire State Building in 1929 and 1930, were published in 1932 by Macmillan as *Men at Work: Photographic Studies of Modern Men and Machines.*

64. Ibid., frontispiece.

65. Carr, "Steel Town," 26.

66. Gilbert, "Marianne Moore," 35; Costello, *Marianne Moore,* 42.

67. M. Moore, "To Statecraft," 104.

68. Bodenheim, "Parade," 7.

69. Sandburg, "Statistics," 181.

70. Sandburg, "Long Guns," 17.

71. Ibid. In his emphasis on the psychic effects of long-range guns, Sandburg may have in mind the infamous "Paris Gun," which the Germans used to bombard Paris from the western front between March and June 1918. This longest of the period's guns shot its projectiles twenty-five miles up into the earth's stratosphere and had an effective target range of about seventy miles. Though its payload was too small and its aim too approximate to match the extent of physical damage done by shorter-range guns, it represented a new level of terror weapon, designed to traumatize an enemy population by eliminating any possibility of safe space and recognizing no distinction between combatant and civilian.

72. Ibid.

73. W. Williams, "Epigramme," 147.

74. W. Williams, *Collected Poems,* vol. 1, 453, 83, 217–19.

75. D'Orge, "Microscope," 223.

76. J. Beach, "Nostalgia," 132.

77. W. Williams, "El Hombre," 24.

78. Seiffert, "The Peddler," 21–22.

79. W. Williams, *Collected Poems,* vol. 2, 54.

80. Tichi, *Shifting Gears,* 16.

81. W. Williams, "To a Solitary Disciple," 145–46.

82. To take but one of many possible examples, in July 1917 William Carlos Williams, notoriously cranky and intemperate in his opinions of other poets, wrote to Harriet Monroe admiring Sandburg's "Cool Tombs" (in *Others* for June) and hoping that he might soon finally meet its creator: "Few men are making any progress in their art. They are adding decoration or repeating the old stuff but Sandburg is really thinking like an artist" (Parisi and Young, *Dear Editor,* 129–30).

83. See Lowell, *Tendencies,* 201–32; Hubbell, "My Friend," 5–17; Crowder, *Carl Sandburg,* 61.

84. Sandburg began receiving honorary degrees in 1928; by 1940 this process had advanced up the academic pecking order to Yale and Harvard, awarded on consecutive days. Also in that year he received the Pulitzer Prize for History and was elected to the American Academy of Arts and Letters.

85. Gregory and Zaturenska, *History of American Poetry,* 242–51. Perhaps the most egregious treatment of Sandburg among major historians of American poetry was by Hyatt Waggoner, who remarked in 1968 that his early work "came as close to being subliterary as the work of any American poet of comparable reputation ever has" (*American Poets,* 452). A fairer estimate came from Bernard Duffey in 1978, who noted without disparagement that "Sandburg stood at the beginning of an avant-garde line departing significantly from the main Imagist emphasis in its willingness to trust more to the possibilities of subject for its expression than to new technique" (*Poetry in America,* 248). Even so, Duffey's book devotes dozens of pages to Pound's line of avant-gardism, less than two to Sandburg's.

86. Even now the Sandburg scholarly tradition is barely more than rudimentary. Other than the inevitable Twayne volume of the early 1960s, Philip Yannella's valuable 1996 study *The Other Carl Sandburg* is, remarkably, still the only full-length scholarly-critical monograph ever published on the poet. Yannella's book, Penelope Niven's 1991 biography, a rather meager selection of letters, two recent compilations of politically provocative verse of the 1910s by George Hendrick and Willene Hendrick, and helpful articles by Mark W. Van Wienen (1991) and John Marsh (2007) have only begun to recover this many-faceted poet.

CHAPTER 5. VOLUNTEERS OF AMERICA

1. C. Miller, "Tongues," 466.
2. Untitled Comment, *Seven Arts,* 1:629.
3. Untitled Comment, *Seven Arts,* 1:52.
4. Ibid.
5. Untitled Comment, *Seven Arts,* 1:266.
6. Ibid.
7. Oppenheim, "'Lazy' Verse," 69.
8. Ibid., 72.
9. Untitled Comment, *Seven Arts,* 1:155–56.
10. Ibid., 1:156.

11. Untitled Comment, *Seven Arts*, 1:266.

12. Gorman, *Left Intellectuals*, 63–64.

13. V. Brooks, "Young America," 144.

14. Ibid., 151.

15. Ibid.

16. V. Brooks, *America's Coming-of-Age*, 21.

17. Ibid., 23.

18. V. Brooks, "Culture of Industrialism," 658.

19. Ibid.

20. Oppenheim, "'Lazy' Verse," 71.

21. Rolland, "America and the Arts," 51.

22. Rosenfeld, "American Composer," 91; W. Frank, "Concerning," 157; V. Brooks, "Splinter," 272.

23. Untitled Comment, *Seven Arts*, 2:68.

24. "Fifth-Month Poet," 117.

25. "Henry David Thoreau," 383.

26. "The American," 555–56.

27. Ibid., 556.

28. Oppenheim, "Memories of Whitman," 10, 12.

29. Untitled Comment, *Seven Arts*, 1:628.

30. Ibid., 1:629.

31. Ibid.

32. Ibid., 1:630.

33. Rolland, "America and the Arts," 47.

34. Untitled Comment, *Seven Arts*, 1:504.

35. Ibid., 1:505–6.

36. Frost, "Mending Wall," 34.

37. Frost, "Bonfire," 25.

38. Paul Fussell describes the notion of an unending war detached from human motivation as coming into general awareness in late 1916: "One did not have to be a lunatic or a particularly despondent visionary to conceive quite seriously that the war would literally never end and would become the permanent condition of mankind. . . . Why indeed not, given the palpable irrationality of the new world?" (*Great War*, 71). Fussell also provides an unforgettable portrait of the physical space of the western front as a "troglodyte world" of mud, metal, pests, blasted vegetation, and living and dead bodies (36–74).

39. Frost, "Bonfire," 26.

40. See Lowell's 1914 poem "The Allies"; and Damon, *Amy Lowell*, 417–21.

41. Lowell, "Flotsam," 30.

42. Lowell, "Orange of Midsummer," 601.

43. McCrae, "In Flanders Fields," 3.

44. Lowell, "Orange of Midsummer," 601.

45. In what is now northern Provence, Orange was a fiefdom of the Holy Roman

Empire given the status of independent principality in 1163. It was governed under the Germanic dynastic system until 1544, when the title Prince of Orange passed to William the Silent, the Dutch noble who solidified the Netherlands as a distinct political entity, creating yet another strong national association for "Orange." The original Provençal territory of Orange became an object of dispute during the Franco-Dutch War, when Louis XIV's armies captured it in 1672 and again ten years later. After the Glorious Revolution of 1688, William III, Prince of Orange, ruled Great Britain, providing the English and Scots a royal dynasty of Orange as well. William's death without issue in 1702 generated further German claims to the principality of Orange and renewed conflict between France and Prussia, resolved finally in 1713 by the Treaties of Utrecht, which placed Orange definitively within the French nation. Henceforward the strongest symbolic resonance of "Orange" shifted to Holland. The Netherlands is still ruled by the royal house of Orange-Nassau, and on April 30, the patriotic holiday known as Queen's Day, its citizens traditionally wear the color as an expression of national identity.

46. Abrahams, *Lyrical Left,* 82.

47. Edward Abrahams notes that well before April 1917, those in charge of the *New Republic* had come to see the war as "a marvelous opportunity to realize their goals of efficient national management, social control, and a revived moral crusade" (ibid., 78).

48. My counterfactual speculation of the 1920s, in which the *Seven Arts* occupies the role assumed by *The Dial,* is supported by reports that in late 1917 Scofield Thayer was strongly interested in taking over funding of the *Seven Arts,* but when that fell through, he turned toward *The Dial* instead (Hoffman, Allen, and Ulrich, *Little Magazine,* 98–99).

49. Untitled Comment, *Seven Arts,* 1:505.

50. Sandburg, "Grass," 474.

51. Brooke, "1914," 115.

52. Untitled Comment, *Seven Arts,* 1:629.

53. Ibid., 1:629–30.

54. Ibid., 1:630.

55. Untitled Comment, *Seven Arts,* 2:68–69.

56. Ibid., 2:69.

57. Ibid., 2:70.

58. Ibid.

59. Ibid., 2:71.

60. Untitled Comment, *Seven Arts,* 2:200.

61. Ibid.

62. Ibid., 2:201.

63. Ibid.

64. Bourne, "War and the Intellectuals," 133.

65. Ibid.

66. Ibid., 145.

67. Ibid., 145–46.

68. Ibid., 146.

69. Ibid.

70. Bourne, "Below the Battle," 270.

71. Ibid., 277.

72. Bourne, "Conspirators," 528–30. Bourne did not name these students, but he had in mind the widely publicized case of Owen Cattell and Charles Phillips, Columbia undergraduates who were convicted, fined, incarcerated, and stripped of their citizenship in July 1917 for "conspiracy to obstruct the operation of the military laws of the United States" (*New York Times,* June 21, 1917); their "co-conspirator" Eleanor Parker of Barnard was acquitted (*New York Times,* July 13, 1917).

73. "'The Masses' and American Rights," 532.

74. Untitled Comment, *Seven Arts,* 1:629.

75. [Oppenheim], Editorial, *Seven Arts* 2:491.

76. Ibid. A prose paean to revolutionary Russia, unsigned but likely by Oppenheim, had already appeared in the May issue ("Holy Russia," 60–61).

77. Bourne, "War Diary," 545.

78. Ibid., 546.

79. Ibid.

80. Russell, "Is Nationalism Moribund?" 676, 680.

81. [Oppenheim], Editorial, *Seven Arts* 2:624–25.

82. Ibid., 2:625.

83. Ibid., 2:625–26.

84. [Oppenheim], "After a Stormy Twilight," 760.

85. Ibid., 760–61.

86. Thomas, "Have We Still Need," 509.

87. Bourne, *World of Randolph Bourne,* 326.

88. Abrahams, *Lyrical Left,* 23; Hoffman, Allen, and Ulrich, *Little Magazine,* 199.

89. Hoffman, Allen, and Ulrich, *Little Magazine,* 199.

90. Abrahams, *Lyrical Left,* 90.

91. Oppenheim, "Randolph Bourne," 14.

92. Hoffman, Allen, and Ulrich, *Little Magazine,* 92.

93. Bourne, "War and the Intellectuals," 143.

94. Ibid.

95. Ibid.

CHAPTER 6. GUTTER AND SKYLINE

1. For a typical example, see George Cabot Lodge's double sonnet "Lower New York" (mid-1900s), whose enthrallment to anti-urban romanticism is announced by the opening line, "Time has no spectacle more stern and strange" (inverting Wordsworth's "Earth has not anything to show more fair"). Here the industrial city before dawn is no more than "a vast necropolis of souls" ruled by "sordid greed

and passions mean and blind" in which life "seems more dead than death, / Aimless and empty as an idiot's mind" (*Poems and Dramas*, 168). Things are no better in the second sonnet, in which dawn in the city is "a hopeless thing to see," bringing nothing but "a vast and sullen rumour" that "for yet another human day, / The world's dull, dreadful labour is begun!"

2. Many of the earliest of these were published in *The Atlantic* under the editorship of Bliss Perry: Harriet Monroe's "The Telephone" in October 1905, followed by Chester Firkins's "A Cry in the Market Place" (July 1907), Firkins's "On a Subway Express" (February 1908), Monroe's "The Hotel" (March 1909) and "The Turbine" (June 1910). Firkins also published "Light in a Tenement Window" and "Night Worker" in *Lippincott's* (March 1908 and March 1909), and "To a City" (*The Independent*, May 1910). Other early city verses include Monroe's "A Power Plant" (*The Century*, January 1906), James Oppenheim's "New York from a Skyscraper" (*American Magazine*, January 1909), Jefferson B. Fletcher's "Seven Sandwichmen on Broadway" (*The Atlantic*, October 1909), Harry Kemp's "An Ode to Sky-Climbers" (*American Magazine*, November 1909), and John Reed's "Foundations of a Sky-scraper" (*American Magazine*, October 1911). In 1909, Charles Hanson Towne published a sonnet sequence entitled *Manhattan*, though its engagement with the material spaces of the city was minimal relative to poems appearing a few years later.

3. Laidlaw, "On Gutter Verse," 635.

4. Kilmer's "The Subway" was also mentioned in "City Poets," an unsigned commentary in *The Independent* in August 1912, and in a somewhat more open-minded editorial comment in *Scribner's* in September 1914 ("Point of View," 407–8).

5. Zurier, Snyder, and Mecklenburg, *Metropolitan Lives*, 210–11.

6. The New Critics' polemical use of Kilmer was exemplified by Allen Tate's 1940 essay "Understanding Modern Poetry," which contemptuously describes the ubiquitous lyric "Trees" as "the 'favorite poem' of the American people, taught piously by every high school teacher, and sometimes aggressively by college professors when they want to show what poetry ought to be; surely one of the preposterously bad lyrics in any language" (160–61).

7. W. Benét, "The City," 28.

8. R. Williams, *Politics of Modernism*, 35.

9. For representative examples of this critical tradition, see Dijkstra, *Cubism, Stieglitz*; Leavell, *Marianne Moore and the Visual Arts*; and MacLeod, *Wallace Stevens and Modern Art*.

10. R. Williams, *Politics of Modernism*, 32.

11. Crary, *Techniques*, 9.

12. Ibid., 1.

13. In the 1950s, Pablo Picasso succinctly described the twentieth-century artist's search for an individual style as a response to the subjectivity of modern perception: "Painters no longer live within a tradition and so each one of us must re-create an entire language" (qtd. in Gilot and Lake, *Life with Picasso*, 67).

14. Crary, *Techniques,* 5.

15. Ibid., 109–10, 119.

16. Simmel, *Philosophy of Money,* 475.

17. W. Benét, "The City," 29.

18. Monroe, "Bigness of the World," 373–74.

19. D'Orge, "Microscope," 223.

20. Crary, *Techniques,* 6.

21. Ibid.

22. Leja, *Looking Askance,* 1.

23. Sandburg, "Broadway," 69; Bodenheim, "Advice," 25.

24. Eliot, "Preludes," 13–14.

25. A widely distributed 1907 account of the origins of photography describes how Nicéphore Niepce coated metal plates with naturally occurring asphalt (also called bitumen) and, after exposing them to an image for several hours, applied lavender oil to dissolve the areas that the exposure had not affected, leaving an imprint of the exposed image (Hasluck, *Book of Photography,* 4–5).

26. Eliot, "Preludes," 15.

27. J. G. Fletcher, "Unquiet Street," 42.

28. Torrence, "Three O'Clock," 23.

29. Bodenheim, "City Streets," 42.

30. Bodenheim, "Garbage Heap," 52.

31. Bodenheim, "Street," 19.

32. Bodenheim, "South State Street," 81.

33. W. Williams, "Epigramme," 147.

34. In 1890, only six buildings in New York City had risen as high as ten stories; by 1908 there were 538 such buildings (Nash, *Manhattan Skyscrapers,* 5), and 1,048 by the end of 1912 (Landau and Condit, *Rise of the New York Skyscraper,* 394).

35. Van Leeuwen, *Skyward Trend,* 84.

36. "Point of View," 409.

37. For a discussion of the ideological impact of this analogical tradition, see Newcomb, *Would Poetry Disappear?* 37–40.

38. Ibid., 14.

39. Schleier, *Skyscraper,* 29.

40. James, *American Scene,* 77.

41. Ibid.

42. Eaton, "Sunrise," 130.

43. Eaton, *New York,* 18.

44. Coates, "New York," 50.

45. Schleier, *Skyscraper,* 35.

46. Coates, "New York," 50.

47. Sharpe, *New York Nocturne,* 244.

48. Coates, "New York," 50.

49. Monroe, "New Beauty."

50. L. Benét, "Gardens of Babylon," 16.

51. S. Benét, "Lunchtime," 41.

52. Wyatt, "To a City Swallow," 298.

53. Eliot, "Morning," 294.

54. Maxwell, *New Negro*, 67.

55. McKay, "White City," 7.

56. Maxwell, *New Negro*, 66; Nelson, *Repression*, 89–90.

57. See, among many other examples, the 1902 *Atlantic* essay "Limitations to the Production of Skyscrapers" by Burton J. Hendrick, which links the economic upheavals that skyscrapers produced with New York City's urgent "tenement problem": both were defined above all by "inadequate light and ventilation" (488). For more on the debates over the deleterious effects of such tall buildings on urban life, see Landau and Condit, *Rise of the New York Skyscraper*, 187–90.

58. Revell, "Regulating the Landscape," 32–33; see also Hendrick, "Limitations," 487–88.

59. "Proper Space," 972–73.

60. Landau and Condit, *Rise of the New York Skyscraper*, 394; Koolhaas, *Delirious New York*, 107; see also Revell, "Regulating the Landscape," 32.

61. Koolhaas, *Delirious New York*, 88.

62. Qtd. in Landau and Condit, *Rise of the New York Skyscraper*, 187.

63. Revell, "Regulating the Landscape," 39.

64. Cushing, "Restraining," 13.

65. Ibid.; see also "Point of View," 410.

66. Bodenheim, "Rear Porches," 51.

67. Untermeyer, "Playground," 12.

68. W. Williams, "Pastoral," 31.

69. Oppenheim, "New York," 216.

70. Carroll, "From a City Street," 41.

71. Sandburg, "Hats," 160.

72. Sandburg, "People Who Must," 158.

Chapter 7. Footprints of the Twentieth Century

1. Some great buildings became such potent emblems of the city that their removal could damage not only its architectural legacy but its communal and historical identity. The authors of the architectural compendium *New York 1960* mourn the 1967 demolition of the Singer Tower, whose "opulent double-height, marble-clad lobby . . . had served several generations as a favorite meeting place" (Stern, Mellins, and Fishman, *New York 1960*, 1126), as a loss to Manhattan's social fabric; likewise, the general lament continues, now nearly fifty years running, over the destruction of the old Penn Station.

2. As Merrill Schleier details, great buildings were taken as subjects by nearly every important American visual artist who came to maturity between 1900 and 1930:

among photographers, Alfred Stieglitz, Alvin Langdon Coburn, Edward Steichen, Paul Strand, Lewis Hine, Charles Sheeler, Margaret Bourke-White; among painters, Charles Sheeler, Georgia O'Keeffe, John Marin, George Bellows, Joseph Stella, John Sloan, Edward Hopper, and Stuart Davis, along with dozens of others (*Skyscraper in American Art*).

3.Van Leeuwen, *Skyward Trend,* 7.

4. Ibid.

5. Hendrick, "Limitations," 487; "Tall Buildings," 837.

6. Though the skyscraper could not have arisen without these economic incentives and technical advances, they do not fully explain the race into the skies after 1900, which enacted a deep psychic need to create spectacular material signs of America's supremacy among modernized nations. In pursuing this argument, Ann Douglas ingeniously situates the skyscraper's "commodification of the air as a marketable product" into the broader category of "airmindedness," which includes plane flight and broadcasting (*Terrible Honesty,* 434).

7. The Eiffel Tower (1889), almost a thousand feet high, was by far the world's tallest structure until 1930. But like the Washington Monument (555 feet), it was not generally considered a *building* as commercial office towers were. As one commentator noted in 1907, "Daily people ascend to the top of each, but they cannot be called inhabited. They are not intended for persons to occupy while at their usual vocations" (Willey, "Coming," 83).

8. According to Rem Koolhaas, in 1911 a "coalition of draftsmen" was busily "'working out the plans for the 100-story building'" (*Delirious New York,* 89). A commentary of that same year in *World's Work* assumed the technological feasability of two-thousand-foot towers, noting that the only remaining hindrance was a scale of diminishing returns in rentable space as more and larger elevators were required the higher a building rose (Forbes, "Skyscraper," 14391). Despite these problems, as he pondered the Woolworth Building's plan to go higher than any existing building, Edgar Forbes was quite certain "that somebody else will come along and climb higher yet" (14389).

9. Not until 1930 did another cluster of iconic modern skyscrapers overtop the group built between 1908 and 1913. This phase was initiated by the Bank of the Manhattan Company Building (1930, H. Craig Severance and Yasuo Matsui, 927 feet; now called 40 Wall Street), enriched by the Chrysler Building (1930, William Van Alen, 1,048 feet), and culminated by the Empire State Building (1931, Shreve, Lamb, and Harmon, 1,250 feet) before the constraints of depression and war encroached once again.

10. Meredith, "New Building," 588.

11. *Cathedral of Commerce,* 8; "Some Statistics Related to the Singer Building."

12. *Metropolitan Life Insurance Company,* 45–46.

13. Qtd. in Nash, *Manhattan Skyscrapers,* 5.

14. Baker, "Modern Skyscraper," 52.

15. Tichi, *Shifting Gears,* 4–5; Schuyler, "Towers of Manhattan," 111.

16. Forbes, "Skyscraper," 14395.

17. Zunz, *Making America Corporate*, 111–12; M. Brooks, *Subway City*, 106–7.

18. Baker, "Modern Skyscraper," 58.

19. Willey, "Coming," 82; Forbes, "Skyscraper," 14389.

20. Eaton, *New York*, 4.

21. William R. Taylor describes Woolworth's strategy for "overwhelming" the public with his spectacular skyscraper but also notes that the tycoon's "legendary" reputation for "practicality and caution about excess" led him to see the project as an ideal combination of "solid investment in Manhattan real estate and unrivalled advertising" (*In Pursuit of Gotham*, 47, 46).

22. Eaton, *New York*, 6.

23. Goodrich, "Biography," 2955; Eaton, *New York*, 6.

24. *Metropolitan Life Insurance Company*, 52; "Some Statistics Related to the Singer Building"; Bruce, *Above the Clouds*, 28–30.

25. Koolhaas, *Delirious New York*, 87.

26. Ibid., 99.

27. Goodrich, "Biography," 2959.

28. Nichols, *Skyline Queen*, 89–90.

29. Greeley, "Age of Invention," 706.

30. Though some discussion of the ruins of the Anasazi Cliff Dwellers had appeared in obscure publications in the mid-1870s, it was not until 1888 that the largest settlements were discovered by archaeological writers (Smith, Introduction, xi). The first widely circulated print accounts—an 1892 article by Frederick Chapin in *American Antiquarian*, Chapin's 1892 book *The Land of the Cliff Dwellers*, and Gustav Nordenskiöld's ethnographic study *The Cliff Dwellers of the Mesa Verde* (1893)—appeared just as the building of steel-frame skyscrapers accelerated in American cities.

31. Some accounts used ethnocentric or openly racist premises to account for the Cliff Dwellers' technological aptitude, refusing to believe they could be the ancestors of the agrarian Pueblo peoples who lived in the plains below, insisting that they must instead have been a "lost fragment of Egyptian civilization" or even a "white people" of "a prehistoric age" (Munk, *Arizona Sketches*, 171–75).

32. *Dream City*.

33. Fuller, *Cliff Dwellers*, 1–2.

34. Ibid., 4.

35. Ibid., 4–5, 12.

36. Ibid., 5.

37. Ibid. This model of the skyscraper as an insular microcosm combining futuristic and ancient elements descends from the Cliff Dwellers metaphor into postmodern science fiction, most vividly in Ridley Scott's dystopian classic film *Blade Runner* (1982), where both the panoptical headquarters of the Tyrell Corporation and the protagonist's fortresslike apartment building feature design motifs reminiscent of ancient Egyptian or Amerindian cultures.

38. "Tall Buildings," 848; Cushing, "Restraining," 13; Carter, "New Problems," 568.

39. Stapley, "City of Towers," 704, 706.

40. Forbes, "Skyscraper," 14397.

41. Eaton, *New York*, 4.

42. Ibid., 5.

43. Ibid., 6–10.

44. Qtd. in "Artistic Aspects," 321.

45. Johns, "Second Avenue," 134.

46. A. Wolff, "Lines," 29.

47. Ibid. In a quirky touch, the building's interior designer had invited this sort of response by installing a grotesque corbel in the lobby that depicted the highest priest of low lucre, F. W. Woolworth himself, feverishly counting nickels and dimes. Wolff's condemnation was particularly pointed, given the well-publicized fact that the Woolworth was built and paid for in cash with no mortgage. Thomas van Leeuwen remarks of this, "The building was conceived . . . as a memorial to the means by which its owner had assembled his fortune, namely nickels and dimes, the 'atomic elements' of capitalism. But it also represented Woolworth's preparations for the hereafter: the money was being returned to the public in the form of a building that was without the sin of usury" (*Skyward Trend*, 67–68). Clearly the poet was not impressed with the tycoon's moral sleight-of-hand. See also Clement Wood's "Woolworth Cathedral" in *The Masses*, which describes the tower as "[r]aised by vice-stained and blood-soaked pennies / Squeezed out of weak and pitiful girls" (20).

48. A. Wolff, "Lines," 29.

49. Reed, "Foundations," 735.

50. Corder, "Skyscraper," 21.

51. Bowen, "Skyscraper," 13.

52. Monroe, "Night in State Street," 8.

53. Eaton, *New York*, 21–22.

54. Ibid., 22.

55. Baker, "Modern Skyscraper," 48, 56.

56. Meredith, "New Building," 588.

57. Teasdale, "From the Woolworth Tower," 15.

58. Holley, "Skyscrapers," 22. Skyscrapers do sway measurably in wind, but their relative stability was one of the features that most astonished people in the early 1900s. Its owners claimed that the Woolworth Building was capable of withstanding winds of two hundred miles per hour without structural damage (*Cathedral of Commerce*, 27); in January 1913, three months before its dedication, the tower did receive gusts of ninety miles per hour with no damage (Landau and Condit, *Rise of the New York Skyscraper*, 359).

59. Holley, "Skyscrapers," 22.

60. W. Benét, "Singing Skyscrapers," 1.

61. Teasdale, "From the Woolworth Tower," 12.

62. Ibid. To New Yorkers of the 1910s, the Woolworth Building's twenty-eight state-of-the-art elevators were objects of intense fascination. The system was monitored from the lobby by an electric dispatcher mechanism, while each car contained a phone capable of contacting any location in the country and enough safety cushions that a seven-thousand-pound cargo was once test-dropped in free fall from the forty-fifth floor to the bottom without spilling a full glass of water in the car (*Cathedral of Commerce,* 14–15, 19). In the 1910s, the two elevators going from the ground to the observation deck in the Woolworth Building were the fastest in the world, routinely running at seven hundred feet per minute (*Cathedral of Commerce,* 14). For a detailed description of the Woolworth's elevators, see the 1913 article in *Technical World* by C. B. Edwards ("Elevators Run").

63. *Cathedral of Commerce,* 13.

64. Nichols, *Skyline Queen,* 136.

65. Teasdale, "From the Woolworth Tower," 13.

66. Eliot, *Waste Land,* 66.

67. Ibid.

68. Ibid., 67.

69. Ibid., 61.

70. Ibid., 67, 55.

71. Ibid., 69.

72. Ibid.

73. Willey, "Coming," 90.

74. Baker, "Modern Skyscraper," 57; Stewart, "Hotels of New York," 292.

75. Koolhaas, *Delirious New York,* 82.

76. *Cathedral of Commerce,* 7, 29–30.

77. Landau and Condit, *Rise of the New York Skyscraper,* 338.

78. Koolhaas, *Delirious New York,* 132.

79. Hungerford, *Story of the Waldorf-Astoria,* 275.

80. Monroe, *Poet's Life,* 190.

81. James, *American Scene,* 102.

82. Ibid., 105.

83. Monroe, *Poet's Life,* 190.

84. Tichi, *Shifting Gears,* 143.

85. Monroe, "Hotel," 324–25.

86. Stern, Gilmartin, and Massengale, *New York 1900,* 257.

87. Orvell, *Real Thing,* 16–29.

88. Ibid., 18.

89. Sandburg, "Skyscraper," 31.

90. Wylie, "Parting Gift," 68.

91. *Metropolitan Life Insurance Company,* 48. The refurbished Metropolitan Tower still offers a nightly light show, although the current effects do not evoke a searchlight, nor do they measure time as the original ones did. But in the building's second century, its great illuminated clock still runs.

92. Teasdale, "Metropolitan Tower," 31.

93. S. Benét, "Chanson," 46.

94. Dublin, *Family of Thirty Million,* 236. Rem Koolhaas describes the Metropolitan as the city's "landlocked lighthouse, ostensibly flashing its beams out to sea, but in fact luring the metropolitan audience to itself" (*Delirious New York,* 94).

95. Ridge, "Time-Stone," 51.

96. Stevens, "Idea of Order," 129.

97. Zunz, *Making America Corporate,* 116.

98. Qtd. in Suárez, "City Space," 103.

99. Eliot, "Love Song," 5.

100. Frost, "Acquainted," 255. Though William Chapman Sharpe stops short, as I do, of claiming that "Acquainted with the Night" specifically describes the Metropolitan Tower, he makes the intriguing suggestion that Frost might have developed the poem's conceptual architecture from his familiarity with Amy Lowell's 1912 cityscape poem "New York at Night" (*New York Nocturne,* 30–31). And yet Teasdale's 1911 poem "The Metropolitan Tower" may be as likely a reference point. Various structures (Memorial Hall at Harvard, the Washtenaw County courthouse or the Michigan Central railway station, both in Ann Arbor) have been advanced as the tower's "true" model (Fleissner, "Frost's 'Acquainted,'" 12–13), but the very profusion of these possibilities, several of them evasively endorsed by Frost at different times, calls them all into question.

101. Frost, "Acquainted," 255.

102. Ibid.

CHAPTER 8. SUBWAY FARE

1. M. Brooks, *Subway City,* 107.

2. Forbes, "Skyscraper," 14397.

3. M. Brooks, *Subway City,* 106–7, 112.

4. Ibid., 46; see also Sharpe, *New York Nocturne,* 113.

5. Berman, *All That Is Solid,* 152.

6. Schivelbusch discusses the practical consequences and connotative meanings of the various conveyance designs seen in nineteenth-century rail travel, particularly the differences between European and American cars. The European compartment model, featuring small chambers furnished like bourgeois parlors and U-shaped seating adapted from the horse-drawn coach or carriage, emphasized privacy, intimate community, and class segregation. Train cars in the United States, their design adapted from the cabins of river steamboats, featured a single long chamber with a central aisle bisecting rows of seats facing forward, emphasizing physical mobility and shifting social interactions among larger groups of people likely to be traveling greater distances (*Railway Journey,* 103–7).

7. Ibid., 73–76.

8. Ibid., 103; see also 100–102.

9. As Michael Brooks points out, 150,000 people rode the New York subway on the long-anticipated opening evening of October 27, 1904; within a month, 425,000 were using it on a typical business day (*Subway City,* 68, 70). By 1920, the annual ridership of New York City's IRT system alone had reached 2.3 billion—about four hundred rides for every one of its 5.6 million inhabitants (1920 Census) and "twice as many as all the steam railroads in the country carried" in the year (*Subway City,* 90).

10. M. Brooks, *Subway City,* 190–205.

11. Simmel, "Metropolis," 331.

12. Spears, *Dionysus,* 74.

13. Baudelaire, "Painter," 12, 13, 5.

14. Whitman, "Crossing Brooklyn Ferry," 308.

15. Whitman, "Sun-Down Poem," 213.

16. Baudelaire, "Painter," 9.

17. Orvell, *Real Thing,* 21–22.

18. Whitman, "Crossing Brooklyn Ferry," 309.

19. Baudelaire, "Painter," 5.

20. Ibid., 13.

21. Ferries were still prominent in the urban scene of the 1910s but had lost their emblematic resonance to subways and trains. For a treatment of a ferry as a thoroughly workaday conveyance, see the 1913 verse "The Ferry Boat" by Berton Braley. Braley's appreciation of the ferry as integral to "[k]eeping up the city's life" (515) suggests the renewed commitment among American poets to address everyday modern experience, as does the curious fact that his poem was first published not in a literary venue but in *Technical World* magazine (and later in his 1917 volume *A Banjo at Armageddon*).

22. During this period in his life, shuttling daily between Manhattan and Mahwah as the literary editor of *The Churchman,* Kilmer became "one of the world's most accomplished commuters," according to the editor of his memoir, Robert Cortes Holliday (Kilmer, *Joyce Kilmer,* 34). Insisting "that it was no life at all, no life at all, for a man not to swing around an orbit of at least sixty miles a day between his office and his home" (34), Kilmer took the metropolitan transport network as the quintessence of twentieth-century experience.

23. Ibid., 174.

24. Sandburg, "Halsted Street Car," 6. The "physical discomforts" of public transportation made "a popular subject" for French political cartoonists from the 1830s, but Daumier in his many vividly observed interiors of omnibuses and railway carriages through the 1860s, such as "Le wagon de troisième classe" (chalk and watercolor 1864; oil 1864–65), elevated the subject from workaday commercial productions into socially resonant high art (Laughton, *Honoré Daumier,* 109; see also 108–20).

25. Sandburg, "Halsted Street Car," 6.

26. Baudelaire, "Painter," 12.

27. Firkins, "On a Subway Express," 181.

28. Ginsberg, "In the Subway," 67–68.

29. Untermeyer, "In the Subway," 119.

30. Ginsberg, "In a Streetcar," 44.

31. Bodenheim, "Summer Evening," 51.

32. Untermeyer, "Lenox Avenue Express," 138.

33. Simmel, "Metropolis," 331.

34. Kilmer, "The Subway," 467.

35. Ibid.; Schivelbusch, *Railway Journey*, 38–39.

36. Kilmer, "The Subway," 467.

37. Mastin, "In the Subway," 26.

38. Masters, "The Subway," 237–38.

39. Sandburg, "Crayon," 53.

40. R. Williams, *Politics of Modernism*, 32.

41. Schocket, *Vanishing Moments*, 150.

42. A "dog collar" could adorn a woman's neck or a dog's, although George Hendrick and Willene Hendrick propose that Sandburg is making reference to the famous *doyenne* of Chicago high society, Mrs. Potter Palmer, born Bertha Honoré, who was frequently photographed wearing a pearl choker (Sandburg, *Poems for the People*, 47).

43. Parsons, *Streetwalking*, 20.

44. Baudelaire, "Painter," 9.

45. Deborah Parsons summarizes the disinclination of some feminist critics of modernism, such as Janet Wolff and Griselda Pollock, to apply the terminology of *flânerie* to women's experience in the city, since *flânerie* has sometimes become "a metaphor for the gendered scopic hierarchy in observations of urban space," and thus implicitly for the gender hierarchies shaping modernism (*Streetwalking*, 4–5). But Parsons's readings of British fiction, along with related work by Rachel Bowlby and Judith Walkowitz, establish the conceptual value of the *flâneuse* by showing that from the mid-nineteenth century woman did indeed "occupy public positions . . . that locate them as observers" of the city (*Streetwalking*, 5).

46. Ibid., 24.

47. Ibid., 43.

48. Bodenheim, *Selected Poems*, 18, 108–9, 18, 109–10, 108, 74–75.

49. Parsons, *Streetwalking*, 6.

50. Mitchell, "Night Court," 35.

51. The playwright and poet Mary Aldis, born Mary Reynolds, was the wife of the Chicago attorney and realtor Arthur Taylor Aldis. Longtime residents of the haute-bourgeois suburb of Lake Forest yet also active participants in various socially progressive causes, the Aldises were good friends of Harriet Monroe and charter guarantors of *Poetry*.

52. One of the five, "Converse," which records a charged yet ambiguous exchange between a bourgeois wife and her husband's lover, does not involve the figure of the

female narrator as fully as the others, but set in a Turkish bath, it certainly inhabits the same world of female labor, leisure, and desire.

53. Aldis, "Love in the Loop," 8.

54. Schocket, *Vanishing Moments*, 150.

55. Aldis, "A Little Old Woman," 20.

56. Aldis, "Window-Wishing," 16–19.

57. Millay, "Recuerdo," 106.

58. Berman, *All That Is Solid*, 152.

59. Ibid.

60. Simmel, "Metropolis," 335.

61. Schivelbusch, *Railway Journey*, 172.

62. Teasdale, "In a Railroad Station," 51.

63. Teasdale, "In a Subway Station," 51.

64. This same irony drives Amy Lowell's powerful love lyric "The Taxi" (from *Sword Blades and Poppy Seed*, 1912), in which, as William Chapman Sharpe notes (*New York Nocturne*, 243), the speaker experiences being carried away from a lover in a taxi as being pierced psychically and physically by the objects and spaces of the city:

> Streets coming fast,
> One after the other,
> Wedge you away from me,
> And the lamps of the city prick my eyes
> So that I can no longer see your face.
> Why should I leave you,
> To wound myself upon the sharp edges of the night? (43).

65. Pound, "In a Station," 12.

66. Sandburg, "Blue Island Intersection," 165.

67. Sandburg, "Speed Bug," 55.

68. Hilton, *The Eastland*, 95–111, esp. 109.

69. Ibid., 72.

70. George Hendrick and Willene Hendrick point out that Sandburg, then in his most fervently socialist phase, published an "angry" article in the September 1915 issue of the *International Socialist Review* blaming the ship's unsafe conditions on the callous imperatives of commerce (Sandburg, *Poems for the People*, xiii; see also Yannella, *Other Carl Sandburg*, 41–42).

71. Sandburg, "The *Eastland*," 11.

72. W. Williams, "Wanderer," 28.

73. Frail, *Early Politics*, 86.

74. The allusion to Kreymborg in Williams's title is noted by Paul Mariani (*William Carlos Williams*, 145).

75. W. Williams, "January Morning," 101.

76. Ibid.

77. Orvell, *Real Thing,* 16–29.

78. Simmel, "Metropolis," 325.

79. Suárez, "City Space," 99.

80. W. Williams, "January Morning," 102.

81. W. Williams, *Collected Poems,* vol. 1, 489.

82. W. Williams, "January Morning," 104.

83. W. Williams, *Collected Poems,* vol 1, 496.

84. Simmel, "Metropolis," 328.

85. Kern, *Culture of Time and Space,* 75.

86. W. Williams, "Overture," 146.

87. Schivelbusch, *Railway Journey,* 39.

88. W. Williams, "Overture," 146.

89. W. Williams, *Collected Poems,* vol. 1, 496; Boccioni qtd. in Kern, *Culture of Time and Space,* 120.

90. W. Williams, "Overture," 146.

91. Tichi, *Shifting Gears,* 280–81; Schmidt, *William Carlos Williams,* 69–70.

92. W. Williams, *Spring and All,* 177.

93. Ibid., 182.

94. W. Williams, "Rapid Transit," 231–32.

95. R. Williams, *Politics of Modernism,* 32.

BIBLIOGRAPHY

Abbott, Craig S. "Magazine Verse and Modernism: Braithwaite's Anthologies." *Journal of Modern Literature* 19 (1995): 151–59.
———. "Publishing the New Poetry: Harriet Monroe's Anthology." *Journal of Modern Literature* 11 (1984): 89–108.
Abrahams, Edward. *The Lyrical Left: Randolph Bourne, Alfred Stieglitz, and the Originals of Cultural Radicalism in America*. Charlottesville: University of Virginia Press, 1986.
Adickes, Sandra. *To Be Young Was Very Heaven: Women in New York before the First World War*. New York: St. Martin's/Griffith, 1997.
Advertisement for *The Masses*. *Poetry* 3 (1914): 228.
Aiken, Conrad. "The Ivory Tower I." *New Republic* 19 (May 10, 1919): 58–60.
———. "Looking Pegasus in the Mouth." *Poetry Journal* 5 (1916): 20–28.
———. "Meretrix: Ironic." *Others* 2.5–6 (May/June 1916): 251–53.
———. "Prizes and Anthologies." *Poetry Journal* 4 (1915): 95–100.
———. *Selected Poems*. New York: Scribner's, 1929.
Albertine, Susan. "Cakes and Poetry: The Career of Harriet Moody." In *A Living of Words: American Women in Print Culture*. Ed. Susan Albertine. Knoxville: University of Tennessee Press, 1995. 94–114.
———, ed. *A Living of Words: American Women in Print Culture*. Knoxville: University of Tennessee Press, 1995.
Alden, Raymond M. "The New Poetry." *The Nation* 96 (April 17, 1913): 387–88.
Aldis, Mary. "The Barber Shop." *The Masses* 8 (April 1916): 23.
———. "Beans." *Others* 3.3 (September 1916): 79–80.
———. "A Little Old Woman." In *Flashlights*. New York: Duffield, 1916. 20–23.
———. "Love in the Loop." In *Flashlights*. New York: Duffield, 1916. 8–11.
———. "Window-Wishing." In *Flashlights*. New York: Duffield, 1916. 16–19.
———. "Words." *The Masses* 8 (October 1916): 20.
Allen, Charles. "*Glebe* and *Others*." *College English* 5 (1944): 418–25.
"The American." *Seven Arts* 1 (1917): 555–56.

"Announcement by Mitchell Kennerley." *Forum* 47 (1912): N.p.

"Announcement of Awards." *Poetry* 5 (1914): 93–95.

"Are You a Poet?" Advertisement for *Poetry: A Magazine of Verse*. *The Masses* 9 (December 1916): 11.

"Artistic Aspects of the Skyscraper." *Current Opinion* 54 (1913): 321–23.

Baker, Ray Stannard. "The Modern Skyscraper." *Munsey's* 22 (1899): 48–58.

Barrington, Pauline B. "Toy Guns." *The Masses* 8 (May 1916): 13.

Baudelaire, Charles. "The Painter of Modern Life." In *The Painter of Modern Life and Other Essays*. Ed. and trans. Jonathan Mayne. London: Phaidon, 1964. 1–40.

Beach, Christopher. *The Politics of Distinction: Whitman and the Discourses of Nineteenth-Century America*. Athens: University of Georgia Press, 1996.

Beach, Joseph Warren. "Nostalgia." *Others* 2.1 (January 1916): 132.

Ben-Merre, David, and Robert Scholes. "War Poems from 1914." *PMLA* 124 (2009): 1747–60.

Benét, Laura. "Gardens of Babylon." *The Masses* 5 (March 1914): 16.

Benét, Stephen Vincent. "Chanson at Madison Square." In *Heavens and Earth*. New York: Doubleday, Doran, and Co., 1920. 46–47.

———. "Lunchtime along Broadway." In *Heavens and Earth*. New York: Doubleday, Doran, and Co., 1920. 41.

Benét, William Rose. "The City." *Munsey's* 69 (1920): 28–29.

———. "Poor Girl." *The Masses* 5 (April 1914): 11.

———. "The Singing Skyscrapers." In *The Burglar of the Zodiac*. New Haven, Conn.: Yale University Press, 1918. 1–5.

Benstock, Shari, and Bernard Benstock. "The Role of Little Magazines in the Emergence of Modernism." *Library Chronicle of the University of Texas* 20 (1991): 69–87.

Berman, Marshall. *All That Is Solid Melts into Air: The Experience of Modernity*. 1982; reprint, New York: Penguin, 1988.

Bernhardi, Friedrich von. *Germany and the Next War*. Trans. Allen H. Powles. New York: Longmans, Green, 1914.

Biggs, Mary. "From Harriet Monroe to AQ: Selected Women's Literary Journals, 1912–1972." *13th Moon* 8 (1984): 183–216.

Bledstein, Burton J. *The Culture of Professionalism: The Middle Class and the Development of Higher Education in America*. New York: Norton, 1976.

Bochner, Jay. "The Marriage of *Rogue* and *The Soil*." In *Little Magazines and Modernism*. Ed. Suzanne W. Churchill and Adam McKible. Aldershot, U.K.: Ashgate, 2007. 49–66.

Bodenheim, Maxwell. "Advice to a Street-Pavement." *Little Review* 6 (June 1919): 25.

———. "After Writing Poetry." *Others* 1.3 (September 1915): 52.

———. "City Streets." In *Introducing Irony*. New York: Boni and Liveright, 1922. 42.

———. "East Side Children Playing." *Others* 4.2 (December 1917): 7.

———. "Garbage Heap." In *Advice*. New York: Knopf, 1920. 52.

———. "Images of Emotions." *Others* 2.4 (April 1916): 209.

———. "Parade of Conscripted Soldiers." *Others* 4.2 (December 1917): 7.

———. "Professional Iconoclasts." *Others* 5.3 (February 1919): 26–28.

———. "The Rear Porches of an Apartment Building." *Others* 1.3 (September 1915): 51.

———. *Selected Poems 1914–1944*. New York: Beechhurst Press, 1946.

———. "South State Street: Chicago." In *Advice*. New York: Knopf, 1920. 81–85.

———. "Street." In *The King of Spain*. New York: Boni and Liveright, 1928. 19.

———. "Summer Evening: New York Subway Station." In *Introducing Irony*. New York: Boni and Liveright, 1922. 51.

Bohan, Ruth L. *Looking into Walt Whitman: American Art, 1850—1920*. University Park: Pennsylvania State University Press, 2006.

"A Boom in Poetry." *Literary Digest* 47 (July 5, 1913): 19–20.

Bourne, Randolph. "Below the Battle." *Seven Arts* 2 (1917): 270–77.

———. "The Collapse of American Strategy." *Seven Arts* 2 (1917): 409–24.

———. "Conspirators." *Seven Arts* 2 (1917): 528–29.

———. "Trans-National America." *The Atlantic* 118 (July 1916): 86–97.

———. "Twilight of Idols." *Seven Arts* 2 (1917): 688–702.

———. "The War and the Intellectuals." *Seven Arts* 2 (1917): 133–47.

———. "A War Diary." *Seven Arts* 2 (1917): 535–47.

———. *The World of Randolph Bourne*. Ed. Lillian Schlissel. New York: Dutton, 1965.

———. *Youth and Life*. Boston: Houghton Mifflin, 1913.

Bowen, Stirling. "Skyscraper." *The Liberator* 5 (November 1924): 13.

Bowlby, Rachel. *Just Looking: Consumer Culture in Dreiser, Gissing, and Zola*. New York: Methuen, 1985.

Bradley, William Aspenwall. "Lyres and Laureates." *Bookman* 37 (1913): 191–99.

Braithwaite, William Stanley, ed. *Anthology of Magazine Verse for 1913*. New York: Laurence Gomme, 1914.

Braley, Berton. *A Banjo at Armageddon*. New York: George Doran, 1917.

———. "The Ferryboat." *Technical World* 18 (1913): 515.

Brody, Alter. *Family Album and Other Poems*. New York: B. W. Huebsch, 1918.

Brogan, Jacqueline Vaught. *Part of the Climate: American Cubist Poetry*. Berkeley: University of California Press, 1991.

Brooke, Rupert. *The Collected Poems of Rupert Brooke*. New York: Dodd, Mead, 1915.

———. "Peace." In *The Collected Poems of Rupert Brooke*. New York: Dodd, Mead, 1915. 111.

Brooks, Michael W. *Subway City: Riding the Trains, Reading New York*. New Brunswick, N. J.: Rutgers University Press, 1997.

Brooks, Van Wyck. *America's Coming-of-Age*. New York: B. W. Huebsch, 1915.

———. "The Culture of Industrialism." *Seven Arts* 1 (1917): 655–66.

———. "On Creating a Usable Past." *The Dial* 64 (1918): 337–41.

———. "The Splinter of Ice." *Seven Arts* 1 (1917): 270–80.

———. "Young America." *Seven Arts* 1 (1916): 144–51.

Brown, Robert Carlton. "Bubbles." *The Masses* 6 (June 1915): 18.

Brownell, Baker. "Irrational Verse." *Others* 5.1 (December 1918): 23–25.

Bruce, H. Addington. *Above the Clouds and Old New York*. Woolworth Building Visitors' Brochure, 1913.

Bryant, Louise. "Lost Music." *The Masses* 9 (January 1917): 43.

Bryant, William Cullen. "The Crowded Street." In *Poetical Works*. Ed. Parke Godwin. New York: Appleton, 1883. 319–20.

Burgess, Gelett. "Darkness before Dawn: A Revolutionary Hymn to the Anthropomorphic God." *The Masses* 4 (June 1913): 3.

Bynner, Witter. "The Highest Bidder." *Others* 3.1 (July 1916): 25.

———. "Outlaws." In *May Days: An Anthology of Verse from Masses-Liberator*. Ed. Genevieve Taggard. New York: Boni and Liveright, 1925. 256.

Calder, E. M. "Personal Recollections of Walt Whitman." *The Atlantic* 99 (1907): 825–34.

Cannell, Skipwith. "Ikons." *Others* 2.2 (February 1916): 158–66.

Carnevali, Emanuel. "Arthur Rimbaud." *Others* 5.4 (March 1919): 20–24.

Carr, Daphne. "Steel Town." *Others* 5.5 (April/May 1919): 26–27.

Carroll, Armond. "From a City Street." In *The Lyric Year: One Hundred Poems*. Ed. Ferdinand Earle. New York: Mitchell Kennerley, 1912. 40–41.

Carter, C. F. "New Problems of Great Cities." *Technical World* 8 (1908): 555–69.

"The Case of Poetry." *The Dial* 53 (1912): 477–79.

The Cathedral of Commerce: Woolworth Building, New York. Woolworth Building Visitors' Brochure, 1918.

Chapin, Frederick H. "Cliff-Dwellers of the Mancos Cañons." *American Antiquarian* 12 (1890): 193–210.

———. *The Land of the Cliff Dwellers*. Boston: Appalachian Mountain Club/ W. B. Clarke, 1892.

Chapple, Joseph Mitchell, ed. *Heart Throbs in Prose and Verse Dear to the American People*. New York: Grosset and Dunlap, 1905.

Chinitz, David. *T. S. Eliot and the Cultural Divide*. Chicago: University of Chicago Press, 2003.

Churchill, Suzanne W. *The Little Magazine* Others *and the Renovation of Modern American Poetry*. Aldershot, U.K.: Ashgate, 2006.

Churchill, Suzanne W., and Adam McKible. Introduction to *Little Magazines and Modernism*. Ed. Suzanne W. Churchill and Adam McKible. Aldershot, U.K.: Ashgate, 2007. 3–18.

"City Poets." *The Independent* 73 (1912): 395–96.

Coates, Florence Earle. "New York: A Nocturne." In *The Lyric Year: One Hundred Poems*. Ed. Ferdinand Earle. New York: Mitchell Kennerley, 1912. 50–52.

Colum, Padraic. "The Beast Shop." *Others* 3.1 (July 1916): 23–24.

———. "Youngest Ireland." *Seven Arts* 2 (1917): 608–23.

Corder, Raymond. "The Skyscraper." *The Liberator* 4 (October 1921): 21.

Correspondence of Arthur Davison Ficke and C. J. Hambleton. Newberry Library, Chicago.

Costello, Bonnie. *Marianne Moore, Imaginary Possessions*. Cambridge, Mass.: Harvard University Press, 1981.

Crane, Hart. *The Bridge*. Paris: Black Sun Press, 1930.

Crapsey, Adelaide. "Cinquains." *Others* 2.3 (March 1916): 167–69.

Crary, Jonathan. *Techniques of the Observer: On Vision and Modernity in the Nineteenth Century*. Cambridge: Massachusetts Institute of Technology Press, 1990.

Croly, Herbert. *The Promise of American Life*. 1909; reprint, New York: Dutton, 1963.

Crowder, Richard. *Carl Sandburg*. New York: Twayne, 1962.

Crunden, Robert M. *American Salons: Encounters with European Modernism, 1885–1917*. Oxford: Oxford University Press, 1993.

Cushing, Charles Phelps. "Restraining the Overambitious Skyscraper." *Collier's* 52 (January 10, 1914): 13.

Damon, S. Foster. *Amy Lowell: A Chronicle*. Boston: Houghton Mifflin, 1935.

Davies, Mary Carolyn. "Later Songs." *Others* 2.4 (April 1916): 198–200.

———. "Songs of a Girl." *Others* 1.1 (July 1915): 3–5.

Davis, Jean. "Our Camilla." *Others* 3.3 (September 1916): 75.

Day, Dorothy. "Mulberry Street." *The Masses* 9 (July 1917): 49.

Dell, Floyd. "Indicted for Criminal Libel." In *Echoes of Revolt*: The Masses, *1911–1917*. Ed. William L. O'Neill. 1966; reprint, Chicago: Ivan R. Dee, 1989. 33–34.

———. Obituary for Randolph Bourne. *New Republic* 17 (January 4, 1919): 276.

———. Papers. Newberry Library, Chicago.

———. "Summer." *The Masses* 9 (February 1917): 23.

Deutsch, Babette. "Petrograd." In *May Days: An Anthology of Verse from* Masses-Liberator. Ed. Genevieve Taggard. New York: Boni and Liveright, 1925. 63.

Dijkstra, Bram. *Cubism, Stieglitz, and the Early Poetry of William Carlos Williams: The Hieroglyphics of a New Speech*. Princeton, N.J.: Princeton University Press, 1978.

Donner, Herman Montagu. "Jetsam—In Memory of the Sinking of the 'Titanic.'" In *The Lyric Year: One Hundred Poems*. Ed. Ferdinand Earle. New York: Mitchell Kennerley, 1912. 79–84.

D'Orge, Jeanne. "The Microscope." *Others* 2.5–6 (May/June 1916): 223.

Dos Passos, John. *Manhattan Transfer*. New York: Harper and Brothers, 1925.

———. "Young Spain." *Seven Arts* 2 (1917): 473–88.

Douglas, Ann. *Terrible Honesty: Mongrel Manhattan in the 1920s*. New York: Farrar Straus Giroux, 1995.

Douglas, Paul H. "Letter to the Editor." In *Echoes of Revolt*: The Masses, *1911–1917*. Ed. William L. O'Neill. 1966; reprint, Chicago: Ivan R. Dee, 1989. 32–33.

Doyle, Charles. Introduction to *Wallace Stevens: The Critical Heritage*. London: Routledge and Kegan Paul, 1986. 1–22.

Drake, William. "Sara Teasdale." In *American Poets 1880–1945*. Vol. 45 of *Diction-*

ary of Literary Biography. Ed. Peter Quartermain. Detroit: Gale Research Press, 1987. 396–405.

The Dream City: A Portfolio of Photographic Views of the World's Columbian Exposition. St. Louis: N. D. Thompson, 1893.

Dublin, Louis I. *A Family of Thirty Million: The Story of the Metropolitan Life Insurance Company.* New York: Metropolitan Life Insurance Company, 1943.

Duffey, Bernard. *Poetry in America: Expression and Its Values in the Times of Bryant, Whitman, and Pound.* Durham, N.C.: Duke University Press, 1978.

Earle, Ferdinand, ed. *The Lyric Year: One Hundred Poems.* New York: Mitchell Kennerley, 1912.

Eastman, Max. "Class War in Colorado." In *Echoes of Revolt:* The Masses, *1911–1917.* Ed. William L. O'Neill. 1966; reprint, Chicago: Ivan R. Dee, 1989. 149–54.

———. "Editorial Notice." *The Masses* 4 (December 1912): 3.

———. *Enjoyment of Poetry.* 1913. New York: Scribner's, 1921.

———. "John Reed." *The Liberator* 4.2 (February 1921): 5.

———. "Lazy Verse." *New Republic* 8 (September 9, 1916): 138–40.

———. "The Nice People of Trinidad." In *Echoes of Revolt:* The Masses, *1911–1917.* Ed. William L. O'Neill. 1966; reprint, Chicago: Ivan R. Dee, 1989. 154–59.

———. "The Policy of *The Masses*: An Editor's Reflections." In *Echoes of Revolt:* The Masses, *1911–1917.* Ed. William L. O'Neill. 1966; reprint, Chicago: Ivan R. Dee, 1989. 301–3.

———. "Science and Free Verse." *Seven Arts* 1 (1917): 426–29.

Eaton, Walter Prichard. *New York.* New York: Grolier Club, 1915.

———. "Sunrise from the Jersey Shore." In *Echoes and Realities.* New York: George H. Doran, 1918. 130.

"Editorials." *The Liberator* 1.1 (March 1918): 5.

Edwards, C. B. "Elevators Run on Schedule of Seconds." *Technical World* 20 (1913): 390–92.

Eliot, T. S. "The Love Song of J. Alfred Prufrock." In *Collected Poems 1909–1962.* New York: Harcourt Brace, 1963. 3–7.

———. "Morning at the Window." *Poetry* 8 (1916): 294–95.

———. "Preludes." In *Collected Poems 1909–1962.* New York: Harcourt Brace, 1963. 13–15.

———. *The Waste Land.* In *Collected Poems 1909–1962.* New York: Harcourt Brace, 1963. 51–76.

Endicoff, Max. "New York Etchings." *Others* 2.1 (January 1916): 137–38.

"An Englishman's View of Whitman." *Living Age* 261 (1909): 384.

Ficke, Arthur Davison. "The Dancer." *Others* 2.3 (March 1916): 178–80.

———. "Of Rupert Brooke and Other Matters." *Little Review* 1.5 (July 1914): 17–21.

———. "Poetry." *Poetry* 1 (1912): 1–2.

———. "Rupert Brooke: A Memory." *Little Review* 2.4 (June 1915): 32.

———. "Tables." *The Masses* 9 (December 1916): 11.

———. "To Rupert Brooke." *Poetry* 6 (1915): 113–16.

"The Fifth-Month Poet." *Seven Arts* 2 (1917): 117–19.

Firkins, Chester. "A Cry in the Market Place." *The Atlantic* 100 (1907): 99; *Current Literature* 43 (1907): 457.

———. "Light in a Tenement Window." *Lippincott's* 81 (1908): 432.

———. "Night Worker." *Lippincott's* 83 (1909): 317.

———. "On a Subway Express." *The Atlantic* 101 (February 1908): 181.

———. "To a City." *The Independent* 68 (1910): 1126.

Fishbein, Leslie. Introduction to *Art for the Masses: A Radical Magazine and Its Graphics, 1911–1917,* by Rebecca Zurier. Philadelphia: Temple University Press, 1988. 3–27.

Fleissner, Robert F. "Frost's 'Acquainted with the Night.'" *Explicator* 37.1 (1978): 11–13.

Fletcher, Jefferson B. "Seven Sandwichmen on Broadway." *The Atlantic* 104 (1909): 516.

Fletcher, John Gould. "Blue Symphony." *Poetry* 4 (1914): 211–15.

———. "Dirge of the Work-Horses." *Others* 3.1 (July 1916): 11.

———. "The Unquiet Street." *Some Imagist Poets: An Annual Anthology* 2 (1916): 42.

Fogelman, Bruce. "The Evolution of Pound's 'Contemporania.'" *Journal of Modern Literature* 15 (1988): 93–103.

Forbes, Edgar Allan. "Skyscraper: An American Creation." *World's Work* 22 (1911): 14384–98.

Frail, David. *The Early Politics and Poetics of William Carlos Williams.* Ann Arbor, Mich.: UMI Research Press, 1987.

Frank, Dana. "Housewives, Socialists, and the Politics of Food: The 1917 New York Cost-of-Living Protests." *Feminist Studies* 11 (Summer 1985): 255–85.

Frank, Waldo. "Concerning a Little Theater." *Seven Arts* 1 (1916): 157–64.

———. *Our America.* New York: Boni and Liveright, 1919.

Freiburger, William. "War Prosperity and Hunger: The New York Food Riots of 1917." *Labor History* 25 (1984): 217–39.

"A Frenchman's Fervid Tribute." *Current Literature* 45 (1908): 286–89.

Freytag-Loringhoven, Elsa von. "The Conqueror." *The Masses* 8 (June 1916): 15.

Frost, Robert. "Acquainted with the Night." In *The Poetry of Robert Frost.* Ed. Edward Connery Lathem. New York: Henry Holt, 1969. 255.

———. "The Bonfire." *Seven Arts* 1.1 (November 1916): 25–29.

———. "Mending Wall." In *The Poetry of Robert Frost.* Ed. Edward Connery Lathem. New York: Henry Holt, 1969. 33–34.

Fuller, Henry Blake. *The Cliff Dwellers.* New York: Harper Brothers, 1893.

Fussell, Paul. *The Great War and Modern Memory.* New York: Oxford University Press, 1975.

Gelpi, Albert. *A Coherent Splendor: The American Poetic Renaissance, 1910–1950.* Cambridge: Cambridge University Press, 1987.

Gibson, Lydia. "Lies." *The Masses* 4 (October 1913): 15.

Gilbert, Sandra. "Marianne Moore as Female Female Impersonator." In *Marianne Moore: The Art of a Modernist*. Ed. Joseph Parisi. Ann Arbor, Mich.: UMI Press, 1990. 27–48.

Gilot, Francoise, and Carlton Lake. *Life with Picasso*. London: Virago Press, 1990.

Ginsberg, Louis. "In a Streetcar." In *Collected Poems*. Ed. Michael Fournier. Orono, Me.: Northern Lights, 1992. 44–45.

———. "In the Subway." In *Collected Poems*. Ed. Michael Fournier. Orono, Me.: Northern Lights, 1992. 67–68.

Giovannitti, Arturo. "The Bum." *The Masses* 4 (January 1913): 15.

———. "The Day of War: Madison Square, June 20th." *The Masses* 8 (August 1916): 20.

Glintenkamp, Henry. Untitled drawing. *The Masses* 8 (December 1915): 12.

Gold, Michael. "The Strange Funeral in Braddock." In *May Days: An Anthology of Verse from Masses-Liberator*. Ed. Genevieve Taggard. New York: Boni and Liveright, 1925. 286.

Goldring, Douglas. "Maisonnettes." *Others* 2.1 (January 1916): 131.

Goodrich, Arthur. "The Biography of an Office Building." *World's Work* 5 (1902–3): 2955–68.

Gorman, Paul R. *Left Intellectuals and Popular Culture in Twentieth-Century America*. Chapel Hill: University of North Carolina Press, 1996.

Greeley, Arthur. "The Age of Invention." *Munsey's* 21 (1899): 706–9.

Greenslet, Ferris. "A Propaganda for Poetry." *Poet-Lore* 11 (1899): 41–54.

Greever, Garland, and Joseph M. Bachelor, eds. *The Soul of the City: An Urban Anthology*. Boston: Houghton Mifflin, 1923.

Gregory, Horace, and Marya Zaturenska. *A History of American Poetry, 1900–1940*. New York: Harcourt Brace, 1946.

Greiner, Donald J. "Robert Frost." In *American Poets 1880–1945*. Vol. 54 of *Dictionary of Literary Biography*. Ed. Peter Quartermain. Detroit: Gale Research Press, 1987. 93–121.

Gruening, Martha. "Prepared." *The Masses* 8 (March 1916): 13.

Hale, Keith, ed. *Friends and Apostles: The Correspondence of Rupert Brooke and James Strachey, 1905–1914*. New Haven, Conn.: Yale University Press, 1998.

Hamilton, Ian. *The Little Magazine: A Study of Six Editors*. London: Weidenfeld and Nicolson, 1976.

Harrington, Joseph. *Poetry and the Public: The Social Form of Modern U.S. Poetries*. Middletown, Conn.: Wesleyan University Press, 2002.

———. "A Response to Lisa Woolley." *Langston Hughes Review* 14 (1996): 49–51.

———. "Why American Poetry Is Not American Literature." *American Literary History* 8 (1996): 496–515.

Hartley, Marsden. "Swallows." *Others* 5.4 (March 1919): 14.

Hartmann, Sadakichi. "To the 'Flat Iron.'" In *Drifting Flowers of the Sea, and Other Poems*. N.p.: Sadakichi Hartmann, 1904. 12.

Hasluck, Paul N., ed. *The Book of Photography*. London: Cassell, 1907.

Heine, Heinrich. "Some Little-Known Poems by Heinrich Heine." Trans. Louis Untermeyer. *Seven Arts* 1 (1917): 590–93.

Henderson, Alice Corbin. "Contemporary Poetry and the Universities." *Poetry* 5
(1914): 176–77.

———. "Lazy Criticism." *Poetry* 9 (1916): 144–49.

———. "A New School of Poetry." *Poetry* 8 (1916): 103–5.

———. "What Would Walt Think?" *Poetry* 7 (1916): 48–49.

Hendrick, Burton J. "Limitations to the Production of Skyscrapers." *The Atlantic*
90 (1902): 486–92.

"Henry David Thoreau." *Seven Arts* 2 (1917): 383–86.

Hervey, John L. "Bryant and 'The New Poetry.'" *The Dial* 59 (1915): 92–93.

Hillyer, Robert. "To Congress Concerning the Bill for Universal Military Service."
The Masses 9 (April 1917): 14.

Hilton, George. Eastland: *Legacy of the* Titanic. Palo Alto, Calif.: Stanford University Press, 1997.

Hine, Daryl. Introduction to *The "Poetry" Anthology, 1912–1977*. Ed. Daryl Hine
and Joseph Parisi. Boston: Houghton Mifflin, 1978. xxxv–xlvii.

Hine, Lewis W. *Men at Work: Photographic Studies of Modern Men and Machines.*
1932; reprint, New York: Dover, 1977.

Hoffman, Frederick. "Research Value of the 'Little Magazine.'" *College and Research
Libraries* 6 (1945): 311–15.

Hoffman, Frederick, Charles Allen, and Carolyn Ulrich. *The Little Magazine: A
History and a Bibliography.* Princeton, N.J.: Princeton University Press, 1946.

Holley, Horace. "Divinations." *Others* 2.5–6 (May/June 1916): 245–48.

———. "Skyscrapers." In *Creation: Post-Impressionist Poems.* London: A. C. Fifield,
1914. 22.

"Holy Russia." *Seven Arts* 2 (1917): 60–61.

Hooker, Brian. "Recent Volumes of Verse." *Bookman* 30 (1910): 465–70.

Hornbrooke, Francis B. "What Should Be the Poet's Attitude toward His Critics."
Poet-Lore 5 (1893): 135–43.

Houston, Margaret Belle. "The Poet in the Market-place." In *The Lyric Year: One
Hundred Poems.* Ed. Ferdinand Earle. New York: Mitchell Kennerley, 1912. 124–27.

Howe, M. A. D. "The Spell of Whitman." *The Atlantic* 98 (1906): 849–55.

Howells, William Dean. *A Hazard of New Fortunes.* New York: Harper and Brothers, 1890.

Hoyt, Helen. Editorial Comment. *Others* 3.3 (September 1916): 54.

———. "Menaia." In *Echoes of Revolt: The Masses, 1911–1917.* Ed. William L.
O'Neill. 1966; reprint, Chicago: Ivan R. Dee, 1989. 82.

Hubbell, Jay B. "My Friend Carl Sandburg." *Library Notes* 48 (December 1978):
5–17.

Hungerford, Edward. *The Story of the Waldorf-Astoria.* New York: G. P. Putnam's
Sons, 1925.

Hutchinson, C. L. Papers. Newberry Library, Chicago.

Hutchinson, James P. "Fenton Johnson: Pilgrim of the Dusk." *Studies in Black Literature* 7.3 (1976): 14–15.

"Improvident Poets." *The Dial* 54 (1913): 368–69.

James, Henry. *The American Scene*. New York: Harper, 1907.

Johns, Orrick. *Asphalt and Other Poems*. New York: Knopf, 1917.

——. "Olives." *Others* 1.1 (July 1915): 9–12.

——. "Second Avenue." In *The Lyric Year: One Hundred Poems*. Ed. Ferdinand Earle. New York: Mitchell Kennerley, 1912. 133–37.

Johnson, Fenton. "Aunt Hannah Jackson." *Others* 5.3 (February 1919): 17.

——. "Aunt Jane Allen." *Others* 5.3 (February 1919): 17.

——. "The Barber." *Others* 5.3 (February 1919): 18.

——. "The Drunkard." *Others* 5.3 (February 1919): 18.

——. "The Gambler." *Others* 5.3 (February 1919): 18.

——. "Tired." *Others* 5.2 (January 1919): 8.

Jones, Margaret C. *Heretics and Hellraisers: Women Contributors to* The Masses, *1911–1917*. Austin: University of Texas Press, 1993.

Kaestle, Carl F., and Janice A. Radway, eds. *Print in Motion: The Expansion of Publishing and Reading in the United States, 1880–1940*. Vol. 4 of *A History of the Book in America*. Chapel Hill: University of North Carolina Press, 2009.

Kalaidjian, Walter. "Incoming: Globalization, Disaster, Politics." *South Atlantic Quarterly* 106 (2007): 825–48.

Keller, E. L. "The Last Days of Walt Whitman." *Putnam's* 5 (1909): 163–69.

Kemp, Harry. "An Ode to Sky-Climbers." *American Magazine* 68 (1909): 16.

Kern, Stephen. *The Culture of Time and Space, 1880–1918*. Cambridge, Mass.: Harvard University Press, 1983.

Kilmer, Joyce. "A Genius Whom the War Made and Killed." *New York Times Magazine,* September 12, 1915, SM19.

——. *Joyce Kilmer*. Ed. Robert Cortes Holliday. Garden City, N.Y.: Doubleday, Doran, and Co., 1931.

——. "The Subway (96th Street to 137th Street)." *The Independent* 69 (1910): 467.

Kirchwey, Freda. "To a Soap-Box Orator." *The Masses* 6 (February 1915): 8.

Knowles, Frederic Lawrence, ed. *The Golden Treasury of American Songs and Lyrics*. Boston: L. C. Page, 1906.

Koolhaas, Rem. *Delirious New York: A Retroactive Manifesto for Manhattan*. New York: Monacelli Press, 1994.

Kreymborg, Alfred. "An Early Impression of Wallace Stevens." *Trinity Review* 8 (1954): 12–16.

——, ed. *Lyric America: An Anthology of Poetry (1630–1930)*. New York: Coward-McCann, 1930.

——. "New York." *Others* 3.4 (December 1916): 43–44.

——, ed. *Others: An Anthology of the New Verse*. New York: Knopf, 1916.

——, ed. *Others: An Anthology of the New Verse*. New York: Knopf, 1917.

———, ed. *Others for 1919: An Anthology of the New Verse*. New York: Nicholas L. Brown, 1920.

———. *Our Singing Strength*. New York: Coward McCann, 1929.

———. "Overheard in an Asylum." *Others* 1.1 (July 1915): 18.

———. *Troubador: An Autobiography*. New York: Liveright, 1925.

———. "Variations." *Others* 1.1 (July 1915): 14–17.

———. "Vers Libre and Vers Librists." *New York Morning Herald*, August 8, 1915, sec. 2, p. 1.

Laidlaw, René. "On Gutter Verse." *The Century* 84 (1912): 634–35.

Landau, Sarah Bradford, and Carl Condit. *The Rise of the New York Skyscraper, 1865–1913*. New Haven, Conn.: Yale University Press, 1996.

"The Latest Word on Whitman." *Current Literature* 47 (July 1909): 45–48.

Laughton, Bruce. *Honoré Daumier*. New Haven. Conn.: Yale University Press, 1996.

Leavell, Linda. *Marianne Moore and the Visual Arts: Prismatic Color*. Baton Rouge: Louisiana State University Press, 1995.

"Leaves from Walt Whitman's Later Life." *The Critic* 41 (1902): 319–27.

Lee, Gerald Stanley. "An Order for the Next Poet." *Putnam's* 1 (1906–07): 697–703; *Putnam's* 2 (1907): 99–107.

———. *The Voice of the Machines: An Introduction to the Twentieth Century*. New York: Doubleday, 1906.

Lee, Muna. "*I thought love would come....*" *Others* 2.5–6 (May/June 1916): 224–25.

Leja, Michael. *Looking Askance: Skepticism and American Art from Eakins to Duchamp*. Berkeley: University of California Press, 2004.

Lentricchia, Frank. *Modernist Quartet*. New York: Cambridge University Press, 1994.

Levere, William C., ed. *The Evanston Poets*. Evanston, Ill.: W. S. Lord, 1903.

Lindsay, Vachel. *The Chinese Nightingale*. New York: Macmillan, 1917.

———. *The Congo and Other Poems*. New York: Macmillan, 1914.

———. "General William Booth Enters into Heaven." *Poetry* 1 (1913): 103–5; *Current Opinion* 54 (1913): 237; *Literary Digest* 46 (1913): 541; *The Independent* 74 (1913): 584.

Lodge, George Cabot. *Poems and Dramas*. Vol. 2. Boston: Houghton Mifflin, 1911.

Long, Augustus White, ed. *American Poets, 1776–1900*. New York: American Book Co., 1905.

Lowell, Amy. "The Allies." In *Complete Poetical Works*. Boston: Houghton Mifflin, 1955. 125.

———. *Complete Poetical Works*. Boston: Houghton Mifflin, 1955.

———. "Flotsam." *Seven Arts* 1 (1916): 30–31.

———. "The Grocery." *The Masses* 8 (June 1916): 17.

———. "Orange of Midsummer." *Seven Arts* 1 (1917): 601.

———. "The Taxi." In *Complete Poetical Works*. Boston: Houghton Mifflin, 1955. 43.

———. *Tendencies in Modern American Poetry*. Boston: Houghton Mifflin, 1917.

Loy, Mina. "Love Songs." *Others* 1.1 (July 1915): 6–8.

———. "Songs to Joannes." *Others* 3.6 (April 1917): 3–19.

MacLeod, Glen G. *Wallace Stevens and Modern Art: From the Armory Show to Abstract Expressionism.* New Haven, Conn.: Yale University Press, 1993.

Macy, John. *The Spirit of American Literature.* Garden City, N.Y.: Doubleday, Page, 1913.

"Major and Minor." *Musical Leader* 28 (1914): 555.

Marek, Jayne. *Women Editing Modernism: 'Little' Magazines and Literary History.* Lexington: University of Kentucky Press, 1995.

Mariani, Paul. *William Carlos Williams: A New World Naked.* New York: McGraw-Hill, 1981.

Marsh, John. "A Lost Art of Work: The Arts and Crafts Movement in Carl Sandburg's *Chicago Poems.*" *American Literature* 79 (2007): 527–51.

Massa, Ann. "'The Columbian Ode' and *Poetry: A Magazine of Verse*: Harriet Monroe's Entrepreneurial Triumphs." *Journal of American Studies* 20 (1986): 51–69.

———. "Form Follows Function: The Construction of Harriet Monroe and *Poetry: A Magazine of Verse.*" In *A Living of Words: American Women in Print Culture.* Ed. Susan Albertine. Knoxville: University of Tennessee Press, 1995. 115–31.

"'The Masses' and American Rights." *Seven Arts* 2 (1917): 532.

Masters, Edgar Lee [Dexter Wallace, pseud.]. *Blood of the Prophets.* Chicago: Rooks, 1905.

———[Webster Ford, pseud.]. *Songs and Sonnets.* Chicago: Rooks, 1910.

———[Webster Ford, pseud.]. *Songs and Sonnets: Second Series.* Chicago: Rooks, 1912.

———. *Spoon River Anthology.* New York: Macmillan, 1915.

———. "The Subway." *Others* 2.5–6 (May/June 1916): 236–39.

Mastin, Florence Ripley. "In the Subway." *The Masses* 8 (August 1916): 26.

Matthews, Brander, ed. *American Familiar Verse: Vers de Société.* New York: Longmans, Green, 1904.

Matthiessen, F. O. *American Renaissance: Art and Expression in the Age of Emerson and Whitman.* New York: Oxford University Press, 1941.

Maxwell, William J. *New Negro, Old Left: African-American Writing and Communism between the Wars.* New York: Columbia University Press, 1999.

McCrae, John. "In Flanders Fields." In *In Flanders Fields, and Other Poems.* New York: G. P. Putnam's Sons, 1919. 3.

McKay, Claude. "America." *The Liberator* 4.12 (December 1921): 9.

———. "The White City." *The Liberator* 4.10 (October 1921): 7.

McKenna, Edmond. "Another Poem." *The Masses* 5 (April 1914): 11.

Meredith, Harry. "New Building Over-Tops All Others." *Technical World* 9 (1908): 588–90.

Metropolitan Life Insurance Company. New York: Metropolitan Life Insurance Co., 1914.

Michailidou, Artemis. "Edna Millay, Muriel Rukeyser, and Adrienne Rich: Political

Poetry, Social Protest, and the Place of the Woman Writer." *European Journal of American Culture* 22 (2003): 7–22.

Millay, Edna St. Vincent. "Recuerdo." In *Collected Lyrics*. New York: Harper and Row, 1939. 106.

———. *Renascence and Other Poems*. New York: Mitchell Kennerley, 1917.

———. "To the Liberty Bell." In *May Days: An Anthology of Verse from* Masses-Liberator. Ed. Genevieve Taggard. New York: Boni and Liveright, 1925. 187.

Miller, Cristanne. "Tongues 'Loosened in the Melting Pot': The Poets of *Others* and the Lower East Side." *Modernism/Modernity* 14 (2007): 455–76.

Miller, Donald L. *City of the Century: The Epic of Chicago and the Making of America*. New York: Simon and Schuster, 1996.

Mitchell, Ruth Comfort. "The Night Court." In *The Soul of the City: An Urban Anthology*. Ed. Garland Greever and Joseph M. Bachelor. Boston: Houghton Mifflin, 1923. 35–38.

Monroe, Harriet. "At Twilight." In *You and I*. New York: Macmillan, 1914. 120–21.

———. "The Audience." *Poetry* 5 (1914): 31–32.

———. "The Bigness of the World." *The Atlantic* 108 (1911): 371–75.

———. "Cantata." In *Valeria and Other Poems*. Chicago: A. C. McClurg, 1892. 213–19.

———. *Chosen Poems*. New York: Macmillan, 1935.

———. "Columbian Ode." In *Chosen Poems*. New York: Macmillan, 1935. 75–85.

———. "Death of Rupert Brooke." *Poetry* 6 (1915): 136–38.

———. "Down East." *Poetry* 8 (1916): 85–89.

———. "The Enemies We Have Made." *Poetry* 4 (1914): 61–64.

———. "The Fight for the Crowd." *Poetry* 5 (1915): 280–83.

———. "The Hotel." *The Atlantic* 103 (1909): 324–25.

———. "Incarnations." *Poetry* 2 (1913): 101–4.

———. "In Danger of Poetry." *Poetry* 2 (1913): 68–70.

———. "In Defense of Poetry." *The Dial* 54 (1913): 409.

———. "The Motive of the Magazine." *Poetry* 1 (1912): 26–28.

———. "The New Beauty." *Poetry* 2 (1913): 22–25.

———. "Newspaper Verse." *Poetry* 19 (1922): 324–30.

———. "Night in State Street." In *You and I*. New York: Macmillan, 1914. 7–14.

———. "The Open Door." *Poetry* 1 (1912): 62–64.

———. Personal Papers. Regenstein Library, University of Chicago.

———. "Poetry and the Other Fine Arts." *The Dial* 54 (1913): 497.

———. "The Poet's Bread and Butter." *Poetry* 4 (1914): 195–98.

———. *A Poet's Life*. New York: Macmillan, 1938.

———. "Poetry a Zest for Life." *Poetry* 2 (1913): 140–42.

———. "A Power Plant." *The Century* 72 (1906): 76.

———. "The Question of Prizes." *Poetry* 7 (1915): 246–49.

———. Rev. of *Challenge*, by Louis Untermeyer. *Poetry* 4 (1914): 203–5.

———. Rev. of *The Lyric Year*, ed. Ferdinand Earle. *Poetry* 1 (1912): 128–31.

———. "'Sobriety and Earnestness.'" *Poetry* 3 (1913): 141–44.

———. "The Telephone." *The Atlantic* 96 (1905): 536.

———. "'That Mass of Dolts.'" *Poetry* 1 (1913): 168–70.

———. "This Southern Number." *Poetry* 20 (1922): 31–34.

———. "The Thunderstorm." In *Chosen Poems*. New York: Macmillan, 1935. 234–67.

———. "Tradition." *Poetry* 2 (1913): 67–68.

———. "The Turbine." *The Atlantic* 105 (1910): 779.

———. "Various Views." *Poetry* 8 (1916): 140–44.

———. "A Word to Our Readers." *Poetry* 4 (1914): 245–49.

———. *You and I*. New York: Macmillan, 1914.

Monroe, Harriet, and Alice Corbin Henderson, eds. *The New Poetry*. New York: Macmillan, 1917.

Moody, William Vaughn. "I Am the Woman." *Poetry* 1 (1912): 3–6.

———. "An Ode in Time of Hesitation." *The Atlantic* 85 (1900): 593–98.

———. "On a Soldier Fallen in the Philippines." *The Atlantic* 87 (1901): 288.

Moore, Charles Leonard. "The Future of Poetry." *Forum* 14 (1893): 768–77.

Moore, Marianne. "To Statecraft Embalmed." *Others* 1.6 (December 1915): 104.

More, Paul Elmer. *Shelburne Essays*. 4th series. New York: G. P. Putnam's Sons, 1906.

Morrisson, Mark S. *The Public Face of Modernism: Little Magazines, Audiences, and Reception, 1905–1920*. Madison: University of Wisconsin Press, 2001.

Munk, Joseph A. *Arizona Sketches*. New York: Grafton Press, 1905.

Munson, Gorham B. *The Awakening Twenties*. Baton Rouge: Louisiana State University Press, 1985.

"The Murder of a Poet." *Little Review* 2.3 (May 1915): 36.

"The Muse in a Pet." *The Dial* 55 (1913): 245–47.

Nadel, Ira B. Introduction to *The Letters of Ezra Pound to Alice Corbin Henderson*. Ed. Ira B. Nadel. Austin: University of Texas Press, 1993. xiii–xxviii.

Naruse, Seichi. "Young Japan." *Seven Arts* 1 (1917): 616–26.

Nash, Eric P. *Manhattan Skyscrapers*. New York: Princeton Architectural Press, 1999.

Naumann, Francis M., and Paul Avrich. "Adolf Wolff: 'Poet, Sculptor, and Revolutionist, but Mostly Revolutionist.'" *Art Bulletin* 67 (1985): 486–500.

Nelson, Cary. *Repression and Recovery: Modern American Poetry and the Politics of Cultural Memory*. Madison: University of Wisconsin Press, 1989.

———. *Revolutionary Memory: Recovering the Poetry of the American Left*. New York: Routledge, 2001.

"New Lamps for Old." *The Dial* 56 (1914): 231–33.

Newcomb, John Timberman. "The Woman as Political Poet: Edna St. Vincent Millay and the Mid-Century Canon." *Criticism* 37 (1995): 261–80.

———. *Would Poetry Disappear? American Verse and the Crisis of Modernity*. Columbus: Ohio State University Press, 2004.

Nichols, John. *Skyline Queen and the Merchant Prince: The Woolworth Story*. New York: Trident Press, 1973.

Niven, Penelope. *Carl Sandburg: A Biography*. New York: Scribner's, 1991.

Nordenskiöld, Gustaf. *The Cliff Dwellers of the Mesa Verde.* Trans. D. Lloyd Morgan. 1893; reprint, New York: AMS Press, 1973.

"Notes and Announcements." *Poetry* 1 (1912): 29–32.

O'Brien, Edward. "Hellenica." *Others* 2.1 (January 1916): 136.

O'Brien, Howard Vincent. *New Men for Old.* New York: Mitchell Kennerley, 1914.

O'Neill, William L. *The Last Romantic: A Life of Max Eastman.* New York: Oxford University Press, 1978.

———, ed. *Echoes of Revolt:* The Masses, *1911–1917.* 1966; reprint, Chicago: Ivan R. Dee, 1989.

[Oppenheim, James]. "After a Stormy Twilight" (editorial). *Seven Arts* 2 (1917): 759–61.

———. Editorial. *Seven Arts* 2 (1917): 489–92.

———. Editorial. *Seven Arts* 2 (1917): 624–26.

Oppenheim, James. "'Lazy' Verse." *Seven Arts* 1 (1916): 66–72.

———. "Memories of Whitman and Lincoln." *Seven Arts* 2 (1917): 8–12.

———. "New York, from a Skyscraper." *American Magazine* 67 (1909): 216.

———. "Pittsburgh." In *The Lyric Year: One Hundred Poems.* Ed. Ferdinand Earle. New York: Mitchell Kennerley, 1912. 198–99.

———. "Randolph Bourne." *The Liberator* 2 (February 1919): 14–15.

Orvell, Miles. *The Real Thing: Imitation and Authenticity in American Culture, 1880–1940.* Chapel Hill: University of North Carolina Press, 1989.

Owen, Wilfred. "Dulce et Decorum Est." In *Poems.* London: Chatto and Windus, 1920. 15.

Page, Curtis Hidden, ed. *The Chief American Poets.* Boston: Houghton, Mifflin, 1905.

Parisi, Joseph, and Stephen Young, eds. *Dear Editor: A History of* Poetry *in Letters; the First Fifty Years, 1912–1962.* New York: Norton, 2002.

Parsons, Deborah L. *Streetwalking the Metropolis: Women, the City, and Modernity.* Oxford: Oxford University Press, 2000.

Partridge, M. H. "The Case of Rupert Brooke." *Little Review* 1.1 (March 1914): 20–22.

Payne, William Morton. Papers. Newberry Library, Chicago.

Pearce, Lelia Miller. "Machine Made." *Others* 2.3 (March 1916): 170.

Pearce, Roy Harvey. *Act of the Mind.* Baltimore: Johns Hopkins University Press, 1965.

———. *The Continuity of American Poetry.* Princeton, N.J.: Princeton University Press, 1961.

"Pecuniary Inducement to Poets." *The Dial* 52 (1912): 118–19.

Peet, Stephen D. "Cliff-Dwellers and Their Works." *American Antiquarian* 12 (1890): 85–104.

Perkins, David. *A History of Modern Poetry: From the 1890s to the High Modernist Mode.* 2 vols. Cambridge, Mass.: Harvard University Press, 1976.

Perry, Bliss. *Whitman: His Life and Work.* Boston: Houghton Mifflin, 1906.

Photograph of Rupert Brooke. *Little Review* 2.4 (June 1915): 33.

Pinchot, Amos. "The Courage of the Cripple." In *Echoes of Revolt: The Masses, 1911–1917*. Ed. William L. O'Neill. 1966; reprint, Chicago: Ivan R. Dee, 1989. 276–80.

"Poetry and Efficiency." *The Dial* 58 (1915): 103.

"Poetry and Prosperity." *The Dial* 57 (1914): 328–29.

"Poetry in General and in Particular." *The Atlantic* 73 (1894): 702–4.

Poetry Magazine Papers. Regenstein Library, University of Chicago.

"The Poet's Bread and Butter." *The Nation* 97 (1913): 117–18.

"Poets Again Best Sellers." *Literary Digest* 48 (1914): 987.

"The Point of View." *Scribner's* 56 (1914): 407–10.

Pollock, Griselda. *Vision and Difference: Femininity, Feminism, and the History of Art*. London: Routledge, 1988.

Portrait of Walt Whitman. *The Century* 79 (1910): 709.

Pound, Ezra. "The Audience." *Poetry* 5 (1914): 29–30.

———. "Contemporania." *Poetry* 2 (1913): 1–12.

———. "In a Station of the Metro." *Poetry* 2 (1913): 12.

———. *The Letters of Ezra Pound to Alice Corbin Henderson*. Ed. Ira B. Nadel. Austin: University of Texas Press, 1993.

———. *Selected Letters 1907–1941*. Ed. D. D. Paige. 1950; reprint, New York: New Directions, 1971.

———. "Small Magazines." *English Journal* 19 (1930): 689–704.

———. "To Whistler, American." *Poetry* 1 (1912): 7.

"Practical Value of Poetry." Rev. of *Enjoyment of Poetry*, by Max Eastman. *Current Opinion* 55 (1913): 126–27.

"Proper Space, Air, and Light in City Streets." *Outlook* 39 (1908): 972–73.

Putzel, Max. *The Man in the Mirror: William Marion Reedy and His Magazine*. Columbia: University of Missouri Press, 1998.

Rai, Lajpat. "Young India." *Seven Arts* 2 (1917): 743–58.

Ransom, John Crowe. "The Woman as Poet." In *The World's Body*. Baton Rouge: Louisiana State University Press, 1938. 76–110.

Read, Mike. *Forever England: The Life of Rupert Brooke*. Edinburgh: Mainstream Publishing, 1997.

Redding, J. Saunders. *To Make a Poet Black*. Chapel Hill: University of North Carolina Press, 1939.

Reed, John. "Foundations of a Skyscraper." *American Magazine* 72 (1911): 735.

———. "One Solid Month of Liberty." In *Echoes of Revolt: The Masses, 1911–1917*. Ed. William L. O'Neill. 1966; reprint, Chicago: Ivan R. Dee, 1989. 294–97.

———. "This Unpopular War." *Seven Arts* 2 (1917): 397–408.

———. "War in Paterson." In *Echoes of Revolt: The Masses, 1911–1917*. Ed. William L. O'Neill. 1966; reprint, Chicago: Ivan R. Dee, 1989. 143–47.

———. "Whose War?" In *Echoes of Revolt: The Masses, 1911–1917*. Ed. William L. O'Neill. 1966; reprint, Chicago: Ivan R. Dee, 1989. 286–88.

"Reminiscences of Walt Whitman." *The Atlantic* 89 (1902): 163–75.

Revell, Keith D. "Regulating the Landscape: Real Estate Values, City Planning, and the 1916 Zoning Ordinance." In *The Landscape of Modernity: Essays on New York City, 1900–1940*. Ed. David Ward and Olivier Zunz. New York: Russell Sage Foundation, 1992. 19–45.

Rev. of *The Enjoyment of Poetry*, by Max Eastman. *North American Review* 197 (1913): 858–59.

Reyher, Ferdinand. "Kaleidoscopics." *Others* 1.6 (December 1915): 116–18.

Rice, Wallace, ed. *A Book of American Humorous Verse*. Chicago: Herbert F. Stone, 1904.

———. "Mr. Ezra Pound and 'Poetry.'" *The Dial* 54 (1913): 370–71.

———. Papers. Newberry Library, Chicago.

Rice, Wallace, and Frances Rice, eds. *The Humbler Poets: A Collection of Newspaper and Periodical Verse, 1885 to 1910*. 2nd series. Chicago: McClurg, 1911.

Ridge, Lola. "Blossoms." *Others* 5.1 (December 1918): 4–5.

———. "Time-Stone." In *Sun-Up*. New York: B. W. Huebsch, 1920. 51.

Rittenhouse, Jessie B., ed. *The Little Book of Modern Verse*. Boston: Houghton Mifflin, 1913.

———. *My House of Life*. Boston: Houghton Mifflin, 1934.

———. *Younger American Poets*. Boston: Little, Brown, 1904.

Robinson, William H. "William Stanley Braithwaite." In *American Poets 1880–1945*. Vol. 54 of *Dictionary of Literary Biography*. Ed. Peter Quartermain. Detroit: Gale Research Press, 1987. 3–12.

Rodker, John. "Dutch Dolls." *Others* 1.4 (October 1915): 64–74.

———. "London Night." *Poetry* 5 (1914): 119–24.

Rogers, Merrill. "The Insolence of Office and the Law's Delay." In *Echoes of Revolt: The Masses, 1911–1917*. Ed. William L. O'Neill. 1966; reprint, Chicago: Ivan R. Dee, 1989. 288–89.

Rolland, Romain. "America and the Arts." *Seven Arts* 1 (1916): 47–51.

Rorty, James. "City Fear." *The Liberator* 6.6 (June 1923): 10.

Rosenfeld, Paul. "The American Composer." *Seven Arts* 1 (1916): 89–94.

"Rupert Brooke on the War." *Little Review* 1.9 (December 1914): 48.

"Rupert Brooke's Visit." *Little Review* 1.4 (June 1914): 33.

Russell, A. J. "The House of Takumi." *Poetry* 4 (1914): 18–21.

Russell, Bertrand. "Is Nationalism Moribund?" *Seven Arts* 2 (1917): 673–87.

Russell, Herbert K. *Edgar Lee Masters: A Biography*. Urbana: University of Illinois Press, 2001.

Sandburg, Carl. *Billy Sunday and Other Poems*. Ed. George Hendrick and Willene Hendrick. New York: Harcourt Brace, 1993.

———. "Blue Island Intersection." In *Complete Poems*. New York: Harcourt Brace, 1950. 165.

———. "Broadway." In *Complete Poems*. New York: Harcourt Brace, 1950. 69.

———. "Buttons." *The Masses* 6 (February 1915): 10.

———. "Chicago." *Poetry* 3 (1914): 191–92.

———. "Chicago Poems." *Poetry* 3 (1914): 191–98.

———. *Complete Poems*. New York: Harcourt Brace, 1950.

———. "Cool Tombs." *Others* 4.1 (June 1917): 17.

———. "Crayon." In *Poems for the People*. Ed. George Hendrick and Willene Hendrick. Chicago: Ivan R. Dee, 1999. 53.

———. "The *Eastland*." In *Billy Sunday and Other Poems*. Ed. George Hendrick and Willene Hendrick. New York: Harcourt Brace, 1993. 11–14.

———. "Grass." *Seven Arts* 1 (1917): 474.

———. "Halsted Street Car." In *Complete Poems*. New York: Harcourt Brace, 1950. 6.

———. "Hats." In *Complete Poems*. New York: Harcourt Brace, 1950. 160.

———. *Letters of Carl Sandburg*. Ed. Herbert Mitgang. New York: Harcourt Brace, 1968.

———. "Long Guns." *Others* 5.5 (April/May 1919): 17.

———. "Louis Mayer's Ice Pictures." *Others* 2.3 (March 1916): 182–83.

———. "People Who Must." In *Complete Poems*. New York: Harcourt Brace, 1950. 158.

———. *Poems for the People*. Ed. George Hendrick and Willene Hendrick. Chicago: Ivan R. Dee, 1999.

———. "Skyscraper." In *Complete Poems*. New York: Harcourt Brace, 1950. 31–32.

———. "Speed Bug." In *Poems for the People*. Ed. George Hendrick and Willene Hendrick. Chicago: Ivan R. Dee, 1999. 55.

———. "Statistics." *Others* 2.3 (March 1916): 181.

———. "The Work of Ezra Pound." *Poetry* 7 (1916): 249–57.

Santayana, George. *Sonnets and Other Verses*. New York: Duffield, 1894.

Saphier, William. "Machine Shop Notes." *Others* 4.1 (June 1917): 18–20.

Schaum, Melita. *Wallace Stevens and the Critical Schools*. Tuscaloosa: University of Alabama Press, 1988.

Schivelbusch, Wolfgang. *The Railway Journey: The Industrialization of Time and Space in the Nineteenth Century*. Berkeley: University of California Press, 1986.

Schleier, Merrill. *The Skyscraper in American Art, 1890–1931*. New York: Da Capo, 1986.

Schmidt, Peter. *William Carlos Williams, the Arts, and Literary Tradition*. Baton Rouge: Louisiana State University Press, 1988.

Schocket, Eric. *Vanishing Moments: Class and American Literature*. Ann Arbor: University of Michigan Press, 2006.

Schoonmaker, Edwin Davies. "The Mob." In *The Lyric Year: One Hundred Poems*. Ed. Ferdinand Earle. New York: Mitchell Kennerley, 1912. 228–29.

Schulze, Robin G. "Harriet Monroe's Pioneer Modernism: Nature, National Identity, and 'Poetry: A Magazine of Verse.'" *Legacy: A Journal of American Women Writers* 21 (2004): 50–67.

Schuyler, Montgomery. "The Towers of Manhattan, and Notes on the Woolworth Building." *Architectural Record* 33 (February 1913): 99–122.

Schweik, Susan. *A Gulf So Deeply Cut: American Women Poets and the Second World War*. Madison: University of Wisconsin Press, 1991.

Seiffert, Marjorie Allen. "The Peddler." *Others* 4.1 (June 1917): 21–22.

Sharpe, William Chapman. *New York Nocturne: The City after Dark in Literature, Painting, and Photography.* Princeton, N.J.: Princeton University Press, 2008.

Simmel, Georg. "The Metropolis and Mental Life." In *On Individuality and Social Forms.* Ed. Donald N. Levine. Chicago: University of Chicago Press, 1971. 324–39.

———. *Philosophy of Money.* Ed. David Frisby. Trans. Tom Bottomore and David Frisby. London: Routledge, 2004.

Sloan, John. "Orango-Tango." *The Masses* 5 (February 1914): 4.

———. "The Past and the Futurist." *The Masses* 8 (January 1916): 4.

———. "A Slight Attack of Third Dimentia Brought on by Excessive Study of the Much-Talked-of Cubist Pictures in the International Exhibition at New York." *The Masses* 4 (April 1913): 12.

Smith, Watson. Introduction to *The Cliff Dwellers of the Mesa Verde,* by Gustaf Nordenskiöld. 1893; reprint, New York: AMS Press, 1973. xi–xiv.

"Some Portraits and Autographs of Walt Whitman." *The Century* 81 (1911): 531–33.

"Some Statistics Related to the Singer Building." Undated pamphlet given to visitors to the Singer Tower.

Soule, George. "Rupert Brooke and Whitman." *Little Review* 1.2 (April 1914): 15–16.

Spears, Monroe K. *Dionysus and the City: Modernism in Twentieth-Century Poetry.* New York: Oxford University Press, 1970.

Stansell, Christine. *American Moderns: Bohemian New York and the Creation of a New Century.* New York: Henry Holt, 2000.

Stapley, Mildred. "The City of Towers." *Harper's* 123 (1911): 697–706.

Stedman, Edmund Clarence, ed. *An American Anthology 1787–1900.* New York: Houghton Mifflin, 1900.

Stern, Robert A. M., Gregory Gilmartin, and John Montague Massengale. *New York 1900: Metropolitan Architecture and Urbanism 1890–1915.* New York: Rizzoli, 1983.

Stern, Robert A. M., Thomas Mellins, and David Fishman. *New York 1960: Architecture and Urbanism between the Second World War and the Bicentennial.* New York: Monacelli Press, 1995.

Stevens, Wallace. *Collected Poems.* New York: Knopf, 1954.

———. "The Idea of Order at Key West." In *Collected Poems.* New York: Knopf, 1954. 128–130.

———. "Pecksniffiana." *Poetry* 15 (1919): 1–11.

———. "Six Significant Landscapes." *Others* 2.3 (March 1916): 174–76.

———. "Thirteen Ways of Looking at a Blackbird." *Others* 4.2 (December 1917): 25–27.

Stevenson, Burton E., ed. *Poems of American History.* Boston: Houghton Mifflin, 1908.

Stevenson, Burton E., and Elizabeth B. Stevenson, eds. *Days and Deeds: A Book of Verse for Children's Reading and Speaking.* New York: Baker and Taylor, 1906.

Stewart, Robert. "The Hotels of New York." *Munsey's* 22 (1899): 281–95.

Stilgoe, John. *Metropolitan Corridor: Railroads and the American Scene.* New Haven, Conn.: Yale University Press, 1983.

Stokes, Rose Pastor. "Paterson." *The Masses* 5 (November 1913): 11.

Suárez, Juan A. "City Space, Technology, Popular Culture: The Modernism of Paul Strand and Charles Sheeler's *Manhatta.*" *Journal of American Studies* 36 (2002): 85–106.

Sullivan, Louis H. "Wherefore the Poet?" *Poetry* 7 (1916): 305–7.

Swasey, Robert. "The City in Summer." *Others* 2.1 (January 1916): 134.

Taggard, Genevieve, ed. *May Days: An Anthology of Verse from* Masses-Liberator. New York: Boni and Liveright, 1925.

Tagore, Rabindrinath. *The Gardener.* New York: Macmillan, 1913.

"Talks with Whitman." *American Magazine* 64 (1907): 281–88.

"The Tall Buildings of New York." *Munsey's* 18 (1898): 833–48.

Tanselle, G. Thomas. "*The Lyric Year*: A Bibliographical Study." *Papers of the Bibliographical Society of America* 56 (1962): 454–71.

Tate, Allen. "Tension in Poetry." In *Essays of Four Decades.* New York: Morrow, 1970. 56–71.

———. "Understanding Modern Poetry." In *Essays of Four Decades.* New York: William Morrow, 1970. 155–68.

Taylor, Lynne. "Food Riots Revisited: Public Protests in the Seventeenth to the Nineteenth Century." *Journal of Social History* 30 (Winter 1996): 483–96.

Taylor, William R. *In Pursuit of Gotham: Culture and Commerce in New York.* New York: Oxford University Press, 1992.

Teasdale, Sara. *Collected Poems.* New York: Macmillan, 1939.

———. "From the Woolworth Tower." In *Rivers to the Sea.* New York: Macmillan, 1915. 12–15.

———. "In a Railroad Station." In *Collected Poems.* New York: Macmillan, 1939. 51.

———. "In a Subway Station." In *Collected Poems.* New York: Macmillan, 1939. 51.

———. "The Metropolitan Tower." In *Collected Poems.* New York: Macmillan, 1939. 31.

Tebbel, John. *A History of Book Publishing in the United States.* Vol. 2. New York: R. R. Bowker, 1975.

Thomas, Calvin. "Have We Still Need of Poetry?" *Forum* 25 (1898): 502–11.

Thurston, Michael. *Making Something Happen: American Political Poetry between the Wars.* Chapel Hill: University of North Carolina Press, 2001.

Tichi, Cecilia. *Shifting Gears: Technology, Literature, Culture in Modernist America.* Chapel Hill: University of North Carolina Press, 1987.

Tietjens, Eunice. "The Drug Clerk." *The Masses* 5 (September 1914): 15.

———. "The Lady of Easy Virtue: An American." *Others* 4.1 (June 1917): 27.

———. Papers. Newberry Library, Chicago.

Torrence, Ridgely. "Three O'Clock." In *Hesperides.* New York: Macmillan, 1925. 23–24.

Towne, Charles Hanson. *Manhattan*. New York: Mitchell Kennerley, 1909.

Trachtenberg, Alan. *Reading American Photographs: Images as History, Mathew Brady to Walker Evans*. New York: Hill and Wang, 1989.

Traubel, Horace. "Sermon to Poets." *The Writer* 23 (1911): 133–37.

———. "Talks with Walt Whitman." *American Magazine* 64 (1907): 281–88.

———. "Walt Whitman at Fifty Dollars a Volume." *Era* 11 (1903): 523–29.

———. "Walt Whitman's Views." *Appleton's* 10 (1907): 465–72.

———. "Whitman in Old Age." *The Century* 74 (1907): 740–55, 911–22.

———. "With Walt Whitman in Camden." *The Century* 71 (1905): 82–98.

———. "With Walt Whitman in Camden." *Forum* 46 (1911): 400–14; 46 (1912): 589–600, 709–19; 47 (1913): 78–89.

———. "With Walt Whitman in Camden." *Seven Arts* 2 (1917): 627–37.

Tripp, Anne Huber. *The IWW and the Paterson Silk Strike of 1913*. Urbana: University of Illinois Press, 1987.

Turbyfill, Mark. "Reality." *Others* 4.1 (June 1917): 28–29.

Untermeyer, Louis. "Any City." *The Masses* 4 (July 1913): 20.

———. "Caliban in the Coal Mines." In *The Lyric Year: One Hundred Poems*. Ed. Ferdinand Earle. New York: Mitchell Kennerley, 1912. 266.

———. "God's Youth." *The Masses* 4 (August 1913): 12.

———. "In the Subway." In *Challenge*. New York, Harcourt, 1914. 119.

———. "The Ivory Tower II." *New Republic* 19 (May 10, 1919): 60–61.

———. "Lenox Avenue Express." In *Roast Leviathan*. New York: Harcourt, Brace, 1923. 138.

———, ed. *Modern American Poetry*. New York: Harcourt, Brace, 1930.

———. *The New Era in American Poetry*. New York: Holt, 1919.

———. Papers. University of Delaware Library.

———. "Playground." In *Roast Leviathan*. New York: Harcourt Brace, 1923. 12.

———. "Sunday." *The Masses* 4 (April 1913): 14.

———. "To a War Poet." *The Masses* 6 (January 1915): 3.

Untitled Announcement. *Others* 2.4 (April 1916): 210–13.

Untitled Comment. *Seven Arts* 1 (1916): 52–56.

———. *Seven Arts* 1 (1916): 152–57.

———. *Seven Arts* 1 (1917): 265–70.

———. *Seven Arts* 1 (1917): 504–6.

———. *Seven Arts* 1 (1917): 627–30.

———. *Seven Arts* 2 (1917): 68–71.

———. *Seven Arts* 2 (1917): 199–201.

Untitled Statement. *Others* 5.1 (December 1918): 1.

Vale, Charles. "The Lyric Year." *Forum* 49 (1913): 91–106.

Van Leeuwen, Thomas A. P. *The Skyward Trend of Thought: The Metaphysics of the American Skyscraper*. Cambridge: Massachusetts Institute of Technology Press, 1988.

Van Wienen, Mark W. *Partisans and Poets: The Political Work of American Poetry in the Great War*. Cambridge: Cambridge University Press, 1997.

————, ed. *Rendezvous with Death: American Poems of the Great War.* Urbana: University of Illinois Press, 2002.

————. "Taming the Socialist: Carl Sandburg's *Chicago Poems* and Its Critics." *American Literature* 63 (1991): 89–103.

Vincent, Leon H. *American Literary Masters.* Boston: Houghton Mifflin, 1906.

Waddell, Elizabeth. "The Tenant Farmer." *The Masses* 8 (August 1916): 8.

Waggoner, Hyatt H. *American Poets, from the Puritans to the Present.* Boston: Houghton Mifflin, 1968.

Walkowitz, Judith. *City of Dreadful Delight: Narratives of Sexual Danger in London.* London: Virago, 1992.

Wasserstrom, William. *The Time of "The Dial."* Syracuse, N.Y.: Syracuse University Press, 1963.

Watson, Steven. *Strange Bedfellows: The First American Avant-Garde.* New York: Abbeville Press, 1993.

Whitman, Walt. *Complete Poetry and Collected Prose.* Ed. Justin Kaplan. New York: Library of America, 1982.

————. "Crossing Brooklyn Ferry." In *Complete Poetry and Collected Prose.* Ed. Justin Kaplan. New York: Library of America, 1982. 308–13.

————. "Drum-Taps." In *Complete Poetry and Collected Prose.* Ed. Justin Kaplan. New York: Library of America, 1982. 416–58.

————. "Long, Too Long America." In *Complete Poetry and Collected Prose.* Ed. Justin Kaplan. New York: Library of America, 1982. 445.

————. "Notes Left Over." In *Complete Poetry and Collected Prose.* Ed. Justin Kaplan. New York: Library of America, 1982. 1050–75.

————. "Reconciliation." In *Complete Poetry and Collected Prose.* Ed. Justin Kaplan. New York: Library of America, 1982. 453.

————. "Sun-Down Poem." In *Leaves of Grass.* Brooklyn: N.p., 1856. 211–22.

————. "When Lilacs Last in the Dooryard Bloom'd." In *Complete Poetry and Collected Prose.* Ed. Justin Kaplan. New York: Library of America, 1982. 459–67.

"Whitman Again." *Outlook* 85 (1907): 862.

"Whitman's Table Talk." *Current Literature* 39 (July 1905): 37–38.

Whittier, John Greenleaf. *Snow-Bound: A Winter Idyl.* Boston: Ticknor and Fields, 1866.

Wilkinson, Marguerite. "The Food Riots." *The Masses* 9 (May 1917): 23.

————, ed. *New Voices: An Introduction to Contemporary Poetry.* New York: Macmillan, 1919.

Willard, Abbie. *Wallace Stevens: The Poet and His Critics.* Chicago: American Library Association, 1978.

Willcox, L. C. "The Personality and Power of Whitman." *North American Review* 183 (1906): 281–96.

Willey, Day Allen. "Coming of the Sky Piercer." *Technical World* 8 (1907): 82–90.

Williams, Ellen. *Harriet Monroe and the Poetry Renaissance: The First Ten Years of Poetry, 1912–22.* Urbana: University of Illinois Press, 1977.

Williams, Kenny J. "An Invisible Partnership and an Unlikely Relationship: William Stanley Braithwaite and Harriet Monroe." *Callaloo* 10 (1987): 516–50.

Williams, Raymond. *The Politics of Modernism: Against the New Conformists.* London: Verso, 1989.

Williams, William Carlos. *Al Que Quiere!* Boston: Four Seas Co., 1917.

———. "Belly Music." *Others* 5.6 (July 1919): 25–32.

———. *Collected Poems, 1921–1931.* New York: Objectivist Press, 1934.

———. *Collected Poems of William Carlos Williams.* Ed. A. Walton Litz and Christopher MacGowan. 2 vols. New York: New Directions, 1986.

———. "Drink." *Others* 3.1 (July 1916): 30.

———. "El Hombre." *Others* 3.4 (December 1916): 24.

———. "Epigramme." *Others* 2.2 (February 1916): 147.

———. "Gloria!" *Others* 5.6 (July 1919): 3–4.

———. "January Morning: Suite." In *Collected Poems of William Carlos Williams.* Ed. A. Walton Litz and Christopher MacGowan. Vol. 1. New York: New Directions, 1986. 100–104.

———. "On First Opening *The Lyric Year.*" *Poetry* 2 (1913): 114–15.

———. "Overture to a Dance of Locomotives." In *Collected Poems of William Carlos Williams.* Ed. A. Walton Litz and Christopher MacGowan. Vol. 1. New York: New Directions, 1986. 146–47.

———. "Pastoral." *Others* 3.4 (December 1916): 31.

———. "Paterson." *The Dial* 82 (1927): 91–93.

———. *Paterson.* New York: New Directions, 1963.

———. "Rapid Transit." In *Collected Poems of William Carlos Williams.* Ed. A. Walton Litz and Christopher MacGowan. Vol. 1. New York: New Directions, 1986. 231–32.

———. *Selected Letters of William Carlos Williams.* Ed. John C. Thirlwall. New York: New Directions, 1957.

———. *Selected Poems.* New York: New Directions, 1949.

———. *Sour Grapes.* Boston: Four Seas Co., 1921.

———. *Spring and All.* In *Collected Poems of William Carlos Williams.* Vol. 1. Ed. A. Walton Litz and Christopher MacGowan. New York: New Directions, 1986. 175–236.

———. "To a Solitary Disciple." *Others* 2.2 (February 1916): 145–47.

———. "The Wanderer." In *Collected Poems of William Carlos Williams.* Vol. 1. Ed. A. Walton Litz and Christopher MacGowan. New York: New Directions, 1986. 27–35.

———. *The Wedge.* In *Collected Poems of William Carlos Williams.* Vol. 2. Ed. A Walton Litz and Christopher MacGowan. New York: New Directions, 1986. 53–55.

———. "The Young Housewife." *Others* 3.4 (December 1916): 18.

Willis, Elizabeth. "A Public History of the Dividing Line: H.D., the Bomb, and the Roots of the Postmodern." *Foreign Literature Studies* 28 (2006): 38–54.

Wolff, Adolf. "Fireflies." *Others* 2.5–6 (May/June 1916): 240–42.

———. "Lines to the Woolworth Building." In *Songs, Sighs, and Curses*. Ridgefield, N.J.: Glebe, 1913. 29.

———. "Mending." *Others* 3.1 (July 1916): 22.

———. "Prison Weeds." *Others* 1.5 (November 1915): 86–92.

Wolff, Janet. "The Invisible *Flâneuse*: Women and the Literature of Modernity." *Theory, Culture, and Society* 2.3 (1985): 37–46.

Wood, Clement. "A Breath of Life." *The Masses* 6 (November 1914): 6.

———. "God's Blunder." *The Masses* 5 (June 1914): 18.

———. "A Lyrical Challenge." *Poetry* 5 (1914): 141–43.

———. "Woolworth Cathedral." *The Masses* 8 (April 1916): 20.

Woolf, Virginia. *A Room of One's Own*. New York: Harcourt Brace, 1929.

Woolley, Lisa. "From Chicago Renaissance to Chicago Renaissance: The Poetry of Fenton Johnson." *Langston Hughes Review* 14 (1996): 36–47.

Wyatt, Edith. "The Old and the New Poetry." *The Dial* 56 (1914): 375–76.

———. "On the Reading of Poetry." *Poetry* 1 (1912): 22–25.

———. "To a City Swallow." In *The Lyric Year: One Hundred Poems*. Ed. Ferdinand Earle. New York: Mitchell Kennerley, 1912. 297–98.

Wylie, Elinor. "Parting Gift." In *Black Armour*. New York: George H. Doran, 1923. 68.

Yannella, Philip. *The Other Carl Sandburg*. Jackson: University Press of Mississippi, 1996.

Zilczer, Judith K. "Robert J. Coady: Forgotten Spokesman for Avant-Garde Culture in America." *American Art Review* 2 (November/December 1975): 77–89.

Zunz, Olivier. *Making America Corporate, 1870–1920*. Chicago: University of Chicago Press, 1990.

Zurier, Rebecca. *Art for the* Masses: *A Radical Magazine and Its Graphics, 1911–1917*. Philadelphia: Temple University Press, 1988.

Zurier, Rebecca, Robert W. Snyder, and Virginia M. Mecklenburg. *Metropolitan Lives: Ashcan Artists and Their New York*. New York: Norton/National Museum of American Art, 1995.

INDEX

JOHN TIMBERMAN NEWCOMB is an associate professor of English at the University of Illinois at Urbana-Champaign and the author of *Would Poetry Disappear? American Verse and the Crisis of Modernity.*

A companion anthology containing the full text of all the poems referred to in this book is available through the University of Illinois Library's scholarly digital repository, the Illinois Digital Environment for Access to Learning and Scholarship (IDEALS), at http://hdl.handle.net/2142/26460.

The University of Illinois Press
is a founding member of the
Association of American University Presses.

University of Illinois Press
1325 South Oak Street
Champaign, IL 61820-6903
www.press.uillinois.edu